Outlier Ensembles

Charu C. Aggarwal · Saket Sathe

Outlier Ensembles

An Introduction

 Springer

Charu C. Aggarwal
IBM T. J. Watson Research Center
Yorktown Heights, NY
USA

Saket Sathe
IBM T. J. Watson Research Center
Yorktown Heights, NY
USA

ISBN 978-3-319-85474-8   ISBN 978-3-319-54765-7   (eBook)
DOI 10.1007/978-3-319-54765-7

Printed on acid-free paper

This Springer imprint is published by Springer Nature
The registered company is Springer International Publishing AG
The registered company address is: Gewerbestrasse 11, 6330 Cham, Switzerland

Charu C. Aggarwal dedicates this book to his wife Lata and his daughter Sayani.

Saket Sathe dedicates this book to his wife Aishwarya and his son Devansh.

Preface

> Talent wins games, but teamwork and intelligence wins championships.
>
> Michael Jordan

Ensemble analysis is a widely used class of meta-algorithms for many data mining problems such as classification and clustering. Numerous ensemble-based algorithms have been proposed in the literature for these problems. Compared to the clustering and classification problems, ensemble analysis has been studied in a limited way in the context of outlier detection. It is only in recent years that the problem of outlier ensembles has been recognized formally, and some techniques for these problems have been proposed. However, the material in the field has not been formally recognized, and it is expected that this book will play a significant role in creating a structured exposition of the topic. This book discusses a variety of methods for outlier ensembles and organizes them by the specific principles with which accuracy improvements are achieved. In addition, a discussion is provided on the techniques with which such methods can be made more effective. A formal classification of these methods has been provided, and the circumstances in which they work well are discussed. A discussion is also provided on how outlier ensembles relate (both theoretically and practically) to the ensemble techniques used commonly for other data mining problems such as classification. The similarities and (subtle) differences in the ensemble techniques for the classification and outlier detection problems are discussed. These subtle differences do impact the design of ensemble algorithms for the latter problem.

Ensemble techniques are increasingly finding their way into the curricula of many data mining courses. This book can be used for such courses. Many illustrative examples and exercises are provided in order to facilitate classroom teaching. A familiarity is assumed to the outlier detection problem and also to the generic problem of ensemble analysis in classification. This is because many of the ensemble methods discussed in this book are adaptations from their counterparts in the classification domain. Some techniques discussed in this book, such as wagging, randomized feature weighting, and geometric subsampling, provide new insights that are not available elsewhere. We have also provided an analysis of the performance of various types of base detectors and their relative effectiveness. This book combines a textbook-style discussion of older topics with new insights. Therefore, we believe that the book will also be of interest to researchers and practitioners for leveraging ensemble methods into optimal algorithmic design.

Yorktown Heights, NY, USA   Charu C. Aggarwal
January 2017   Saket Sathe

Acknowledgements

We would like to thank our families for their support during the writing of this book. Charu C. Aggarwal would like to thank his wife Lata and his daughter Sayani. Saket Sathe would like to thank his wife Aishwarya for her love and support. He would like to especially thank his four-year-old son Devansh for his affection and playfulness.

We are grateful to the support of our management at IBM. In particular, we would like to thank Nagui Halim and Deepak Turaga for their support during the writing of this book.

We would like to thank our numerous collaborators whose insights have helped make this book a success. Charu Aggarwal would like to thank Tarek F. Abdelzaher, Jing Gao, Quanquan Gu, Manish Gupta, Jiawei Han, Alexander Hinneburg, Thomas Huang, Nan Li, Huan Liu, Ruoming Jin, Daniel Keim, Arijit Khan, Latifur Khan, Mohammad M. Masud, Jian Pei, Magda Procopiuc, Guojun Qi, Chandan Reddy, Jaideep Srivastava, Karthik Subbian, Yizhou Sun, Jiliang Tang, Min-Hsuan Tsai, Haixun Wang, Jianyong Wang, Min Wang, Suhang Wang, Joel Wolf, Xifeng Yan, Philip Yu, Mohammed Zaki, ChengXiang Zhai, and Peixiang Zhao. Charu Aggarwal would also like to thank Lata Aggarwal for her help in some of the diagrams drawn using Powerpoint in the book. Saket Sathe would like to thank Karl Aberer, Timos Sellis, Dipanjan Chakraborty, Arun Vishwanath, Hoyoung Jeung, Sue Ann Chen, and Tian Guo for their collaborations over the years. We also thank Leman Akoglu for several general discussions on ensemble methods.

Contents

About the Authors

Charu C. Aggarwal is a Distinguished Research Staff Member (DRSM) at the IBM T. J. Watson Research Center in Yorktown Heights, New York. He completed his undergraduate degree in computer science from the Indian Institute of Technology at Kanpur in 1993 and his Ph.D. from the Massachusetts Institute of Technology in 1996.

He has worked extensively in the field of data mining. He has published more than 300 papers in refereed conferences and journals and authored over 80 patents. He is the author or editor of 16 books, including textbooks on data mining, recommender systems, and outlier analysis. Because of the commercial value of his patents, he has thrice been designated a Master Inventor at IBM. He is a recipient of an IBM Corporate Award (2003) for his work on bioterrorist threat detection in data streams, a recipient of the IBM Outstanding Innovation Award (2008) for his scientific contributions to privacy technology, a recipient of two IBM Outstanding Technical Achievement Awards (2009, 2015) for his work on data streams and high-dimensional data, respectively. He received the EDBT 2014 Test of Time Award for his work on condensation-based privacy-preserving data mining. He is also a recipient of the IEEE ICDM Research Contributions Award (2015), which is one of the two highest awards for influential research contributions in the field of data mining.

He has served as the general co-chair of the IEEE Big Data Conference (2014) and as the program co-chair of the ACM CIKM Conference (2015), the IEEE ICDM Conference (2015), and the ACM KDD Conference (2016). He served as an associate editor of the IEEE Transactions on Knowledge and Data Engineering from 2004 to 2008. He is an associate editor of the ACM Transactions on Knowledge Discovery from Data, an associate editor of the IEEE Transactions on Big Data, an action editor of the Data Mining and Knowledge Discovery Journal, editor-in-chief of the ACM SIGKDD Explorations, and an associate editor of the Knowledge and Information Systems Journal. He serves on the advisory board of the Lecture Notes on Social Networks, a publication by Springer. He has served as the vice president of the SIAM Activity Group on data mining and is a member of the SIAM industry committee. He is a fellow of the SIAM, ACM, and the IEEE, for "contributions to knowledge discovery and data mining algorithms."

Saket Sathe has worked at IBM Research Australia/USA since 2013. Saket received a Ph.D. degree in computer science from EPFL (Lausanne) in 2013. At EPFL, he was associated with the Distributed Information Systems Laboratory. Before that he received a Master's (M.Tech.) degree in Electrical Engineering from the Indian Institute of Technology at Bombay in 2006. Prior to joining EPFL, he spent one year working for a start-up. His primary areas of interest are data mining and data management. Saket has served on program committees of several top-ranked conferences and has been invited to review papers for prominent peer-reviewed journals. His research has led to more than 20 papers and 5 patents. His work on sensor data management received the runner-up Best Paper Award in IEEE CollaborateCom, 2014. He is a member of the ACM, IEEE, and the SIAM.

Chapter 1
An Introduction to Outlier Ensembles

*Music is not math. It's science. You keep mixing the stuff up until
it blows up on you, or it becomes this incredible potion.*

Bruno Mars

1.1 Introduction

The outlier analysis problem has been widely studied by database, data mining, machine learning and statistical communities. Numerous algorithms have been proposed for this problem in recent years [6, 9, 11, 14, 35, 36, 39, 40, 53, 55]. A detailed survey [19] classifies the different types of algorithms for anomaly detection, and a book on the subject [3] provides a comprehensive treatment of various algorithms. This chapter and the remainder of this book assumes a familiarity with the basic algorithms that are commonly used for outlier detection. The book will also assume a familiarity with the common ensemble methods used in clustering and classification. Detailed discussions on classification ensemble methods may be found in [71].

The modeling process in some data mining problems like outlier detection is often an inherently subjective process, where the objective function or model defined for a particular problem depends on an analyst's understanding of the generative behavior of the data. For example, a nearest-neighbor algorithm for outlier detection might provide very different results from a one-class support vector machine. These differences are caused by the differences in the underlying assumptions. Clearly, such assumptions are very subjective, and a specific algorithm being used may often model the underlying generative process in a limited way. In such cases, effective results can be obtained on some parts of the data which are modeled well, whereas the results on other parts of the data may not be very accurate. Similarly, a given model may sometimes behave well on a given data set, but may not behave well on other data sets. In many cases, the model may be extremely sensitive to the choice of parameters used in a particular outlier detection model. For example, a particular choice of the number of nearest neighbors may work well for an exact *k*-nearest neighbor outlier detector in a given data set, but it might not work well for another data set. Furthermore, it is often difficult to tune parameters or select the most appropriate algorithm in a problem like outlier detection because of the absence of ground truth. All these issues often make the evaluation of the quality of outlier detection algorithms more challenging. In the absence of ground-truth, this can cause uncertainty in the analyst about the true effectiveness of her algorithm.

Ensemble analysis is a method that is commonly used in data mining problems to reduce the dependence of the model on the specific data set or data locality. This greatly increases the robustness of the data mining process. The ensemble technique is used very commonly in problems such as clustering and classification. Ensemble analysis can include any approach that combines the results of *either* dependent or independent executions of data mining algorithms. For example, the boosting technique in classification, in which the different executions of the classification algorithm are clearly dependent on one another, can also be considered an ensemble approach. The idea here is that the final result is an ensemble score from the results of different models, no matter how each of these models is derived.

The problem of ensemble analysis has been widely studied in the context of many data mining problems such as clustering and classification [58, 63, 71], although the approaches are different in supervised and unsupervised problems. In fact, each of these areas of meta-algorithm analysis is considered an active and vibrant subfield in its own right. To provide a specific example, the seminal paper [26] on boosting in classification has several thousand citations, and many different variants of the basic boosting approach have been proposed in the literature. The common methods used for ensemble analysis in clustering and classification are as follows:

- In clustering, the areas of alternative clustering, multiview clustering, and ensemble clustering are closely related subtopics of ensemble analysis. The idea in each of these variants is that the clustering process is inherently subjective, and a single clustering may not reflect the complete insights about how the data may cluster. Therefore, it is useful to examine the different and *alternative* clusters [13, 49, 50, 65] and combine the results. Alternative clustering is also sometimes referred to as *multiview clustering*. The goal here is to determine clusterings which are significantly different from one another in order to obtain different insights. In some cases, the exploration of the clusters is performed visually [1, 32] in order to obtain the best results. A notable cluster-ensemble, referred to as *extremely-randomized clustering forest (ERC-Forest)* [47], is closely related to an outlier ensemble method known as isolation forests [43].
- In the context of the classification problem, a variety of ensemble based methods have been proposed as as bagging [15], boosting [26], stacking [22, 64, 68], random forests [16, 33], model averaging [23], and bucket of models [70]. Ensemble analysis is considered particularly important in noisy and streaming scenarios in which the quality of the results from individual classifiers is not considered robust because of limitations in data quality or processing time. Some recent methods

also design techniques for outlier detection in the rare-class setting [20, 37, 45, 46] although this setting is fundamentally different from the unsupervised case.

These different methods for ensemble analysis in clustering and classification enjoy wide popularity, and have been explored extensively in the literature. Furthermore, the different sub-topics (e.g., bagging, boosting, and so on) in the ensemble analysis area are very well formalized. Ensemble analysis methods have regularly won several data mining contests in fields as diverse as clustering, classification, and recommender systems. For example, the winning entry in the Netflix prize contest contained hundreds of different collaborative filtering models [12]. Similarly, some ensemble methods in classification like random forests [16, 33] are almost legendary in their ability to consistently win [25] over a wide variety of competing classification models. All these observations suggest that it makes sense to explore such methods in the outlier analysis domain.

1.1.1 Motivations for Ensemble Methods in Outlier Analysis

The successes of ensemble methods in various problem settings have not been recognized in outlier analysis even though many existing methods show considerable promise; this is not so much because the outlier analysis problem provides less potential for improvements but primarily because the research in the field has been rather limited and it is often difficult to crisply evaluate the improvements resulting from ensemble analysis in the unsupervised setting.

Most meta-algorithms require crisp evaluation criteria in order to show their relative merits over the base algorithm. Furthermore, evaluation criteria are often used in the intermediate steps of an ensemble algorithm (e.g., boosting or stacking), in order to make future decisions about the precise construction of the ensemble. Among all core data mining problems, outlier analysis is the hardest to evaluate (especially on real data sets) because of a combination of its small sample space and unsupervised nature. The small sample space issue refers to the fact that a given data set may contain only a small number of outliers, and therefore the correctness of an approach is often hard to quantify in a statistically robust way. This is also a problem for making robust decisions about future steps of the algorithm, without causing over-fitting. The unsupervised nature of the problem refers to the fact that no ground truth is available in order to evaluate the quality of a component in the ensemble. This necessitates the construction of simpler ensembles with fewer qualitative decisions about the choice of the components in the ensemble. These factors have been a significant impediment in the development of effective meta-algorithms. On the other hand, since the classification problem has the most crisply defined criteria for evaluation, it also has the richest meta-algorithm literature among all data mining problems. This is because the problem of model evaluation is closely related to quality-driven meta-algorithm development. However, recent years have seen a number of significant advances in the topic of outlier ensembles both from an algorithmic [2, 5] and application [30] point of view. In particular, it has been shown in [5] that the theoretical foundations of outlier ensembles are fundamentally not very different from those of classification ensembles. In particular, it was shown that the bias-variance trade-off for outlier ensembles is not very different from that in classification.

Another issue with unsupervised problems is that the evaluation process is less concrete, and therefore the success of ensemble methods is not as well recognized even when there are significant performance improvements under the covers. Since the modeling of ground truth is subjective in these settings, a highly-performing algorithm might not be as well-recognized as in another field like classification in which the ground-truth is more concrete and also used for training. These factors also make it difficult to design data mining contests around unsupervised problems like outlier analysis, which also reduces the ability to showcase the effectiveness of ensemble methods for outlier detection. For example, ensemble methods were used more widely in recommender systems after the victory of ensemble methods in the Netflix prize contest. In other words, the absence of eye-catching contests in unsupervised problems like outlier analysis has been a factor that impedes popularity about the obvious potential of ensemble methods in this domain.

Interestingly, even though the unsupervised nature of the outlier detection problem makes ensemble analysis more challenging, it also makes it more essential. Unlike classification, in which one can perform *model selection* (i.e., selection of the best algorithm) and parameter tuning with the use of labels, this is not possible in outlier detection. Therefore, the results of outlier detection algorithms often vary more significantly over different data sets. For example, kernel methods are among the best-performing techniques for classification; yet such methods are rarely favored in unsupervised problems like outlier detection. This is because of the extreme *instability* of these methods to the choice of the kernel and its parameters. We will show in this book (with specific examples in Chap. 6) that outlier ensembles can help make such techniques extremely competitive. Furthermore, outlier ensembles have great *equalizing* power in making different algorithms behave in a more similar way. In other words, the performance gains in outlier ensembles are often inherently more useful and significant because they partially overcome the weak performances resulting from lack of supervision. In general, an important function of ensemble analysis in unsupervised problems is to partially overcome the lack of certainty caused by the unavailability of ground truth.

1.1.2   Common Settings for Existing Ensemble Methods

Several practical examples exist in the literature for outlier ensembles. These cases show that when ensemble analysis is used properly, the potential for algorithmic improvement is significant. Ensemble analysis has been used particularly effectively in high-dimensional outlier detection [31, 38, 41, 48, 50, 51], in which multiple subspaces of the data are often explored in order to discover outliers. In fact, the earliest *formalization* [41] of outlier ensemble analysis finds its origins in high-dimensional outlier detection, although informal methods for ensemble analysis were proposed much earlier to this work. The high-dimensional scenario is an important one for ensemble analysis, because the outlier behavior of a data point in high-dimensional space is often described by a subset of dimensions, which are rather hard to discover in real settings. In fact, most methods for localizing the subsets of dimensions can be considered *weak guesses* to the true subsets of dimensions which are relevant for outlier analysis. The use of multiple models (corresponding to different subsets of dimensions) reduces the uncertainty arising from an inherently difficult subspace selection process, and provides greater robustness for the approach. The feature bagging work discussed in [41] may be considered a first *formal* description of outlier ensemble analysis in a real setting. However, as we will see in this chapter, numerous methods were proposed earlier to this work which could be considered ensembles, but were never formally recognized as ensembles in the literature. As noted in [31], even the first high dimensional outlier detection approach [6] may be considered an ensemble method, though it was not formally presented as an ensemble method in the original paper. High-dimensional data can be considered one of the most important applications of outlier ensemble analysis. This is primarily because of the great uncertainty caused by the specific choice of subspace on the outlier ensemble method. For example, the isolation forest method [43] (roughly) quantifies the dimensionality of the local subspace in which a point can be isolated as an outlier after using random splits in a decision tree-like fashion. The basic premise is that outliers can be isolated in low-dimensional subspaces on randomly partitioning the data space. Another method known as rotated bagging [5] generalizes the feature bagging ideas in [41] to subspaces defined by combinations of arbitrarily oriented vectors and not just axis-parallel combinations of features.

It should also be pointed out that while high-dimensional data is an important case for ensemble analysis, the potential of ensemble analysis is much broader, and is extremely useful in any scenario in which there is *significant uncertainty about the specific effect of model design*. The choice of ensemble method is also influenced by the specific application and data type at hand. For example, the ensembles may sometimes need to be designed in a customized way for specific applications such as network anomaly detection [69]. A time-series ensemble may require one to account for the dependencies among different data items in order to design the ensemble method.

Although ensemble components are usually independent of one another, many types of ensembles such as sequential ensembles can be used in order to successively refine data-centric insights. A position paper summarizing the state-of-the-art is found in [2], and this introductory chapter is, in fact, an extended version of this position paper. In addition to providing a more detailed and updated exposition over the original position paper [2], this chapter also introduces the organization of the book within the context of a broader overview.

This book will discuss the different methods for outlier ensemble analysis in the literature. In addition, we will introduce several new ensemble methods that are not discussed in the literature. Therefore, the contribution of this book is not just to summarize and provide an overview of the state-of-the-art, but also to advance the state-of-the-art to a large extent. This chapter will provide a categorization of the different types of ensembles, and the key parts of the algorithmic design of ensembles. The specific importance of different parts of algorithmic design will also be discussed, and the various chapters of this book will be organized in the context of this discussion. Finally, an important part of the discussion in this book will be about the sensitivity of base algorithms to ensemble methods. We will show that different base algorithms provide different scopes of improvement with various ensemble methods.

1.1.3 Types of Ensemble Methods

Ensemble algorithms can be categorized in various ways. The earliest position paper [2] categorized outlier ensembles in two different ways:

- *Categorization by component independence*: Are the different components of the ensemble independent of one another or do they depend on one another? To provide an analogy with the classification problem, boosting can be considered a problem in which the different components of the ensemble are not independent of one another. This is because the execution of a specific component depends on the result from previous executions. On the other hand, many forms of classification ensembles such as bagging allow the base models to be independent of one another. One can also categorize outlier ensemble methods using similar principles.
- *Categorization by component type*: Each component of an ensemble can be defined on the basis of either *data choice* or *model choice*. The idea in the former is to carefully pick a subset of the data or data dimensions (e.g., boosting/bagging in classification) or to select a specific algorithm (e.g., stacking or different base algorithms). The former types of ensembles are referred to as data-centric ensembles, whereas the latter types are referred to as model-centric ensembles.

It should be pointed out that the aforementioned categorizations of different types of ensembles is inherently incomplete, and it is impossible to fully describe every possibility. For example, it is possible for the different components to be heterogeneous, which are defined on the basis of different aspects of the data and models [52]. In other words, different algorithms are used to create different components of the ensemble. However, such models are less frequent in the outlier analysis literature, because of the complexity of reasonably evaluating the importance of different ensemble components. Nevertheless, such methods are important because they increase the robustness of ensemble methods. In fact, this book will provide one such heterogeneous ensemble method, referred to as *TRINITY*, in Chap. 6.

Another way of categorizing outlier ensembles is with the use of the *theoretical mechanism* with which accuracy is improved by an ensemble method. As discussed in [5], the bias-variance theory of outlier ensembles is not very different from that of classification ensembles. Just as the error of a classifier can be decomposed into squared bias and variance, it is also possible to decompose the error of an outlier detector into squared bias and variance (with respect to an unobserved ground truth). Therefore, outlier ensembles can improve the accuracy of base detectors with the use of the following two mechanisms:

- *Bias reduction*: Bias reduction is generally hard to achieve in the context of out-lier detection because of the unavailability of ground-truth. It is hard to gener-ate analogs to methods like boosting for outlier detection because these methods almost always use the ground-truth in intermediate steps of the algorithm. A num-ber of recent schemes such as *SELECT* [56], CARE [57], and FVPS [57] fall into this category. These techniques use heuristic tricks that might often work in several practical settings, although this is not always the case.
- *Variance reduction*: These methods reduce variance by making the combination method more robust. Many of the classification ensemble methods like bagging and subsampling can be directly adapted to outlier detection. Most of the existing ensemble methods in outlier detection are variance reduction methods.

In addition, there are a number of schemes that combine bias and variance reduction.

The chapters of this book will be largely organized along these theoretical varia-tions corresponding to bias and variance reduction. This is because these variations are inherently more fundamental in terms of how they improve accuracy of the outlier detector. Historically, the vast majority of outlier ensemble methods are variance-reduction methods. This is primarily because of the unsupervised nature of the outlier detection problem in which bias reduction methods are harder to adapt from classi-fication. Variance reduction methods usually do not require knowledge of the class labels and are relatively easy to adapt from classification to outlier detection. Most bias reduction methods like boosting (in classification) require knowledge of the class labels. Nevertheless, a small number of methods are still designed for bias reduction in outlier ensemble analysis. Most of these methods are heuristics, and do not always provide an improvement in performance. This is because of their sensitivity to the specific data set at hand. We will devote a single chapter of this book to bias reduction in outlier ensemble analysis.

1.1.4 Overview of Outlier Ensemble Design

The design of a typical outlier ensemble method contains a number of different components, which are used to construct the final result. The first step in outlier ensembles is to select the base model at hand. The outputs of these base models are normalized and then combined in order to yield the final result. In the following, we provide a brief overview of these three components of outlier ensemble design:

- *Base model choice*: This is the individual methodology or algorithm which is used to create the corresponding component of the ensemble. The nature of the model depends on the goals of the base method. For example, in a high-dimensional method, the individual ensemble components might contain outlier detection methods in subspace projections. In a parameter-centric method, the individual ensemble component might be an execution of the same algorithm with a different choice of parameters. In other cases, the base components might contain entirely different outlier detection algorithms.

- *Normalization*: Different methods may create outlier scores which are on very different scales. For example, a k-nearest neighbor detector will report a score on a completely different scale than the LOF algorithm. In some cases, the scores may be in ascending order, whereas in others, they may be in descending order. In such cases, normalization is important in being able to combine the scores meaningfully, so that the outlier scores from different components are roughly comparable.
- *Model combination*: This refers to the final combination function, which is used in order to create the outlier score. For example, one might average the normalized scores of a data point output by different detectors in order to create the final results. The use of averaging is the most common combination, and is an adaptation from known variance-reduction results in the classification literature [71].

This chapter will discuss each of these components of ensemble analysis briefly. Later chapters will discuss each of these aspects in greater detail. In particular, the issues of normalization and model combination will be discussed in detail in Chap. 5.

This chapter is organized as follows. The next section will discuss the categorization of ensembles on the basis of component independence. Section 1.3 will discuss the categorization of ensembles on the basis of model type. Section 1.4 discusses the categorization of outlier ensemble methods on the basis of the theoretical approach used for accuracy improvements. In particular, the accuracy improvements are achieved through either bias or variance reduction. Section 1.5 will study the role of the combination function in different kinds of ensemble analysis. Section 1.6 discusses an overview of the different adaptations of ensemble-based algorithms in the classification literature to outlier analysis. Many of these algorithms will also be discussed in more detail in the book. Therefore, this section will also discuss the various chapters of the book where these algorithms are discussed. Section 1.7 contains the conclusions and summary.

1.2   Categorization by Component Independence

This categorization examines whether the executions of the components are independent of one another, or whether they depend on one another in terms of the input of one component depending on the output of the previous component. There are two primary types of ensembles that can be used in order to improve the quality of outlier detection algorithms:

- In *sequential ensembles*, a given algorithm or set of algorithms are applied sequentially, so that future applications of the algorithms are impacted by previous applications, in terms of either modifications of the base data for analysis or in terms of the specific choices of the algorithms. The final result is either a weighted combination of, or the final result of the last application of an outlier analysis algorithm. For example, in the context of the classification problem, boosting methods may be considered examples of sequential ensembles. There are relatively few methods for outlier detection in this category, although a few methods exist that remove outliers from the data in the preliminary executions in order to provide more robust results.

- In *independent ensembles*, different algorithms, or different instantiations of the same algorithm are applied to either the complete data or portions of the data. The choices made about the data and algorithms applied are independent of the results obtained from these different algorithmic executions. The results from the different algorithm executions are combined in order to obtain accuracy improvements.

In this section, both types of ensembles will be discussed in detail.

1.2.1 Sequential Ensembles

In sequential-ensembles, one or more outlier detection algorithms are applied sequentially to either all or portions of the data. The core principle of the approach is that each application of a base algorithm provides a better understanding of the data, so as to enable a more refined execution with either a modified algorithm or data set. Thus, depending on the approach, either the data set or the algorithm may be changed in sequential executions. If desired, this approach can either be applied for a fixed number of times, or be used in order to converge to a more robust solution. The broad framework of a sequential-ensemble algorithm is provided in Fig. 1.1.

In each iteration, a successively refined algorithm may be used on a refined data, based on the results from previous executions. The function $f_j(\cdot)$ is used to create a refinement of the data, which could correspond to data subset selection, attribute-subset selection, or generic data transformation methods. The description above is provided in a very general form, and many special cases can be instantiated from this

Fig. 1.1 Sequential ensemble framework

Algorithm SequentialEnsemble(Data Set: $\mathcal{D}$
     Base Algorithms: $\mathcal{A}_1 \ldots \mathcal{A}_r$)
begin
  $j = 1$;
  repeat
    Pick an algorithm $\mathcal{A}_j$ based on results from
      past executions;
    Create a new data set $f_j(\mathcal{D})$ from $\mathcal{D}$ based
      on results from past executions;
    Apply $\mathcal{A}_j$ to $f_j(\mathcal{D})$;
    $j = j + 1$;
  until(termination);
  report outliers based on combinations of results
    from previous executions;
end

general framework. For example, only a single algorithm may be used on successive modifications of the data, as data is refined over time. Furthermore, the sequential ensemble may be applied in only a small number of constant passes, rather than a generic convergence-based approach, as presented above. The broad principle of sequential ensembles is that a greater knowledge of data with successive algorithmic execution helps focus on techniques and portions of the data that can provide fresh insights.

Sequential ensembles have not been sufficiently explored in the outlier analysis literature as general purpose meta-algorithms. However, many *specific* techniques in the outlier literature use methods that can be recognized as special cases of sequential ensembles. A classical example of this is the use of two-phase algorithms for building a model of the normal data. In the first phase, an outlier detection algorithm is used in order to remove the obvious outliers. In the second phase, *a more robust* normal model is constructed after removing these obvious outliers. Thus, the outlier analysis in the second stage is more refined and accurate. Such approaches are commonly used for cluster-based outlier analysis (for constructing more robust clusters in later stages) [10], or for more robust histogram construction and density estimation. However, most of these methods are presented in the outlier analysis literature as specific optimizations of *particular* algorithms, rather than as general meta-algorithms that can improve the effectiveness of an *arbitrary* outlier detection algorithm. There is significant scope for further research in the outlier analysis literature by recognizing these methods as general-purpose ensembles, and using them to improve the effectiveness of outlier detection. In these models, the goal of the sequential ensemble is data refinement. Therefore, the score returned by the last stage of the ensemble is the most relevant outlier score. However, it is possible, in principle, to combine the scores obtained from earlier executions with the final score. The effectiveness of a particular choice of strategy may depend on the base algorithm and data set at hand.

Another example of a sequential ensemble is proposed in [48] in which different subspaces of the data are *recursively* explored, on the basis of their discriminative behavior. A subspace is explored only if one of its predecessor[1] subspaces is also sufficiently discriminative. Thus, this approach is sequential, since the construction of future models of the ensemble is dependent on the previous models. The goal of the sequential ensemble is the discovery of other related subspaces which are also discriminative. Nevertheless, since the sequential approach is combined with enumerative exploration of different subspace extensions, the combination function in this case needs to include the scores from the different subspaces in order to create an outlier score. The main point here is that the designs of the individual ensemble components are not independent of one another. The work in [48] uses the product of the outlier scores of the discriminative subspaces as the final result. This is equivalent to using an arithmetic sum on the logarithmic function of the outlier score.

A model-centric sequential ensemble, referred to as *SELECT*, has recently been proposed in [56]. This approach firsts executes the base detectors in order to compute a pseudo-ground truth by averaging the scores of the detectors. This artificial ground

---

[1] A predecessor is defined as a subspace with one dimension removed.

truth is then used to prune the detectors that deviate too much from the average performance. Such an approach tends to remove the poorly performing detectors and therefore improves the overall performance. Although the final execution averages the scores of independently executed detectors, the selection step requires sequential evaluation and addition of detectors to the ensemble. Interestingly, most of the sequential ensemble methods are bias reduction methods, and the performance gains obtained are often heuristic in nature (as is the case for all bias reduction methods).

1.2.2 Independent Ensembles

In independent ensembles, different instantiations of the algorithm or different portions of the data are used for outlier analysis. Alternatively, the same algorithm may be applied, but with either a different initialization, parameter set or even random seed in the case of a randomized algorithms. The results from these different algorithm executions can be combined in order to obtain a more robust outlier score. Independent ensembles represent the most common setting in outlier detection. A general-purpose description of independent ensemble algorithms is provided in the pseudo-code description of Fig. 1.2.

The broad principle of independent ensembles is that different models provide different (and valid) insights about diverse aspects of the data, and combining these insights provides more robust results which are not dependent on specific artifacts of a particular algorithm or data set. Independent ensembles have been explored much more widely and formally in the outlier analysis literature, as compared to sequential ensembles. Independent ensembles are particularly popular for outlier analysis in high-dimensional data sets, because they enable the exploration of different subspaces of the data in which different types of deviants may be found. In general, independent ensembles may be used in any setting with a randomized base component in which there is high variability in prediction from each component.

Examples exist of both picking different algorithms and data sets, in order to combine the results from different executions. For example, the methods in

Fig. 1.2 Independent ensemble framework

Algorithm IndependentEnsemble(Data Set: $\mathscr{D}$
      Base Algorithms: $\mathscr{A}_1 \ldots \mathscr{A}_r$)
begin
  $j = 1$;
  repeat
    Pick an algorithm $\mathscr{A}_j$;
    Create a new data set $f_j(\mathscr{D})$ from $\mathscr{D}$;
    Apply $\mathscr{A}_j$ to $f_j(\mathscr{D})$;
    $j = j + 1$;
  until(termination);
  report outliers based on combinations of results
    from previous executions;
end

[29, 41–43] sample subspaces from the underlying data in order to determine outliers from each of these executions independently. Then, the results from these different executions are combined in order to determine the outliers. The idea in these methods is that results from different subsets of sampled features may be bagged in order to provide more robust results. Some of the recent methods for subspace outlier ranking and outlier evaluation can be considered independent ensembles which combine the outliers discovered in different subspaces in order to provide more robust insights. Numerous methods in the classification literature such as bagging and subsampling can also be trivially adapted to outlier ensembles [5, 72]. As we will see in Chap. 2, the outlier ensemble problem is very similar to that of classification in some settings. However, some modest adaptations are required in order to address the uncertainty arising from the unsupervised nature of the outlier detection problem [5]. Most of these methods fall under the category of independent ensembles. Furthermore, many of these methods are variance reduction techniques, although some of them combine bias and variance reduction.

1.3 Categorization by Constituent Components

In general, a particular base component of the ensemble may use a different model, or a particular component might use a different subset or subspace of the data. Although it is possible to combine data selection with model selection, there are only a few methods such as [52] that do this in practice. Typically, each component of the model is either defined as a specific model, or as a specific part of the data. The former type of ensemble is referred to as *model-centered*, whereas the latter type is referred to as *data-centered*. Each of these specific types will be discussed in detail in this section.

1.3.1 Model-Centered Ensembles

Model-centered ensembles attempt to combine the outlier scores from different models built on the same data set. The major challenge in this type of ensemble is that the scores from different models are often not directly comparable with one another. For example, the outlier score from a k-nearest neighbor approach is very different from the outlier score provided by a detection model based on principal component analysis (PCA) because of the different scales of the scores. In some cases, larger scores indicate a greater degree of outlierness, whereas in other cases, smaller scores indicate a greater degree of outlierness. This causes issues in combining the scores from these different outlier models. Therefore, it is critical to be able to convert the different outlier scores into normalized values which are directly comparable, and also preferably interpretable, such as a probability [28]. This issue will be discussed in the next section on defining combination functions for outlier ensembles.

Another key challenge is in terms of the choice of the specific combination function for outlier detection. Should we use model averaging, best fit or worst fit? This problem is of course not specific to model-centered ensembles. Nevertheless, it is particularly relevant in this context because of the propensity of different outlier models to create scores with very different characteristics. For example, a model based on the raw distances will provide very different ranges of scores than a normalized method like LOF [14].

A particular form of model-centered ensembles which is commonly used in outlier analysis, but not formally recognized as ensembles is the issue of using the same model over different choices of the underlying model parameters, and then combining the scores. This is done quite frequently in many classical outlier analysis algorithms such as LOCI [53] and LOF [14]. However, since the approach is interpreted as a question of parameter tuning, it is not recognized formally as an ensemble. In reality, any systematic approach for parameter tuning, *which is dependent on the output scores and directly combines or uses the outputs of the different executions* should be interpreted as an ensemblar approach. This is the case with the LOF and LOCI methods. Specifically, the following ensemblar approach is used in the two methods.

- In the LOF method, the model is run over a range of values of k, which defines the neighborhood of the data points. The work in [14] examines the use of different combination functions such as the minimum, average or the maximum of the LOF values as the outlier score. It is argued in [14], that the appropriate combination function is to use the *maximum* value in order to prevent dilution of the outlier scores by inappropriate parameter choices in the model. In other words, the specific model which *best enhances* the outlier behavior for a data point is used. However, in many cases, the averaging function can provide robust results.
- The LOCI method uses a multi-granularity approach, which uses a sampling neighborhood in order to determine the level of granularity in which to compute the outlier score. Different sampling neighborhoods are used, and a point is declared as an outlier based on the neighborhood in which its outlier behavior is *most* enhanced. It is interesting to note that the LOCI method uses a very similar combination function as the LOF method in terms of picking the component of the ensemble which *most* enhances the outlier behavior.

It should be pointed out that when the different components of the ensemble create comparable scores (e.g., different runs of a particular algorithm such as LOF or LOCI), then the combination process is greatly simplified, since the scores across different components are comparable. However, this is not the case, when the different components create scores which are not directly comparable to one another. This issue will be discussed in a later section on defining combination functions.

Model-centered ensembles can be used in natural way by constructing randomized variations of a base detector. The randomization of the base detector may be performed by using a variety of different techniques, such as the injection of randomness in different steps of the base detector. For example, one may choose to use a randomized clustering algorithm in order to score outliers (as their distance to the nearest centroid). The averaged score from different executions may be reported as the final outlier score. A specific approach is this kind of technique is the use of *randomized autoencoder ensembles* [21]. The basic idea is to perform nonlinear dimensionality reduction with randomized autoencoders, and then use the average (or median) residuals from the output units across all ensemble components in order to create the outlier scores. Randomization is incorporated by randomly dropping connections in the neural network. Good results have been reported in [21] with the use of this technique.

Model-centered ensembles are often used for subspace outlier detection. Recently, a method called *OutRank* [51] has been proposed, which can combine the results of multiple rankings based on the relationship of data points to their nearest subspace clusters. It has been shown in [51] that the use of even traditional subspace clustering algorithms like PROCLUS [8] can provide good results for outlier analysis, when the ensemble method is used. The basic idea is to score each data point based on its relationship to its nearest cluster as well as the properties of its nearest cluster. In particular, the *OutRank* method uses the aggregate of the normalized fraction of points and the normalized fraction of dimensions in a subspace cluster in order to score all points present in it. In the case of overlapping clusters, the score of a point in a single ensemble component is obtained by summing this value over all clusters in which the point lies. The averaged score over multiple randomized executions is used to quantify the outlier score of the data point. This approach is referred to as *Multiple-Proclus*. Thus, the work in [51] conclusively shown the power of ensemble analysis for high dimensional data. In general, methods like clustering and histograms are naturally designed for an ensemble-centric setting because the resulting outlier scores show a large amount of variability across different runs. Furthermore, methods like isolation forests [43] use weak models for each component, but the combination often provides extremely powerful results.

1.3.2   Data-Centered Ensembles

In data-centered ensembles, different parts, samples, projections, or functions of the data are explored in order to perform the analysis. It should be pointed out that a function of the data could include either a sample of the data (horizontal sample) or a relevant subspace (vertical sample). More general functions of the data are also possible, though have rarely been explored in the literature. The core idea is that each part of the data provides a specific kind of insight, and by using an ensemble over different portions of the data, it is possible to obtain different insights.

One of the earliest data-centered ensembles was discussed in [41]. In this approach, random subspaces of the data are sampled, and the outlier scores of data points are computed in these projected subspaces. The final outliers are declared as a combination function of the outlier scores from the different subspaces. This technique is also referred to as the *feature bagging* or *subspace ensemble* method, and it is a generalization of similar ideas in the classification domain [17, 33, 34]. The core algorithm discussed in [41], as applied to a data set $\mathscr{D}$ with dimensionality

d, is as follows:

Algorithm *FeatureBagging*(Data Set $\mathcal{D}$);
begin
  repeat
  Sample an integer r between $d/2$ and $d - 1$;
  Select r dimensions from the data randomly to
    create an r-dimensional projection;
  find *LOF* score for each point in projected representation;
  until n iterations;
  Report combined scores from different subspaces;
end

Two different methods are used for combining scores in feature bagging. The first uses the best rank (i.e., rank indicative of greatest degree of outlierness) of each data point (over all ensemble components) in order to score it. This approach can be viewed as a maximization combination function, except that it is applied to the ranks. One issue with this method is that it can cause many ties between the scores of different data points because (discrete) ranks are used for scoring. The second method averages the scores over the different executions. Another method discussed in [28] converts the outlier scores into probabilities before performing the bagging. This normalizes the scores, and improves the quality of the final combination.

The feature bagging method uses axis-parallel projections. Recently, the idea has been generalized to use arbitrary random projection. This method is referred to as *rotated bagging* [5]. the basic idea is to select a randomly rotated axis-system of low dimensionality (which is $2 + \lceil \sqrt{d}/2 \rceil$). However, the axis system is randomly rotated and data points are projected on this rotated system. This type of rotation provides better diversity and also discovers subspace outliers in arbitrarily oriented views of the data.

A number of techniques have also been proposed for statistical selection of relevant subspaces for ensemble analysis [38, 48]. The work in [48] determines subspaces that are relevant to each data point. The approach is designed in such a way, that For the discriminative subspaces found by the method, the approach uses the *product* of (or the addition of the logarithm of) the outlier scores in the different discriminative subspaces. This can be viewed as a combination of model averaging and selection of the most discriminative subspaces, when the scores are scaled by the logarithmic function. The work in [38] is much closer to the feature bagging method of [41], except that statistical selection of relevant subspaces is used for the outlier analysis process. By statistically selecting particular subspaces, the bias characteristics of the ensemble method can be improved. The final score is computed as the average of the scores over different components of the ensemble.

A different data-centered ensemble that is commonly used in the literature, but often not recognized as an ensemblar approach is that of using initial phases of removing outliers from a data set, in order to create a more refined model for outlier analysis. An example of such an approach in the context of intrusion detection is discussed in [10]. In these cases, the combination function can be simply defined as the result from the very last step of the execution. This is because the data quality is improved by removing the outliers in early phases of the algorithm. This improvement in data quality results in better modeling of the outliers in the last phase of algorithm execution. This approach is essentially a sequential ensemble in which the primary goal is that of successive data refinement.

It should be pointed out that the distinction in this section between model-centered and data-centered ensembles is a somewhat semantic one, since a data-centered ensemble can also be considered a specific type of model-centered ensemble in which the process of creating the data set is part of the modeling algorithm. Some methods like feature bagging is tricky to classify from this point of view because they seem to be data-centered ensembles at least from a semantic point of view because the different data sets of the ensemble components are created using subspace projections. However, as we will see in Chap. 3, it is much easier to explain methods like feature bagging from a model-centric point of view rather than data-centric point of view from a theoretical perspective. Nevertheless, this semantic categorization is useful, because the exploration of different segments of the data requires inherently different kinds of techniques than the exploration of different models which are data-independent. The choices in picking different functions of the data for exploration requires data-centric insights, which are analogous to classification methods such as boosting, especially in the sequential case. Therefore, we view this categorization as a convenient way to stimulate different lines of research on the topic.

1.3.3   Discussion of Categorization Schemes

The two different categorization schemes are clearly not exhaustive, though they represent a significant fraction of the ensemble functions used in the literature. In fact, these two categorization schemes can be combined in order to create four different possibilities. This is summarized in Table 1.1. We have also illustrated how many of the current ensemblar schemes map to these different possibilities. Interestingly, do not have too many examples of a sequential model-based ensemble in the literature. The only such method we are aware of in this context is the *SELECT* scheme, which sequentially adds detectors to an ensemble of models based on the correlations between the current ensemble and candidate components. Since there is not much work in this area, it would be an interesting avenue for future exploration. The work by Nguyen et al. [52] cannot be classified as either a data-centered or a model-centered scheme, since it uses some aspects of both. Furthermore, the work in [28] converts outlier scores into probabilities as a general pre-processing method for normalization, and it is not dependent on whether the individual components are data-centered or model-centered. The issue of model combination is a critically tricky one both in terms of how the individual scores are normalized, and in terms of how they are combined. This issue will be discussed in detail in the next section.

Table 1.1 Categorization of ensemble techniques

	Data centered	Model centered
Independent	Feature bagging [41]	LOF tuning [14]
	HiCS [38]	LOCI tuning [53]
	Subsampling [5, 7, 18, 43, 72]	Isolation forests [43]
	Rotated bagging [5]	Multiple-Proclus [51]
	RS-Hash [60]	OutRank [51]
	Nguyen et al. [52]	
	Converting scores into probabilities [28]	
	Calibrated bagging [28]	
Sequential	Intrusion bootstrap [10]	*SELECT* [56]
	OUTRES [48]	

1.4 Categorization by Theoretical Approach

Recently, it has been shown [5] that the theoretical foundations for classification ensembles can be adapted to outlier ensembles with some modifications. A helpful way of viewing the relationship between outlier detection and classification is that outlier detection can be considered an unsupervised analog of the rare class detection problem. This analogy helps in building a parallel bias-variance theory for outlier detection, albeit with some differences from that in classification. *A key difference is that labels are unobserved in outlier detection, whereas they are observed in classification.* Furthermore, the noise term is treated differently between classification ensembles and outlier ensembles. However, the consequences of these differences are primarily *algorithmic* in that one no longer has the availability of class labels in order to develop effective algorithms. Depending on the specific methodology at hand, it may or may not be easy to adapt as specific classification ensemble algorithm to outlier detection.

Broadly speaking, even though the ground-truth is not *available* in unsupervised problems, it can still be assumed that some hypothetical (but unknown) ideal ground-truth does exist. This ground-truth can be defined either in terms of the outlier scores, or in terms of the underlying binary labels. The former case is similar to that of regression modeling in the supervised domain, whereas the latter case is similar to that of classification. As in the case of the supervised domain, one can defined a mean-squared error (MSE) with respect to this ground truth. Subsequently, this mean-squared error can be decomposed into two terms:

1. *Squared bias*: This represent the squared difference between the *expected* output of the algorithm and the ideal outlier score (which is unobserved in unsupervised problems). Nevertheless, in spite of the unobserved nature of outlier scores, it can still be defined as a *theoretical* quantity.
2. *Variance*: This represents the mean-squared deviation in the outlier scores over various randomized instantiations of the base data or randomized instantiations

of the base detectors. Thus, the variance is often a result of the nuances of the specific data set, which causes variation in the output.

The overall error of an outlier detection algorithm can be decomposed into the bias and the variance [5]:

$$MSE = Bias^2 + Variance \tag{1.1}$$

This relationship will also be studied in greater detail in Chap. 2. It is also noteworthy that the right-hand side of the aforementioned equation contains an intrinsic error term in classification. However, this intrinsic error term is missing in outlier detection because of the ideal nature of the outlier scores. This point will be discussed in greater detail in Chap. 2.

Outlier ensemble analysis is a methodology for using repeated applications of one or more *base* algorithms in order to reduce the bias or the variance. These correspond to the two primary classes of algorithms discussed in this book, and we briefly revisit them here.

1.4.1 Variance Reduction in Outlier Ensembles

Variance reduction methods often improve the robustness of base detectors by using different randomized instantiations of the base data or different randomized instantiations of base detectors, and then averaging the predictions. The basic idea is to create an approach that provides more similar results over different training data sets. Since the variance is a component of the overall error, reducing the variance will also reduce the error of the detector. The vast majority of outlier ensemble methods such as feature bagging and subsampling, are variance reduction methods. Many variance-reduction techniques are discussed in detail in Chap. 3. Furthermore, an experimental comparison between many variance reduction techniques is also provided in the chapter.

1.4.2 Bias Reduction in Outlier Ensembles

In bias reduction, the goal is to improve the accuracy of the outlier detector in *expectation*. An example of a bias reduction method in the classification domain is boosting. However, such methods are often hard to generalize to outlier detection. A reason for this is that bias reduction methods typically require the availability of the ground truth in order to guide the algorithm. For example, in the case of classification, boosting requires the availability of ground truth in order to guide the algorithm. when such ground-truth is not available, it becomes more difficult to guide the algorithm in a reliable way. Nevertheless, even in these cases, it is often possible to use heuristic methods to reduce bias. A number of these methods will be discussed in detail in Chap. 4.

1.5 Defining Combination Functions

A crucial issue in outlier analysis is the definition of combination functions which can combine the outlier scores from different models. There are several challenges which arise in the combination process:

- *Normalization issues*: The different models may output scores which are not easily comparable with one another. For example, a k-nearest neighbor classifier may output a distance score, which is different from an LOF score, and the latter is also quite different from the MDEF score returned by the LOCI method. Even a feature bagging approach, which is defined with the use of the same base algorithm (LOF) on different feature subsets, may sometimes have calibration issues in the scores [28]. Therefore, if a combination function such as the average or the max is applied to the constituent scores, then one or more the models may be inadvertently favored.
- *Combination issues*: The second issue is the choice of the combination function. Given a set of normalized outlier scores, how do we decide the specific choice of the combination function to be used? Should the average of the scores be used, or the maximum of the scores be used? It turns out that the answer to this question may sometimes depend on the size of the data and the level of instability of the model at hand. However, there are some typical effects of using specific types of combination functions, and it is even possible to combine the effects of using different types of combination functions in a robust way.

In the following section, we will discuss some of these issues in detail.

1.5.1 Normalization Issues

The major factor in normalization is that the different algorithms do not use the same scales of reference and cannot be reasonably compared with one another. In fact, in some cases, high outlier scores may correspond to larger outlier tendency, whereas in other cases, low scores may correspond to greater outlier tendency. This causes problems during the combination process; when combining scores on incomparable scales, it is likely to inadvertently weight one outlier detection algorithm more than the other. Furthermore, combining algorithms with different conventions on the ordering of the scores can lead to completely unpredictable results. One simple approach for performing the normalization is to use the ranks from the different outlier analysis algorithms; furthermore, the ranking uses the consistently convention to order the scores from the greatest outlier tendency to least outlier tendency.

These ranks can then be combined in order to create a unified outlier score. One of the earliest methods for feature bagging [41] uses such an approach in one of its combination functions.

The major issue with such an approach is that it does lose a lot of information about the relative differences between the outlier scores. For example, consider the cases where the top outlier scores for components A and B of the ensemble are $\{1.71, 1.71, 1.70\ldots\}$ and $\{1.72, 1.03, 1.01\ldots\}$ respectively, and each component uses (some variation of) the LOF algorithm. It is clear that in component A, the top three outlier scores are almost equivalent, and in component B, the top outlier score is the most relevant one. However, a ranking approach will not distinguish between these scenarios, and provide them the same rank values. Clearly, this loss of information is not desirable for creating an effective combination from the different scores.

The previous example suggests that it is important to examine both the ordering of the values and the distribution of the values during the normalization process. Ideally, it is desirable to somehow convert the outlier scores into probabilities, so that they can be reasonably used in an effective way. An approach was proposed in [28] which uses mixture modeling in conjunction with the EM-framework in order to convert the scores into probabilities. Two methods are proposed in this work. Both of these techniques use parametric modeling methods. The first method assumes that the posterior probabilities follow a logistic sigmoid function. The underlying parameters are then learned from the EM framework from the distribution of outlier scores. The second approach recognizes the fact that the outlier scores of data points in the outlier component of the mixture is likely to show a different distribution (Gaussian distribution), than the scores of data points in the normal class (Exponential distribution). Therefore, this approach models the score distributions as a mixture of exponential and Gaussian probability functions. As before, the parameters are learned with the use of the EM-framework. The posterior probabilities are calculated with the use of the Bayes rule. This approach has been shown to be effective in improving the quality of the ensemble approach proposed in [41]. A second method has also been proposed recently [28], which improves upon this base method for converting the outlier scores, and converting the scores into probabilities.

1.5.2 Combining Scores from Different Models

The second issue is the choice of the function which needs to be used in order to combine the scores. Given a set of r (normalized) outlier scores $Score_i(\overline{X})$ for the data point $\overline{X}$, should we use the model average or the maximum? For ease in discussion in this section, we will assume the convention without loss of generality that greater outlier scores correspond to greater outlier tendency. Therefore the use of the maximization function always uses the outlier ensemble component for each point, in which its outlier behavior is most magnified.

The earliest work on ensemble-based outlier analysis (not formally recognized as ensemble analysis) was performed in the context of model-centric parameter tuning [14, 53]. Most outlier analysis methods typically have a parameter, which controls the *granularity* of the underlying model. The outliers may often be visible to the algorithm only at a specific level of granularity. For example, the value of k in the k-nearest neighbor approach or LOF approach, the sampling neighborhood size in the LOCI approach, the number of clusters in a clustering approach all control the granularity of the analysis. What is the optimal granularity to be used? While this is often viewed as an issue of parameter tuning, it can also be viewed as an issue of ensemble analysis, when addressed in a certain way.

In particular, the methods in [14, 53] run the algorithms over a range of values of the granularity parameter, and pick the parameter choice which best enhances the outlier score (maximum function for our convention on score ordering) for a given data point. In other words, we have:

$$Ensemble(\overline{X}) = \text{MAX}_i\{Score_i(\overline{X})\} \tag{1.2}$$

This reason for this has been discussed in some detail in the original LOF paper. In particular, it has been suggested that the use of other combination function such as the average or the minimum leads to a dilution in the outlier scores from the irrelevant models. However, as we will see later, the relative performance of the maximization function and the averaging function depends on far more subtle factors than one might imagine. There are cases in which the averaging function performs better and there are also cases in which the maximization function performs better. However, the former turns out to be a more robust approach than the latter, whereas the maximization function turns out to be more unstable. Nevertheless, as we will see in Chap. 5, it is possible to combine the two in order to obtain the best of both worlds.

The common functions that are used for score combination are as follows:

- *Maximum function*: This is one of the most common functions used for combining ensemblar scores both in implicit (LOF and LOCI parameter tuning) and explicit ensemblar models. One variation on this model is to use the ranks instead of the scores in the combination process. Such an approach was also used in feature bagging [41]. An important aspect of the process is that the different data points need to have the same number of components in the ensemble in order to be compared meaningfully.
- *Averaging Function*: In this case, the model scores are averaged over the different components of the ensemble. The risk factor here is that if the individual components of the ensemble are poorly derived models, then the irrelevant scores from many different components will dilute the overall outlier score. Nevertheless, such an approach has been used extensively, and it does have the advantage of robustness because it reduces the variance of the overall prediction. As we will discuss in Chap. 3, variance reduction often results in superior performance. Examples of methods which use this method are one of the models in feature bagging [41] and the HiCS method [48].

- *Damped averaging*: In this model, a damping function is applied to the outlier scores before averaging, in order to prevent it from being dominated by a few components. Examples of a damping function could be the square root or the logarithm. It should be pointed out that the use of the product of the outlier scores (or geometric averaging) could be interpreted as the averaging of the logarithm of outlier scores. Such an approach is particularly appropriate for outlier scores that are interpreted as probabilities or fit values, since the logarithms of the probabilities correspond to log-likelihood estimates.
- *Pruned averaging and aggregates*: In this case, the low scores are pruned and the outlier scores are either averaged or aggregated (summed up) over the relevant ensembles. The goal here is to prune the irrelevant models for each data point before computing the combination score. The pruning can be performed by either using an absolute threshold on the outlier score, or by picking the top-k models for each data point, and averaging them. When using absolute thresholds, it is important to normalize the scores from the different ensemble components. For example, the work in [5] advocates the conversion of scores to standardized Z-values, and then using a threshold of 0 on the scores. Aggregates are more appropriate than averages, since they implicitly count the number of ensemble components in which a data point is relevant. A data point will be more relevant in a greater number of ensemble components, when it has a greater tendency to be an outlier. Such an aggregated score, which is referred to as *Thresh* in [5], combines the benefits of maximization and averaging. This type of approach can often provide more robust results.
- *Result from last component executed*: This approach is sometimes used in sequential ensembles [10], in which each component of the ensemble successively refines the data set, and removes the obvious outliers. As a result, the normal model is constructed on a data set from which outliers are removed and the model is more robust. In such cases, the goal of each component of the sequential ensemble is to successively refine the data set. Therefore, the score from the last component is the most appropriate one to be used.

Which combination function provides the best insights for ensemble analysis? Clearly, the combination function may be dependent on the structure of the ensemble in the general case, especially if the goal of each component of the ensemble is to either refine the data set, or understand the behavior of only a very *local* segment of the data set.

However, for the general case, in which the function of each component of the ensemble is to provide a reasonable and comparable outlier score for each data point, the two most commonly used functions are the *maximum* and the *averaging* functions. While pruned averaging combines these aspects, it is rarely used in ensemble analysis. Which combination function is best? Are there any other combination functions that could conceivably provide better results? These are open questions, the answer to which is not completely known because of the sparse literature on outlier ensemble analysis. A recent paper [5] sheds some light on the issue. The maximum function tends to help in terms of bias, whereas the averaging function works well in terms of the variance. The bias reduction of the maximization function is a heuristic one, and it tends to work quite well on a variety of data sets. The scores of outlier points often turn out to be far more brittle and unstable than the scores of inlier points. As a result, the use of the maximization function significantly improves the overall performance in most cases (when measured with objective performance metrics like the are-under-curve or receiver operating characteristic), whereas the use of the minimization function can have the opposite effect. The main problem with the maximization approach is that even though it often improves bias heuristically, it can sometimes increase the variance of the combination. By combining the maximization combination function with averaging (for variance reduction), it is possible to obtain accurate and robust results [5]. On the other hand, using a function such as minimization is generally absolutely disastrous in the context of outlier detection whether it is combined with averaging or not. The model tends to get diluted by the worst components in the data and the performance is often worse than the median base performance. Many variants have been proposed in [5] that combine the benefits of maximization and averaging. These variants will be discussed in Chaps. 3 and 5.

1.6 Research Overview and Book Organization

The area of outlier ensemble analysis is still in its infancy, although it is rapidly emerging as an important research area in its own right. In some ways, ensemble methods are far more crucial for unsupervised methods like outlier detection, because such methods can provide the robustness needed in cases where tuning is not possible (because of lack of ground truth). One encouraging aspect of outlier ensemble analysis is that it is very similar in some respects to the classification problem. Therefore, much of the classification work can be easily generalized to outlier ensembles. In fact, many methods for outlier ensembles analysis like bagging and subsampling are adapted directly from the classification domain.

As discussed earlier, a major challenge for ensemble development in unsupervised problems is that the evaluation process is highly subjective, and the ground truth cannot be assumed to be available to the detector itself. Therefore, the performance-centric effects of the intermediate steps cannot be assessed by the algorithm with objective metrics, and the intermediate decisions must be made with the use of outlier scores only. In comparison, methods like classification allow the use of concrete evaluation criteria on hold-out sets. Therefore, in this context, we believe that the major similarities and differences in supervised and unsupervised methods are as follows:

- **Intermediate evaluation**: In unsupervised methods, ground truth is typically not available. While one can use measures such as classification accuracy in supervised methods, this is not the case with unsupervised methods. Intermediate evaluation is particularly important for sequential methods (such as boosting in classification). This is one of the reasons that sequential methods are much rarer than independent methods in outlier ensemble analysis. Furthermore, bias-reduction methods are more difficult to reliably construct in outlier detection.

- **Diversity and consensus issues**: Both supervised and unsupervised methods seek greater diversity with the use of an ensemble in terms of the methodology used for creating the model. In many cases, this is done by selecting models which are different from one another. For example, in clustering, diversity is achieved by using either randomized clustering or explicitly picking orthogonal clusterings [4]. However, in the case of supervised methods, the level of consensus is also measured *at the end* in terms of the ground truth. This is not the case in unsupervised methods, since no ground truth is available. Nevertheless, the (unsupervised) randomized methods used in classification, such as bagging and subagging, can be easily generalized to outlier ensemble analysis.

Some of the properties in supervised learning (e.g., presence of class labels) cannot obviously be transferred to outlier analysis. In spite of these differences, many of the key ideas from classification ensembles can still be generalized to outlier ensembles. In the following, we discuss some common methods used for different supervised and unsupervised problems, and whether they can be transferred to the problem of outlier analysis. In some cases, the ensemble ideas from classification have already been adapted to outlier analysis. These cases will also be discussed below:

- *Boosting*: Boosting [26, 27] is a common technique used in classification. The idea is to focus on successively difficult portions of the data set in order to create models which can classify the data points in these portions more accurately, and then crate the ensemble scores by averaging the score over all the components. This type of focus on difficult portions of the data set is achieved by increasing the weight of incorrectly classified training instances in each iteration, and decreasing the weight of correctly classified training instances. The basic idea is to assume that the errors are caused by the limitations of the model, and by averaging the predictions of the model over the weighted data sets, one can create a model that does not have these limitations. Such an approach clearly does not seem to be applicable to the unsupervised version of the problem because of the difficulty in computing the accuracy of the model on different data points in the absence of ground truth. On the other hand, since the supervised version of the problem (rare class detection) is a skewed classification problem, the boosting approach is applicable almost directly. A number of learners [20, 37] have been proposed for the supervised version of the outlier analysis problem. These classifiers have been shown to achieve significantly superior results because of the use of boosting. This is difficult to achieve in outlier ensemble analysis because of the fact that the problem is unsupervised. Nevertheless, a number of heuristic bias reduction methods can still be developed in the context of the outlier detection problem. Some recent methods [57, 59] have developed ideas along these lines.

- *Bagging*: Bagging [15] is an approach that combines the predictions from models constructed on different *bootstrapped* samples of the training data. The basic idea is to sample training data points with replacement and predict each test point repeatedly using a model constructed on each sample. The predictions of a test point across different samples are averaged to yield the final prediction. The effect of bagging is to reduce the variability in prediction of a test instance over the specific choice of the training data set. Such a reduction in variability leads to accuracy improvements.

As shown in Chap. 3, it is easy to generalize bagging to outlier detection. The main problem with the use of bagging is that many outlier detectors are not very robust to the presence of repeated data points. As we will see later in this book, many detectors like LOF perform poorly in the presence of repeated data points. Therefore, it is important to make appropriate modifications to the base detectors to ameliorate the effect of repeated points. Although bagging is a well-known technique in classification, this book provides the first study of bagging in the context of the outlier detection problem. An interesting conclusion from the results of Chap. 3 is that bagging is a very attractive option for improving detector performance as long as it is possible to modify the base algorithm appropriately to adjust for the effect of repeated points. Unfortunately, the specific technique used to adjust for the effect of repeated points depends on the base algorithm at hand.

Instead of bagging, one can use subsampling or subagging [18] in order to reduce variance. In this case, the points are sampled without replacement from the data. Just like bagging, subsampling can be generalized trivially from classification to outlier detection. The first application of subsampling for outlier detection was proposed in the work on isolation forests primarily for its computational benefits [43], although occasional accuracy improvements were also observed. The subsampling method tends to perform better with distance-based detectors [5, 72]. The work in [72], however, provides an incorrect theoretical explanation of the accuracy improvements of distance-based methods, and the specific implementation is somewhat unreliable in terms of its accuracy effects. A correct explanation of the accuracy improvements of subsampling (along with a more reliable implementation) may be found in [5].

It is noteworthy that one can subsample either the entries of a matrix or the rows of a matrix in order to build outlier detection models. The appropriateness of a specific methodology depends on the particular data type at hand. For example, in graphs and recommender systems, it makes sense to subsample entries (edges or ratings), whereas in the case of multidimensional data, it makes sense to subsample rows. An example of entry-wise subsampling of graph adjacency matrices is proposed in [7]. This method samples edges from a graph in order to score the outlier tendency of edges and then uses the median score of different models as the final outlier score.

- *Feature bagging*: The well known *feature* bagging approach for outlier analysis [28, 41] is a generalization of a similar idea that was already proposed in the classification domain [17, 34]. The basic idea in feature bagging is to preselect a random subset of features on which the classifier or outlier detector) is applied. The final classifier prediction (or outlier score) is obtained by averaging the predictions from different base algorithms.

- *Random forests*: A random forest [16, 33] is a method that constructs multiple decision trees on the training data by restricting the split criteria at each node, and then averages the prediction from the different trees. The split criterion is restricted at each node by pre-selecting a random subset of features at each node, and the splitting feature is selected only from this node-specific set of features. Note that restricting the feature set at each node would seem to be detrimental from the perspective of the prediction accuracy of a *single tree*; however, the averaged performance from multiple trees is extremely accurate. Random forests can be seen as a way of explicitly injecting randomness into the base classifier in order to induce diversity. It uses a similar principle to feature bagging [17, 34], which injects randomness into the classifier by *globally* selecting subsets of features on which the entire classifier is applied. Thus, feature bagging is different from a random forest in that the former preselects a subset of features up front on which the entire algorithm is applied, whereas a random forest might select a different subset of features at each node. In this sense, the random forest method is a generalization of the idea of feature bagging, when applied to decision trees. In fact, the early versions [33] of random forests in classification show that the basic idea of a random forest is a generalization of the idea of feature bagging (or random subspace sampling).

While decision trees were not originally designed for the outlier analysis problem, it has been shown in [43] that the broad concept of decision trees can also be extended to outlier analysis by examining those paths with unusually short length, since the outlier regions tend to get isolated rather quickly. An ensemble of such trees is referred to as an *isolation forest* [43], and has been used effectively for making robust predictions about outliers. Interestingly, the isolation forest approach can be viewed as an indirect way of performing subspace outlier detection, by relating the outlierness of the data point with its tendency to be isolated in a subspace of low dimensionality. In fact, the dimensionality of the subspace in which one can isolate the point is a rough proxy of its outlier score. Outliers can be generally isolated in subspaces of relatively low dimensionality. It is noteworthy that the goals with which an isolation forest is constructed are different from those of a decision tree, and therefore the comparison between the two is somewhat superficial in nature.

- *Model averaging and combination*: This is one of the most common models used in ensemble analysis and is used both for the clustering and classification problems. In fact, the random forest method discussed above is a special case of this idea. In the context of the classification problem, many Bayesian methods [23] exist for the model combination process. Some recent works [52, 56] have focused on creating a bucket of models from which the scores are combined through either averaging or using the maximum value. Even the parameter tuning methods used in many outlier analysis algorithms such as LOF and LOCI can be viewed to be drawn from this category. A related model is *stacking* [22, 68], in which the combination is performed in conjunction with model evaluation. This can sometimes be more difficult for unsupervised problems such as classification. Nevertheless, since stacking has been used for some unsupervised problems such as density estimation [64], it is possible that some of the techniques may be generalizable to outlier analysis, as long as an appropriate model for quantifying performance can be found. In this book, we will discuss some unsupervised generalizations of stacking for supervised outlier detection.

- *Bucket of models*: In this approach [70], a "hold-out" portion of the data set is used in order to decide the most appropriate model. The most appropriate model is one in which the highest accuracy is achieved in the held out data set. In essence, this approach can be viewed as a competition or bake-off contest between the different models. While this is easy to perform in supervised problems such as classification, it is much more difficult for small-sample and unsupervised problems. No ground truth is available for evaluation in unsupervised problems. It is unlikely that a precise analogue of the method can be created for outlier analysis, since exact ground truth is not available for the evaluation process.

To summarize, we create a table of the different methods, and the different characteristics such as the type of ensemble, combination technique, or whether normalization is present. This is provided in Table 1.2. It is noteworthy that this type of categorization is not exact; for example, methods like rotated bagging and feature bagging (which transform the data) can also be considered either model-centered ensembles or data-centered ensembles depending on whether one considers the transformation process a part of the base algorithm. Although we have classified these methods as data-centered ensembles, we will see in later chapters that the model-centered view of these methods is more convenient from the point of view of theoretical analysis.

1.6.1 Overview of Book

In this book, we will explore several of the aforementioned models and issues in outlier ensemble analysis. In particular, the following topics will be covered by the various chapters:

1. *Theory of outlier ensembles*: Chap. 2 will set the stage for the generalization of outlier ensemble analysis from the classification domain. The bias-variance theory will be derived for the outlier analysis domain. This derivation is closely related to (and in fact simpler than) the corresponding derivation in the classification domain. We will show how the theoretical models from classification can be generalized to outlier detection. Furthermore, we will study several natural generalizations of bias-variance theory in terms of how the overall error of a model can be decomposed into the bias and variance components. This chapter can be viewed as a generalization of the ideas presented in [5].

2. *Variance reduction methods*: We will investigate different variance-reduction methods in Chap. 3. Since variance reduction is one of the most important classes of methods in unsupervised problems, we will study numerous methods in detail. A proper explanation of subsampling will also be provided in this chapter. Several new variance-reduction methods will also be proposed in this chapter, which have not been proposed anywhere else in the literature. A detailed experimental study of the different variance-reduction methods will also be provided in this chapter.

Table 1.2 Characteristics of outlier ensemble methods

Method	Model-centered or Data-centered	Sequential or Independent	Combination function	Normalization
LOF tuning [14]	Model	Independent	Max	No
LOCI tuning [53]	Model	Independent	Max	No
Feature bagging [41]	Data	Independent	Max/Avg	No
Rotated bagging [5]	Data	Independent	Max/Avg.	Yes
HiCS [38]	Data	Independent	Selective Avg	No
Calib. bagging [28]	Both	Independent	Max/Avg	Yes
OutRank [51]	Model	Independent	Harmonic mean	No
Multiple-Proclus [51]	Model	Independent	Harmonic mean	No
Converting scores to probabilities [28]	Both	Independent	Max/Avg	Yes
Intrusion bootstrap [10]	Data	Sequential	Last component	No
OUTRES [48]	Data	Sequential	Product	No
Nguyen et al. [52]	Both	Independent	Weighted Avg.	No
Entry subsampling [7] (Graph Matrix)	Both	Independent	Median	Yes
Isolation forest [43]	Model	Independent	Average	Yes
Bagging (Chap. 3)	Data	Independent	Average	Yes
Variable subsampling [5]	Data	Independent	Many	Yes
One-class [66]	Data	Independent	Avg./Product	No
SELECT [56]	Model	Sequential	Average	Yes
LODA [54]	Model	Independent	Average	Yes
RS-Hash [60]	Both	Independent	Average	No
CARE [57]	Both	Sequential	Weighted Avg.	Yes
FVPS [57]	Data	Sequential	Average	Yes
RandNet [21]	Model	Independent	Median	Yes
BSS/DBSS [59]	Data	Independent	Average	Yes

3. *Bias reduction methods*: Bias reduction is much more difficult in outlier ensemble analysis as compared to classification. In classification, bias-reduction methods such as boosting require the computation of accuracy in intermediate phases of the algorithm. This is generally difficult in the context of outlier ensemble analysis because of the unsupervised nature of the problem. Nevertheless, several unsupervised heuristics can be used to improve the effectiveness of outlier-detection algorithms. Chapter 4 will study the effect of using different types of bias-reduction methods. Several of these methods are new, and have not been discussed elsewhere in the literature.
4. *Model combination methods*: Chap. 5 will introduce several model combination methods. This chapter will study different model combination methods from the perspective of the bias-variance trade-off, and discuss their relative effects in these settings.
5. *Effect of base detectors*: The choice of base detectors has a significant effect on the outlier detection algorithm at hand. This issue will be discussed in Chap. 6. It is often an article of faith in the research community that locally normalized algorithms like LOF are more effective than unnormalized k-nearest neighbor detectors or multivariate extreme value analysis methods. However, it turns out that raw distance-based detectors are far more *stable* to various parameter settings and choices of data sets.

In Chap. 6, the effect of combining different types of detectors is also explored. An experimental study comparing several important outlier detectors will be provided in this chapter. It will also be shown that the use of ensemble methods tends to have an *equalizing effect*; it tends to make many base methods more similar in terms of overall performance, which is very close to the best performance that one can hope to achieve. This is a natural consequence of the fact that the variance component of all detectors is reduced drastically by many ensemble techniques like variable subsampling [5]. Since worse detectors tend to have larger variance components, the use of an ensemble method often has an equalizing effect on different detectors. Although base detectors that use kernel transformations are often not fully reliable in outlier detection, the use of ensemble methods is often able to raise these methods to more robust performance. A particularly interesting method in this context is the *kernel Mahalanobis* method, which has not been explored elsewhere in the literature. Unlike other kernel methods like one-class SVMs [61, 62], this approach has a score-centric approach, which can be easily generalized to ensemble-centric settings. Although it has been shown in the literature [24, 44], that kernel methods (like one-class SVMs [61, 62] and support vector data description [67]) are rather unpredictable, we show that the ensemble-centric approach of the kernel Mahalanobis method is extremely robust. We will also examine the robustness effects of combining different base detectors.
6. *Combining supervised and unsupervised models*: Although this book is primarily focused on unsupervised outlier ensembles, it will also touch on a few settings in which supervised methods are used. For example, mild forms of supervision can

be used in the final step of model selection and combination by bringing the user into the loop. Similarly, the output of unsupervised outlier detection methods can be used as a feature engineering method for supervised outlier detection [45, 46]. These different aspects of mild supervision will be discussed in Chaps. 4 and 5.

In summary, this book will not only cover the state-of-the-art in ensemble analysis, but will also introduce several new ideas. Therefore, this book can be viewed both as an overview book, as well as a book introducing new ideas into the ensemble analysis literature.

1.7   Conclusions and Discussion

This chapter provides an overview of the emerging area of outlier ensemble analysis, which has seen increasing attention in the literature in recent years. We also discuss how the material in this chapter relates to the various chapters in this book. Many ensemble analysis methods in the outlier analysis literature are not recognized as such in a formal way. This paper provides an understanding of how these methods relate to other techniques used explicitly as ensembles in the literature. We provided different ways of categorizing the outlier analysis problems in the literature, such as independent or sequential ensembles, and data- or model-centered ensembles. We discussed the impact of different kinds of combination functions, and how these combination functions relate to different kinds of ensembles. The issue of choosing the right combination function is an important one, though it may depend upon the structure of the ensemble in the general case. We also provided a mapping of many current techniques in the literature to different kinds of ensembles. Finally, a discussion was provided on the feasibility of adapting ensemble techniques from other data mining problems to outlier analysis.

Ensemble analysis is a recent field in the outlier analysis domain as compared to other data mining problems such as clustering and classification. The reason for this is rooted in the greater difficulty of judging the quality of a component of the ensemble, as compared to other data mining problems such as classification. Many models such as stacking and boosting in other data mining problems require a crisply defined judgement of different ensemble components on hold-out sets, which are not readily available in data mining problems such as outlier analysis. The outlier analysis problem suffers from the problem of small sample space as well as lack of ground truth (as in all unsupervised problems). The lack of ground truth implies that it is necessary to use the intermediate outputs of the algorithm (rather than concrete quality measures on hold-out sets), for making the combination decisions and ensemble-centric choices. These intermediate outputs may sometimes represent poor estimations of outlier scores. When combination decisions and other choices are made in an unsupervised way on an inherently small sample space problem such as outlier analysis, the likelihood and consequences of inappropriate choices can be high as compared to another unsupervised problem such as clustering, which does not have the small sample space issues.

While outlier detection is a challenging problem for ensemble analysis, the problems are not unsurmountable. It has become clear from the results of numerous recent ensemble methods that such methods can lead to significant qualitative improvements. Therefore, ensemble analysis seems to be an emerging area, which can be a fruitful research direction for improving the quality of outlier detection algorithms. This book will provide an overview of this emerging area and also advance the state-of-the-art in outlier ensembles.

Exercises

1. Consider a randomized algorithm that predicts whether a data point is an outlier or non-outlier correctly with a probability of 0.6. Furthermore, all executions of this algorithm are completely independent of one another. A majority vote of 5 independent predictions of the algorithm is used as the final result. What is the probability that the correct answer is returned for a given data point?
2. Discuss the similarities and differences between rare-class detection and outlier detection. What do these similarities imply in terms of being able to adapt the ensembles for rare-class detection to outlier analysis?
3. Discuss how one can use clustering ensembles to measure similarities between data points. How can these computed similarities be useful for outlier detection?

References

1. C. C. Aggarwal. A Human-Computer Interactive Method for Projected Clustering. *IEEE Transactions on Knowledge and Data Engineering*, 16(4), pp. 448–460, 2004.
2. C. C. Aggarwal. Outlier Ensembles: Position Paper, *ACM SIGKDD Explorations*, 14(2), pp. 49–58, December, 2012.
3. C. C. Aggarwal. Outlier Analysis, Second Edition, *Springer*, 2017.
4. C. C. Aggarwal, C. Reddy. Data Clustering: Algorithms and Applications, *CRC Press*, 2013.
5. C. C. Aggarwal and S. Sathe. Theoretical Foundations and Algorithms for Outlier Ensembles, *ACM SIGKDD Explorations*, 17(1), June 2015.
6. C. C. Aggarwal and P. S. Yu. Outlier Detection in High Dimensional Data, *ACM SIGMOD Conference*, 2001.
7. C. C. Aggarwal and P. S. Yu. Outlier Detection in Graph Streams. *IEEE ICDE Conference*, 2011.
8. C. C. Aggarwal, C. Procopiuc, J. Wolf, P. Yu, and J. Park. Fast Algorithms for Projected Clustering, *ACM SIGMOD Conference*, 1999.
9. F. Angiulli, C. Pizzuti. Fast Outlier Detection in High Dimensional Spaces, *PKDD Conference*, 2002.
10. D. Barbara, Y. Li, J. Couto, J.-L. Lin, and S. Jajodia. Bootstrapping a Data Mining Intrusion Detection System. *Symposium on Applied Computing*, 2003.
11. S. D. Bay and M. Schwabacher, Mining distance-based outliers in near linear time with randomization and a simple pruning rule, *KDD Conf.*, 2003.
12. R. Bell and Y. Koren. Lessons from the Netflix prize challenge. *ACM SIGKDD Explorations Newsletter*, 9(2), pp. 75–79, 2007.
13. S. Bickel, T. Scheffer. Multi-view clustering. *ICDM Conference*, 2004.

14. M. Breunig, H.-P. Kriegel, R. Ng, and J. Sander. LOF: Identifying Density-based Local Outliers, *ACM SIGMOD Conference*, 2000.
15. L. Brieman. Bagging Predictors. *Machine Learning*, 24(2), pp. 123–140, 1996.
16. L. Brieman. Random Forests. *Journal Machine Learning archive*, 45(1), pp. 5–32, 2001.
17. R. Bryll, R. Gutierrez-Osuna, and F. Quek. Attribute Bagging: Improving Accuracy of Classifier Ensembles by using Random Feature Subsets. *Pattern Recognition*, 36(6), pp. 1291–1302, 2003.
18. P. Buhlmann. Bagging, subagging and bragging for improving some prediction algorithms, *Recent advances and trends in nonparametric statistics*, Elsevier, 2003.
19. V. Chandola, A. Banerjee, V. Kumar. Anomaly Detection: A Survey, *ACM Computing Surveys*, 2009.
20. N. Chawla, A. Lazarevic, L. Hall, and K. Bowyer. SMOTEBoost: Improving prediction of the minority class in boosting, *PKDD*, pp. 107–119, 2003.
21. J. Chen, S. Sathe, C. Aggarwal, and D. Turaga. Outlier Detection with Autoencoder Ensembles. *SIAM Conference on Data Mining*, 2017.
22. B. Clarke. Bayes Model Averaging and Stacking when Model Approximation Error cannot be Ignored, *Journal of Machine Learning Research*, pp 683–712, 2003.
23. P. Domingos. Bayesian Averaging of Classifiers and the Overfitting Problem. *ICML Conference*, 2000.
24. A. Emmott, S. Das, T. Dietteerich, A. Fern, and W. Wong. Systematic Construction of Anomaly Detection Benchmarks from Real Data. arXiv:1503.01158, 2015. https://arxiv.org/abs/1503.01158
25. M. Fernandez-Delgado, E. Cernadas, S. Barro, and D. Amorim. Do we Need Hundreds of Classifiers to Solve Real World Classification Problems? *The Journal of Machine Learning Research*, 15(1), pp. 3133–3181, 2014.
26. Y. Freund and R. Schapire. A Decision-theoretic Generalization of Online Learning and Application to Boosting, *Computational Learning Theory*, 1995.
27. Y. Freund and R. Schapire. Experiments with a New Boosting Algorithm. *ICML Conference*, pp. 148–156, 1996.
28. J. Gao and P.-N. Tan. Converting output scores from outlier detection algorithms into probability estimates. *ICDM Conference*, 2006.
29. S. Guha, N. Mishra, G. Roy, and O. Schrijver. Robust Random Cut Forest Based Anomaly Detection On Streams. *ICML Conference*, pp. 2712–2721, 2016.
30. M. Grill and T. Pevny. Learning Combination of Anomaly Detectors for Security Domain. *Computer Networks*, 2016.
31. Z. He, S. Deng and X. Xu. A Unified Subspace Outlier Ensemble Framework for Outlier Detection, *Advances in Web Age Information Management*, 2005.
32. A. Hinneburg, D. Keim, and M. Wawryniuk. Hd-eye: Visual mining of high-dimensional data. *IEEE Computer Graphics and Applications*, 19:22–31, 1999.
33. T. K. Ho. Random decision forests. *Third International Conference on Document Analysis and Recognition*, 1995. Extended version appears as "The random subspace method for constructing decision forests" in *IEEE Transactions on Pattern Analysis and Machine Intelligence*, 20(8), pp. 832–844, 1998.
34. T. K. Ho. Nearest Neighbors in Random Subspaces. *Lecture Notes in Computer Science*, Vol. 1451, pp. 640–648, *Proceedings of the Joint IAPR Workshops SSPR'98 and SPR'98*, 1998. http://link.springer.com/chapter/10.1007/BFb0033288
35. W. Jin, A. Tung, and J. Han. Mining top-n local outliers in large databases, *ACM KDD Conference*, 2001.
36. T. Johnson, I. Kwok, and R. Ng. Fast computation of 2-dimensional depth contours. *ACM KDD Conference*, 1998.
37. M. Joshi, V. Kumar, and R. Agarwal. Evaluating Boosting Algorithms to Classify Rare Classes: Comparison and Improvements. *ICDM Conference*, pp. 257–264, 2001.
38. F. Keller, E. Muller, K. Bohm. HiCS: High-Contrast Subspaces for Density-based Outlier Ranking, *IEEE ICDE Conference*, 2012.

39. E. Knorr, and R. Ng. Algorithms for Mining Distance-based Outliers in Large Datasets. *VLDB Conference*, 1998.
40. E. Knorr, and R. Ng. Finding Intensional Knowledge of Distance-Based Outliers. *VLDB Conference*, 1999.
41. A. Lazarevic, and V. Kumar. Feature Bagging for Outlier Detection, *ACM KDD Conference*, 2005.
42. F. T. Liu, K. N. Ting, and Z.-H. Zhou. On Detecting Clustered Anomalies using SCiForest. *Machine Learning and Knowledge Discovery in Databases*, pp. 274–290, Springer, 2010.
43. F. T. Liu, K. M. Ting, and Z.-H. Zhou. Isolation Forest. *ICDM Conference*, 2008. Extended version appears in: *ACM Transactions on Knowledge Discovery from Data (TKDD)*, 6(1), 3, 2012.
44. L. M. Manevitz and M. Yousef. One-class SVMs for Document Classification, *Journal of Machine Learning Research*, 2: pp. 139–154, 2001.
45. B. Micenkova, B. McWilliams, and I. Assent. Learning Outlier Ensembles: The Best of Both Worlds Supervised and Unsupervised. *ACM SIGKDD Workshop on Outlier Detection and Description, ODD*, 2014.
46. B. Micenkova, B. McWilliams, and I. Assent. Learning Representations for Outlier Detection on a Budget. arXiv preprint arXiv:1507.08104, 2014.
47. F. Moosmann, B. Triggs, and F. Jurie. Fast Discriminative Visual Codebooks using Randomized Clustering Forests. *Neural Information Processing Systems*, pp. 985–992, 2006.
48. E. Muller, M. Schiffer, and T. Seidl. Statistical Selection of Relevant Subspace Projections for Outlier Ranking. *ICDE Conference*, pp, 434–445, 2011.
49. E. Muller, S. Gunnemann, I. Farber, and T. Seidl, Discovering multiple clustering solutions: Grouping objects in different views of the data, *ICDM Conference*, 2010.
50. E. Muller, S. Gunnemann, T. Seidl, and I. Farber. Tutorial: Discovering Multiple Clustering Solutions Grouping Objects in Different Views of the Data. *ICDE Conference*, 2012.
51. E. Muller, I. Assent, P. Iglesias, Y. Mulle, and K. Bohm. Outlier Ranking via Subspace Analysis in Multiple Views of the Data, *ICDM Conference*, 2012.
52. H. Nguyen, H. Ang, and V. Gopalakrishnan. Mining ensembles of heterogeneous detectors on random subspaces, *DASFAA*, 2010.
53. S. Papadimitriou, H. Kitagawa, P. Gibbons, and C. Faloutsos, LOCI: Fast outlier detection using the local correlation integral, *ICDE Conference*, 2003.
54. T. Pevny. Loda: Lightweight On-line Detector of Anomalies. *Machine Learning*, 102(2), pp. 275–304, 2016.
55. S. Ramaswamy, R. Rastogi, and K. Shim. Efficient Algorithms for Mining Outliers from Large Data Sets. *ACM SIGMOD Conference*, pp. 427–438, 2000.
56. S. Rayana and L. Akoglu. Less is More: Building Selective Anomaly Ensembles. *ACM Transactions on Knowledge Disovery and Data Mining*, 10(4), 42, 2016.
57. S. Rayana, W. Zhong, and L. Akoglu. Sequential Ensemble Learning for Outlier Detection: A Bias-Variance Perspective. *IEEE ICDM Conference*, 2016.
58. L. Rokach. Pattern classification using ensemble methods, *World Scientific Publishing Company*, 2010.
59. M. Salehi, X. Zhang, J. Bezdek, and C. Leckie. Smart Sampling: A Novel Unsupervised Boosting Approach for Outlier Detection. *Australasian Joint Conference on Artificial Intelligence*, Springer, pp. 469–481, 2016. http://rd.springer.com/book/10.1007/978-3-319-50127-7
60. S. Sathe and C. Aggarwal. Subspace Outlier Detection in Linear Time with Randomized Hashing. *ICDM Conference*, 2016.
61. B. Scholkopf, J. C. Platt, J. Shawe-Taylor, A. J. Smola, and R. C. Williamson. Estimating the support of a high-dimensional distribution. *Neural Computation*, 13(7), pp. 1443–1472, 2001.
62. B. Scholkopf, R. C. Williamson, A. J. Smola, J. Shawe-Taylor, and J. C. Platt. Support-vector Method for Novelty Detection, *Advances in Neural Information Processing Systems*, 2000.
63. G. Seni, J. Elder, and R. Grossman. Ensemble Methods in Data Mining: Improving Accuracy through combining predictions. *Morgan and Claypool*, 2010.

64. P. Smyth and D. Wolpert. Linearly Combining Density Estimators via Stacking. *Machine Learning Journal*, 36, pp. 59–83, 1999.
65. A. Strehl and J. Ghosh. Cluster ensembles: A Knowledge Reuse Framework for Combining Multiple Partitions. *Journal of Machine Learning Research*, 3, pp. 583–617, 2001.
66. D. Tax and R. Duin. Combining One-Class Classifiers. *Multiple Classifier Systems*, pp. 299–308, 2001.
67. D. Tax and R. Duin. Support Vector Data Description. *Machine learning*, 54(1), 45-66, 2004.
68. D. Wolpert. Stacked Generalization, *Neural Networks*, 5(2), pp. 241–259, 1992.
69. H. Xiao, J. Gao, D. Turaga, L. Vu, and A. Biem. Temporal Multi-view Inconsistency Detection for Network Traffic Analysis. *WWW Conference*, pp. 455–465, 2015.
70. B. Zenko. Is Combining Classifiers Better than Selecting the Best One. *Machine Learning*, pp. 255–273, 2004.
71. Z.-H. Zhou. Ensemble Methods: Foundations and Algorithms. *Chapman and Hall/CRC Press*, 2012.
72. A. Zimek, M. Gaudet, R. Campello, J. Sander. Subsampling for efficient and effective unsupervised outlier detection ensembles, *KDD Conference*, 2013.

Chapter 2
Theory of Outlier Ensembles

Theory helps us to bear our ignorance of facts.

George Santayana

2.1 Introduction

Outlier detection is an unsupervised problem, in which labels are not available with data records [2]. As a result, it is generally more challenging to design ensemble analysis algorithms for outlier detection. In particular, methods that require the use of labels in intermediate steps of the algorithm cannot be generalized to outlier detection. For example, in the case of boosting, the classifier algorithm needs to be evaluated in the intermediate steps of the algorithm with the use of training-data labels. Such methods are generally not possible in the case of outlier analysis. As discussed in [1], there are unique reasons why ensemble analysis is generally more difficult in the case of outlier analysis as compared to classification. In spite of the unsupervised nature of outlier ensemble analysis, we show that the theoretical foundations of outlier analysis and classification are surprisingly similar. A number of useful discussions on the theory of classification ensembles may be found in [27, 29, 33]. Further explanations on the use of the bias-variance decomposition in different types of classifiers such as neural networks, support vector machines, and rule-based classifiers are discussed in [17, 30, 31]. It is noteworthy that the bias-variance decomposition is often used in customized ways for different types of base classifiers and combination methods; this general principle is also true in outlier detection.

Several arguments have recently been proposed on the theory explaining the accuracy improvements of outlier ensembles. In some cases, incorrect new arguments (such as those in [32]) are proposed to justify experimental results that can be explained by well-known ideas, and an artificial distinction is made between the theory of classification ensembles and outlier ensembles. A recent paper [4]

© Springer International Publishing AG 2017
C.C. Aggarwal and S. Sathe, *Outlier Ensembles*,
DOI 10.1007/978-3-319-54765-7_2

clarifies these misconceptions and establishes that the theoretical foundations of outlier analysis are very similar to those of classification. Bias-variance theory [13, 16, 20, 21] is a well-known result in the classification domain, which explains the varying causes of error in different classification methods. This chapter will revisit these results and provide deeper insights behind some of these results. A observation is that even though labels are unobserved in outlier analysis (unlike classification), it does not change the basic foundations of bias-variance theory for outlier ensemble analysis in a significant way. In fact, it was shown in [4] that a minor modification of the existing theory for classification ensembles can also be used for outlier ensembles.

Bias-variance theory characterizes the output of learning processes in terms of the *expected* error of an algorithm over a set of randomized instantiations of the algorithm. It is noteworthy that the applicability of an algorithm on a specific data set is often dependent on a number of randomized choices, some of which are hidden and others are visible. For example, the specific choice of the training data is often achieved through a data collection process that is (often) hidden from the analyst. Nevertheless, the specific choice of the training data induces a random element into the accuracy, which is characterized by a component of bias-variance theory. Similarly, the choice of a specific model or the randomized selection of a particular design choice of the detector is more obviously visible during execution. These randomized choices induce errors, which can be defined as random variables. Bias-variance theory decomposes these randomized errors into two parts, each of which can be reduced with a specific type of ensemble-centric design. Therefore, a proper understanding of the theoretical foundations of outlier ensembles is crucial in designing accurate algorithms that reduce bias or variance.

Intuitively, the model *bias* defines the basic "correctness" of a model. For example, consider a data set in which all the normal points are distributed on the surface of a unit sphere in three dimensions. A single outlier is located in the empty central region of the sphere. In this case, a multivariate extreme value analysis method (e.g., distance from centroid) is the worst possible model to use because it is based on a wrong model of how outliers are distributed. This portion of the error is referred to as the bias. Now, consider a setting in which we used a 1-nearest neighbor algorithm in order to score the points. Even though this model will generally provide good results, it is possible for a *particular* draw of the data from the base distribution to score some of the points on the unit sphere as outliers. This is because such points may be isolated with respect to particular draw, which is regulated by random variance. This portion of the error is referred to as the variance. Bias-variance theory quantifies the error as a combination of these two quantities.

Traditionally, bias-variance theory is defined over a *random process*, which corresponds to the selection of training data sets from a base distribution. Although this view is very useful for explaining several methods like bagging, it is often not quite as useful for explaining the effectiveness of methods like random-forests. In fact, random-forests have not been fully explained [12] even today, even though they are widely recognized to be variance-reduction methods. Therefore, this book will take a more generalized view of bias-variance theory in which the random process is not only allowed to be draws of the training data but also allowed to be random-ized choices made in the base detector itself. This provides a *model-centric* view of bias-variance theory rather than a data-centric view. For the same algorithm, there are therefore multiple ways in which the bias-variance decomposition can be performed. These different ways provide different insights into explaining the effectiveness of the ensemble. We will also explain these differences with a number of simulations on synthetically generated data sets. It is noteworthy that even though the model-centric approach for bias-variance decomposition is proposed for outlier ensembles (in this book), it can be easily extended to classification ensembles, where it has not been explored previously.

This chapter is organized as follows. In the next section, we provide a review of the bias-variance trade-off for outlier detection, and its similarity and differences with the corresponding trade-off in classification. This section will also discuss the effect of the specific random process used for bias-variance decomposition. The applications of these theoretical foundations to the outlier detection problem are discussed in Sect. 2.3. An experimental illustration of bias-variance theory is provided in Sect. 2.4. The effect of using different types of random processes for performing the bias-variance decomposition is also described in this section. Section 2.5 discusses the conclusions and summary.

2.2 The Bias-Variance Trade-Off for Outlier Detection

The bias-variance trade-off is often used in the context of supervised learning prob-lems such as classification and regression. Recent work [4] has shown how a parallel bias-variance theory can also be developed for outlier detection. Although labels are not available in outlier detection, it is still possible to create bias and variance quantifications with respect to an unknown but ideal ground-truth. In other words, the bias and variance can be quantified as a *theoretical* construct (with respect to the unobserved ground-truth) but it cannot be evaluated in practice for a particular application. This point of view turns out to be useful in adapting supervised ensemble methods to the unsupervised setting, as long as these methods do not use the ground truth in their intermediate steps. Furthermore, as we will study in this chapter, the bias and variance can be roughly quantified on an experimental basis when rare class labels are used as substitutes for outlier labels in real applications. These relation-ships between the theoretical foundations of classification ensembles and those of outlier ensembles were first discussed in [4]. The discussion in this section is based on this work.

Most outlier detection algorithms output scores to quantify the "outlierness" of data points. After the scores have been determined, they can be converted to binary labels. All data points with scores larger than a user-defined threshold are declared outliers. An important observation about outlier scores is that they are *relative*. In other words, if all scores are multiplied by the same positive quantity, or translated by the same amount, it does not change various metrics (e.g., receiver operating characteristic curves [ROC]) of the outlier detector, which depend only on the ranks of the scores. This creates a challenge in quantifying the bias-variance trade-off for outlier analysis because the *uniqueness* of the score-based output is lost. This is because the ROC provides only an incomplete interpretation of the scores (in terms of *relative* ranks). It is possible to work with crisper definitions of the scores which allow the use of more conventional error measures. One such approach, which preserves uniqueness of scores, is that the outlier detectors always output standardized scores with zero mean, unit variance, and a crisp probabilistic interpretation. Note that one can always apply [1] a standardization step as a post-processing phase to any outlier detector without affecting the ROC; this also has a natural probabilistic interpretation (discussed below).

Consider a data instance denoted by $\overline{X_i}$, for which the outlier score is modeled using the training data $\mathscr{D}$. We can assume that an ideal outlier score y_i exists for this data point, even though it is unobserved. The ideal score is output by an unknown function $f(\overline{X_i})$, and it is assumed that the scores, which are output by this ideal function, also satisfy the zero mean and unit variance assumption over all possible points generated by the base data distribution:

$$y_i = f(\overline{X_i}) \tag{2.1}$$

The interpretation of the score y_i is that by applying the (cumulative) standard normal distribution function to y_i, we obtain the relative outlier rank of $\overline{X_i}$ with respect to all possible points generated by the base data distribution. In a sense, this crisp definition directly maps the score y_i to its (percentile) outlier rank in (0, 1). Of course, *in practice*, most outlier detection algorithms rarely output scores exactly satisfying this property even after standardization. In this sense, $f(\overline{X_i})$ is like an oracle that cannot be computed in practice; furthermore, in unsupervised problems, we do not have any examples of the output of this oracle.

This score y_i can be viewed as the analog to a numeric class variable in classification/regression modeling. In problems like classification, we add an additional term to the right-hand side of Eq. 2.1 corresponding to the *intrinsic noise* in the dependent variable. However, unlike classification, in which the value of y_i is a part of the *observed* data for training points, the value y_i in unsupervised problems only represents a theoretically ideal value (obtained from an oracle) which is *unobserved*. Therefore, in unsupervised problems, the labeling noise[1] no longer remains relevant, although including it makes little difference to the underlying conclusions.

Since the true model $f(\cdot)$ is unknown, the outlier score of a test point $\overline{X_i}$ can only be *estimated* with the use of an outlier detection model $g(\overline{X_i}, \mathscr{D})$ using base data set $\mathscr{D}$. The model $g(\overline{X_i}, \mathscr{D})$ is only a way of approximating the unknown function $f(\overline{X_i})$, and

---

[1]If there are errors in the feature values, this will also be reflected in the hypothetically ideal (but unobserved) outlier scores. For example, if a measurement error causes an outlier, rather than an application-specific reason, this will also be reflected in the ideal but unobserved scores.

it is typically computed algorithmically. For example, in k-nearest neighbor outlier detectors, the function $g(\overline{X}_i, \mathscr{D})$ is defined as follows:

$$g(\overline{X}_i, \mathscr{D}) = \alpha \text{KNN-distance}(\overline{X}_i, \mathscr{D}) + \beta \qquad (2.2)$$

Here, α and β are constants which are needed to standardize the scores to zero mean and unit variance. It is important to note that the k-nearest neighbor distance, α, and β depend on the specific data set $\mathscr{D}$ at hand. This is the reason that the data set $\mathscr{D}$ is included as an argument of $g(\overline{X}_i, \mathscr{D})$. *We note that the above example of $g(\overline{X}_i, \mathscr{D})$ is only for illustrative in nature and the theoretical results do not assume any particular form of the outlier score such as a density estimator or a k-nearest neighbor detector.*

   If the function $g(\overline{X}_i, \mathscr{D})$ does not properly model the true oracle $f(\overline{X}_i)$, then this will result in errors. This is referred to as *model bias* and it is directly analogous to the model bias used in classification. For example, the use of k-nearest neighbor algorithm as $g(\overline{X}_i, \mathscr{D})$, or a specific choice of the parameter k, might result in the user model deviating significantly from the true function $f(\overline{X}_i)$. Similarly, if a linear model is used to separate the outliers and inliers, whereas a nonlinear model is more appropriate, then it will lead to a *consistent error* in the scoring process, which corresponds to the bias. A second source of error is the *variance*. The variance is caused by the fact that the outlier score directly depends on the data set $\mathscr{D}$ at hand. Any data set is finite, and even if the *expected* value of $g(\overline{X}_i, \mathscr{D})$ correctly reflects $f(\overline{X}_i)$, the estimation of $g(\overline{X}_i, \mathscr{D})$ with limited data would likely not be exactly correct. In other words, $g(\overline{X}_i, \mathscr{D})$ will not be the same as $E[g(\overline{X}_i, \mathscr{D})]$ over the space of various random choices of training data sets $\mathscr{D}$. Therefore, variance is a manifestation of *inconsistent behavior* by the algorithm over the space of different random choices of training data sets in which the same point receives very different scores across different choices of training data sets.. This phenomenon is caused by the algorithm adjusting too much to the specific nuances of a data set, and is also sometimes referred to as *overfitting*.

   Although one typically does not distinguish between training and test points in unsupervised problems, one can easily do so by cleanly separating the points used for model building, and the points used for scoring. For example, a k-nearest neighbor detector would determine the k closest points in the training data for any point $\overline{X}_i$ in the test data. We choose to demarcate training and test data because it makes our analysis cleaner, simpler, and more similar to that of classification; however, it does not change[2] the basic conclusions. Let $\mathscr{D}$ be the training data, and $\overline{X}_1 \ldots \overline{X}_n$ be a set of test points whose (hypothetically ideal but unobserved) outlier scores are $y_1 \ldots y_n$. It is assumed that these out-of-sample test points remain fixed over different instantiations of the training data $\mathscr{D}$, so that one can measure statistical quantities such as the score variance. We use an unsupervised outlier detection algorithm that

---

[2]It is noteworthy that the most popular outlier detectors are based on distance-based methods. These detectors are lazy learners in which the test point is itself never included among the k-nearest neighbors at prediction time. Therefore, these learners are essentially out-of-sample methods because they do not include the test point within the model (albeit in a lazy way).

uses the function $g(\cdot, \cdot)$ to *estimate* these scores. Therefore, the resulting scores of $\overline{X_1} \ldots \overline{X_n}$ using the training data $\mathscr{D}$ are $g(\overline{X_1}, \mathscr{D}) \ldots g(\overline{X_n}, \mathscr{D})$, respectively. The mean-squared error, or MSE, of the detectors of the test points over a particular realization $\mathscr{D}$ of the training data is:

$$MSE = \frac{1}{n} \sum_{i=1}^{n} \{y_i - g(\overline{X_i}, \mathscr{D})\}^2 \tag{2.3}$$

The *expected MSE, over different realizations of the training data*, generated using some random process, is as follows:

$$E[MSE] = \frac{1}{n} \sum_{i=1}^{n} E[\{y_i - g(\overline{X_i}, \mathscr{D})\}^2] \tag{2.4}$$

The different realizations of the training data $\mathscr{D}$ can be constructed using any crisply defined random process. In the traditional view of the bias-variance trade-off, one might assume that the data set $\mathscr{D}$ is generated by a hidden process that draws it from a true distribution. The basic idea is that *only one instance of a finite data set* can be collected by the entity performing the analysis, and there will be some variability in the results because of this limitation. This variability will also lead to some loss in the accuracy over a setting where the entity actually had access to the distribution from which the data was generated. To the entity that is performing the analysis, this variability is hidden because they have only one instance of the finite data set. Other unconventional interpretations of the bias-variance trade-off are also possible. For example, one might construct each instantiation of $\mathscr{D}$ by starting with a larger base data set $\mathscr{D}_0$ and use random subsets of points, dimensions, and so on. In this alternative interpretation, the expected values of the *MSE* is computed over different instantiations of the random process extracting $\mathscr{D}$ from $\mathscr{D}_0$. Finally, one might even view the randomized process of extracting $\mathscr{D}$ from $\mathscr{D}_0$ as a part of the base detector. This will yield a randomized *base detector* $g(\overline{X_i}, \mathscr{D}_0)$, but a fixed data set $\mathscr{D}_0$. Therefore, the random process is now defined with respect to the randomization in base detector, rather than the training data selection process.

These different interpretations will provide different bias-variance decompositions of the same (or almost the same) MSE. We will provide specific examples of the different types of decomposition in a Sect. 2.4 with synthetic simulations. It is important to define the underlying random process clearly in order to properly analyze the effectiveness of a particular ensemble method. Note that even though the training data $\mathscr{D}$ might have different instantiations because it is generated by a random process, the test points $\overline{X_1} \ldots \overline{X_n}$ always remain fixed over all instantiations of the random process. This is the reason that we chose to demarcate the training and test data; it allows us to evaluate the effects of changing the training data (with a random process) on the same set of test points. If the predictions of the same test points vary significantly over various instantiations of the random process, we say that the model has high *variance*. Note that high variance will increase the overall error even if the prediction of the test point is accurate *in expectation*. On the other hand, if the expected prediction of each test point is inaccurate, we say that the model has high *bias*. The basic idea is to decompose the error of the classifier into these two components. This type of decomposition provides the intuition needed to design algorithms that can reduce error by reducing one of these components.

The term in the bracket on the right-hand side of Eq. 2.4 can be re-written as follows:

$$E[MSE] = \frac{1}{n}\sum_{i=1}^{n} E[\{(y_i - f(\overline{X_i})) + (f(\overline{X_i}) - g(\overline{X_i}, \mathcal{D}))\}^2] \tag{2.5}$$

Note that we can set $(y_i - f(\overline{X_i}))$ on the right-hand side of aforementioned equation to 0 because of Eq. 2.1. Therefore, the following can be shown:

$$E[MSE] = \frac{1}{n}\sum_{i=1}^{n} E[\{f(\overline{X_i}) - g(\overline{X_i}, \mathcal{D})\}^2] \tag{2.6}$$

This right-hand side can be further decomposed by adding and subtracting $E[g(\overline{X_i}, \mathcal{D})]$ within the squared term:

$$E[MSE] = \frac{1}{n}\sum_{i=1}^{n} E[\{f(\overline{X_i}) - E[g(\overline{X_i}, \mathcal{D})]\}^2]$$
$$+ \frac{2}{n}\sum_{i=1}^{n} \{f(\overline{X_i}) - E[g(\overline{X_i}, \mathcal{D})]\}\{E[g(\overline{X_i}, \mathcal{D})] - E[g(\overline{X_i}, \mathcal{D})]\}$$
$$+ \frac{1}{n}\sum_{i=1}^{n} E[\{E[g(\overline{X_i}, \mathcal{D})] - g(\overline{X_i}, \mathcal{D})\}^2]$$

The second term on the right-hand side of the aforementioned expression evaluates to 0. Therefore, we have:

$$E[MSE] = \frac{1}{n}\sum_{i=1}^{n} E[\{f(\overline{X_i}) - E[g(\overline{X_i}, \mathcal{D})]\}^2] + \frac{1}{n}\sum_{i=1}^{n} E[\{E[g(\overline{X_i}, \mathcal{D})] - g(\overline{X_i}, \mathcal{D})\}^2]$$
$$= \frac{1}{n}\sum_{i=1}^{n} \{f(\overline{X_i}) - E[g(\overline{X_i}, \mathcal{D})]\}^2 + \frac{1}{n}\sum_{i=1}^{n} E[\{E[g(\overline{X_i}, \mathcal{D})] - g(\overline{X_i}, \mathcal{D})\}^2]$$

The first term in the aforementioned expression is the (squared) bias, whereas the second term is the variance. Stated simply, one obtains the following:

$$E[MSE] = \text{Bias}^2 + \text{Variance} \tag{2.7}$$

This derivation is very similar to that in classification although the intrinsic error term is missing because of the ideal nature of the score output by the oracle. The bias and variance are specific not just to the algorithm $g(\overline{X_i}, \mathcal{D})$ *but also to the random process used to create the training data sets* $\mathcal{D}$. Although this random process is generally assumed to be that of selecting a training data set from a base distribution, it could, in principle, be any random process such as the randomized algorithmic choices inside the base detector. The second view is non-traditional, but is more helpful in explaining the performance of certain types of outlier detectors.

A second issue is about the nature of the assumptions on the scores that were used at the very beginning of the analysis. Although we did make an assumption on the scaling (standardization) of the scores, the basic result holds as long as the outputs of the base detector and oracle have the same mathematical interpretation. For example, we could very easily have made this entire argument under the assumption that both the base detector $g(\overline{X_i}, \mathcal{D})$ and the oracle $f(\overline{X_i})$ directly output the relative ranks in $(0, 1)$. *In other words, the above arguments are general, and they are not specific to the use of any particular outlier detector or assuming that outlier detectors are density estimators.*

2.2.1 Relationship of Ensemble Analysis to Bias-Variance Trade-Off

Ensemble analysis is a way of combining different models in order to ensure that the bias-variance tradeoff is optimized. In general, one can view the output of a base detector $g(\overline{X}, \mathcal{D})$ as a random variable, depending on a random process over either the selection of the base data $\mathcal{D}$, or the construction of the detector $g(\cdot, \cdot)$ itself, which might be randomized. The overall mean-squared error of this random variable is reduced with respect to the unknown oracle output $f(\overline{X})$ by the ensemble process. This is achieved in two ways:

1. *Reducing bias*: Some methods such as boosting reduce bias in classification by using an ensemble combination of highly biased detectors. The design of detectors is based on the performance results of earlier instantiations of the detector in order to encourage specific types of bias performance in various components. The final combination is also carefully designed in a weighted way to gain the maximum advantage in terms of overall bias performance. However, it is generally much harder to reduce bias in outlier ensembles because of the absence of ground truth. Nevertheless, some methods have been designed to heuristically reduce bias in the context of outlier ensemble analysis [25, 26, 28].

2. *Reducing variance*: Methods such as bagging, bragging, wagging, and subbagging (subsampling) [9–11], can be used to reduce the model-specific variance in classification. In this context, most classification methods generalize *directly* to outlier ensembles. In most of these methods the final ensemble score is computed as an average of the scores of various detectors. The basic idea is that the average

of a set of random variables has lower variance. In a sense, many of the variance reduction methods like bagging try to roughly simulate the process of drawing the data repeatedly from a base distribution. We will explain this point in greater detail in later chapters.

The "unsupervised" nature of outlier detection does not mean that bias and variance cannot be defined. *It only means that the dependent variables are not available with the training data, even though an "abstract," but unknown ground truth does exist.* However, the bias-variance trade-off does not rely on such an availability *to the base algorithm*. None of the steps in the aforementioned computation of mean-squared error rely on the need for $g(\overline{X_i}, \mathscr{D})$ to be computed using examples of the output of oracle $f(\cdot)$ on points in $\mathscr{D}$. This is the reason that variance-reduction algorithms for classification generalize so easily to outlier detection.

2.2.2 Out-of-Sample Issues

It is noteworthy that the test points $\overline{X_1} \ldots \overline{X_n}$ are cleanly separated from the training data $\mathscr{D}$ in the aforementioned analysis, and are therefore out-of-sample with respect to $\mathscr{D}$. Note that the random process varies the training data sets over different instantiations but the same fixed set $\overline{X_1} \ldots \overline{X_n}$ of test points is used for each instantiation of the training data. Even in classification, the bias-variance trade-off is always understood in terms of the performance of the detector on out-of-sample test points that are fixed over the various instantiations of the training data.

However, in outlier detection, one typically does not distinguish between the training and test data. A natural question, therefore, arises as to whether this difference can affect the applicability of the bias-variance trade-off. We argue that even when the training data is the same as the test data, the bias-variance trade-off still holds approximately, as long as a *leave-one-out* methodology is used to construct the outlier scores. The leave-one-out methodology means that, when scoring a test point $\overline{X} \in \mathscr{D}$, one uses only $\mathscr{D} - \{\overline{X}\}$ to construct the model. Such an approach is common in outlier detection settings, especially when instance-based methods are used. For example, in a k-nearest neighbor outlier detector or LOF detector, one typically does not include the data point itself, while computing the k-nearest neighbors of a data point. In other words, the outlier scores are almost always determined using a leave-one-out methodology.

As a result, the score of each point is computed in out-of-sample fashion, although each test point is drawn from the same data set $\mathscr{D}$. The leave-one-out methodology is a special case of the cross-validation methodology in classification, in which the data is divided into several folds, and one fold is classified using the remaining folds (as the training data set). In the particular case of leave-one-out, each fold contains exactly one data point, which is viewed as an extreme case of cross-validation. The cross-validation methodology is known to estimate the bias and variance characteristics of the out-of-sample setting very well, especially when the number of folds is large (as in the extreme case of leave-one-out). Although there are tiny differences among the training data sets for various test points, the differences are small enough to provide an excellent approximation of the bias-variance characteristics of the out-of-sample setting.

2.2.3   Understanding How Ensemble Analysis Works

The bias-variance trade-off is defined in terms of a random process that creates the different training data sets. Note that the definition of the random process is crucial because the bias and variance are statistical quantities derived from this random process. In fact, for the same algorithm, one might use different random processes to describe it. Correspondingly, the error of the classifier will be decomposed into the bias and the variance in many different ways depending on the random process that is used. Furthermore, the overall error is also different depending on whether on assumes the availability of the base distribution or not. Traditionally, the bias-variance trade-off is understood from the perspective of sampling from a true distribution. In such cases, the errors are computed with respect to the availability of infinite data, and therefore the effect of finite size of the data is included in the error. In other types of model-centric random processes, the availability of the base distribution is not assumed, and therefore the overall error is lower (since it does not include the portion caused by the finiteness of the data). In order to explain this point, we will use a specific example.

Consider a mortgage application in which three banks collect data about the transactions of various customers to make predictions about which (outlier) customers are the ones most likely to default on their mortgage by using[3] outlier analysis. The banks collect different types of data about the customers such as their demographics, their past payment history, their salary, assets, and so on. Therefore, each bank has its own set of training data which might be different. It is assumed that the training data of each bank is drawn from the same base distribution, although each bank receives a different instantiation of the training data. Furthermore, the banks see only their own instantiation of the training data, and they have no access to each other's instantiations. Therefore, even though there is an inherent variance in the output over these instantiations (even if all banks use the same detector), the banks are unable to see each other's data sets or results to fully appreciate the nature of this variance.

Consider a setting in which each of the three banks receives a mortgage application from John. Therefore, John is a test point for which each bank needs to compute the outlier score using the training data. Note that the training data across the three banks are different, whereas the test point (John) is the same. This is the general assumption in the bias-variance setting, where we compute the bias and variance on the same

---

[3]In practice, such unsupervised methods are never used in such real-life scenarios. This example is only for illustrative purposes in order to provide a concrete example of the workings of the bias-variance trade-off.

set of test points using training data, which are generated by different instantiations
of the random process. For example, each bank could apply a k-nearest neighbor
outlier detector on its respective training data set to compute the outlier score for
John. Furthermore, let us assume for the purpose of argument that each bank uses
exactly the same value of k to execute the algorithm. In other words, the k-nearest
neighbor distance of John is computed with respect to its training data set to report
an outlier score. Clearly, each bank would receive a different outlier score for John
because of the difference in their training data sets. This difference corresponds to the
variance in the algorithm over different choices of training data sets. For *theoretical*
purposes, it is assumed that each bank uses the same random process to draw the
training data from the same base distribution. In *practice*, the banks use some data
collection mechanism to create the training data sets, and therefore the assumption of
drawing from a base distribution is simply a (hidden) theoretical assumption for the
purposes of analysis. The basic idea of variance in the context of a hidden process of
generating the training data sets is illustrated in Fig. 2.1. It is appropriate to consider
this variance as "hidden" in real settings, because each bank would have only one
instance of the training data, and may not notice the fact that some of the error in
their computation of John's scores is explained by the variability in John's scores by
other banks. After all, if all banks get very different scores for John with their data
sets, at least some of them are very wrong. In variance-reduction ensemble methods,
the goal is to minimize this *hidden* variability across the banks, with each entity

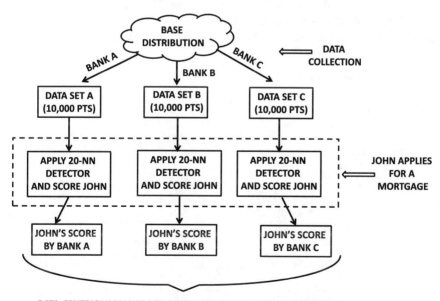

**DATA-CENTRIC VARIANCE REFLECTS INCONSISTENCY OF JOHN'S SCORES
OVER DIFFERENT RANDOM CHOICES OF TRAINING DATA (DURING COLLECTION)**

Fig. 2.1 Hidden variance caused by finite data set size

using only their *local* instance of the training data (assuming that each entity used the ensemble on its instance).

The variance in John's scores depends on the size of the training data sets are drawn. One can view the available data as a finite resource that affects the variance in the results. Smaller data sets have a negative impact on the accuracy of the approach because of larger variance; after all, the variance is a component of the mean-squared error. For example, if each bank draws a training data of the same small size from the base distribution (i.e., collects a smaller training data set), the variance of their scores on John would be larger. On the other hand, if each bank decides to use a larger size of the training data, then the variance will be much smaller in the scores of John. In general, when the variance is high, the quality of the scores obtained for John will be lower because the variance is one of the components of the error. For example, for bank A, its contribution to the variance is proportional to $\{g(John, \mathscr{D}^A) - E[g(John, \mathscr{D})]\}^2$. Here, $\mathscr{D}^A$ represents the training data of bank A. The expected score $E[g(John, \mathscr{D})]$ can be (very roughly) estimated as John's average score over the three different banks. The difference between this expected score and the ground-truth score yields the bias performance. Unfortunately, in unsupervised settings, this ground-truth is usually not available because of which the bias performance remains purely a theoretical construct.

The bias often has a significant impact on the quality of the scores obtained for John. In unsupervised problems, the bias is the most unpredictable part of the performance that cannot be easily controlled. Consider a setting in which John occurs together with a small cluster of similar anomalies. This example is illustrated in Fig. 2.2 where 4 outliers occur together in the vicinity of John. Such scenarios are quite common in real settings; for example a small percentage of mortgage defaulters

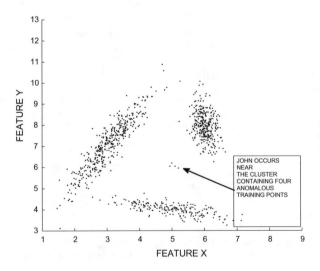

Fig. 2.2 Effects of parameter choice on bias

might exhibit their anomalous behavior for the same underlying causes (e.g., low salary and high indebtedness). The training data for each bank will typically contain this small cluster, and therefore the choice of the value of k is important for the k-nearest neighbor detector. If each bank used a small value of k such as 1, then they would *consistently* obtain incorrect outlier scores for John. This is because the *expected* score $E[g(John, \mathcal{D})]$ of the 1-nearest neighbor detector no longer reflects $f(John)$, when the value of k is set to 1. Given that the training data sets (of size 10,000) of all banks are drawn from the same base distribution, all of them are likely to contain a small number of training points in the anomalous region populated by John. Therefore, even through John should be considered an anomaly, it will typically not be reflected as such with the use of $k = 1$. This portion of the error $\{f(John) - E[g(John, \mathcal{D})]\}^2$ corresponds to the (squared) bias. Note that the bias heavily depends on the data distribution at hand. For example, in the particular case of Fig. 2.2, the use of a small value of k leads to high bias. It is also possible (and relatively easy) to construct data distributions in which small values of k lead to less bias. For example, in a data distribution with randomly distributed (but isolated) outliers, small values of k would be more effective. In a data distribution with anomalous clusters of varying sizes, different choices of k would exhibit better bias on different points. This aspect of outlier detection is very challenging because it is often difficult to tune outlier ensemble algorithms to reduce the bias. Furthermore, it is often more difficult to predict the bias trends in an unsupervised problem like outlier detection as compared to classification. When a k-nearest neighbor classifier is used in the supervised setting, the bias generally increases with the value of k and the variance generally reduces. However, in outlier detection (with a k-nearest neighbor detector), the bias could either increase or decrease with k but the variance almost always reduces with increasing k. It is noteworthy that it is not always necessary for the bias and variance trends to be opposite one another even in classification, although such a trade-off is *often* observed because of better ability to supervise the tuning of the algorithm towards a pareto-optimal frontier of the bias-variance trade-off.

How can one reduce the variance in the scores? Consider an ideal *theoretical* setting, in which each bank could draw as many training data sets as they wanted from the base distribution. In such a case, each bank could repeat the process of drawing training data sets over an infinite number of trials, determine the score for John over each training data set, and average John's scores over these different computations. The result would be that all banks would obtain exactly the same score for John, and the quality of the score would also be better because the variance component in the error has dropped to 0. This scenario is shown in Fig. 2.3a. However, this is impossible to achieve in practice, because each bank only has *one* instantiation of a finite data set, and therefore one cannot fully simulate the draws from a base distribution, which is an infinite resource of data. The finite nature of the resource (training data) ensures that some portion of the variance will always be irreducible. Therefore, we somehow need a way to make use of this finite resource (data) as *efficiently* as possible to minimize the variance. For example, running the detector once on a data set containing 10,000 points is not the most efficient way of reducing variance for the resource of 10,000 points. Very often, the quality of the scores

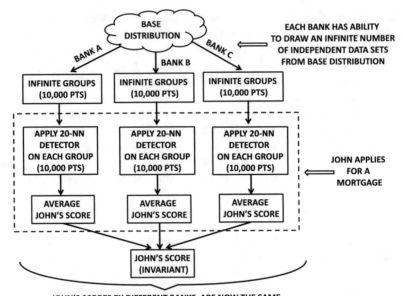

(a) Reducing variance to 0 with infinite data resources

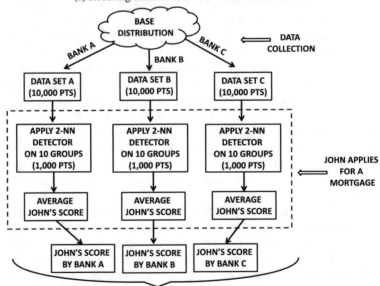

(b) Reducing variance partially with finite data resources

Fig. 2.3 Reducing variance in data-centric ensembles

obtained from using a 20-NN detector on 10,000 points are only marginally better than those obtained using a 2-NN detector on 1,000 points, and one does not gain much from increasing the size of the data by 10 times.

In order to reduce the variance more *efficiently*, we need multiple instantiations of the training data set, which are derivatives of the original training data instance and then average the scores from the different instantiations *at the very end*. By doing so, one is roughly trying to simulate the process of drawing the scores from the base distribution by using the finite resource (data set) available to us. To achieve this goal, one can divide the data set of 10,000 points into 10 equal parts and then compute the outlier score of John with respect to each of these 1,000 points. Note that the value of k can be adjusted to the same relative value to ensure greater similarity in the two settings. For example, if we use $k = 20$ with 10,000 points, we can use $k = 2$ with 1,000 points. By making this adjustment, the bias performance is roughly similar in the two cases for an exact k-NN detector. By averaging John's outlier score across the 10 runs, the variance is greatly reduced, and the error closely reflects the bias of using $k = 2$ on 1000 points (or $k = 20$ on 10,000 points). Of course, the variance of an outlier detector with $k = 2$ on 1,000 sampled training points is greater than that on an outlier detector with $k = 20$ on 10,000 sampled training points. However, using averaging across 10 buckets of 1,000 points is a more efficient way of reducing variance rather than simply increasing the size of the base data to 10,000 points. As a result, higher-quality results will generally be obtained by the bucketing approach because the variance of John's score will be smaller. For example, if all three banks used this approach to determine John's outlier score, their scores will be more similar to one another with the bucketing approach. This is because they have reduced the variance component of their scores. This scenario is illustrated in Fig. 2.3b. Interestingly, this example is s simple variant of a well-known technique in classification referred to as subagging [9–11], and it provides a simple idea of how a *variance-reduction* scheme works in ensemble analysis. The idea is to use the finite data set available to us in the most efficient way possible to reduce variability in the scores caused by the finite nature of the data set. It is noteworthy, that unlike the case of Fig. 2.3a, some part of the variance is irreducible in Fig. 2.3b because we only have access to a finite resource. It is also important to note that this type of simulation is imperfect because it improves the accuracy in the vast majority of the cases, but can also occasionally fail in some circumstances. This example provides an understanding of the type of tricks that one commonly uses in order to gain accuracy improvements. Since variance reduction is more common in outlier ensemble analysis, as compared to bias reduction, much of our discussion will be based on this aspect.

2.2.4 Data-Centric View Versus Model-Centric View

The aforementioned discussion of the bias-variance trade-off is designed from the perspective of a random process for choosing the training data set $\mathscr{D}$. In other words, the expected values in the bias term $\frac{1}{n}\{f(\overline{X_i}) - E[g(\overline{X_i}, \mathscr{D})]\}^2$ and the variance term $\frac{1}{n}\sum_{i=1}^{n} E[\{E[g(\overline{X_i}, \mathscr{D})] - g(\overline{X_i}, \mathscr{D})\}^2]$ are both computed over various random choices of training data sets. The basic idea here is that the training data set is chosen from a true distribution by a random process that is hidden from us. This hidden process induces variability in the scores. Furthermore, we have only one instantiation of this hidden process, because the analyst (e.g., the bank in the previous section) has only one instantiation of the data set, and one must reduce the variability in the scores from this single instantiation. This is a more challenging setting than a case in which an infinite resource of data, such as the base distribution, is available to each bank. In the example in the previous section, all three banks were able to make their outlier scores more similar to one another by using ensembles on their *own* data sets (i.e., without using each other's data sets) with the use of draws from the base distribution. In the process, the quality of John's scores typically improves for each of the three banks because the variance component in the error has been reduced.

A common way in which the variability in the scores is reduced by many ensemble analysis methods, is by using a random process to construct randomized derivatives of the data set, and then averaging the scores from these different data sets. One can view each derivative as a sample from the base distribution, although it does not represent a theoretically ideal simulation because there will be correlations and overlaps among these derivative data sets, which would not have occurred if they had truly been drawn directly from the base distribution. This is the reason that ensemble analysis only provides imperfect simulations that almost always improve accuracy, but are not guaranteed to do so.

In our earlier example with the banks, the process of dividing the training data set into ten segments and then averaging the scores reduces the variability of the output. A theoretical explanation of this (imperfect) variance reduction process is provided in Chap. 3. However, from the perspective of bias-variance theory and ensemble analysis, this random process need not be applied to the training data set $\mathscr{D}$. The randomness could easily be directly injected into the detector $g(\overline{X_i}, \mathscr{D})$ rather than the data sets. This leads to a model-centric view of the bias-variance trade-off. We emphasize that this view of bias-variance is unconventional, and we have not seen it discussed elsewhere. The traditional random process of sampling from a base distribution is excellent for explaining certain ensemble methods like bagging and subsampling, but its often not very good at explaining many other types of variance reduction methods in which the detector is itself randomized.

In practice, there are several ways in which one can use the bias-variance trade-off from the perspective of an ensemble method:

1. Consider an ensemble method like subsampling in which the training data sets from drawn from the same base data set $\mathscr{D}_0$. How should one view the random process for analyzing the bias-variance trade-off? In practice, one would need to

break up the random process into two separate steps. The first random process, which is hidden, produces a training data set $\mathcal{D}_0$ from an unknown base distribution. The second random process of ensembling produces different choices of training data sets $\mathcal{D}$, each of which is a subset of $\mathcal{D}_0$. This is the scenario discussed in the previous section. This is equivalent to saying that each data set $\mathcal{D}$ is directly selected from the (hidden) base distribution, although different instantiations of the data might have overlaps because of the dependencies in the sampling process. Therefore, the ensemble method simulates the process of generating training data sets from the base distribution although the simulation is imperfect because of dependencies among the base detectors caused by the finiteness of the resource with which we are attempting to perform the simulation.

For methods like subsampling there is an alternative way in which one can view the random process for the bias-variance trade-off. For example, one can perform bias-variance analysis under the assumption that the random process generates the training data directly from $\mathcal{D}_0$, and simply omit the first step of sampling $\mathcal{D}_0$ from the base distribution. The use of such a random process results in dividing the same error into bias and variance in a different way as the case in which we assume the existence of a base distribution. Furthermore, the overall error is also different because we no longer have the variability of drawing $\mathcal{D}_0$ from the base distribution. We will provide a better understanding of these decompositions later in this chapter. The main point to keep in mind is that the bias and variance will depend not only on the choice of the detector $g(\overline{X_i}, \mathcal{D})$ but also on the random process to construct the training data sets $\mathcal{D}$. Traditionally, the selection of $\mathcal{D}_0$ from a base distribution is always assumed in order to capture the variance of the hidden process that generates a finite data set. Note that this type of randomized process is relevant to the data-centered ensembles discussed in Chap. 1.

2. The random process injects randomness within the detector $g(\overline{X_i}, \mathcal{D})$ but the data set $\mathcal{D}$ is fixed. For example, while using a k-nearest neighbor detector, one might simply choose the value of k randomly from a range. Therefore, the bias and variance of a randomized detector is defined by its randomized design choices over a *fixed* data set. In such a case, it is important to note that the expectation $E[MSE]$ of bias-variance theory is no longer over the randomized choices of training data, but over the randomized choices in model design. For example, a user might not be certain over the value of k to use, and might guess the choice of k, which is virtually equivalent to making a random choice within a range. By modeling k to be drawn randomly from a range of values, the bias-variance decomposition provides a model-centric variability, which is specific to parameter choice. However, by ensembling over different values of k, one is able to reduce this randomness.

This second form of the bias-variance trade-off is unconventional, but it is more useful for the analysis of model-centered ensembles discussed in Chap. 1. The key point to understand is that the bias-variance trade-off is designed with respect to a random process, and this random process can be different, depending on the kind of ensemble algorithm one is looking at. Furthermore, this form of the bias-variance trade-off is more general because data-centered ensembles can be considered special cases of model-centered ensembles. For example, the data selection process in bagging can be considered a part of the randomized algorithm $g(\overline{X}, \mathcal{D}_0)$, where $\mathcal{D}_0$ is the fixed base data from which the points are selected. The randomized algorithm $g(\overline{X}_i, \mathcal{D}_0)$ samples the points randomly with replacement, and therefore the data sampling process is part of the detector g. A datacentric view would be that the algorithm g is deterministic but the data set $\mathcal{D}$ is selected randomly from $\mathcal{D}_0$ in order to run $g(\overline{X}_i, \mathcal{D})$. Furthermore, one can assume that $\mathcal{D}_0$ is itself selected from an unknown base distribution by a hidden process. This is equivalent to saying that the data set $\mathcal{D}$ is directly selected from the (hidden) base distribution, although different instantiations of the data might have overlaps because of the dependencies in the sampling process. The data-centric view is more useful in methods like bagging (and its variants like subagging/subsampling), which reduce the variance resulting from the *hidden* process. Therefore, for any given ensemble algorithm, it is important to properly select the random process that best explains its performance. The model-centric view is more useful in methods that reduce the uncertainty arising from model selection choices. An example is the choice of the parameter k in distance-based algorithms. In fact, different values of k may be more suitable for different data points, and the ensemble will often do better than the median performance over these different choices. Such methods cannot be explained with a data-centric view. We believe that one of the reasons that methods like random forests have not been properly explained [12] in supervised settings like classification is that the literature has generally taken an (inflexible) data-centric view to the biasvariance trade-off.

3. It is possible for the random process to choose both the detector $g(\overline{X}_i, \mathcal{D})$ and the data set $\mathcal{D}$. For example, one might use different choices of the parameter k in a distance-based algorithm over different bags of the data.

Variance reduction methods can be explained very easily with the use of the biasvariance trade-off. The basic idea in all variance reduction algorithms follows the same framework:

1. Use a data-centric or model-centric random process to generate randomized outputs from various base detectors. For example, one might generate randomized versions of the data sets (subsets of points or dimensions), or one might generate randomized versions of the detector $g(\overline{X}_i, \mathcal{D})$. An example of the latter case in one in which we use random choices of the parameters of the algorithm.

2. Average the outputs of these base detectors to reduce variance. The basic idea is that the average of a set of random variables has lower variance than the individual variables. The variance is best reduced when the outputs of various detectors are uncorrelated with one another.

This basic idea is invariant across classification and outlier detection, and therefore virtually all variance-reduction ensembles from classification can be generalized easily to outlier detection. In particular, many of the natural ensemble methods like bagging [5], subagging [10] and random forests [6, 18] have corresponding analogs

in outlier analysis. It is noteworthy that the generation of randomized variants of
the detector has a detrimental effect on the bias, as compared to a fully optimized
algorithm. For example, if one applied a detector to a subset of points or with a random
choice of the parameters, one might not do as well (in bias performance) as compared
to an algorithm with all the points or specific choices of the parameters. However,
the variance reduction effects of averaging are often sufficient to compensate for
the poorer bias performance of individual components in such settings. In fact, it
is possible (and common) for the ensemble performance to be better than the *vast
majority* of the base component detectors. This type of performance jump is, however,
not guaranteed and it is sometimes also possible for the ensemble performance to
degrade below the median base performance. Section 3.3 of Chap. 3 discusses the
circumstances under which such methods can degrade.

Let us try to understand the effect of a model-centered ensemble on the bias-
variance trade-off. The crucial point to understand is that the randomized process
for model-centered ensembles is inherently different from the randomized process
used in the case of data-centered ensembles. We restate the bias-variance trade-off
introduced earlier in this chapter:

$$E[MSE] = \frac{1}{n} \sum_{i=1}^{n} \{f(\overline{X_i}) - E[g(\overline{X_i}, \mathcal{D})]\}^2 + \frac{1}{n} \sum_{i=1}^{n} E[\{E[g(\overline{X_i}, \mathcal{D})] - g(\overline{X_i}, \mathcal{D})\}^2]$$

(2.8)

In the original statement of the bias-variance trade-off, the expectation *E[MSE] is
typically computed over different choices of training data sets drawn from a base
distribution.* However, in the model-centric point of view, we assume that we have
a set of *m* alternative models, and we select one of these *m* alternative *models* over
the same data set. Therefore, the data set is fixed, whereas the model might be
randomized. For example, the choice of the parameter *k* in a *k*-NN detector might
provide one of these alternative models. In this case, the *expectation in the bias-
variance trade-off is over the different choices of models.* We emphasize that this is
an unconventional view of the bias-variance trade-off and is generally not discussed
elsewhere in the literature. Although it is more general to think of a model-centric
view of the bias-variance trade-off, the expectation in the traditional view of the
bias-variance trade-off is usually computed over different choices of training data
sets. However, a model-centric view of the bias-variance trade-off helps to explain
many types of ensembles, which cannot be easily explained purely by using a data-
centric view. The difference between the model-centric view and data-centric view
of outlier ensembles roughly corresponds to the categorization of ensemble analysis
into data-centric ensembles and model-centric ensembles [1].

Why is this approach to the bias-variance trade-off more general? This is because
one can also understand the data-centric processes of selecting a randomized derivative of the data set as a special case of this setting. For example, in the case where
John was scored on 10 different randomly drawn partitions of the training data sets,
one can view the randomized process of creating 10 partitions of the data as a part
of the model itself. Therefore the bias and variance is computed over this *random*

process of creating the 10 partitions, rather than over random process of drawing data from a true distribution. In such a case, the variance of John's score can be viewed as its expected variation over all possible groupings of the data over a fixed base training data (without taking into account the additional hidden random process of drawing the training data). The bias is defined by determining John's expectation score over all possible groupings, and they computing the difference between John's (unknown) ground-truth score and the expected score. The key here is that the expectation is *over the process of creating the different groupings* rather than the choice of the data set. This distinction is crucial because this different random process will have a different bias and a different variance. Although the mean-squared error will always be the same for a particular algorithm, this model-centric decomposition will provide a different view of the bias and variance, *because it is a model-centric view of the bias-variance trade-off.* In other words, one can decompose the error of a randomized detector into bias and variance in multiple ways, depending on the kind of random process that one is looking at. Any data-centric ensemble can be analyzed either from the perspective of a data-centric bias-variance trade-off, or a model-centric bias-variance trade-off. In the latter case, the process of extracting the training data is considered a part of the model. However, a model-centric ensemble can be analyzed only from the perspective of a model-centric bias-variance trade-off.

The model-centric view of the bias-variance trade-off can also handle settings that cannot be easily handled by the data-centric view. Just as data-centric ensembles are designed to address the uncertainty in choice of training data sets, model-centric ensembles are designed to address the uncertainty in the choice of models. The design choice of a model plays a crucial role in many problems like outlier detection. In unsupervised problems like outlier detection, there is significantly greater uncertainty in the design choices of the models, as compared to supervised problems like data classification. This is because one can use techniques like cross-validation in classification in order to make important choices, such as the optimal value of k in a k-nearest neighbor classifier. However, since the ground-truth is not available in problems like outlier detection, it is impossible to know the optimal value of the parameter k. Just as the choice of training data set is imposed on the analyst (and creates some hidden variance), the choice of such model parameters (or other design choices) creates uncertainty for the analyst. In this case, the analyst has greater control on selecting such parameters (as compared to training data determination), but may often set these values in an arbitrary way because of lack of guidance. Such arbitrary choices (implicitly) result in a kind of variance in the output of the detector because they might vary with the specific analyst, and one cannot easily view any of these choices as inherently better than the other in an unsupervised setting. In other words, all choices of the parameter k within a reasonable range are as good as random guessing, and the variability caused by this random guessing is not very different in principle than the variability caused by different random choices of training data sets.

It is noteworthy that in the data-centric view of outlier ensembles, design-choices (such as the parameter k) affect the bias of the model *over the space of different randomly selected training data sets* (see Fig. 2.2). However, in the model-centric view, this variability in bias (caused by changing k) is now viewed as a part of the variance *of the randomized model-centric process of selecting k*, which can be reduced with ensemble analysis. It is here that the model-centric view of the bias-variance trade-off is particularly useful.

In order to understand this point, let us revisit the problem in which John's mortgage application is scored by banks A, B, and C with the use of an outlier detector. Consider a setting, where the three banks have access to *exactly the same training data set* of 10,000 points. Note that this setting is already different form the previous case because we are no longer assuming that the different banks have different training data sets drawn from the same base distribution. However, in this case, the uncertainty is caused by the fact that none of the analysts seem to know what value of k to use for their k-nearest neighbor detector. For some data sets, a value of 5 might be effective, whereas for others a value of 100 might be effective. Therefore, there is significant uncertainty about the effect of choosing a particular value of k, particularly in the context of unsupervised problems in which the specific accuracy cannot be known even after the fact. As a result, the different analysts use different values of k for their respective detectors. The result of this approach is that they all obtain different results, and there is an inherent variability in their results caused by the specific choice of the parameter k. This variability is shown in the different outputs for John in Fig. 2.4a. However, it is possible for the analysts to run the detector over 10 different randomly chosen values of k, and average the performance of the detector over these choices to reduce the variance. As a result, John's scores from the three banks become more similar. Furthermore, the quality of the scores is improved because of reduced variability. This scenario is shown in Fig. 2.4b. It is important to note that in this model-centric view, the data set is assumed to be fixed, and the variability is caused because of uncertainty in the specific choice of the model. In the model-centric view, one is often improving the bias performance of individual models in the data-centric view by averaging over the variability in the bias over different randomized models. For example, a specific choice of k has a particular bias in the data-centric view; however this variability in bias over different choices of k in the data-centric view is converted to variance in the model-centric view. One can then reduce this aspect of the variance with the ensemble approach. In practical settings, this often means that one might be able to obtain better results with the ensemble scheme, compared to any particular value of k. For example, a value of $k \leq 4$ is clearly suboptimal to discover John as an outlier. It may be possible that for some other test points, a value of $k = 5$ may be too large and may therefore provide incorrect results. By ensembling over a "well-chosen" range of k, it is often possible to obtain better results than any specific value of the parameter (over all points). This is because of the *variability* in performance of different portions of the data over different values of k. Herein, lies the power of variance reduction in the model-centric setting. This principle is also related to the notion of reducing *representational bias* [13] of any specific model design by ensembling over different randomized models. We will discuss this issue in greater detail in Chap. 3.

The differences between data-centric and model-centric views of the bias-variance trade-off are shown in Fig. 2.5. The traditional view, which is the data-centric view,

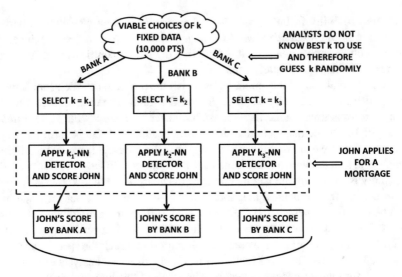

(a) Model-centric random process with high variance

(b) Model-centric random process with low variance

Fig. 2.4 Reducing variance in model-centric ensembles

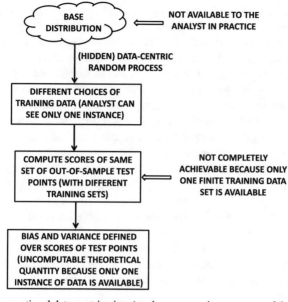

(a) Conventional data-centric view (random process is over space of data sets)

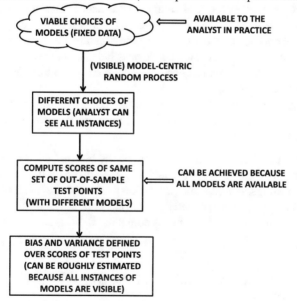

(b) Unconventional model-centric view (random process is over space of models)

Fig. 2.5   Different perspectives on the bias-variance trade-off

is shown in Fig. 2.5a. Here, the expectation $E[MSE]$ (in the bias-variance equation) is computed *over different random choices of training data sets*. Since a particular analyst usually has access to only one training data set and does not have access to the base distribution, it is generally hard to estimate the bias and variance in this setting. In other words, the *finiteness* of the available data causes limitations in our ability to estimate the bias and variance of a particular model. One typically reduces variances in such settings by using methods like bagging, which can be (approximately) viewed as the process of drawing different training data sets from the same base distribution. By averaging the results from the different draws, one is able to effectively reduce variance, although the approximate process of performing the draws leads to significant constraints. A more unconventional view of the bias-variance trade-off, which is the model-centric view, is shown in Fig. 2.5b. Here, the expectation is computed over *different randomized choices of models* over the same training data set. In this case, the expectation is computed over different randomized choices of models. Note that this process is often directly controlled by the analyst, and (in most cases) it is not a hidden process outside the control of the analyst. Therefore, the analyst can actually run the model over different randomized choices of the model and estimate the bias and variance as follows:

1. The analyst can run the model over a very large number of trials and compute the expected score over each out-of-sample test instance. The bias of the model is the difference between the true (ground-truth) scores and the averaged scores. Of course, since one typically does not have the ground-truth available in problems like outlier detection, it may often not be possible to compute the bias in practice, except for some bench-marking settings in which ground-truths are set on the basis of some assumption.
2. The analyst can determine the variance in the scores over different test instances relatively easily. Therefore, the variance can be easily computed whether the ground-truth is available or not.

In unsupervised problems, it is hard to compute the bias in both model-centric and data-centric settings. However, it is much easier to estimate the variance in most model-centric settings, unless some part of the random process is hidden from the analyst. Furthermore, it is also generally much easier to develop variance-reduction algorithms in the unsupervised setting, as compared to bias-reduction algorithms.

2.3 Examples and Applications of the Bias-Variance Tradeoff

In the following, we provide a few examples of how the bias-variance trade-off is used in different settings related to classification, and the corresponding adaptations to outlier detection. These examples also show that many ideas from classification can be adapted easily to outlier detection. However, the adaptation is not always a simple matter because of the unsupervised nature of outlier detection. In general, we will see that variance-reduction methods are much easier to adapt to the unsupervised settings, as compared to bias-reduction methods such as boosting. The main difference among these methods is in terms of how the combination is constructed in order to reduce either the bias or the variance. Correspondingly, the accuracy improvements of each of these methods can be explained with an appropriate definition of the random process over which the corresponding bias-variance trade-off is defined.

2.3.1 Bagging and Subsampling

Bagging and subsampling are well-known methods in classification for reducing variance [5, 6, 9–11]. The basic idea is to draw different training data sets from the same base data by sampling with or without replacement. The predictions over these different components are averaged to yield the final result. The basic idea in these methods is to reduce the variance with the averaging process. We describe these two approaches in some detail below, along with their corresponding effects on bias and variance:

1. *Bagging*: In bagging, samples of the data are drawn from a base data set with replacement, so that a bootstrapped sample is constructed. The bootstrapped sample typically has the same size as the original data set, although it is not essential to impose this restriction. Because of the fact that the sampling is performed with replacement, the sample will contain duplicates, and many points from the original data set will typically not be included. In particular, when a sample of size n is drawn from a data set of size n, the probability that a particular data point is not included is given by $(1 - 1/n)^n \approx 1/e$. A separate classification (or outlier detection) model is constructed on each of the bootstrapped samples, and the predictions across different samples are then averaged in order to create a final score. This basic idea of bagging is discussed in [1].

   The basic idea in bagging is to reduce the variance of the prediction. Each individual detector has roughly similar bias characteristics as the original data. However, by averaging, it is possible to significantly reduce the variance of the prediction. As a result, the accuracy of the prediction is improved. The theoretical and intuitive arguments for bagging are very similar in the case of classification and outlier detection. A detailed discussion of bagging together with experimental results is provided in the variance reduction chapter (Chap. 3). To the best of our knowledge, this book provides the first detailed experimental results on bagging in the context of outlier detection.

2. *Subsampling*: Subsampling is a straightforward variation of bagging. The approach is also referred to as *subagging*. In subsampling, samples of the data are constructed *without* replacement. Therefore, the sampled data set is much smaller than the original data set. Note that if we use the same algorithm parameters over a smaller data set, the subsampled data set is likely to have very different bias characteristics. Nevertheless, the variance reduction is often likely to more

significant because the individual ensemble components are more diverse. The basic idea of subsampling was proposed in [9–11] and it can be generalized trivially to outlier detection with virtually no changes. The first use of subsampling for outlier detection was proposed in the context of *edge* subsampling in the graph domain [3]. Subsampling methods were also sometimes used in the context of *efficiency improvements* [23], although the accuracy improvements were only limited with this specific implementation. Subsequent discussions on the use of subsampling for outlier detection with the use of distance-based detectors are provided in [4, 32]. However, the work in [32] provides an implementation of subsampling that has unpredictable bias-centric effects and also provides an incorrect theoretical explanation. The incorrectness of this reasoning was clarified in [4], and the theoretical foundations for outlier analysis/ensembles were also established in this work. These foundations were used to propose more accurate and reliable subsampling by varying the subsampling rate [4]. A detailed discussion of subsampling will also be provided in Chap. 3.

Note that the natural adaptation of the bagging family of techniques from classification to outlier detection has also been published in an earlier position paper [1] on outlier detection. The key idea of subsampling (as it applies to classification) should be credited to the original subsampling papers [9, 10]. Although subsampling methods were subsequently investigated in [3, 23, 32], a proper explanation of the effects of subsampling, as it applies to outlier detection, may be found in [4]. Further exposition of these effects are provided in greater detail in Chap. 3.

Both the methods of bagging and subsampling rely on a random process generating the ensemble components, and then using a combination method to reduce the variance of the final output. However, these principles apply to any approach for randomly perturbing a detector to improve the variance-reduction characteristics of the method. Bagging and subsampling methods are discussed in detail in Chap. 3.

2.3.2 Feature Bagging

Feature bagging is a method that is used commonly in classification [7, 8, 19, 24] to create individual ensemble methods with sufficient diversity. The averaging of the predictions of different ensemble members can reduce (model-centric) variance. Subsequently, a natural adaptation of the feature bagging method to outlier detection was proposed in [22].

The basic idea in feature bagging, as it applies to outlier detection, is to sample a number r between $\lfloor d/2 \rfloor$ and $d - 1$, where d is the total number of dimensions in the data. Subsequently, r randomly chosen dimensions are sampled from the underlying data and the outlier detection algorithm is applied to this r-dimensional projection. Note that the individual ensemble components in feature bagging often have deteriorated (model-centric) bias characteristics because of the fact that dimensions are dropped from the data set. On the other hand, they are somewhat diverse, and therefore variance can be reduced by the averaging process. The deteriorated bias characteristics of feature bagging are somewhat of a concern because they can sometimes affect the final ensemble performance as well. Nevertheless, in most cases, it has been shown that the use of feature bagging generally improves accuracy. This improvement in accuracy is attributed to variance reduction. However, one needs to be careful of using the right random process to describe the bias-variance trade-off of this ensemble method. In particular, feature bagging can be best explained with a model-centric random process, even though the the approach seems to be a data-centric ensemble at first sight. Feature bagging methods are discussed in detail in Chap. 3. A proper theoretical explanation of feature bagging is also provided in the same chapter.

2.3.3 Boosting

The boosting method is used popularly in classification [14, 15], but it is harder to generalize to outlier detection. Boosting uses a combination of highly biased detectors, so that the final detector has less bias than the individual components. The basic idea is to create biased data sets in which the misclassified training examples are given greater weight. The basic assumption is that the errors in the misclassified examples are caused by instance-specific bias, and weighting them to a larger degree will result in a training model that will classify them correctly. This is achieved by using a base detector with low variance, so that most of the error is caused by the bias component. A weighted combination detector is created to combine the bias characteristics of various components to create a final detector, which has lower bias than its individual components.

An important observation about boosting is that it requires the computation of accuracy on the training examples. The accuracy computation of a classifier requires the comparison of the predictions with the ground truth. This can often be difficult in an unsupervised problem like outlier detection. Nevertheless, a number of heuristic methods can also be used in the context of the outlier detection problem. Such methods are discussed in Chap. 4.

2.4 Experimental Illustration of Bias-Variance Theory

In this section, we will provide an experimental illustration of bias-variance theory with the use of a number of synthetic data sets. We will also show the impact of using ensemble methods on the bias-variance analysis. Since variance reduction is particularly valuable in the context of bias-variance theory, much of our focus will be on the effect of ensemble methods on variance. In particular, we will show the following effects:

1. We show the effect of methods like subsampling on variance reduction.
2. We show the effect of finiteness of the data set on the limits of data-centric variance reduction.
3. We show the differences in the data-centric and model-centric view of the bias-variance trade-off.

These different insights set the stage for introducing the different ensemble methods discussed in subsequent chapters.

2.4.1   Understanding the Effects of Ensembles on Data-Centric Bias and Variance

In this section, we will study the effect of ensemble methods like subsampling on *data-centric* bias and variance. In this case, the assumption is that the training data sets are drawn from the same base distribution. The data-centric bias and variance are only theoretical quantities in real settings (which cannot be actually computed) because they are based on the variability of drawing training data sets from a base distribution. In practice, this base distribution is not available to the analyst, but only a *single finite instantiation* of the data set is available. This finite instantiation can be viewed as a finite resource that must be exploited as *efficiently* as possible to maximize the benefits of ensemble analysis. Knowing the base distribution is equivalent to having an infinite resource of data at one's disposal. Although the data-centric bias and variance are difficult to quantify in real settings (because of the finiteness of the data resource), we can still use a synthetic setting in which it is assumed that the base distribution is known. This synthetic setting can be used to show the effects of ensemble analysis on various measures of outlier detection accuracy, such as the rank-wise accuracy, the mean-squared error, bias, and variance. A preliminary version of these results is available in [4], although this expanded version provides significantly more insights in terms of data-centric and model-centric analysis.

In order to show the effects of ensemble analysis, we use some simulations with the subsampling method [3, 4, 9–11, 23, 32] discussed earlier in this chapter. This approach can be viewed as a variant of the example of scoring mortgage applications with averaged predictions on randomized partitions of the data. Instead of creating randomized partitions, we draw random subsamples of the training data, and then score each point with respect to the subsample whether that point is included in the subsample or not. The scores of a test point across the different subsamples are then averaged in order to provide the final outlier score of that point.

The subsampling approach has been used earlier for both classification and outlier detection. The use of subsampling for classification is discussed in [9–11]. The earliest accuracy-centric work on subsampling in outlier detection was done in the context of *edge* subsampling for graph data (for detecting edge outliers), and the approach was also used in the context of efficiency-centric improvements for outlier detection in multidimensional data [23]. Note that the former implicitly subsamples *entries* in an adjacency matrix, whereas the latter subsamples *rows* in a multidimensional data matrix. The approach was also explored for nearest neighbor detectors like the average k-nearest neighbor detector [4] and the LOF method [4, 32]. The work in [4] already provides a number of experimental illustrations of bias-variance theory although it does not specifically decompose the error into the bias and variance components. This section will show some further simulations with synthetic data, which explain the nature of the bias-variance decomposition discussed in [4].

In the following, we will use some simple synthetic distributions to generate data sets. One advantage of using synthetic distributions is that we can explicitly test the effects of drawing truly independent training data sets from from an infinite resource of data; these independent data sets can be used to properly characterize the bias and variance performance of training data sets drawn from a particular base distribution.

We used two 1-dimensional locally uniform distributions and a 2-dimensional distribution with clusters of uniformly distributed points. Consider a data set $\mathscr{D}$ containing the points $\overline{X_1} \ldots \overline{X_n}$, with local probability densities $f_1 \ldots f_n$, which are known from the parameters of the generating distribution. Therefore, these represent ground-truth scores. Let the corresponding scores output by the outlier detection algorithm be $r_1 \ldots r_n$. We say that an inversion has occurred if $f_1 < f_2$ and $r_1 < r_2$. In other words, if a data point with a lower probability density (i.e., in a sparse region), has smaller 1-nearest neighbor distance than a data point in a dense region, then an inversion is assumed to have occurred. For each of the $n \cdot (n-1)/2$ pairs of points in the data set, we computed a non-inversion credit $C(\overline{X_i}, \overline{X_i})$ as follows:

$$C(\overline{X_i}, \overline{X_j}) = \begin{cases} 0 & f_i < f_j \text{ and } r_i < r_j \\ 0 & f_i > f_j \text{ and } r_i > r_j \\ 1 & f_i < f_j \text{ and } r_i > r_j \\ 1 & f_i > f_j \text{ and } r_i < r_j \\ 0.5 & f_i = f_j \text{ or } r_i = r_j \end{cases} \tag{2.9}$$

The average non-inversion credit $NI(\mathscr{D})$ over all pairs of data points in data set $\mathscr{D}$ is defined as follows:

$$NI(\mathscr{D}) = \frac{\sum_{i<j} C(\overline{X_i}, \overline{X_j})}{n(n-1)/2} \tag{2.10}$$

In other words, this measure computes the fraction of pairs of points in which the inversion does not occur. Larger values indicate that outliers and inliers will not be inverted. In the ideal case, when no inversions occur, the the value of $NI(\mathscr{D})$ is 1. A value of 0.5 would be expected from a random detector. Therefore, the non-inversion credit provides an intuitive idea of how well a particular detector performs in a given setting.

Since our primary argument on the effectiveness of subsampling is based on variance reduction, one of the challenges that we faced in our testing was the effect of correlations across multiple ensemble components. Because of the overlaps among the training data sets from various subsamples, the outlier scores (1-nearest neighbor distances) from various ensemble components are correlated. As a result, the variance reduction effects of averaging were curtailed. The problem is that the base data set is finite, and larger subsamples from a base data set always lead to correlated detectors. Even though one can view the process of drawing a subsample from the base data as equivalent to drawing the sample from the base distribution over a *single* sample, this is not true over multiple samples in which the finiteness of the base data comes into play and causes correlated samples. Correlated detectors generally have a negative effect on any form of variance reduction in ensemble analysis. Furthermore, one cannot meaningfully estimate the bias performance of a particular detector from a data-centric point of view, if the base distribution is unavailable. If the base distribution is available, one can use the approach of Fig. 2.1a to repeatedly draw training data sets and average the results to reduce the variance to 0. The remaining error reflects the bias-performance of the algorithm.

In this section, we simulate the scenario where the base distribution is available. In effect, the availability of the base distribution provides the resources of an infinite data set. One can study the effects of such infinite resources on a procedure such as subsampling to see how much one can improve the performance. In such a case, the results of any pair of subsamples (drawn from the base distribution) would be truly independent, and the full effect of variance reduction could be realized because of the infiniteness of this resource. The original base data $\mathcal{D}$ is only used to test the outlier scores against each such generated model, whereas the training data sets are generated directly from the base distribution. We also study the limits of this variance reduction caused by the finite data size available in real settings. As we will show, a portion of the variance caused by training data variability is always irreducible in the setting, where a finite data set is used for variance reduction. Therefore, we generated two different variants of base detectors and ensembles:

1. We constructed the base detectors by drawing subsamples from the original data set $\mathcal{D}$. This data set was also used as the test data set, but the 1-NN computation of each point in the test data $\mathcal{D}$ was computed only on the subsample of $\mathcal{D}$. The average of the 1-NN scores provided the ensemble score. The resulting base detector was referred to as *BASE-F* and the ensemble detector was referred to as *ENSEMBLE-F*. The "-F" corresponds to the fact that the base data is finite.
2. In this case, the test data set is fixed to the original data set $\mathcal{D}$, but the subsamples are drawn from an infinite base data set of the same distribution as the test set. This scenario is simulated by generating the subsamples and the test set from the same probability distribution. Note that it is not meaningful to talk of sampling "rates" in this case, because the training data set size is infinite. However, in order to ensure comparability of results with the finite base data, we defined the sampling rate of the subsample with respect to the original (test) data set $\mathcal{D}$. Note that the same test data set $\mathcal{D}$ is used in both finite and infinite sampling. The resulting base detector was referred to as *BASE-I* and the ensemble detector was referred to as *ENSEMBLE-I*. The "-I" at the end of the name refers to the fact that subsampling is performed from a infinite data set. Using an infinite base data has the advantage

that it allows us to test the performance once the effects of correlation between base detectors have been removed.

The results in this section used 300 trials. The accuracy of the base detector is computed by averaging the accuracy over each of these 300 instantiations, whereas the accuracy of the ensemble approach is computed using the averaged 1-NN score of the ensemble. We used 300 trials because the accuracy usually leveled out after this point, and not much advantage was obtained by further increasing the number of trials.

First, we used a data set $\mathscr{D}$ containing 2000 points drawn from locally uniform distributions in a single dimension. The data distribution is shown in Fig. 2.6a. In this case, the data is distributed in 20 1-dimensional buckets. All 1-dimensional points in the ith bucket take on uniformly random values in the range $(i, i + 1)$. The relative number of points in each bucket is a uniform random variable drawn from $(0, 1)$, and it is illustrated on the Y-axis of Fig. 2.6a. Therefore, the lower bars correspond to regions which are outlier regions in this 1-dimensional data, albeit uniformly distributed. The values on the Y-axis of Fig. 2.6a, are used as the ground-truth values of f_i in Eq. 2.9 for the corresponding data points in that bucket. The 1-NN distance is used as r_i in Eq. 2.9. The fraction of non-inversions (i.e., $NI(\mathscr{D})$) of the base system (a 1-NN detector) and ensemble systems both for the case of finite and infinite sampling are illustrated in Fig. 2.6b. Note that the performance of both base detectors *improves with* the sampling rate, and no advantage was observed for smaller subsamples. The main improvements were achieved with the use of the variance reduction impact of the ensemble. The *ENSEMBLE-F* detector did indeed perform quite well for smaller subsamples, but the improvements were achieved *because of less correlation among the base components*, and therefore better variance reduction. When the subsample size was exactly equal to the size of the full data, no performance improvement was observed because of perfect correlations among the base detectors in *ENSEMBLE-F*. This is substantiated by the fact that the performance of the *ENSEMBLE-I* detector *improves* with increasing subsample size, when the correlations are removed. The gap between the two reflects the gap in variance reduction which arises as a result of increasingly correlated base detectors in *ENSEMBLE-F*. The performance of *ENSEMBLE-I* almost always improves with increasing subsample size, which is a result of the statistical effects of using more data. We repeated the same experiment with the use of 40 buckets instead of 20 and present the results in Fig. 2.6c, d. The results are very similar to the case of Fig. 2.6a, b. Note that some forms of the bias-variance trade-off [17] explicitly take this correlation into account. This form of the decomposition is referred to as the *bias-variance-covariance* decomposition.

We also tested the effects with 2-dimensional locally uniform distributions of 2000 points. In this case, 30 clusters of uniformly distributed squares were generated, with lower-left corners chosen uniformly at random in $(0, 1)$. Each square had a side of length 1/15. The relative number of points in each cluster was a uniform random variable in $(0, 1)$, and it represented the ground-truth value of f_i in Eq. 2.9. The corresponding scatter plot is shown in Fig. 2.7a. The corresponding effects on

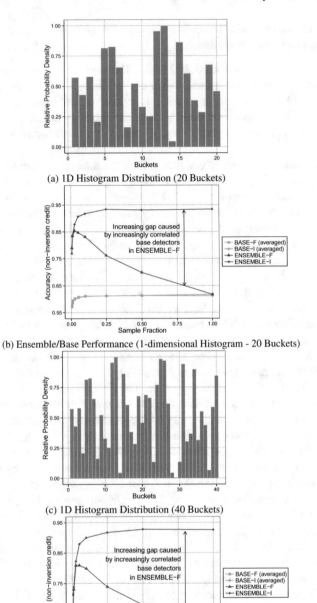

(a) 1D Histogram Distribution (20 Buckets)

(b) Ensemble/Base Performance (1-dimensional Histogram - 20 Buckets)

(c) 1D Histogram Distribution (40 Buckets)

(d) Ensemble/Base Performance (1-dimensional Histogram - 40 Buckets)

Fig. 2.6 Effectiveness of base and ensemble on locally uniform data sets (Sampling "rates" for infinite data set are defined with respect to finite base data set $\mathcal{D}$)

Fig. 2.7 Effectiveness of base and ensemble on locally uniform data sets (Sampling "rates" for infinite data set are defined with respect to finite base data set $\mathscr{D}$)

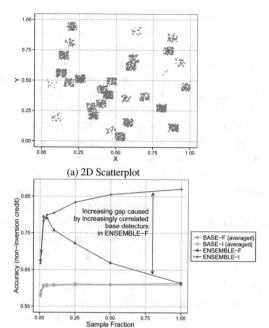

(a) 2D Scatterplot

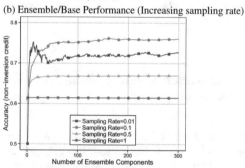

(b) Ensemble/Base Performance (Increasing sampling rate)

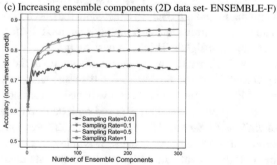

(c) Increasing ensemble components (2D data set- ENSEMBLE-F)

(d) Increasing ensemble components (2D data set- ENSEMBLE-I)

the non-inversion credit with increasing subsample size are illustrated in Fig. 2.7b. As in the case of the 1-dimensional distributions, the non-inversions reduced with increasing subsample size. The ensemble based approach *ENSEMBLE-F* initially improved with increasing subsample size, and then the performance started reducing because of increasing correlations among detectors. Here, we have also shown the effect of increasing the number of ensemble components in Fig. 2.7c, d. The former (Fig. 2.7c) is for the case of the *ENSEMBLE-F* method with the 2d-distribution, whereas the latter is for the case of *ENSEMBLE-I* method with the 2d-distribution. It is noteworthy that larger subsamples generally level off sooner and no advantage is observed by increasing the number of ensemble components. Smaller subsamples initially perform poorly, but because of increasing variance reduction, they can often perform better with increasing number of ensemble components. However, there is a limit to this improvement. Subsamples, which are too small, lose too much information in individual detectors to be effective overall, even with a large number of components. For example, at the lowest sampling rate of 0.005, each subsample contained only 10 points, which was not sufficient to meaningfully represent the 30 clusters. Therefore, the ensemble performance at this sampling rate could not outperform the ensemble performance at higher sampling rates, even after increasing the number of ensemble components. Note that for the case of *ENSEMBLE-I*, larger subsampling rates almost always provided better performance because the ensemble components were independent, and one could make better use of the greater amount of data.

2.4.2 Experimental Examples of Bias-Variance Decomposition

The synthetic nature of the data sets allow us a way to show the bias-variance decomposition experimentally. In real settings, one can never construct ensemble performances like *ENSEMBLE-I* with a single instance of a finite data set. Although some sampling methods exist [20] to *estimate* the bias and variance experimentally for real data sets, we argue that such methods are too unreliable/approximate to provide any meaningful insights. This is in part because the base distribution of a real data set is unavailable and there are correlations among the results from different samples. However, for synthetic data sets, where one has access to the base distribution, it is possible to simulate the bias and variance performance very closely.

In the previous section, we used rank-centric measures for test the performance of *ENSEMBLE-I* and *ENSEMBLE-F*. In this section, we will study the more conventional *MSE* measure because it is relevant to the bias-variance decomposition. In order to compute the *MSE*, we do need to standardize both the ground-truth and the predicted scores for comparability. Therefore, just before the computation of the *MSE*, the ground-truth scores and the predicted scores (both for the base and the ensembles) are standardized to zero mean and unit variance. In the following, we will assume that the size of the test data $\mathscr{D}$ is n_0.

It is important to remember that the bias-variance decomposition depends on the *choice of the random process* over which the expected value $E[MSE]$ is computed. Therefore, we will consider the following two ways of defining the random process:

1. *Random Process A (Data-centric)*: The base distribution is available to the analyst. We can describe the random process for *BASE-I* as follows. For a given test data set $\mathscr{D}$ of size n_0, we repeatedly draw samples of size $f \cdot n_0$ from the base distribution in order to compute the scores.

   We can describe the random process of *BASE-F* as follows. The training data of size n_0 is drawn from the base distribution and then a fraction f sample of size $f \cdot n_0$ is subsampled from it to create the training data. Note that this process is equivalent to drawing a sample of size $f \cdot n_0$ from the base-distribution, although there are overlaps among the samples drawn for a particular run of subsampling. However, the bias and variance are computed not over a particular run of subsampling but *over all possible draws* of the base data of size n_0. This is an important point, because it makes the bias-variance decomposition of *BASE-F* and *BASE-I* very similar. It is important to note that the variance of the prediction of a given test point needs to include the variance caused by initially selecting a particular base data set of size n_0 from the distribution for subsampling. For example, if one drew a subsample of fraction $f = 1$, then the same subsample will be drawn every time from a particular base data set, but the variance of the prediction of a test point by *BASE-F* will still be non-zero because it includes the variance of drawing a training data set of size n_0 from the base distribution. In this context, the variance of predicting each test point, when computed over a very large number of instantiations of the base data set (followed by subsampling in each case), is not very different between *BASE-F* and *BASE-I*. As we will see later, a portion of this variance of *BASE-F* is always irreducible in practice, because of correlations among subsampled base detectors. This irreducible variance is an artifact of the fact that an analyst has access to only a *single finite instance* of this data set, and there are fundamental limitations to the variance reduction process with this finite resource.

2. *Random Process B (Model-Centric)*: In this case, it is not assumed that the base distribution is available. Rather a single finite data set is available, and the random process of *BASE-F* is simply that of subsampling this finite data set. Note that the subsampling is now part of the detector itself, and therefore we have a randomized detector with a particular bias and variance on a finite data set. The expected values of the MSE, bias and variance are computed with respect to the random process implied by the stochastic behavior of this *detector*. This is the reason that this way of defining the bias-variance trade-off is referred to as model-centric. Note that although both *BASE-I* and *BASE-F* can be captured by random process A, only *BASE-F* can be captured by random process B. Therefore, the former approach is more general. However, the model-centric approach of bias-variance decomposition is more valuable in some ensemble settings where one cannot

relate the variance reduction directly with statistical variations in the training data, but with the randomized variations in the detector. In some ensembles (such as the example discussed in this sections), one can use both decomposition, but the data-centric decomposition provides better insights.

Although we do not distinguish between training and test points in the simulation of *BASE-F*, the predictions are still (roughly) similar to the case when training and test data were different, because distance-based detectors exclude the test point at hand while computing the nearest neighbors for the prediction. It does cause a small difference in training data size of a single point; this effect is negligible. Note that if we draw a different data set $\mathscr{D}'$, which is of the same size as the test data $\mathscr{D}$ (for creating the subsampled training data sets), we will get roughly similar results. This fact is validated by the similar performance of *BASE-F* and *BASE-I* in Fig. 2.6.

In the following, we will run the process of 1000 trials; our basic assumption is that 1000 trials are sufficient to stabilize the ensemble performance from a practical point of view. Therefore, we can roughly estimate these results to be reflective of an infinite number of trials, which are required for accurately computing quantities like bias and variance.

We show the performance of both the base and ensemble performance in Fig. 2.8. In this case, we present the results for the 2-dimensional distribution discussed earlier in this section. Note that Fig. 2.8a, b are respectively identical to Fig. 2.8c, d. However, they are annotated differently. In Fig. 2.8a, b, the annotation is designed to show the bias-variance decomposition according to the data-centric setting. The first observation is that the data-centric bias of *BASE-I* is simply the MSE of *ENSEMBLE-I* after a large number of trials. This is because *ENSEMBLE-I* has zero variance after a large number of subsamples, and all the *MSE* is simply the bias of its base detector. It is, however, less obvious why the bias of *BASE-F* and *BASE-I* should be the same. Note that the random process defining *BASE-F* includes the variance of the initial step of choosing the base data of size n_0, even though we see only one instance of this finite data set. After this variance is included, the variances of *BASE-F* and *BASE-I* are equivalent to sampling a training data of size $f \cdot n_0$ directly from the base distribution. Furthermore, the expected *MSE* of *BASE-F* is also the same as that of *BASE-I*, even though there are minor differences in the *particular* case of Fig. 2.8 due to statistical fluctuations. In fact, the *MSE* of *BASE-I* in Fig. 2.8 reflects the *expected MSE* of *BASE-F* more closely than the specific instantiation of *BASE-F* in the figure. This is because *BASE-F* is constructed using a subset of the test points as the training data, whereas the data-centric random process assumes that the base detectors are constructed using a different sample from the same distribution (as in *BASE-I*)). Therefore, the data-centric bias, variance, and *MSE* of both *BASE-F* and *BASE-I* are identical, and are defined completely by the *BASE-I* and *ENSEMBLE-I* simulations. Interestingly, both the *BASE-F* and *ENSEMBLE-F* simulations are completely irrelevant for defining the data-centric bias and variance of *BASE-F*. However, the *ENSEMBLE-F* plot is still interesting, in that it shows how much of the variance one can heuristically reduce, while working within the limitations of a finite resource (data set). Because of the finiteness of the data set, there are correlations among

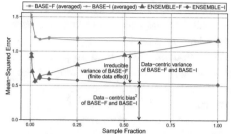

(a) Random Process A: Data-centric bias-variance decomposition (1000 components)

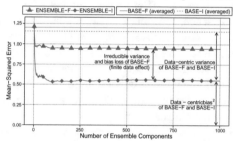

(b) Random Process A: Data-centric bias-variance decomposition (sampling rate 0:5)

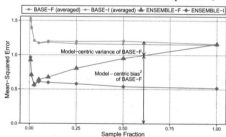

(c) Random Process B: Model-centric bias-variance decomposition (1000 components)

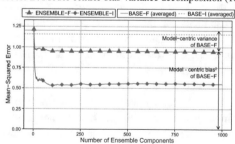

(d) Random Process B: Model-centric bias-variance decomposition (sampling rate 0.5)

Fig. 2.8 Two different ways of performing the bias-variance decomposition of the same MSE (data-centric view and model-centric view). One can define the bias-variance decomposition in any number of ways by choosing the appropriate random process over which the expectation is computed. An important assumption is that 1000 base detectors are sufficient for stabilization of ensemble performance, and therefore we are treating the (ensemble) variance to be negligible at that point

the base detectors of *ENSEMBLE-F*, and therefore only a portion of the variance can be reduced. The portion of the irreducible variance because of intra-detector correlations are annotated in Fig. 2.8a, b.

The bias-variance decomposition with random process B is shown in Fig. 2.8c, d. This model-centric approach can no longer decompose the error of *BASE-I* since it starts with a finite data set, and does not assume that the training data sets are drawn from a base distribution. Therefore, even though the plots of *BASE-I* and *ENSEMBLE-I* are shown in the figure, they are irrelevant from a bias-variance decomposition perspective. The draws of data from an infinite data set are relevant to the model-centric random process B. After a large number of trials *ENSEMBLE-F* is assumed to have zero variance, and therefore the variance of base *BASE-F* is simply the difference between *BASE-F* and *ENSEMBLE-F*. The remaining part of the *MSE* is the (model-centric) bias. It is interesting to note that the model-centric view does not provide a particularly satisfactory explanation of variance reduction in this particular setting of subsampling. However, as discussed in the next chapter, there are indeed several settings in which the model-centric view provides better insights. For example, methods like feature bagging can be better explained from a model-centric view of variance reduction. Therefore, an appropriate form of the bias-variance trade-off can be used to justify different types of ensemble methods.

2.5 Conclusions

This chapter introduces the theory of outlier ensembles. The ideas in this chapter show that the theoretical underpinnings of ensemble analysis for classification are not very different from those in outlier detection. As a result, many of the existing ensemble schemes for classification can be generalized directly to outlier detection. In this chapter, we provide both a data-centric and a model-centric view of outlier ensembles. These ideas can be used to explain both data-centric and model-centric outlier ensembles. By designing ensemble methods to reduce either the bias or the variance or both, one can design more accurate outlier detection methods. Bias-reduction methods are generally harder to adapt from classification to outlier detection because of the fact the accuracy needs to be computed in intermediate steps in most such methods. Accuracy computation requires the knowledge of labels that are not available in unsupervised settings. On the other hand, variance-reduction methods can be adapted more easily from classification to outlier detection. The theoretical ideas discussed in this chapter set the stage to view the rich literature in classification as a reservoir of ideas, which can be adapted in various ways to the outlier detection domain.

Exercises

1. Consider a randomized outlier detection algorithm, $g(\overline{X}, \mathcal{D})$, which is almost ideal in the sense that it correctly learns the function $f(\overline{X})$ most of the time. The value of $f(\overline{X})$ is known to be finite. At the same time, because of a small

bug in the program, the randomized detector $g(\overline{X}, \mathcal{D})$ outputs an ∞ score about 0.00001% of the time. Furthermore, every test point is equally likely to receive such a score, although this situation occurs only 0.00001% of the time for any particular test instance. What is the model-centric bias of the bug-infested base detector $g(\overline{X}, \mathcal{D})$?

2. Would you recommend running the randomized base detector of Exercise 1 multiple times, and averaging the predictions of the test instance? How about using the median?

3. Does the data-centric variance of an average k-nearest neighbor outlier detector increase or decrease with k? What about the bias?

References

1. C. C. Aggarwal. Outlier Ensembles: Position Paper, *ACM SIGKDD Explorations*, 14(2), pp. 49–58, December, 2012.
2. C. C. Aggarwal. Outlier Analysis, Second Edition, *Springer*, 2017.
3. C. C. Aggarwal and P. S. Yu. Outlier Detection in Graph Streams. *IEEE ICDE Conference*, 2011.
4. C. C. Aggarwal and S. Sathe. Theoretical Foundations and Algorithms for Outlier Ensembles, *ACM SIGKDD Explorations*, 17(1), June 2015.
5. L. Brieman. Bagging Predictors. *Machine Learning*, 24(2), pp. 123–140, 1996.
6. L. Brieman. Random Forests. *Journal Machine Learning archive*, 45(1), pp. 5–32, 2001.
7. G. Brown, J. Wyatt, R. Harris, and X. Yao. Diversity creation methods: a survey and categorisation. *Information Fusion*, 6:5(20), 2005.
8. R. Bryll, R. Gutierrez-Osuna, and F. Quek. Attribute Bagging: Improving Accuracy of Classifier Ensembles by using Random Feature Subsets. *Pattern Recognition*, 36(6), pp. 1291–1302, 2003.
9. P. Buhlmann, B. Yu. Analyzing bagging. *Annals of Statistics*, pp. 927–961, 2002.
10. P. Buhlmann. Bagging, Subagging and Bragging for Improving Some Prediction Algorithms. *Recent advances and trends in nonparametric statistics*, Elsevier, 2003.
11. A. Buja, W. Stuetzle. Observations on bagging. *Statistica Sinica*, 16(2), 323, 2006.
12. M. Denil, D. Matheson, and N. De Freitas. Narrowing the Gap: Random Forests In Theory and in Practice. *ICML Conference*, pp. 665–673, 2014.
13. T. Dietterich. Ensemble Methods in Machine Learning. *First International Workshop on Multiple Classifier Systems*, 2000.
14. Y. Freund and R. Schapire. A Decision-theoretic Generalization of Online Learning and Application to Boosting. *Computational Learning Theory*, 1995.
15. Y. Freund and R. Schapire. Experiments with a New Boosting Algorithm. *ICML Conference*, pp. 148–156, 1996.
16. J. Friedman. On Bias, Variance, 0/1loss, and the Curse-of-Dimensionality. *Data Mining and Knowledge Discovery*, 1(1), pp. 55–77, 1997.
17. S. Geman, E. Bienenstock, and R. Doursat. Neural Networks and the Bias/Variance Dilemma. *Neural computation*, 4(1), pp. 1–58, 1992.
18. T. K. Ho. Random decision forests. *Third International Conference on Document Analysis and Recognition*, 1995. Extended version appears in *IEEE Transactions on Pattern Analysis and Machine Intelligence*, 20(8), pp. 832–844, 1998.
19. T. K. Ho. Nearest Neighbors in Random Subspaces. *Lecture Notes in Computer Science*, Vol. 1451, pp. 640–648, *Proceedings of the Joint IAPR Workshops SSPR'98 and SPR'98*, 1998. http://link.springer.com/chapter/10.1007/BFb0033288

20. R. Kohavi and D.H. Wolpert. Bias plus variance decomposition for zero-one loss functions, *ICML Conference*, 1996.
21. E. Kong and T. Dietterich. Error-Correcting Output Coding Corrects Bias and Variance. *Proceedings of the Twelfth International Conference on Machine Learning*, pp. 313–321, 1995.
22. A. Lazarevic, and V. Kumar. Feature Bagging for Outlier Detection, *ACM KDD Conference*, 2005.
23. F. T. Liu, K. M. Ting, and Z.-H. Zhou. Isolation Forest. *ICDM Conference*, 2008. Extended version appears in: *ACM Transactions on Knowledge Discovery from Data (TKDD)*, 6(1), 3, 2012.
24. R. Michalski, I. Mozetic, J. Hong and N. Lavrac. The Multi-Purpose Incremental Learning System AQ15 and its Testing Applications to Three Medical Domains, *Proceedings of the Fifth National Conference on Artificial Intelligence*, pp. 1041–1045, 1986.
25. S. Rayana, L. Akoglu. Less is More: Building Selective Anomaly Ensembles with Application to Event Detection in Temporal Graphs. *SDM Conference*, 2015.
26. S. Rayana, L. Akoglu. Less is More: Building Selective Anomaly Ensembles. *ACM Transactions on Knowledge Disovery and Data Mining*, to appear, 2016.
27. L. Rokach. Pattern classification using ensemble methods, *World Scientific Publishing Company*, 2010.
28. M. Salehi, C. Leckie, M. Moshtaghi, and T. Vaithianathan. A Relevance Weighted Ensemble Model for Anomaly Detection in Switching Data Streams. *Advances in Knowledge Discovery and Data Mining*, pp. 461–473, 2014.
29. G. Seni and J. Elder. Ensemble Methods in Data Mining: Improving Accuracy through Combining Predictions. *Synthesis Lectures in Data Mining and Knowledge Discovery, Morgan and Claypool*, 2010.
30. R. Tibshirani. Bias, Variance, and Prediction Error for Classification Rules, *Technical Report, Statistics Department, University of Toronto*, 1996.
31. G. Valentini and T. Dietterich. Bias-variance Analysis of Support Vector Machines for the Development of SVM-based Ensemble Methods. *Journal of Machine Learning Research*, 5, pp. 725–774, 2004.
32. A. Zimek, M. Gaudet, R. Campello, J. Sander. Subsampling for efficient and effective unsupervised outlier detection ensembles, *KDD Conference*, 2013.
33. Z.-H. Zhou. Ensemble Methods: Foundations and Algorithms. *Chapman and Hall/CRC Press*, 2012.

Chapter 3
Variance Reduction in Outlier Ensembles

Bagging goes a ways toward making a silk purse out of a sow's ear, especially if the sow's ear is twitchy.

Leo Brieman

3.1 Introduction

The theoretical discussion in the previous chapter establishes that the error of an outlier detector can be decomposed into the squared bias and the variance. Ensemble methods attempt to reduce the overall error by reducing either the squared bias or the variance. The latter is more common in unsupervised problems like outlier detection. This chapter will focus on the more common scenario of variance-reduction techniques, whereas the next chapter will focus on the scenario of bias reduction.

A particular outlier detection algorithm may behave very differently for different instantiations of the same data distribution, especially if these instantiated data sets are small. Furthermore, the specific design choices of a particular algorithm may often have a significant impact on the final result. In such cases, these unpredictable effects of data and design choices can result in significant variability in the output of the algorithm. For example, with a particular training data set, John may be predicted to be an outlier, whereas with another training data set (collected under similar circumstances), John may be predicted to be an inlier. As discussed in the previous chapter, this variability in prediction, referred to as variance, has a negative effect on the performance of the algorithm because the variance is a component of the overall *expected* error (over different choices of the training data). In the example discussed above, the prediction for John will be incorrect in at least one of the two training data instantiations; this will increase the expected error. The goal of variance-reduction methods is to minimize the negative impact of this variability by designing ensemble methods that are more robust to the choice of the training data.

Variance-reduction methods are used commonly in a variety of classification applications [59, 62, 72]. In fact, variance-reduction is also used implicitly in many

© Springer International Publishing AG 2017
C.C. Aggarwal and S. Sathe, *Outlier Ensembles*,
DOI 10.1007/978-3-319-54765-7_3

supervised and unsupervised learning methods such as clustering [9] and recommendations [7]. In recent years, such methods have also been used effectively in semi-supervised scenarios [46, 47]. The ensemble techniques discussed in this chapter also have significant usability in various applications such as computer security [33], intrusion detection, and fraud detection.

One can view the variability in an algorithm and the corresponding ensemble techniques to minimize this variability in two different ways:

1. *Data-centric variability*: One can view the training data set available to an analyst as a single instance of a data set drawn from a (hidden) base distribution. For example, consider a setting in which three banks evaluate John's outlier score based on training records of other individuals. If three banks draw training data sets from the same base distribution to score John, they will all obtain different results for John. This difference contributes to the error in the form of the variance component. Even though each bank sees only one instance of the data (and the score), it is this hidden variability that needs to be minimized (without access to each other's data sets). Many variance-reduction techniques such as bagging and subagging reduce this variability (i.e., make the scores from all three banks more similar), by using their available finite resource (data set) in a more *efficient* way. An implicit assumption in many of these methods is that the training data are drawn from some hidden base distribution which is unknown to the analyst. The variation in a particular draw induces the corresponding variability in the output of the method.

2. *Model-centric variability*: In many settings, there is significant uncertainty in the design of a model that will work best in a particular setting. For example, a randomized model in which decisions are made in a stochastic way will exhibit variability in the output. An example is the case of a gradient-descent method for matrix-factorization methods in recommender systems, in which the randomized initialization point of the descent might have a significant effect on the final output (rating prediction). Therefore, instead of using a single initialization point, one might average the prediction with the use of multiple initialization points. In most cases, this averaged prediction is better *in expectation* than the use of a randomly chosen initialization point; furthermore, in some settings, it does better than the use of smart heuristics to select initialization points.

   In fact, one can even view parameter choice in such algorithms from the perspective of model-centric variance by setting the parameters in a randomized way within a reasonable range. In such a case, the randomized process of selecting the parameters is considered a part of the modeling algorithm. It is noteworthy that the problem of model-centric uncertainty is greater in unsupervised problems like outlier detection, as compared to supervised problems like classification. This is because one can use the available ground-truth in problems like classification to perform model selection and parameter tuning. This type of ground-truth is not available in problems like outlier detection, and therefore choosing one set of parameters over another is no better than random guessing.

In all these cases, ensemble analysis is a useful tool to reduce variability and improve the output accuracy. It is noteworthy that most variance-reduction techniques in classification can be adapted in a straightforward way to outlier detection. The easy adaptation of variance-reduction techniques from classification to outlier detection is facilitated by the fact that they do not require the availability of the ground-truth. This makes their adaptation from classification relatively simple. One can adapt most variance-reduction techniques from classification, such as bagging, bragging, wagging, and subagging (subsampling) [16, 20–22, 32], in a fairly straightforward way from classification to outlier detection. There are also some methods [13] to perform feature bagging in classification. The broader idea in most of these methods is that an averaged score of diverse detectors often provides more accurate results than the individual detectors [18]. Nevertheless, there are some unique aspects to outlier detection with respect to the unavailability of the ground truth. These aspects will be discussed in this chapter in terms of their effects on variance-reduction techniques.

The data-centric and model-centric views of variability are complementary to one another. In many cases, one can relate the effects of data-centric variability and model-centric variability to one another. For example, in bagging, the act of bootstrapped sampling of a subset of points can be considered a part of the base detector itself, rather than viewing the bootstrapped sample as a drawn sample from some base distribution. In such a case, one can view the variance reduction from a model-centric point of view. However, as discussed in the experimental results of the previous chapter, such a view does not provide insights into the hidden data-centric variability that is reduced by bagging. In other cases, such as varying the value of the parameter k in a k-nearest neighbor detector, a model-centric view would be most effective in understanding the variance-reduction effects. The reduction of model-centric variability is also different in a subtle way from the reduction of data-centric variability because it often leads to models that are actually more powerful than their base detectors. This is an issue that we will discuss in greater detail in a later section as to how reduction in model-centric variability implicitly leads to reduction in *representational bias* of the base detector. The broader idea here is that combining different randomized versions of a model leads to a model that is inherently superior in terms of modeling complexity.

The most basic template of variance-reduction is as follows:

1. Use a random process repeatedly either on the base training data (to create multiple training data sets) or on a base detector (to create multiple randomized models). Obtain different randomized predictions for a given data point using these multiple training data sets and/or models.
2. Average the scores of each point to create a stable prediction for each data point.

This template is borrowed from the seminal bagging and random forest works in the supervised domain [15, 16, 24, 36]. The notion of *averaging* is fairly standard for variance reduction, and was proposed in the context of classification [16, 20–22]. Since the bias-variance trade-off is also applicable to outlier detection, the generalization to the new setting of outlier detection is trivial. In fact, many of the variance reduction methods in outlier detection like isolation forests [41] and feature

bagging [40] have adapted it from classification. In this chapter, we will also study
several other centralized measures for variance reduction, such as the median and
trimmed mean, to investigate their effectiveness.

This chapter is organized as follows. Section 3.2 discusses the key motivations for
variance-reduction methods. Section 3.3 discusses the circumstances under which
variance-reduction methods are effective, and those in which they tend to degrade.
Variance reduction methods are discussed in Sect. 3.4. Many of these methods can
be used for either for classification or outlier detection. Some new methods for
variance reduction, which are specially tailored to anomaly detection, are discussed
in Sect. 3.5. These new methods are proposed for the first time in this book and are
not discussed elsewhere. We will investigate the use of some stable combination
functions like the median and the trimmed mean in Sect. 3.6. Experimental results
are discussed in Sect. 3.7. These experiments include the new methods proposed
in this chapter and provide the first comprehensive evaluation of many different
variance-reduction methods. Conclusions are presented in Sect. 3.8.

3.2 Motivations for Basic Variance Reduction Framework

A learning algorithm $g(\overline{X}, \mathscr{D})$ can be viewed as a search through the space of all possible *hypotheses* to perform a particular task of predicting the value of the (unknown)
oracle function $f(\overline{X})$ with a particular training data set $\mathscr{D}$. Each of these hypotheses
provides different instantiations of the prediction $g(\overline{X}, \mathscr{D})$. Therefore, each instantiation of $g(\overline{X}, \mathscr{D})$ can be considered a possible hypothesis. Typically, these instantiations are constructed either by using a random process to select $\mathscr{D}$ from a base
distribution, or by randomness injection into the function $g(\overline{X}, \mathscr{D})$. In the former case,
the base distribution is only a theoretical construct that is used for better analysis of
ensemble methods; in practice, an analyst only has access to one finite instance of
the data rather than the base distribution.

Imagine a setting in which we have a binary prediction task of predicting whether
or not a point is an outlier, and each detector is able to make a correct prediction
for a point with probability 0.51. Note that this performance is only slightly better
than that of flipping a coin for each data point to make a prediction. If we could
have m *independent* instantiations of the scores, and we *average* the predictions, we
can use the Chernoff bound [8, 49] to show that obtain the correct prediction with
probability almost 100% [28]. Of course, in practice, one can never really construct
truly independent hypothesis with a finite data set; as a result, one will always have a
residual error, corresponding to irreducible variance of the prediction. The situation
in learning problems is similar in which the accuracy improvements are limited by
the finiteness of the data.

In learning problems, the nature of the variance of the prediction of a detector can take on many forms. The previous chapters have discussed two different
types of the bias-variance trade-off corresponding to the data-centric version and the

model-centric version. These two versions correspond to various types of variance that one tries to reduce in these algorithms [28]:

1. *Statistical variance*: The variances in the solution are caused by the statistical fluctuations in the choice of the training data. In the previous chapter, we introduced one such example, where three banks score the same individual, and they each obtain a different score for the same individual because of their different choices of training data. This difference in individual score across different training data sets is a result of statistical variance. The bagging method [16] is designed to reduce statistical variance in classification.

   The notion of statistical variance is best explained by Fig. 3.1a. A learning algorithm might construct a set of hypothesis $\mathscr{H} = \{h_1 \ldots h_r\}$, which might be generated by learning the training model on different instantiations of the training data. These hypotheses might be considered equally good based on the specific model at hand, but can only be evaluated accurately, if the ground-truth were available. Therefore, these is no way of the analyst to know which ones of $h_1 \ldots h_r$ reflect the true model f the best. In other words, there is an inherent risk associated with any particular training data set, which cannot be quantified without knowledge of the ground-truth. This hypothesis space is illustrated by the outside contour of the diagram. Consider a setting, where a learning algorithm has a high level of accuracy and is able to find solutions within the inner contour of Fig. 3.1a. This algorithm is able to find six different hypothesis $h_1 \ldots h_6$, all of which are good approximations to the true hypothesis f, but still have a certain amount of error to the true hypothesis f. By averaging these different hypotheses, however, one is able to obtain a good approximation to f than any of the individual models. For example, the model learned by averaging the predictions over different training data sets will almost always be a better approximation to the true hypothesis, especially if the training data sets are independent.

2. *Computational variance*: Computational variance is caused by the fact that the different choices in model design often yield local optima because of the effect of variance. For example, a gradient-descent approach of a one-class SVM outlier detector [1] might get stuck in a local optimum. However, upon repeating the process multiple times with different starting points and averaging, one might obtain a better prediction. The random forest method in classification [15, 36] is designed to reduce computational variance. This situation is illustrated in Fig. 3.1b. In this case, the different starting points lead to different hypotheses, but the average of these different hypothesis is very close to the true hypothesis.

3. *Representational variance*: Although one often uses the notion of "representational bias," of a model over different samples of the training *data*, one can also use an equivalent notion of "representational variance" with a randomized *model*. This is because traditional bias-variance analysis is usually performed only from a data-centric point of view, whereas this book also considers a model-centric point of view for bias-variance analysis. Representational variance is caused by the fact that an individual instantiation of a randomized learning algorithm is unable to fully capture the complexity of the function to be learned. The former can be

viewed as the data-centric bias of $g(\overline{X}, \mathscr{D})$ using a fixed instantiation of the randomized model (i.e., fixing the random seeds that control model randomization). However, in cases in which the random seeds in the algorithm $g(\overline{X}, \mathscr{D})$ are allowed to vary, the variability in *data-centric* bias over different (deterministic) instantiations of $g(\overline{X}, \mathscr{D})$ now becomes a part of this randomized detector's *model-centric* variance. Note that this form of the variance is relevant to the unconventional notion of model-centric variance. For example, in feature bagging, any particular subset of dimensions is inadequate to capture all outliers (representational bias of that particular projection) because different data points may be relevant to different subspaces; however, by using an ensemble combination of these different hypotheses, one is often able to predict the outlier scores based on the locally relevant dimensions of each point. Clearly, each individual detector is unable to capture this complex function, but the ensemble is able to do so. Therefore, *certain model-centric variance reduction methods are able to capture more complex models than their individual constituents.*

This scenario is best illustrated in Fig. 3.1c. In this case, the hypothesis space $\mathscr{H}$ *does not contain* the true hypothesis f. Yet, upon averaging the hypothesis $h_1 \ldots h_6$ in Fig. 3.1c, one is able to approximate f reasonably well. Therefore, in many settings, ensembles can actually *expand* the hypothesis space explored by a particular algorithm, and determine solutions that could not be found by any particular instantiation. This explains why the feature bagging method is an excellent example of this type of scenario.

The notion of representational variance is sometimes indistinguishable from computational variance. As discussed in Chap. 2, the error of a detector can be decomposed into bias and variance in different ways depending on how one understands the random process used for bias and variance quantification. Each such decomposition provides a different view of the effect of a particular ensemble method. It is crucially important to use the correct random process for describing the bias-variance decomposition in order to explain an ensemble method properly.

The first of these forms of variance is relevant to the data-centric version of the bias-variance trade-off, whereas the other two are relevant to the model-centric version. These different forms of variance are illustrated in Fig. 3.1. In many cases, it is not easy to cleanly separate the portions of the improvement arising from reduction in statistical variance with those arising from computational or representational variance. This is because the model fluctuations and statistical fluctuations can interact with one another to add to the error.

It is also noteworthy that the errors caused by representational limitations are traditionally viewed in terms of the (data-centric) bias of the individual components of the ensemble. However, the model-centric view (of the bias-variance trade-off) allows us to view the variability in data-centric bias as a part of this randomized detector's model-centric variance. This variance can be reduced by averaging over different components. In this sense, variance reduction methods, when designed properly, *do* address the bias limitations of individual detectors. The ensemble can often (implicitly) create a model that is more representationally sophisticated than

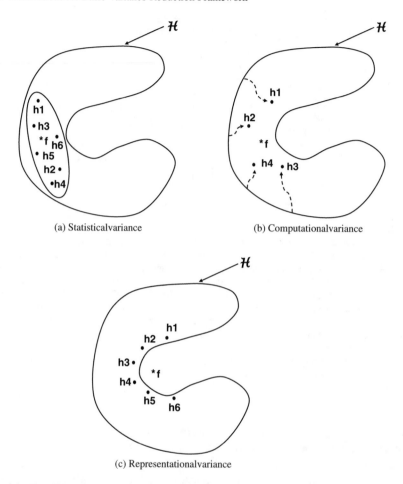

(a) Statistical variance   (b) Computational variance

(c) Representational variance

Fig. 3.1 The different types of variance in ensemble methods

its individual components. A classical example of this scenario is feature bagging, which will be discussed later in this chapter.

This highly-desirable property of variance-reduction methods is often overlooked by researchers and practitioners, and it applies to both classification and outlier detection. For example, the great accuracy of random forests in classification can be explained from a model-centric point of view; even to this date, there are few classifiers and ensemble methods that can *consistently* outperform [30] the random forest model. The greater accuracy of a random forest is because of its inherent ability to reduce the representational limitations of a decision tree model when applied to a finite data set. When applied to an finite data set, a decision tree has inherent representational limitations because of its piecewise linear boundaries although it can discover an arbitrary decision boundary with an infinite data set [28]. The representational limitation of a decision tree is partially caused by the fact that the attributes

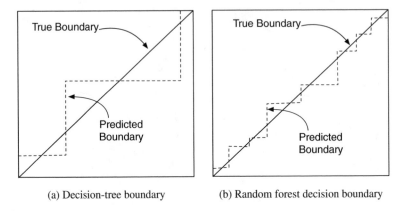

(a) Decision-tree boundary   (b) Random forest decision boundary

Fig. 3.2 Even though a decision tree can model an arbitrary boundary with an infinite amount of data, it tends to have a large data-centric bias with a small amount of data, which is caused by the piecewise boundaries and the attribute selected for splits at the top levels of the tree. In other words, different training samples of small size, which are selected from the base distribution would give correlated (biased) results. This is evidence of the fact that data-centric bias also depends on the size of the training data drawn from the base distribution. One can convert a portion of this data-centric bias into model-centric variance by constructing a randomized decision tree with randomized choices of split attributes and using a model-centric random process to describe the bias-variance decomposition of the (randomized) decision tree. One can then reduce this variance with predictive averaging in a random forest. As a result, the boundaries of the random forest reflect the true boundaries more closely. Using the correct random process to decompose the error into bias and variance is important for explaining the effectiveness of an ensemble method both in classification and in outlier detection

selected at the top level of the decision tree are often invariant with choice of training sample. This bias can only be corrected with sufficient numbers of splits at lower levels. With a limited amount of data, this is not possible because the height of the decision tree is limited. This situation is illustrated in Fig. 3.2a. Indeed, the representational bias of an algorithm depends on the size of the training data because it restricts the space of hypotheses being considered by the algorithm. Therefore, if one used bagging with a decision tree or were even provided access to the base distribution to generate independent samples of restricted size, then the averaged performance of the runs would never be able to overcome this consistent *data-centric* bias. On the other hand, an ensemble combination of decision trees with *randomized* split points is often able to discover a smoother decision boundary than the individual decision trees, even when applied to the same data set. This situation is illustrated in Fig. 3.2b. Note that in this case, we are randomizing the *model* rather than the draws of the training data, although one can construct an analytical explanation[1] for this, which is not too different from that for data-centric variance reduction. Just as each individual ensemble component of a data-centric variance reduction method like bagging has slightly deteriorated (data-centric) bias characteristics (because of repeated points in

---

[1] An analytical explanation for data-centric variance reduction is provided in Sect. 3.3.1.

bootstrapped sample), each randomized component of a random forest has slightly deteriorated (model-centric) bias characteristics (because of restricted splits at each node). However, the variance reduction in both cases is able to more than make up for this bias deterioration and in fact improve overall accuracy in both cases. A more detailed analytical explanation of how variance reduction more than makes up for bias deterioration in the data-centric setting is provided in Sect. 3.3.1. Model-centric variance reduction is consistent with a similar analytical explanation of the effectiveness of random forests. It is noteworthy that in spite of the widespread success of random forests, its theory is still not well understood [26]. Therefore, we believe that the (unconventional) notions of model-centric variance reduction discussed in this book will also be helpful in explaining the theoretical effects of many classification ensembles like random forests. An interesting property of a random forest is that it is able to reduce *data-centric* bias with *model-centric* variance reduction.

Model-centric variance reduction is not just related to the finiteness of the data (which is a common justification for many variance-reduction methods). For example, feature bagging often provides improvements even when used on very large data sets because of its inherent ability to reduce representational bias. In general, the specific instantiation of any randomized model (by fixing the random seed) has a (data-centric) bias that depends on the value of the random seed. However, by allowing this random seed to vary, one converts a lot of this representational bias into representational variance. This variance can be reduced by variance reduction. In other words, the model-centric view of variance reduction provides a more appropriate bias-variance decomposition for the purposes of theoretical explanation of the effectiveness of the method. We will revisit this aspect of feature bagging in Sect. 3.4.1.

3.3   Variance Reduction Is Not a Panacea

Brieman's humorous statement on making a silk purse out of a "twitchy" sow's ear [16] has often been misinterpreted to mean that variance-reduction methods provide a risk-free approach to improving the effectiveness of ensemble methods. Indeed, the no-free-lunch theorem of [70] states that for a given setting, one algorithm may be able to derive more information from the same data than another, but it is impossible for a particular algorithm to win in all settings. In fact, because of the consistent victories of ensemble methods in data science competitions, a (misunderstood) view has arisen that such ensemble methods (and not just variance-reduction methods) provide a "free lunch" approach to improving base algorithms.

Although specific ensemble methods like bagging generally perform better than a single application of the base algorithm, examples abound in which the ensemble can do worse than even the median performance of the base detectors. Variance reduction methods generally improve performance by using a more efficient way of reducing data-centric variance, while slightly deteriorating bias characteristics. Tricks like bagging and subsampling often improve overall accuracy because the gains from variance reduction are often greater than the deterioration in bias. However, there is no guarantee that such an approach will always work, because these are heuristic methods with no theoretical guarantees.

In Brieman's original paper on bagging [16], it was made clear that such methods are not a panacea and do not work in every setting. Some experimental results were also provided for cases in which bagging deteriorates performance. In fact, with some types of stable learners, it is possible for the approach to degrade the performance. Variance-reduction methods simply provide a more *efficient* way of minimizing the variance of an algorithm with a finite resource (data set) in certain types of settings that are common in classification and outlier detection. With only one instance of the finite training data (and no access to the base distribution), it is impossible to always reduce variance without affecting the bias. Although the attempt to reduce the variance (with heuristic methods like bagging and subagging) can often lead to a slight increase in bias, the overall effect is *often* favorable in *practical* settings.

The basic idea in variance reduction is that any statistical learning method, when applied to a finite training data set, will always have a "hidden" variance in the prediction of a (out-of-sample) test point, even though we see only one instance of the data set (and therefore only one prediction). For example, if we could send a data collector out to collect a training data set again under exactly similar circumstances, we would not obtain the same prediction on a particular out-of-sample test point with the new training data set. We repeat the example from the earlier chapter (Chap. 2) in Fig. 3.3a, which illustrates the hidden variance in the scores of John, who is the test instance. As discussed in Chap. 2, this hidden variability is a component of the error, and the accuracy can be improved with variance-reduction methods only if such a variability is present in the interaction of a particular algorithm with the base distribution in the first place. The greater the variability, the greater the hidden error is, and therefore the greater the scope of improvement. In order to understand this point, we will provide an analytical explanation.

3.3.1 When Does Data-Centric Variance Reduction Help?

If one had access to the base distribution from which a data set was generated, one can always eliminate the variance component by repeatedly drawing samples from the base distribution and then averaging the results. We repeat the example from the earlier chapter (Chap. 2) in Fig. 3.3b in which the base distribution is leveraged to reduce the variance. Data-centric variance reduction methods such as bagging and subagging [16, 20–22] attempt to use a finite resource to minimize variance by artificially *simulating* a setting in which one had access to the base distribution. An example of such a simulation is shown in Fig. 3.3c in which the data set is divided into groups for averaging purposes. Since this simulation (with a finite resource) is not as effective as using the base distribution, some of its steps[2] can actually *increase* either

---

[2]For example, in the case of Fig. 3.3c, each individual detector is run on a smaller data set with a correspondingly adjusted value of k. This smaller detector will have larger variance.

Fig. 3.3 Reducing the hidden variance from a finite resource by simulating the infinite resource setting (Revisiting Figs. 2.1 and 2.2 of Chap. 2)

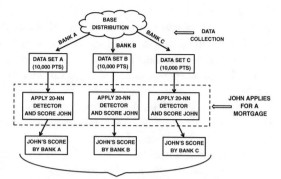

(a) Hidden variance caused by finite data set size

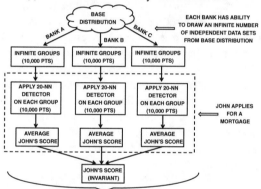

(b) Reducing variance to 0 with infinite data resources

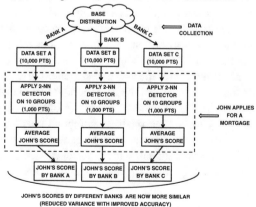

(c) Simulating variance-reduction with finite data resources

bias or variance or both; however, in many *practical* settings, the overall process is often able to reduce variance over an algorithm that uses the entire data set in a naive way. The general condition for being successful is for the algorithm to be sufficiently "twitchy;" in other words, the base detector should be unstable and therefore does not achieve its optimal performance when the full data set is used in a naive way. However, in cases where the base detector is stable, there is not much variance to reduce in the first place. Therefore, the intermediate steps of the simulation that increase the error can actually dominate. On the other hand, the problem with using an unstable detector is that it is sometimes possible to do better with the use of a more stable detector on the full data set, as compared to an unstable detector with ensembling, when the stable detector also has low bias. Therefore, one must always be careful about interpreting the overall advantages obtained with the use of variance-reduction methods.

In order to understand the effect of instability on data-centric variance reduction, let us consider a setting where we have a training data set $\mathcal{D}$, and the ground-truth outlier score for a test point $\overline{X}$ is given by $f(\overline{X})$. Furthermore, consider a setting where the outlier score $g(\overline{X}, \mathcal{D})$ denotes the output of an algorithm with the use of the training data set $\mathcal{D}$ of size n. Note that these are the same notations as used in Chap. 2. Consider a setting, where the outlier detector is able to estimate the true ground-truth to within an error, depending on the size of the training data. Let V be a random variable drawn from the standard normal distribution, and $b(n)$ be the bias of the detector when a subsampled data set $\mathcal{D}$ of size $b(n)$ is used. For analytical purposes, we assume the following model that relates the algorithm prediction $g(\overline{X}, \mathcal{D})$ to the true prediction $f(\overline{X})$:

$$g(\overline{X}, \mathcal{D}) = f(\overline{X}) + \frac{V}{n^\alpha} + b(n) \tag{3.1}$$

Note that this model may not necessarily hold for a particular learning problem, although we believe that it is a natural model to explore the effect of ensemble methods. Note that V is a random variable because the data set $\mathcal{D}$ is drawn randomly from the base distribution, and therefore the value of V will depend on the specific instantiation of $\mathcal{D}$. For simplicity, V is assumed to be a normally distributed error (variance) term with mean 0 and standard derivation 1. The variance term reduces with increasing size n of the data set based on the value of α. We *model* the constant bias term $b(n)$ to depend on the size n of the data set $\mathcal{D}$ drawn from the base distribution. This is a reasonable assumption only with certain types of detectors that are adjusted with data set size. In general, the trend of $b(n)$ with changing value of n is often unpredictable [6] in unsupervised problems like outlier detection, but for appropriately adjusted[3] detectors, the value of $b(n)$ often increases slightly with

---

[3] An example of such an adjusted k-nearest neighbor detector is discussed in [6]. In this case, when subsamples of the data are drawn at sample fraction f, the value of k is also adjusted with fraction f. In such a case, the bias becomes less unpredictable and increases only slightly at smaller subsample sizes.

reducing values of n. This is because of the information loss associated with small samples although the change is only slight in modest range of n. The information loss becomes particularly evident[4] at very small values of n where it starts increasing drastically. For simplicity, we assume that we have a wonderful detector, for which the bias is negligible for data sets of size $n > n_0$, and thereafter takes the following form for any (smaller) value of $n = f \cdot n_0$ for $f < 1$ (because of irretrievable information loss in being able to represent the distribution):

$$b(n) = \beta \frac{(n_0 - n)}{n} = \beta \frac{(1 - f)}{f} \qquad (3.2)$$

Here, $\beta > 0$ is a parameter that regulates the sensitivity of the bias to the size of the data set. However, this term always blows up at very small values of f. This is because extremely small values of n will almost always increase bias significantly because of irretrievable information loss (even in real settings). This is reflected in the functional form of $b(n)$ in the aforementioned equation. The expected MSE is $b(n)^2/n^{2\alpha} + E[V^2/n^{2\alpha}] = b(n)^2 + 1/n^{2\alpha}$. Therefore, the ensemble process needs to yield an expected MSE less than $1/n^{2\alpha} + b(n)^2$, for the approach to work. Note that if our base data set is of size $n > n_0$, then the bias term vanishes.

It is evident that $\alpha > 0$ is a parameter that regulates the stability (variance) of the outlier detector. Larger values of α tend to make the detector more stable. In most real settings, the error would be much larger than that obtained by setting α to the value of[5] 0.5. As we will show, the value of α has a significant influence on the effectiveness of bagging as a strategy. Note that if we could consistently draw training samples from the base distribution, estimate $g(\overline{X}, \mathcal{D})$, and average the results, one would obtain the prediction $f(\overline{X}) + b(n)$ in expectation. Furthermore, if the base data set is of size $n \geq n_0$, this wonderful (though theoretical) detector is able to achieve zero error. For simplicity in analysis, we will assume that the base data is *exactly* of size n_0. Therefore, with access to the base distribution (i.e., infinite resources), one is able to predict the ground-truth exactly with ensembles with a base data of size n_0.

Of course, in *practice*, one never has access to the base distribution. In other words, we need to work with the finite data set available to us, and derive the new training data sets from the original data. It is in this step that additional errors are introduced into the ensemble, and our goal is to examine the circumstances in which these additional errors would be sufficient to bring the final ensemble result below the original performance $g(\overline{X}, \mathcal{D})$. Imagine that the data set $\mathcal{D}_L$ is derived from $\mathcal{D}$ in a procedure that inevitably leads to some increase in error because of the lossy

---

[4]For example, if a clustering-based detector is used, some of the normal clusters might persistently disappear at small values of n, each time a training data set of size n is drawn from the base distribution. This will cause bias.

[5]Even for simple functions such as computing the mean of a set of data points, the standard deviation reduces with the inverse of the square-root of the number of data points. Complex functions (such as those computed in outlier detection) generally have a much larger standard deviation.

nature of the process. For example, in bagging, bootstrapped samples are drawn that lead to repeated data points, whereas only a random subset of the data $\mathscr{D}$ is used to derive the training data $\mathscr{D}_L$ in subagging. Clearly, these processes tend to increase the error of the detector, and are a natural consequence of trying to derive $\mathscr{D}_L$ from the finite resource $\mathscr{D}$ rather than the base distribution. This increase in error will typically result in an increase of both the bias and variance. Clearly, the variance component will be related to that of the original detector $g(\overline{X}, \mathscr{D})$, but will typically be larger. In the case of methods like subagging, the change in the bias and variance terms are relatively easy to compute because the subsample has the same distribution as the original data, and we have already assumed their functional dependency on the size of the data set. For methods like bagging, it is generally much harder to crisply characterize these quantities in terms of the original distribution. Therefore, for this discussion, we will assume the simpler case of subagging. Assume that $\mathscr{D}_L$ is derived from $\mathscr{D}$ with the use of subagging at fraction f, where a random fraction f of the training data is used to derive $\mathscr{D}_L$. Since the base data is of size n_0, the size of $\mathscr{D}_L$ is fn_0. Therefore, we have:

$$g(\overline{X}, \mathscr{D}_L) = f(\overline{X}) + \frac{V}{f^\alpha n_0^\alpha} + b(fn_0) \tag{3.3}$$

$$= f(\overline{X}) + \frac{V}{f^\alpha n_0^\alpha} + \beta \left(\frac{1-f}{f} \right) \tag{3.4}$$

At first sight, it would seem that we can repeatedly draw $\mathscr{D}_L$ from $\mathscr{D}$, and average the results to obtain an error that depends only on the bias. Therefore, if the amount of bias (value of β) is small compared to the variance of V (1 unit), one can always hope to improve the performance at modestly large values of f.

There is, however, a problem here that is directly related to the *finiteness* of the base data $\mathscr{D}$ from which $\mathscr{D}_L$ is drawn. In subagging (or any other process like bagging), there will be overlaps in the different sets $\mathscr{D}_L$ drawn from $\mathscr{D}$. The overlap will increase with the value of the subagging fraction f, and therefore the correlation among base detectors will also increase. This correlation in the base detectors means that a portion of the variance V is always irreducible. Assume for simplicity that the coefficient of correlation between the base detectors is given by $f^{1/\gamma}$. Larger values of $\gamma > 0$ increase the correlation among detectors and are therefore bad for reducing variance, and typically values of γ are greater than 1. This irreducible portion of the variance is reflected by the gap between *ENSEMBLE-I* (sampling from base distribution) and *ENSEMBLE-F* (sampling from fixed data) in Figs. 2.6, 2.7, and 2.8 of Chap. 2.

Consider the case where the data sets $\mathscr{D}_1 \ldots \mathscr{D}_m$ are drawn from $\mathscr{D}$ using subagging. Then, by using Eq. 3.4, it is easy to show that the expected MSE_m of the ensemble on data point $\overline{X}$ is given by the following:

$$E[MSE_m] = E\left[\left\{ \frac{\sum_{i=1}^m g(\overline{X}, \mathscr{D}_i)}{m} - f(\overline{X}) \right\}^2 \right] \tag{3.5}$$

$$= \beta^2 (1-f)^2 / f^2 + \frac{E[(\sum_{i=1}^m V_i/m)^2]}{f^{2\alpha} n_0^{2\alpha}} \tag{3.6}$$

Here $V_1 \ldots V_m$ are standard normal variables, which are *not* independent but positively correlated due to the overlaps between subsamples. Specifically, the pairwise correlation between them is given by $f^{1/\gamma}$. Note that the expression $E[(\sum_{i=1}^{m} V_i/m)^2]$ represents the variance of the mean of $V_1 \ldots V_m$, since each V_i has zero mean in expectation. For *large* values of m, the variance of the mean of m *positively* correlated random variables with pairwise correlation ρ and variance σ is equal to $\rho\sigma^2$ in the limit of increasing m. This is exactly equal to $f^{1/\gamma}$ by substituting $\rho = f^{1/\gamma}$ and $\sigma = 1$. In other words, the expected MSE of an ensemble with a large number of components is given by the following:

$$E[MSE]_{ensem} = \lim_{m \to \infty} E[MSE_m] = \beta^2 (1 - f)^2/f^2 + \frac{f^{1/\gamma - 2\alpha}}{n_0^{2\alpha}} \qquad (3.7)$$

We care about the MSE Loss Ratio between the ensemble performance and the original algorithm. Recall that the original algorithm has an expected MSE of $1/n_0^{2\alpha}$ at base data size of n_0 since the bias is 0. The loss ratio is then given by the following:

$$\frac{E[MSE]_{ensem}}{E[MSE]} = \underbrace{n_0^{2\alpha} \beta^2 (1 - f)^2/f^2}_{\text{Bias Effects}} + \underbrace{f^{1/\gamma - 2\alpha}}_{\text{Variance Effects}} \qquad (3.8)$$

In the above equation, larger values of f increase (hidden) variance, whereas they reduce bias. We would like the loss-ratio to be less than 1 in order for the approach to work. We make a number of observations, which naturally show the settings in which variance reduction works:

1. The loss ratio always improves (i.e., becomes smaller) for smaller values of α. Small values of α represent unstable detectors in which the variance decreases only slowly with increasing data size.
2. The loss ratio worsens with increasing value of β because it captures the detrimental (information loss) effect of simulating draws from the base distribution with a smaller data set.
3. At $f = 1$ the loss ratio is exactly 1 and therefore the ensemble performs exactly like the base detector. When f reduces, the detector gains in terms of variance reduction but it loses in terms of bias (irretrievable information loss). Therefore, there is often an optimal value of the subsampling rate at which the scheme performs the best. This is also true in most real settings. The optimal value of the subsampling fraction depends on α and β.
4. Increasing the value of γ (correlation tendency) increases the loss ratio. In such cases, a larger fraction of the variance is irreducible. A larger correlation reduces the likelihood of the loss ratio improving over the base performance.

In order to show these effects, we use the default values of the parameters $\alpha = 0.2$, $n_0 = 1000$, $\beta = 0.01$, and $\gamma = 1$, and show the loss ratio with increasing sampling fraction f. These parameters were selected because the corresponding shape of the curve tends to reflect the performance of ensembles in real-world settings. The results

Fig. 3.4 Effect of detector
properties in viability of
data-centric variance
reduction. A loss ratio of 1 is
break-even and shown by a
horizontal line (smaller
values are better)

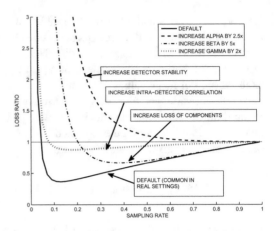

are shown in Fig. 3.4. We also increased each of α, β, and γ (over default values
while keeping other values unchanged) to respectively show the effect of increasing
stability, lossiness, and detector correlation on the performance. It is evident that in
the *normal case* of default parameters, the loss reaches an optimal performance at an
intermediate value of f, although it matches the base detector performance at $f = 1$,
and blows up at very small values of f because of irretrievable information loss. The
similarities of the performances in Fig. 3.4 with the performance of *ENSEMBLE-
F* in Fig. 2.8 of Chap. 2 are striking. This normal case (with default values of the
parameters) is the most common situation in real-world settings. However, in some
cases, the pathological performances shown by the other three curves can also be
achieved. These are cases in which the ensemble approach breaks down; it is simply
unable to reduce variance effectively without irretrievably losing information because
of the lossy ensemble simulation.

The most interesting case was when the value of α was increased to yield a very
stable detector. In this case, the loss ratio is *always* greater than 1 and therefore the
ensemble performance can never be better than the base detector. By increasing the
lossiness of the simulation process (information loss due to bootstrapping or subsampling) by increasing β, the error obviously increases, though the effect is mostly
visible at small values of f. This is because the bias effects are greatly magnified
at small values of f. Finally, some detectors may be more correlated than others,
when working with schemes like subagging. Clearly, correlated detectors have a
disadvantage in the variance reduction process.

We point out that many of the rigorous theoretical results underpinning these ideas
are presented in [16, 20–22], although the analysis presented in this section is much
simpler and easy to understand (albeit with some assumptions). This analysis also
provides an intuitive understanding of the circumstances in which variance reduction
works well, and is not found elsewhere in the literature in this simplified form.

One can also understand these concepts in terms of the intuitive explanation that
many complex learning algorithms try to estimate the parameters of a learner, and

the prediction is a higher-order function of the estimates of the learned parameters. However, many outlier detection algorithms are inherently non-parametric in nature. Even in such cases, one can often view of the intermediate quantities of a non-parametric algorithm (which are estimated from the data) to be learned parameters; for example, the final score in LOF can be viewed as a function of neighborhood statistics that are estimated from the data. Friedman and Hall [31] specifically showed that no advantage of bagged ensembling was gained for a (simple) linear function of the learned parameters, whereas even for a (slightly more complex) quadratic function, significant variance reduction advantages of ensembling were gained. This is the general rule in variance reduction methods, where greater model complexity helps the algorithm in gaining advantages from variance reduction methods in almost all settings.

3.3.2 When Does Model-Centric Variance Reduction Help?

Model-centric variance reduction can generally be explained with an unconventional version of the bias-variance trade-off, in which the expectation of the random process is computed over different models rather than over different points. However, it is also possible to understand these improvements from a data-centric point of view. Examples of such model-centric schemes include ensembling over different values of k in a k-nearest neighbor outlier detector, feature bagging [40], or the random-forest technique in classification [15]. However, all these schemes can also be understood from a data-centric point of view, albeit loosely.

How does the model-centric variance-reduction approach work? Consider a large number of models $g_1(\overline{X}, \mathscr{D}) \ldots g_m(\overline{X}, \mathscr{D})$. In the simplest version of this scheme, we compute the outputs of all the algorithms and average the score. In the *data-centric* point of view, it is much easier to explain this approach from the point of view of *bias*-reduction rather than variance reduction. The basic idea is that the direction of bias (i.e., sign of $g_i(\overline{X}, \mathscr{D}) - f(\overline{X})$) can be different for different detectors. Averaging the predictions from different detectors will lead to some of these bias terms canceling each other out. Therefore, the overall bias of the averaged detector $g_{avg}(\overline{X}, \mathscr{D})$ can sometimes be lower in *absolute* terms than any of the individual detectors. Furthermore, the (data-centric) variances can also be lower because of the averaging process. However, it is also possible to understand these improvements purely from a model-centric variance-reduction point of view. The first step is construct a *single* randomized detector $g_{random}(\overline{X}, \mathscr{D})$ as follows:

1. Select i at random from $\{1 \ldots m\}$
2. Report the output of $g_i(\overline{X}, \mathscr{D})$.

Assuming that the detector $g_i(\overline{X}, \mathscr{D})$ is deterministic, the average of a large number of trials of this random process will yield almost the same result as the simple round-robin averaging scheme discussed earlier. However, the improvements of this detector are best explained in terms of *model-centric* variance reduction.

It is noteworthy that $g_{random}(\overline{X}, \mathcal{D})$ is a randomized detector with a particular *model-centric* bias for *fixed* data set $\mathcal{D}$ (i.e., not drawn from a hidden base distribution), and the relevant random process for the bias-variance trade-off is the selection of i in the first step of the process. In other words, the expectation $E[MSE]$ in the bias-variance trade-off is now over different randomized choices of i. The aforementioned *data-centric* variability in bias between different $g_i(\overline{X}, \mathcal{D})$ now becomes a part of this randomized detector's *model-centric* variance. It is this variance that is reduced by the averaging process. Even though methods like feature bagging [40] and random forests [15] can be explained in terms of the data-centric bias-variance trade-off, it is much easier to view them in terms of model-centric variance reduction. This view of the bias-variance trade-off is unconventional, but it is more useful in these settings. This view is also helpful in explaining the variance-reduction effects of many classification methods like random forests, the theory of which is still not well understood [26].

Why does model-centric variance-reduction help? The basic idea is that for a given out-of-sample test point, there is an *uncertainty* in the model-design that best enhances its outlier characteristics. Furthermore, different model designs may be more suitable for different parts of the data. Model-centric variance reduction reduces this variability in performance over different parts of the data with a specific model design. In order to understand this point, consider the scenario where the value of k for a k-nearest neighbor detector needs to be selected. Depending on the nature of the underlying data distribution, a single value of k might not be appropriate for all parts of the data. In such cases, the use of ensembles can significantly improve the overall accuracy of the outlier detection process.

This factor is generally crucial in model-centric ensembles. *Data sets in which different randomized instantiations of the model are more effective in different localities of the data are particularly suitable for model-centric variance reduction.* This is because the score combination process (such as maximization or averaging) in the ensemble is local to each data point. As a result, the final combination is often able to design a more general *local* model for each point, which is not possible with the individual ensemble components. This situation is illustrated in Fig. 3.1c. This particular chapter will focus on averaging because of its relevance to variance reduction. One can also relate this point to the issue of *representational variance* [28] discussed earlier in this chapter. We will explain this point with the help of the example of high-dimensional data in the next section. For model-centric variance reduction to work, it is crucial to use models that work better in specific localities of the data. It is only in such a setting that the overall ensemble will generally perform significantly better than its base detectors. Therefore, even in the case of model-centric variance reduction, there are fundamental limitations on the type of settings and design choices that will make the approach work effectively in practice.

3.3.3 The Subtle Differences Between AUCs and MSEs

It is noteworthy that the averaging process in variance reduction is geared towards minimizing the mean-squared error, as is evident from the way in which bias-variance theory is formulated. Lowering the mean-squared error generally leads to lowered AUCs, although this is not guaranteed. Therefore, it is occasionally possible to see an averaged ensemble AUC performance, which is worse than the expected AUC performance of the base detectors. Although this situation is rare, it does happen occasionally. For example, imagine a situation where each ensemble component performs excellently, but it makes mistakes on 1% of the inlier points in an extreme way by giving them ∞ scores. This type of base detector has excellent AUC performance but very poor MSE performance. Furthermore, if different base detector components assign ∞ scores to different points, then the final ensemble result will not only have a poor MSE, but it will also have a poor AUC that is lower than the base detectors. We will see a specific example of this scenario with the Lymphography data set in Fig. 3.23b of Sect. 3.7. Although this scenario does not occur often, it is useful to keep in mind when one sees an ensemble AUC lower than the median of the base detectors. One sometimes sees results in anomaly detection that are slightly unexpected because errors are measured differently than in classification. In general, the AUC trends can be different from the MSE trends in the following cases:

1. When inlier points generally get low scores in most ensemble components but inappropriately get very large scores in a few ensemble components (resulting in false positives in the ensemble), the AUC trends can be worse than MSE trends. This occasionally occurs with some methods like LOF in combination with some variance reduction methods.
2. When outlier points generally get low scores in most ensemble components but appropriately get very large scores in a few ensemble components (resulting in prevention of false negatives in the ensemble), the AUC trends can be better than MSE trends. This occasionally occurs with some methods like subsampling.

It does need to be kept in mind that the AUC is not the only appropriate measure for the effectiveness of a particular ensemble method.

3.4 Variance Reduction Methods

In the following, we discuss some of the key variance-reduction methods that have been proposed in the literature. Some of these methods, such as bagging, have been studied only in the context of classification, and they will be extensively tested in the context of outlier detection for the first time in this book. Furthermore, in a later section, we will also propose a few new techniques that have not been proposed elsewhere in the literature. Some of these methods can be better explained from the perspective of the data-centric bias-variance trade-off, whereas others can only be explained from the perspective of the model-centric bias-variance trade-off.

3.4.1 Feature Bagging (FB) for High-Dimensional Outlier Detection

As discussed earlier, model-centric variance reduction overcomes the global representation bias of individual detectors, when different models are more suitable to different data localities. This observation about sensitivity to data locality is particularly relevant to high-dimensional outlier detection. The basic idea of subspace outlier detection methods [10] is that different subsets of dimensions are suitable to detect the outlier characteristics of different data points. The first subspace outlier detection paper [10] provides a pictorial illustration as to why different outliers are suitable in different localities. We show a similar illustration in Fig. 3.5. The original subspace outlier detection work [10] explains the importance of locally relevant features as follows:

> "Thus, by using full dimensional distance measures, it would be difficult to detect outliers effectively because of the noisy and irrelevant dimensions. Furthermore, it is impossible to prune specific features a-priori, since different points may show different kinds of abnormal patterns, each of which use different features or views."

The importance of the *locality* of the *relevant* features in the aforementioned quotation is noteworthy. Feature bagging [40] is a technique that is designed to exploit the effect of data-locality in high-dimensional outlier detection. Feature bagging repeatedly samples subsets of the dimensions, scores the points on these subsets, and then averages the scores. We repeat the basic pseudo-code of feature bagging from Chap. 1 for a data set of dimensionality d:

Algorithm *FeatureBagging*(Data Set $\mathscr{D}$, Ensemble Components: T);
begin
  repeat
  Sample an integer r from $\lfloor d/2 \rfloor$ to $d - 1$;
  Select r dimensions from the data $\mathscr{D}$ randomly to
    create an r-dimensional projection;
  Use base detector on projected representation to compute scores;
  until T iterations;
  Report combined scores of each point as a combination
    function of its score from different subspaces;
  {The most common combinations are maximization and averaging}
end

The basic idea in feature bagging is to sample an integer r between $\lfloor d/2 \rfloor$ and $d - 1$. Subsequently, r dimensions are sampled from the data set. The data is then scored in this projection, and the original work [40] used the LOF method as the base detector In principle, however, one could use virtually any type of detector as long as the scores from each detector are properly normalized to the same mean

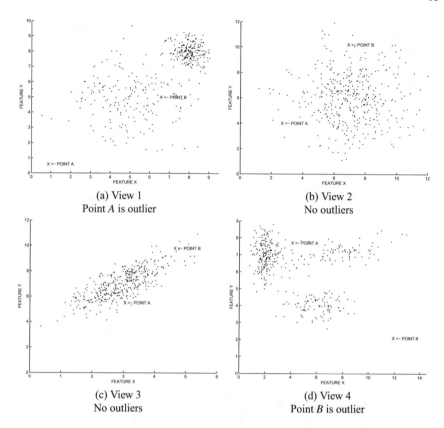

Fig. 3.5 Effect of data locality in high-dimensional outlier detection [1, 10]

and standard deviation. Subsequently, the scores of each data point over different ensemble components are combined. The two most common combination functions are the maximization and averaging functions. In the averaging combination function, the scores of each data point are averaged. In the maximization function, a rank-centric process is used. However, since lower ranks are better, a maximization on the scores maps to a minimization on the ranks. Therefore, for each data point, its lowest rank is used as the score.

In the following, we will focus on the averaging approach because of its relevance to variance reduction. By sampling different subsets of dimensions and averaging [40] one is able to achieve model-centric variance reduction for each data point. If the LOF algorithm is used for feature bagging (as in the original work [40]), it is not necessary to normalize the scores, because LOF returns inherently normalized scores. However, if a different algorithm is used for feature bagging, it is important to normalize the scores because different algorithms work on data sets of different dimensionality. It has been shown in [6] that the use of the average k-nearest neighbor detector is more effective with feature bagging than the use of the LOF detector; this is largely because

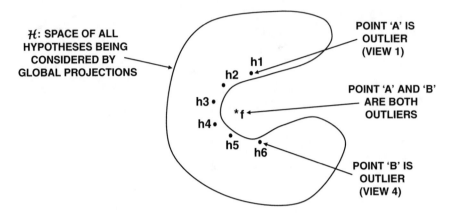

Fig. 3.6 Explaining feature bagging from the point of view of representational variance

the average k-nearest neighbor detector is more robust than LOF. It is noteworthy that feature bagging can be used in conjunction any outlier detector; in fact, this broader idea has also been used successfully in the classification domain [18, 19, 37].

As long as sufficient numbers of subspaces for each point capture the relevant dimensions, feature bagging is likely to lead to improvements. This is a result of model-centric variance reduction. As discussed in [10], different subspaces are relevant for discovering outliers in different subsets of dimensions. Feature bagging is able to find locally optimized subspaces for each point in an implicit way, even though each detector uses a globally selected subspace. The feature bagging work also provides an illustration similar to Fig. 3.5 to explain this effect. In fact, the original subspace outlier detection work [10] can also be viewed as an ensemble method in which the maximization combination function is used over a more carefully selected set of subspaces, instead of using the averaging function over all subspaces. Similarly, the work in [40] also allows the use of the rank-centric maximization combination function with feature bagging. Although the maximization combination function is not optimized for variance reduction, it is specifically focused on optimizing the bias-centric aspects of data locality, especially in the feature-bagging setting [6]. These issues will discussed in more detail in Chap. 5.

The averaging combination function can be explained from the point of view of representational variance [28]. The notion of representational variance is illustrated in Fig. 3.1c. Here, we show an application of this principle to model-centric variance reduction in general, and feature bagging in particular. Note that each *particular* subset of dimensions is simply inadequate to model the outlier behavior of all data points. As discussed in [10], different sets of dimensions are relevant to different points, and therefore selecting a single subset is unable to properly represent the outlier behavior of all regions of the space adequately. This is a *representational* inadequacy of the model, and therefore the outlier detector when applied to a particular subset of dimensions has a (data-centric) bias, that depends on the set of dimensions being selected. Consider a setting, where we consider the process of selecting a particular subset of dimensions to be a part of the detector itself. Now the aforementioned variability in the (data-centric) bias of the different detectors becomes a part of this randomized detector's *model-centric* variance. The relevant random-process for this model-centric variance is the process of selecting different subsets of dimensions. By averaging over different subsets of dimensions, one is able to partially overcome the representational limitations of each instantiation of the detector. An example of this situation is shown in Fig. 3.6, which is based on the views illustrated in Fig. 3.5. In this case, point 'A' is an outlier in view 1 (Fig. 3.5a), which corresponds to the hypothesis h_1 in Fig. 3.6. Similarly, point 'B' is an outlier in view 4 (Fig. 3.5d), which corresponds to the hypothesis h_6 in Fig. 3.6. Clearly, neither the hypotheses h_1 and h_6 are sufficient to capture both outliers 'A' and 'B', because these hypotheses correspond to the detection of outliers in global views of the data. However, the averaging or maximization combination function on the scores of individual data points can often discover locally relevant outliers in the various views. In particular, the averaging function is best explained from the perspective of reducing representational variance. This example shows how model-centric variance reduction is often able to construct decision boundaries that are more general than those implied by the individual detectors. In other words, model centric variance reduction is actually able to reduce the representational limitations (i.e., *data-centric bias*) of the individual detectors after fixing the dimensions used in the model. Therefore, there are interesting settings in which the variability in data-centric bias of individual models can be reduced by the averaging effect of model-centric variance. These distinctions between the data-centric view and the model-centric view of the bias-variance trade-off are discussed in Chap. 2. Fundamentally, data-centric bias refers to the expected error of a fixed model over different training data sets drawn from the same distribution. However, model-centric bias is different when the underlying model is allowed to vary over different ensemble components; for example, the random selection of a particular set of dimensions can be viewed as a part of a randomized model. In such a case, the model-centric bias *over all the random selections of features* will be very different from the data-centric bias of using a particular subset of features.

This broader principle is a useful one because it can explain many model-centric ensembles. For example, averaging the outlier scores of an algorithm over various (reasonable) choices of the parameters of an outlier detection method (e.g., value of k in a k-NN method) often provides better performance than the median performance of these different runs. Since the correct parameter choice of any outlier detection method cannot be known, such an approach is a viable technique for improving the expected performance over the default choice of guessing the parameters, which is virtually the same as setting it randomly in an unsupervised problem.

3.4.1.1 Other Subspace Outlier Ensembles

Several variations of the subspace sampling framework have been explored, that perform a more directed exploration of various subspaces. Examples of these methods include *HiCS* [38] and *OUTRES* [50]. An approach that uses multiple randomized subspace clusters is proposed in [51]. A biased subspace sampling method that uses an information-theoretic measure is discussed in [53]. Random subspace sampling has also been combined with the use of heterogeneous base detectors [52]. These methods are described in detail in [1] and they are all variants of subspace methods [10] for high-dimensional data. Many of these methods combine variance reduction with a *heuristic* element of bias reduction. This is because purely random subspaces are not used, but a statistical approach is used to preselect subspaces in methods like *HiCS*, which are likely to better identify outliers. The basic idea in *HiCS* is to use statistical testing up front in order to discover subspaces in which the data distribution is non-uniform. Once such subspaces have been identified, an approach similar to feature bagging is used to combined the scores. Such an approach translates to using base detectors with better bias characteristics. Some of these issues will be discussed in greater detail in Chap. 4. A detailed discussion of various subspace ensemble methods is provided in [35] and in Chaps. 5 and 6 of [1]. According to the discussion in [35], most of the subspace outlier detection methods are ensemble methods including the first technique proposed in [10]. We argue that the combination of outlier scores from different subspaces is inherently suited to high-dimensional outlier detection. As we will discuss later in this chapter, some of the successful outlier detection methods like isolation forests [41] also indirectly leverage local subspaces in order to isolate points in low-dimensional subspace projections.

3.4.1.2 Weaknesses of Feature Bagging

Although the feature bagging algorithm is an excellent idea from the perspective of the principle it illustrates, it is not necessarily the best implementation of the broader principle. In particular, it is implemented in a somewhat naive way, as a result of which the performance gains from subspace exploration are somewhat limited. In the following, we discuss some of these weaknesses. This discussion naturally leads to a scheme that ameliorates many of these weaknesses.

The feature bagging method proposes to always randomly select between $\lfloor d/2 \rfloor$ and $d - 1$ dimensions; one does not always gain the best variance reduction by selecting so many dimensions because of correlations among different detectors. When two subspace samples have many dimensions in common, distance computations and outlier scores will be highly correlated across these different samples (ensemble components). Correlations among detectors hinder variance reduction. One might even select the same subset of dimensions repeatedly, while providing drastically worse bias characteristics. In particular, consider a 6-dimensional data set. The number of possible 3-dimensional projections is 20, the number of possible 4-dimensional projections is 15, and the number of 5-dimensional projections is 6. The total number of possibilities is 41. Therefore, most of the projections (and especially the 4- and 5-dimensional ones) will be repeated multiple times in a set of 100 trials, and not much variance can be reduced from such repetitions. On the other hand, the 3-dimensional projections, while more diverse in overlap and repetition, will have deteriorated bias characteristics. This will also be reflected in the final ensemble performance. Here, it is important to note that the most diverse dimensions provide the worst bias characteristics and vice versa. The rotated bagging method [6] solves some of these problems.

3.4.2   Rotated Bagging (RB)

A natural solution to reduce the problems with feature bagging is to devise a randomized sampling scheme that reduces the correlations among detectors. In *rotated bagging* [6], the data is rotated to a random axis system before selecting the features. The random rotation provides further diversity. A salient observation is that real data sets often have significant correlations, and the projections along different directions are correlated with one another. This means that one can afford to use a much lower dimensionality than $\lfloor d/2 \rfloor$ to represent the data without losing too much information. In real data sets, the implicit dimensionality usually does not grow much faster than $\sqrt{d}$ with increasing dimensionality d. Therefore, a total of $2 + \lceil \sqrt{d}/2 \rceil$ orthogonal directions are selected from the rotated axis-system as the set of relevant feature bags. Using a lower dimensional projection helps in increasing diversity and therefore it leads to better variance reduction. At the same time, the $2 + \lceil \sqrt{d}/2 \rceil$ dimensions are able to roughly capture most of the salient modeling information in the data because of the random orientation of the axis system. In other words, one is able to increase the potential of better variance reduction without compromising the quality of the individual detectors too much.

The approach is not designed to work for 3 or less dimensions. Therefore, a constant value of 2 is added up front to prevent its use in such cases. The component detectors will be more uncorrelated in high dimensional cases, which yields a better opportunity for variance reduction. The overall algorithm works as follows:

1. Determine a randomly rotated axis system in the data.
2. Sample $r = 2 + \lceil \sqrt{d}/2 \rceil$ directions from rotated axis system. Project data along these r directions.
3. Run the outlier detector on projected data.

After running the detector, the scores can be averaged with a primary goal of variance reduction. It is important to use standardization on the scores before the combination. However, other choices for combination such as maximization are possible, as with other detectors.

How can one determine $r = 2 + \lceil \sqrt{d}/2 \rceil$ randomly rotated mutually orthogonal directions? The basic idea is to generate a $d \times r$ random matrix Y, such that each value in the matrix is uniformly distributed in $[-1, 1]$. Let the tth column of Y be denoted by $\overline{y_t}$. Then, the r random orthogonal directions $\overline{e_1} \ldots \overline{e_r}$ are generated using a straightforward Gram-Schmidt orthogonalization of $\overline{y_1} \ldots \overline{y_r}$ as follows:

1. $t = 1; \overline{e_1} = \frac{\overline{y_1}}{|\overline{y_1}|}$
2. $\overline{e_{t+1}} = \overline{y_{t+1}} - \sum_{j=1}^{t} (\overline{y_{t+1}} \cdot \overline{e_j}) \overline{e_j}$
3. Normalize $\overline{e_{t+1}}$ to unit norm.
4. $t = t + 1$
5. if $t < r$ go to step 2

Let the resulting $d \times r$ matrix with columns $\overline{e_1} \ldots \overline{e_r}$ be denoted by E. The $n_0 \times d$ data set D is transformed and projected to these orthogonal directions by computing the matrix product DE, which is an $n_0 \times r$ matrix of r-dimensional points.

There is another important reason that rotated bagging is more powerful than the feature bagging method, when viewed from the perspective of subspace outlier detectors. Rotated bagging can also be viewed as a subspace outlier detection in which data points from arbitrary subspaces (i.e., randomly oriented views of the data) are captured. This point of view is discussed in detail in [1] (see Chap. 5 of that book). Just as feature bagging can be viewed as an axis-parallel outlier detection method, rotated bagging can be viewed as an outlier detection method that discovers outliers in subspaces constructed from a randomly rotated axis system. This makes the rotated bagging method a more powerful detector than the feature bagging method, and it also provides another explanation of why the rotated bagging method consistently outperforms the feature bagging method. By using the same argument as shown in Fig. 3.6, one can infer that the rotated bagging method is often able to leverage locally relevant subspaces (which are not necessarily axis-parallel) to compute the outlier scores for each data point. Rotated bagging also has computational benefits for high-dimensional data because it *drastically* reduces the dimensionality of the data within each ensemble component. For example, for a 400-dimensional data set, the approach will create projections in only 12 dimensions. As a result, distance computations and space requirements will be quite modest.

It is noteworthy that a related (and independently proposed) ensemble method, referred to as *LODA* [55], also uses arbitrary random projections in order to obtain high-quality results. However, the approach builds histograms on 1-dimensional projections, each of which has $\sqrt{d}$ non-zero elements. In other words, the vector for each random projection has only $\sqrt{d}$ nonzero values, each of which is generated from a standard normal distribution with zero mean and unit variance. Therefore, LODA resembles rotated bagging slightly, although it is much more specialized in using histogram-based methods and it uses $\sqrt{d}$ non-zero elements in each projection.

3.4.3   Projected Clustering and Subspace Histograms

Projected clustering methods have also been used for subspace outlier detection. Although many subspace clustering methods discover outliers as a side product of the algorithm, this approach often does not work well because the outliers that are discovered as side products of algorithms are often weak outliers. A more effective approach is to use a scoring mechanism tied to the objective function of clustering, such as the distance to the nearest cluster centroid. Even when using such an approach, there is often a very high variability in prediction with the specific choice and initialization of the clustering algorithm. Such a variability is indicative of a high level of variance, which significantly reduces the accuracy of the underlying detector. Therefore, it is *crucial* for using ensemble methods in making clustering-based outlier detection techniques work.

Among these works, the work in [51] is notable because it relates subspace clustering to subspace outlier detection within the *OutRank* framework. The basic idea is to use multiple randomized runs of a subspace clustering algorithm on the data and score a point in each run depending on the properties of the cluster it belongs to. For example, if a data point belongs to a small cluster, or a subspace cluster of low dimensionality, it is more likely to be an outlier. The work in [51] proposes several different quantifications of the outlier score of a data point based on the properties of its relevant cluster. The basic approach in each base detector uses the following two steps:

1. Execute a subspace clustering algorithm on the data in order to create clusters.
2. Score a point based on its frequency of presence in a cluster, the size of the cluster it belongs, and the dimensionality of the cluster to which it belongs. Points belonging to many clusters with a large number of points and many dimensions are unlikely to be outliers.

It is noteworthy that subspace clusters are often overlapping, and therefore it is important for the quantification to account for this fact. One of the quantifications used in [51] is to identify the cluster(s) to which the point belongs, and compute the fractions of these cluster sizes with respect to maximum cluster size. The maximum cluster size is computed with respect to all clusters, whether the point is included in it or not. Similarly, the fractions of dimensionalities to the maximum dimensionality (of various clusters) is computed. These two quantities are then added over all the clusters to which the point belongs and divided by the number of clusters in the entire data set. This provides a score of a point in each ensemble component, in which a lower value is more indicative of the data point being an outlier. This score is then added over multiple subspace clusterings of the data. This approach can handle cases in which the subspace clusters have overlap and also those cases in which they do not have overlap. While this scoring mechanism can give reasonable results, some advanced scoring mechanisms with even better results are discussed in the paper. The PROCLUS algorithm [4] was used as the base clustering method in order to obtain high-quality results. This algorithm is referred to as *Multiple-proclus*. Even though the score from each cluster is not particularly strong, it was shown in [51] that the results from each ensemble combination often provided effective results.

In fact, it has been shown in [29] that such clustering ensembles are useful even in cases where the base clustering method does not use subspace projection. The reason for this is that randomized clustering methods tend to discover very different clusters over different runs. This increases the variance in the outlier scores, which can be reduced using ensemble techniques. A notable method in this respect is the extremely-randomized clustering forest (ERC-Forest) [48], the use of which is almost equivalent to that of an isolation forest (see Sect. 3.4.3.4). Since, an ERC-Forest inherently discovers subspace clusters, one can view this approach as a robust implementation of subspace clustering ensembles.

A key point to understand in the case of clustering methods is that the nature of the outliers found will be sensitive to the type of model used for clustering. For example, subspace outliers will often be found by projected clustering algorithms, locally sensitive outliers will be found by locality sensitive clustering algorithms, and correlation sensitive outliers will be found by correlation clustering algorithms (also referred to as generalized projected clustering) [5].

Recently, subspace histograms have also been used in combination with hashing for identification of subspace outliers in *linear time* [61]. The basic idea is to sample a subspace of a given dimensionality r, and a fractional grid size f on a sample of the data of constant size s. A hashing approach is used to count the frequency of the points in various grid cells. The test points are then scored based on the frequency of their grid cell. The approach is repeated over multiple ensemble components and the logarithms of the scores are averaged. This approach is referred to as RS-Hash and its streaming variant is referred to as RS-Stream. The *RS-Hash* method is described in greater detail in Sect. 6.3.1.2 of Chap. 6.

3.4.3.1   Isolation Forests

The isolation forest has been included in the section on clustering and histograms, because it is essentially a histogram method under the covers (although this is not obvious). The isolation forest[6] is also referred to as *iForest*. An isolation forest is an outlier detection method that shares some intuitive similarities with random forests in classification, although the objective of tree construction is quite different. At the same time, the isolation forest can also be viewed as a subspace method in which the scoring function quantifies the ease with which a local subspace of low dimensionality can be found to isolate a particular point with a randomized exploration process. In this sense, the isolation forest exhibits intuitive similarities with feature bagging as well.

An isolation forest is constructed using a set of isolation trees. Each isolation tree is constructed like a decision tree in top-down fashion. The algorithm starts with the entire data set at the root node. An attribute is randomly chosen, and then a binary split is executed at a random point between the minimum and maximum ranges of that attribute. Therefore, the data is split into the two children of that node. This process is recursively repeated until each node contains a single point. This tree will typically not be balanced, because points in dense regions will tend to require a larger number of splits whereas nodes in sparse regions will get isolated earlier on. Therefore, the outlier score of a data point is equal to its depth in the isolation tree. In other words, the number of edges (splits) from the root to the leaf is used as the outlier score. An isolation forest contains multiple isolation trees. Therefore, the scores from the different trees are averaged in order to obtain the final outlier score. In high-dimensional data, the number of splits from the root to the leaf often correlates very well with the dimensionality of the local subspace in which a point is isolated as an outlier. From this point of view, the isolation forest defines outliers as data points that can be isolated easily in lower dimensional subspaces using random splits. Although the original description of isolation forests does not emphasize its connections to

---

[6]The description in this chapter is repeated almost identically in Sect. 6.3.1.3 of Chap. 6. This is because this detector is important both from the perspective of variance-reduction methods as well as base detectors. The description is repeated in both places for the benefit of readers who have electronic access to only one of the chapters of this book.

subspace outlier detection, this view provides an interesting perspective on the inner workings of the approach.

A single iteration of the recursive splitting process during isolation tree building can be described as follows:

1. Select any node in the (current) isolation tree with more than one point, which has not been split so far.
2. Select any attribute x for splitting.
3. Select a random split point a between the minimum and maximum ranges of that attribute.
4. Create two children of the node based on the random split point and distribute the points to the two children. All points with $x \leq a$ are assigned to one child and all points with $x > a$ are assigned to the other child. Store the split predicate of the form $x \leq a$ or $x > a$ at each of the children. This split predicate can also be used for scoring out-of-sample points that are not included within the training data for *iForest* construction.

The process is repeated until each node in the isolation tree contains exactly one point. For a data set containing n points, the process requires $\theta(n \cdot \log(n))$ time in the average case, although it is possible for it to require $O(n^2)$ time, if the tree is fully unbalanced. However, the average case performance is almost always achieved in practical settings. The approach also requires $O(n)$ space. When the entire data set is used for tree-building (i.e., there are no out-of-sample points), a separate testing phase is not required because the depth of each point can be computed during tree building.

However, to make the approach more efficient, subsampling is used. The *iForest* approach samples 256 points from the data set and constructs an isolation tree on this sample. Note that such an approach requires constant time for construction of the isolation tree. When subsampling is used, a separate testing phase is required in order to score the data points. During the training phase, each split point is stored as a split *predicate*. For example, if the ith attribute is split at value of a, then the two branches of the tree will defined by the condition (or *predicate*) whether $x_i \leq a$ is satisfied. For each test points, we use the split predicates in order to traverse the appropriate path in the isolation tree. The number of edges from the root to the leaf provides the final outlier score. The subsampling approach requires constant space and constant time for training because the tree contains only 256 points. Furthermore, for a tree containing 256 points, the testing time for each point is a small constant dependent on the average depth of the tree. Therefore, the approach requires $O(n)$ time for testing with a small constant factor.

The isolation forest can be interpreted from the perspective of a subspace method. One can view the isolation tree as a randomized test of the ease of being able to isolate a point in a local subspace of low dimensionality. Note that the path length from the root to the leaf node isolates a local subspace, and is roughly[7] indicative of the dimensionality required to isolate the point with randomized partitioning. For example, consider a setting in which we have various physical measurements of an individual, and it is unusual for individuals of height less than 5 feet to have weight greater than 200 pounds. In such a case, a sequence of splits like *Height* $\leq$ 5, *Weight* $\geq$ 200 might quickly isolate a point in a path of length only 2. Furthermore, this sequence of splits is also highly interpretable. Therefore, the decision tree provides a high level of interpretability, and the relevant regions may be determined by examining those ensemble components for which the score for a particular test instance is low.

The isolation forest is an accurate approach for many "typical" real-world data sets. However, the approach does have its "blind spots" for specific types of pathological data sets. For example, the isolation forest faces challenges in data sets where too many dimensions are relevant. It also faces challenges in cases where outliers occur in small clusters or in interior regions of the data. This point will be discussed in Chap. 6. In a later section of this chapter, we will compare the isolation forest with other variance-reduction methods. Here, we present some summary results with 200 trials over a small number of data sets. These data sets are described in detail in Sect. 3.7.1.

The results are illustrated in Fig. 3.7. We have shown box-plots illustrating the performance of base detectors as well as the ensemble performance. The boxplots have been split into the Fig. 3.7a, b to accommodate the large number of data sets. The identities of the relevant data sets are indicated below each of the figures. For each data set, the performance on the full data set and a subsample of size 256 is shown. Some data sets like Lymphography contained fewer than 256 points. In those cases, the entire data set was used in lieu of the sample of 256 points. In other words, both the data-specific box plots are simply different instantiations of identical runs on the full data set in such cases. It is interesting to see that the performance with the subsample is better on many data sets because of the diversity benefits gained from subsampling. Therefore, in addition to its interesting approach based on random forests, the *iForest* approach introduced subsampling ideas into outlier detection. In Sect. 3.7, we will also show comparative experimental results with respect to other ensemble methods.

3.4.3.2   Other Optimizations

The isolation forest allows the use of a few other optimizations, such as thresholding the maximum height of the isolation tree. The idea is that the growth of the isolation tree is stopped beyond a certain height, or if all points in the nodes are duplicates. In

---

[7]Although the same dimension may be used to split a node along a path of the tree, this becomes increasingly unlikely with increasing dimensionality. Therefore, the outlier score is roughly equal the dimensionality required to isolate a point with random splits in very high dimensional data. For a subsample of 256 points, roughly 8 dimensions are required to isolate a point, but only 4 or 5 dimensions might be sufficient for an outlier. The key is in the power of the ensemble, because at least some of the components will isolate the point in a local subspace of low dimensionality.

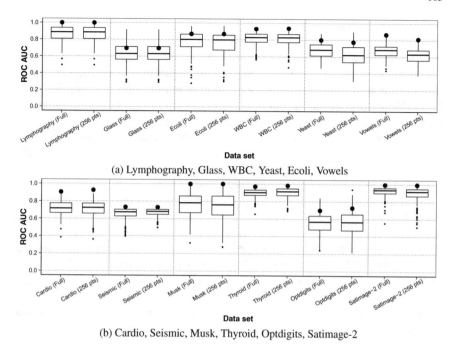

Fig. 3.7 Performance of full-data and subsampled version of *iForest* on several data sets. A sample size of 256 is used for the subsampled version. If the data size is less than 256, then the entire data set is used

such cases, all points in the node are credited with a height defined by the expected height of a random binary tree containing these points. For a node containing r points, the credit $C(r)$ is defined as follows:

$$c(r) = \ln(r - 1) - \frac{2(r - 1)}{r} + 0.5772 \qquad (3.9)$$

The value of $C(r)$ is added to the depth of the leaf node in the case of early termination. However, setting a maximum height is often not required when a subsample of size 256 is used. This is because the expected height of the tree is only 8 in these settings, which is quite modest in practice. The small height of the subsampled isolation forest also explains why it is so efficient at the time of scoring outliers. With an isolation forest, it is often feasible to use more ensemble components than many of the other detectors because of its efficiency. This tends to improve the accuracy of the approach.

3.4.3.3   Variations

Several variants of the basic isolation forest idea have been explored in the literature. Because of its speed, it is relatively easy to adapt to the case of streaming data. For example, the work in [65] proposes the notion of streaming HS-Trees, which uses the basic idea of isolation forests. However, there are some differences in terms of how scoring is done. In this case, the trees are scored on the basis of the notion of *mass* [67], and a split point is chosen in the middle of the range. A related method, referred to as *SCiForest* [42], shows how to discover clustered anomalies. The basic idea is that anomalies often occur in small clusters, which are sometimes hard to detector. The SciForest approach is able to detect such anomalies effectively. It uses arbitrarily oriented hyperplanes, rather than the axis-parallel hyperplanes used in iForest. The works in [34, 71] developed random forest methods for the case of streaming data. The use of artificial data to create one-class random forests is discussed in [27]. This work also clarifies the connections between decision tree-based methods and subspace outlier detection methods for high-dimensional data. One advantage of the random forest class of techniques is that they implicity separate out the outliers in local subspaces of low dimensionality and ensemble over them. Therefore, the approach can also be viewed from the perspective of subspace outlier detection. This particular perspective of random forest methods is discussed in detail in [39] with the notion of *sapling forests*. The basic ideas in the isolation forest have also been extended to similarity computation [68]. Enhancements of the basic isolation forest idea, such as random cut forests [34], have also been proposed recently in the streaming context.

3.4.3.4   Relationship to Clustering Ensembles

Isolation forests are closely related to clustering ensembles. An isolation tree is a hierarchical subspace clustering of the data, in which the sequence of axis-parallel splits to reach a node defines the bounding box of the relevant cluster of points in that node. When data points cannot be clustered easily in a subspace containing a sufficiently large subset of dimensions, they tend to be outliers. Such points will show up as shorter path lengths in the isolation tree. Interestingly, an earlier clustering ensemble, referred to as the *extremely randomized clustering forests (ERC-Forests)* [48] is very similar to the isolation forest. The only difference is that instead of using a single randomized split at each node, it uses a fixed number of trials on the randomized split to measure "goodness" of the split, and selects the best one. This measure of goodness could be supervised (e.g., entropy) or unsupervised (e.g., tree balance). However, setting the number of trials to 1 and growing the tree to full height will result in the creation of an isolation tree.

A number of subspace clustering ensembles are discussed in the *OutRank* work [51]. This approach is also discussed in Sect. 3.4.1.1 of this chapter. In the *OutRank* work, it is shown that the use of multiple randomized (subspace) clusterings, such as the multiple use of the PROCLUS algorithm [4], provides better results than the use of a single application of an optimized clustering algorithm. The isolation forest may be viewed as an extreme example of creating a randomized clustering with little focus on optimizing the quality of the clustering (since random splits are used). The good results of the isolation forest seem to suggest that diversity is often more important in outlier ensemble methods than the optimization of the base components.

3.4.4 The Point-Wise Bagging and Subsampling Class of Methods

Bagging is used commonly in classification to reduce variance. Typically, a *bootstrapped* sample (i.e., sample with replacement) is drawn in order to construct the training data. Each test point is predicted with the use of this sample as the training data. The prediction of each test point is averaged over multiple training samples because the averaged prediction has lower variance. Although it is possible to use bagging for outlier detection, the main problem with doing so is that many base detectors like LOF are not very robust to the presence of repeated points, which increases bias. In some variants of bagging for classification, subsampling is used instead of bootstrapping [20–22]. In this variant of bagging methods, bootstrapping is not used. Rather, training samples are selected from the data *without* replacement. The prediction of each test point is computed by constructing a model on each subsample, and then averaging the prediction from various subsamples. This variant is referred to as *subagging* or *subsampling* [20–22]. As in the case of bagging it has been shown [20–22] that the primary effect of subagging is to reduce the variance. Even though subagging is less popular than bagging, it has been shown that subagging is virtually equivalent to bagging and might even have accuracy and computational advantages under many circumstances [20–22].

3.4.4.1 Subsampling

In the context of multidimensional data, the *rows* of the data matrix are sampled in order to create models for scoring data points. However, methods are entry-wise subsampling of the graph adjacency matrix have also been proposed for outlier detection in graph data [2]. Since the multidimensional case is primarily discussed in this book, we will focus on the latter case of subsampling the rows of a data matrix. An early use of subsampling for multidimensional data was proposed in [41], although the primary goal of this approach was efficiency improvements, and accuracy improvements were inconsistent. Subsampling works much better in the case of distance-based detectors, and such scenarios were explored in [6, 73]. However, the specific implementation in [73] uses a fixed subsample of the data, which tends to have unpredictable effects, and the theoretical reasoning provided in this paper is incorrect as well. A correct theoretical explanation of the ensemble improvements is proposed in [6] (see Chap. 2).

The subsampling (subagging) approach can be generalized to outlier detection as follows. Each point in the data is scored with respect to the subsample by a base outlier detector, whether the point is included in the subsample or not. The scores across different subsamples are then averaged. Note that the bagging scheme can be generalized to outlier detection in an almost identical way as the subsampling scheme. Effective variations of subagging may be found in [6] along with several new combination techniques. This chapter will also study some new combination techniques that are not discussed elsewhere.

Understanding the Trade-Offs

As discussed earlier in this chapter, bagging-like variance-reduction methods try to simulate multiple draws from the base distribution with multiple draws from the *base data set*. Such draws have two primary shortcomings, which are sometimes encountered in different circumstances:

1. The detectors constructed on draws from the finite base data set tend to be correlated with one another. For example, in subagging, the overlaps increase with the value of the subsampling fraction f, and therefore the correlations between base-detectors increase. This hinders the reduction of the data-centric variance associated with truly independent draws from a *base distribution*. After all, subsampling is only an imperfect simulation of draws from the base distribution. For example, at subsampling fraction of 1, all the hidden variance (associated with draws from a theoretical base distribution) is irreducible because we are trying to simulate it with identical draws from the base data. This irreducible hidden variance corresponds to the gap between *ENSEMBLE-F* and *ENSEMBLE-I* in Figs. 2.6 and 2.7 of Chap. 2.
2. The detectors constructed on draws from the finite base data irretrievably lose valuable information from the original data set. In spite of the loss of information associated with subsampling, base detectors often behave unpredictably with subsample size if a heuristic mechanism for adjusting the algorithm parameters to data size does not exist. For example, in an exact k-nearest neighbor detector, two subsample sizes can be compared fairly only if the value of k is proportionally adjusted with data size. This is not possible in a parameter-free detector. In such cases, a specific subsample size might have unpredictable effects. However, even in this case, if the subsample size is too small, there will generally be bias-deterioration effects.

In spite of the unpredictable effect of data size, a peak in performance is typically achieved at some intermediate value of f (see Fig. 2.6) with the finite data simulation. This is reflected in Eq. 3.8 by the contradicting effect of f towards the bias and variance components, and it is also reflected by the trough in the loss ratio of Fig. 3.4. As we will see in experimental results with real data sets, this performance is typical in real settings. An important caveat to show this type of trend is to adjust the parameters of the detector to the data set size drawn in subagging. For example, the value of

k in a k-nearest neighbor detector will depend on the size of the subsample drawn, because larger subsamples will require larger values of k. As discussed in [6], such nuances can cause significant confusion on the effects of data set size on bias, when the parameters of the detectors are not adjusted to data set size. We will discuss this issue in the next section.

The Unpredictable Effect of Data Size on Algorithm Performance

It is important not to be misled by the effect of data set size on parameter choice in methods like subsampling. Often it is not possible to fairly compare the performance of a detector on the full data to that on the subsampled data, if the parameters of the algorithm are fixed. The optimal choice of parameters of a detector is highly sensitive to the base data set size. For example, for a k-nearest neighbor detector, the bias performance of an algorithm that uses $k = 7$ on a data set of 100 points is (roughly) similar to the bias performance of an algorithm that uses $k = 70$ on a data set of 1000 points. Even this adjustment is not exact, and in most cases, it is impossible to adjust the parameters exactly to data set size. For very small data sets, an adjusted set of parameters might not even exist. For example, for a data set with 10 points, there is no corresponding value of k to simulate the bias performance of the aforementioned example. This is reflected by our bias-centric loss term in Eq. 3.8. The difficulty in adjusting the parameters exactly to the base data set is particularly true for more complex variations of distance-based detectors like LOF. For example, LOF is generally more sensitive to the choice of the parameter k as compared to raw distance-based detectors.

In general, for distance-based detectors, smaller values of k work better for smaller data sets and larger values of k work well for larger data sets. If one used the same choice of the parameters both on the base data and the subsample, the effect is completely unpredictable and data-distribution specific. This effect is important to keep in mind because if one selected a fixed set of parameters that are optimized to the smaller subsample (e.g., a very small value of k in a k-nearest neighbor detector), then one might do better with the subsample than on the larger base data set *even with a single detector*. This provides an illusion of suggesting better performance with less data. We refer to this effect as an "illusion" because it is caused by using a detector with *asymptotically poor characteristics*. As pointed out in [6], some past works in the literature have used this fact to make grandiose (but absurd) claims [73] about this being a *desirable* property of a detector or an inherent property of outlier detection in general [64, 66]. In general, it is true that any particular parameter setting of a detector might work best with a specific sample size of the base data *distribution*. However, this *optimal* sample size of the distribution is unknown in practice and can even be ∞ for some distributions; furthermore, in unsupervised problems, there is no way of knowing whether this optimal data size is larger or smaller than the base data set provided to us. In general, for a k-nearest neighbor detector, if one used a very small value of k like 2 or 3, then the optimal data size to be drawn from the base distribution would be very small, whereas if we use $k = 10$, then the optimal data size to be used would be much larger. The key point here is that the works in [64, 73] use very small values of k in their experiments, as a result of which they make conclusions that are not broadly generalizable to arbitrary parameter settings or outlier detectors. Although it is true that a *specific setting* of a particular detector might work well[8] for smaller subsamples of a specific data set, one cannot say anything about the performance on an arbitrary detector on a particular data set in general.

It is noteworthy that if we use random draws of data sets with a particular data size, then the bias of a particular algorithm will depend on the size of the subsample being drawn. We repeat the bias-variance equation here:

$$E[MSE] = \text{Bias}^2 + \text{Variance} \tag{3.10}$$

A different way of understanding this is that if we apply Eq. 3.10 to only the universe of data sets of a particular size S (without adjusting the parameters for the data size), the bias term will be sensitive to the value of S. As the value of S increases, the bias might increase or decrease. The effect is, of course, highly data distribution-, algorithm-, and parameter-specific. On the other hand, the variance term in Eq. 3.10 will almost always increase with smaller subsamples (i.e., smaller S) because of the statistical unreliability of using less data. Therefore, the overall accuracy can be affected in an unpredictable way, although it is dragged down to some extent by increased variance effects for smaller subsamples. In general, knowing the optimal value of S for obtaining the best bias performance in unsupervised problems is impossible because of the unavailability of ground truth.

In order to understand this point, consider a data set in which a k-nearest neighbor algorithm shows improved performance with increasing values of k. In this case, the *size* of the sampled data set is important; if one fixed the value of k, and down-sampled the data by a factor of $f < 1$, one has effectively increased the *percentile* value of k by a factor of $1/f$. Therefore, if you used a 9-nearest neighbor algorithm on a sample of 100 points, the bias would be similar to a 90-nearest neighbor algorithm on a sample of 1000 points, and it would not be comparable to the bias of a 9-nearest neighbor algorithm on a sample of 1000 points. *In data sets, where the accuracy of a k-nearest neighbor algorithm increases with k on the full data set, subsampling with fixed k will generally improve the accuracy of an individual detector on a single subsample.* Even though reduced subsample size has a tendency to reduce accuracy because of increased variance, the accuracy can increase when the bias effects in a particular data set are sufficiently large. On the other hand, *in data sets, where the accuracy of a k-nearest neighbor algorithm reduces with k on the full data set, subsampling with fixed k will generally have significantly reduced accuracy of individual detectors because of the double whammy of greater bias and variance from smaller subsample size.* In general, it is not necessary for a data set to show a monotonic trend with increasing values of k, in which case the bias is entirely unpredictable *and completely dependent on the value of k selected for the*

---

[8]Perhaps the claims in [73] were motivated by the superior performance [41] of the isolation forest on smaller samples from the *Mulcross* data generator [58]. This is caused by a *swamping* effect of other data instances on the algorithm. Another related behavior is *masking*. However, the claims in [41] are very specific to a particular data set and it is impossible to predict the size of the base data at which phenomena like swamping or masking might occur.

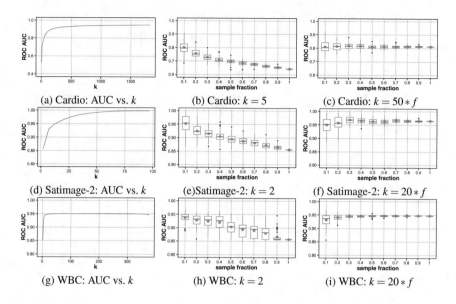

Fig. 3.8 AUC of Avg-KNN increases with k on these data sets. The results show improvement of component detectors at fixed k with smaller subsamples. However, adjusting the value of k by subsample size nullifies (and slightly reverses) this effect because the bias component has been removed and larger subsamples have an inherent statistical advantage

base method. Therefore, no general statement can be made about the base detectors, although the ensemble performance might improve because of the reduced variance of the *ensemble combination*; this is not a new argument [20–22]. The aforementioned observations for unnormalized k-nearest neighbor distances are also roughly true for LOF-like algorithms, but more approximately so.

In order to show this effect, we performed simulations with a number of real data sets with varying accuracy trends with k. The details of these data sets are provided in Sect. 3.7.1. In this approach, the *average* distance to the k-nearest neighbor distances [11] is reported as the outlier score. We first used the unnormalized distances because adjusting the value of k for bias is easier in this case than in the case of LOF. Generally, an exact adjustment is impossible, and even more difficult (from a practical point of view) with algorithms like LOF. The data sets with increased accuracy with increasing values of k are shown in Fig. 3.8, and the data sets with reduced accuracy with increasing values of k are shown in Fig. 3.9. We reported the Area Under Curve (AUC) of Receiver Operating Characteristics (ROC) curves. Each row contains three figures for a single data set. The leftmost figure of each row shows the performance of the full data set with increasing values of k. The middle figure of each row shows the performance of the subsample with fixed values of k, but varying subsample size n_i. The box-plots provide an idea of the variation in the quality of the component detectors over the different runs. In the rightmost figure of each row, we adjusted the value of k proportionally to subsample size with the formula $k_i = \lceil k_0 \cdot (n_i/n_0) \rceil$,

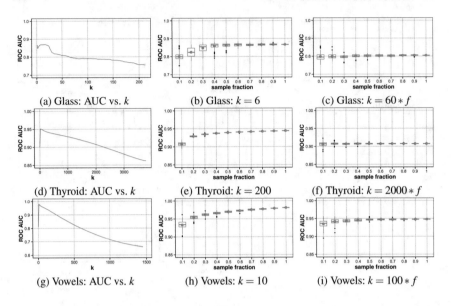

Fig. 3.9 AUC of Avg-KNN decreases with increasing k on these data sets. The results show significant worsening of component detectors at fixed k with smaller subsamples. However, adjusting the value of k by subsample size ameliorates this effect because the bias component has been removed

where n_0 was the size of the full data set and $k = k_0$ was used for the full data set. The value of k_0 in the rightmost figure was always selected to be 10 times the fixed value of k in the middle figure. As a result, the same[9] value of k was used at subsampling rates of 0.1 in both the fixed-k and adjusted-k cases. However, the performance on the full data would be very different in these cases because of a value of k, which is different by a factor of 10. We ran the base detector 100 times with randomly chosen subsamples, and report the box plots, which show the median (blue line in middle of box) and mean (red dot) performances of the *component detectors*. Note that we are only focusing on component detector performance here in order to understand the bias effects. It is understood that the ensemble will perform better because of known variance reduction effects of subsampling [20–22]. Nevertheless, we will show in a later section that the performance of component detectors do affect the final ensemble performance to a large extent.

It is evident that for all data sets with increasing accuracy with k, reduction of subsample size improved the performance of the base detector (Fig. 3.8b, e, g), when the value of k was fixed across different subsample sizes. On the other hand, for data sets with reducing accuracy with increasing value of k, the performance was drastically reduced (Fig. 3.9b, e, g) by reducing subsample size. In other words, exactly *opposite* trends were obtained in the two types of data sets represented by Figs. 3.8 and 3.9, respectively.

---

[9]The (roughly similar) boxplots show random variations.

The most interesting results were obtained for the case where an adjusted value of $k = \lfloor k_0 \cdot (n_i/n_0) \rfloor$ was used. In these cases, the bias effects have been largely removed, and one can see only the impact of the variance. In this case, *consistent* trends were observed in the two types of data sets. In most cases, the accuracy reduced (modestly) with smaller subsample sizes, in *both* types of data sets (Figs. 3.8c, f, i, and 3.9c, f, i). This suggests that smaller subsamples provide worse performance because of increased variance, once the *data-dependent bias component* has been removed. Furthermore, it is often not possible to fully adjust for data-dependent bias, and the closest possible adjustment at different data sizes will often show some (bias-centric) degradation because of irretrievable information loss of smaller subsamples. This degradation becomes particularly obvious at smaller subsamples, which is reflected by the nature of the bias-centric term in Eq. 3.8. It is noteworthy that if the optimal value of k_0 on the full data set is less than n_0/n_i, then subsampling with n_i points has an inherent disadvantage for the component detectors, because there is no way of simulating this bias performance on the subsample at any adjusted value of $k \geq 1$. This is a simple artifact of the fact that *randomly* throwing away data leads to irretrievable loss in ability to represent the underlying distribution accurately for outlier detection.

In some data sets, such as the Lymphography data set, we found that the behavior of the algorithm with increasing values of k was algorithm dependent (e.g., average k-nearest neighbor versus LOF-like algorithms). The results are shown in Fig. 3.10a. The corresponding behavior of the component detectors in subsampling mirrored this behavior. For example, by fixing $k = 2$, the average k-nearest neighbor detector

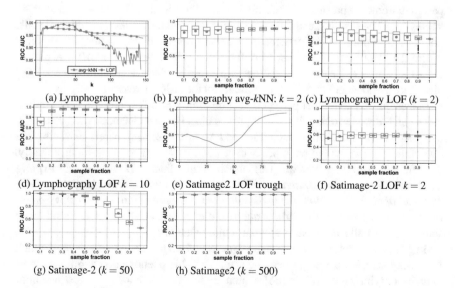

(a) Lymphography (b) Lymphography avg-kNN: $k = 2$ (c) Lymphography LOF ($k = 2$)

(d) Lymphography LOF $k = 10$ (e) Satimage2 LOF trough (f) Satimage-2 LOF $k = 2$

(g) Satimage-2 ($k = 50$) (h) Satimage2 ($k = 500$)

Fig. 3.10 Effects of using different algorithms and parameter settings. The bias is highly dependent on the choice of algorithm and parameter setting. However, given the ground-truth, it is easy to predict by plotting *AUC* versus k

(Fig. 3.10b) showed opposite trends to LOF (Fig. 3.10c). This is roughly consistent with the expected trends suggested by Fig. 3.10a. Furthermore, if the value of k was increased to $k = 10$ for LOF in the subsampling of Lymphography, the results were vastly different, as shown in Fig. 3.10d. This is simply because LOF already performs quite well at $k = 10$ on the full data set, and subsampling at fraction f and $k = 10$ is (roughly) equivalent to using the algorithm on the full data at a much larger value of k than 10. Such values of $k \lg 10$ on the full data would be suboptimal (see Fig. 3.10a). In Satimage-2, we found the performance with k to be unpredictable and not monotonic. This result is shown in Fig. 3.10e. The value of $k = 50$ provided almost the trough in the performance of LOF on the full data set, as shown in Fig. 3.10e. This value of k seemed to be one of the worst choices for the performance on the full data, and therefore subsampling is guaranteed to improve the bias performance. Therefore, we tried other values of k. The trends at $k = 2$ and $k = 500$ are shown in Fig. 3.10f, h, and they are exactly the opposite of the trends at $k = 50$ (Fig. 3.10g).

These results show that the bias induced by subsampling on the component detectors is completely *unpredictable*, *data-dependent*, *algorithm-dependent*, and *parameter-dependent*, although it can be (roughly) predicted simply by plotting[10] the ground-truth AUC performance versus k on the full data set. Of course, since we do not have the ground-truth available in unsupervised problems like outlier detection, there is no way of practically making use of this fact in real settings.

The sensitivity of the base detectors to the subsample size also has an important impact on the ensemble performance. The unpredictable effect on base detectors, when adverse, can and will swamp the ensemble performance. Data sets in which pareto-extremes represent outliers often show improved accuracy with increasing values of k. The simplest example is a single Gaussian distribution in which the tails are viewed as outliers. We generated a standard normal distribution of 2000 points where the 3% of points furthest from the mean were tagged as outliers. A plot of the AUC versus k for both the average k-nearest neighbor algorithm and the LOF algorithm is shown in Fig. 3.11. It is evident that the AUC increases rapidly with k and stabilizes quickly to almost perfect detection after $k = 50$. Therefore, subsampling at small fixed values of k will show improved bias. For raw distance-based detectors, using subsamples of similar magnitude as k results in scoring pareto-extremes in a favorable way even with other types of distributions. With increasing dimensionality, this effect is magnified even when k is much smaller than n. *Therefore, subsampling at fixed values of k has a tendency to increase the relative outlier ranks of the pareto-extremes of high-dimensional data distributions, but pareto-extremes are not generic outliers.* Therefore, if most outliers are pareto-extremes in a data set, it would make sense to use small sample sizes at a particular value of k.

In general, an optimal sample size *might* exist *for a fixed* value of k beyond which increasing sample size might degrade accuracy. This phenomenon is referred to as "gravity-defying behavior" in [66], which studies the behavior of nearest neighbor

---

[10]The prediction is even rougher for LOF because of reachability smoothing and the quirky harmonic normalization.

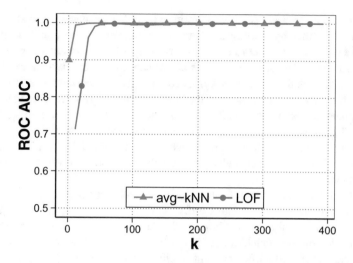

Fig. 3.11 The AUC-vs-k always increases at small values of k in the normal distribution. Therefore, subsampling at very small values of k would be beneficial

detectors at $k = 1$ and suggests using extremely small subsample sizes (and even considers the use of a subsample size of 1 as a reasonable choice). There is nothing surprising about the existence of an optimal sample size for 1-NN detectors, or even inconsistent with the results already presented in [6], although the work in [66] does not provide a clear picture of the fact that this *empirical* phenomenon works in frequently recurring special cases that are easy to solve anyway. The *possible* existence of an optimal sample size is consistent with the arguments in [6]. The work in [66] fixes $k = 1$ while computing optimal sample size, whereas the work in [6] emphasizes the *incomparable* performances at a fixed value of k for data sets of varying sizes because it is an implicit way of varying the *relative* value of k. As long as an optimal value of k exists for the full data set, so will an optimal sample size at $k = 1$. Furthermore, the work in [66] incorrectly states that the bias-variance theory in [6] is derived for density-estimation rather than outlier detection. This is not the case, because the bias-variance theory in [6] is directly derived for the error of anomaly detection as an unsupervised adaption of classification/regression rather than density estimation. In fact, the bias-variance results in [6] do not even assume the use of a particular detector such as k-nearest neighbor or LOF, and the arbitrary interpretation of outlier scores as hypothetical but unobserved (ideal) values is explicitly emphasized. Although the arguments in [66] emphasize the effect of "anomaly contamination," the classification/regression setting automatically models[11] the effect of both the outlier and inlier distributions. A particularly common form of anomaly contamination in the context of a 1-NN detector is a small cluster of outliers, which often disappears from a subsample. One can reduce the risk caused by anomaly con-

---

[11]For example, if we have an anomalous cluster (i.e., contaminant) and a normal cluster, the bias at a particular subsample size and k would depend on the relative size of the anomalous cluster.

tamination in a k-nearest neighbor algorithm by either increasing the value of k for fixed data size (thereby ignoring a cluster of k anomalies) or by reducing sample size at fixed $k = 1$. Let $f = k/n$ be the *relative value* of the parameter k with respect to base data size. The data-centric bias performance of an exact k-nearest neighbor detector at the relative value $f = k/n$ is equal to that of scoring test points at their f-percentile distance with respect to the *data distribution*. If we assume that the bias is minimized at some intermediate (finite) value $f = f^* > 0$, an optimal value of the sample size will also exist for a 1-nearest neighbor detector, which is (roughly) equal to $1/f^*$. For some distributions, such as those in Fig. 2.6a, c, it is possible for the value of f^* to be infinitesimally small and therefore no finite value of the optimal base data size exists.

Although "anomaly contamination" does have obvious detrimental effects with increased sample sizes in the rather unfair case of fixing $k = 1$ (and not adjusting k with data size), it is not the most important factor in explaining the successful use of very small subsamples (such as 1) with 1-nearest neighbor detectors. The main issue is that real benchmarks often present relatively simple cases of outlier detection. An important aspect of subsampling is that it shifts the bias of 1-nearest neighbor detectors, so that *it increases the relative outlier ranks of the pareto-extremes of the data distribution*. For example, the expected 1-NN score at a subsample size of 1 is the average distance of the test point to all training points, which is often at its highest at the pareto-extremes of the data. Furthermore, at very small subsample sizes greater than 1, there are several reasons that pareto-extremes will tend to be *heuristically* favored, especially with increasing dimensionality. Although such pareto-extremes are obviously not generic outliers (and easy to trivially discover by other methods) [56, 57], surprisingly[12] many real data sets derived from classification benchmarks predominantly contain pareto-extremes as outliers. One cannot use these properties of typical benchmarks to make generic inferences. The reported claim in [66] that subsample sizes of 1 achieve near-optimal results on many data sets is an almost certain indicator of the preponderance of pareto-extreme outliers in these data sets.

Consider a d-dimensional *ball-and-speck* data set (see p. 265) without significant anomaly contamination in which a single outlier is placed at the center of a unit sphere, and whose surface contains all the normal points. Subsampling this data will always worsen bias characteristics of 1-NN to the extent that even the variance reduction of the ensemble does not recover the accuracy achieved by a single execution of 1-NN on the full data set. Using a sample size of 1 (with ensembles) earns the dubious distinction of the single outlier being ranked as the strongest inlier. Increasing the dimensionality d increases the minimum sample size required to avoid this dubious distinction. Making a very small change to the data set by moving the

---

[12]Perhaps, it is not so surprising. The rare class often has a very different mean from the normal class (and by implication the full data). Features in classification data tend to have high Fisher's scores [8], indicating at least partial separability on individual dimensions. This separability is sharpened over multiple dimensions. The increasing tendency of tiny classes to be separable with increasing dimensionality is also well known [43, 48]. Even partial separability can often guarantee a decent AUC for a pareto-extreme detector. See also comments on real benchmarks on p. 267.

single outlier to a position just *outside* the sphere drastically changes the bias characteristics of subsampling so that a subsample size of 1 is now a perfect detector (when used in an ensemble-centric setting). Sufficiently increasing dimensionality without changing the sphere radius or the distance of the outlier from the center of the sphere sharpens this effect in the sense that a single base component might do really well with a subsample size of 1. Note that in both the unusually contrasting cases, the distributions can be equally well-represented by a particular sample size and have equal (negligible) amounts of anomaly contamination. These factors are not the key in deciding the optimal sample size. In the first case, it is far more important to describe the exact shape of the data manifold[13] with the sample because of the nature of the outlier placement. When outliers are placed deep in the sparse interior regions of a high-dimensional data set, large subsamples are needed whose size can increase exponentially with data dimensionality. On the other hand, if outliers can be described in large part by their pareto-extreme characteristics, then the shape of the data manifold is mostly irrelevant and even a subsample size of 1 might work very well (with the effect being more pronounced in higher dimensions). Pareto-extreme values require global analysis with very few points, whereas interior outliers need local analysis with many points especially if the dimensionality is high. In other words, reducing subsample size (without adjusting parameters) results in a fundamentally *different* model rather than a *better* model, which often works well for outlier placements that are *biased towards pareto-extremes* in real distributions. This fact, however, needs to be understood only as an *empirical* observation about the pareto-extreme biases of rare classes in labeled benchmarks rather than a *theoretical* one about the conventional-wisdom-defying merits of nearest neighbor detectors. Pareto-extreme outliers are almost trivial to model and interior outliers are difficult to model. Conventional wisdom states that we do not need large sample sizes or complicated models in easily solvable cases, and unnecessarily changing (localizing) the model with increased sample size is counterproductive. The real problem in the unsupervised setting is that we can never be sure whether our data set is in the easily solvable category.

Finally, we would like to mention that "gravity-defying" behavior is not specific to the anomaly detection problem, but it *can* occur in any unsupervised algorithm with *data size-sensitive* parameters where it is impossible to perform supervised parameter tuning. Inducing inflexibility by designing parameter-free methods can also cause this problem. For unsupervised algorithms, one can *sometimes* adjust parameters so that bias is roughly stable with increasing data size, which results in more reasonable accuracy behavior with increasing data. In almost all of our experiments we have observed improved accuracy with increased data of nearest neighbor (base) detectors

---

[13]In high-dimensional space, it is often more meaningful and general to talk of data manifolds describing the distribution structure rather than clusters.

with proportionally increasing k (or fixed *relative* value of k), although this choice of k is only a heuristic adjustment. The reasoning for this observation is not very difficult to deduce from variance-reduction effects. An exact 10-NN detector on 1000 points would be more stable (i.e., have lower variance) than a 1-NN detector on 100 points but in both the cases the expected scores would be roughly equal to the top-1 percentile distribution distance (i.e., same bias). It is noteworthy that the work in [66] seems to question[14] this simple observation without providing a convincing explanation. The main accuracy advantage of using $k = 1$ over larger values of k occurs only in the *ensemble-centric* and small-finite-data setting where the proportionally reduced subsample size reduces *correlations* among diverse base detectors and therefore reduces variance more efficiently.

Learning problems are "gravity-compliant" only when it is possible to learn optimized algorithmic design or parameter choices (or at least *similar* models) with increased data, which is generally not done in unsupervised settings. One can view a 1-NN detector as a parameterized detector in which the hidden parameter corresponding to the (all-important) *relative* value of k changes asymptotically as $1/n$. This results in a fundamentally *different* model with changing n in terms of the locality of computation and its effect on pareto-extreme scores. There will usually be some optimal value of $1/n$ for this trade-off, beyond which the detector almost always starts becoming asymptotically poor. Poor (asymptotic) choices of parameters can even make a supervised algorithm show this type of unreasonable behavior. For example, if we change the bandwidth of a Gaussian kernel proportionally to $1/n$ in a supervised support-vector machine (as in Fig. 3.12), it can sometimes show worse performance with more data! The only difference is that asymptotically poor design choices are often less visible or obvious[15] in unsupervised problems than in supervised problems. This lack of visibility also means that the optimal data size at $k = 1$ cannot be known in advance for a particular data set (when it does exist). Furthermore, heuristic rules for setting sample sizes based on distances to predicted anomalies will work only when the anomaly detection algorithm is correctly identifying anomalies to begin with (which is also not possible to know in unsupervised settings). This necessitates the use of methods like variable subsampling.

---

[14] The work in [66] states that the result in [6] is based on "stretching" results from density estimation. This is incorrect because the notion of density-estimation is not discussed in [6]. It is recognized that the proportional adjustment factor is a heuristic one and is slightly different between the average k-NN detector and exact k-NN detector, especially at small values of k. For some algorithms like LOF, the exact adjustment factor is even more difficult to analytically compute.

[15] Another example of a less visible design choice is that parametrization is generally necessary to create flexible learning methods in the supervised setting. However, parameter-free methods are very much desirable in the unsupervised setting. Unfortunately, this comes at the price that parameter-free methods will often work well at specific data sizes because of inflexibility in design. Non-monotonicity in performance with increased data is also common in data types like graphs and networks where controlling performance with increased data is hard.

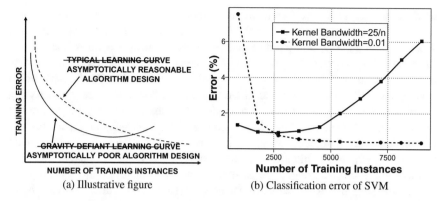

(a) Illustrative figure   (b) Classification error of SVM

Fig. 3.12 The performance in **b** is illustrative of a Gaussian kernel SVM on 2-dimensional uniformly distributed data in the unit square with the two classes corresponding to $x_1 \leq x_2$ and $x_1 > x_2$. The weighting of the slack term is $C = 1$. The only lesson here is one of perspective– "gravity-defying" behavior is not a *desirable* property of an algorithm but that of the *failure* to design algorithms with asymptotically optimal characteristics. Inflexible algorithm design can be used to induce asymptotically suboptimal behavior in almost any learning algorithm

3.4.4.2 Variable Subsampling (VS)

The variable subsampling approach [6] was designed to address the problem of unpredictable bias induced by data size. The simplest solution to this problem is to vary the subsampling rate. As we will see, varying the subsampling rate results in more diverse detectors. Let n_0 be the number of points in the base data set $\mathcal{D}$. The algorithm proceeds as follows:

1. Select f uniformly at random between $\min\{1, \frac{50}{n_0}\}$ and $\min\{1, \frac{1000}{n_0}\}$, where n_0 is the number of points in the original data set $\mathcal{D}$.
2. Select $f \cdot n_0$ randomly sampled points from the original data $\mathcal{D}$, and apply the base outlier detector on this sample to create an outlier detection model. Score each point in $\mathcal{D}$ using this model.

At the end of the process, the scores of each data point in different components are averaged to create a unified score. However, before averaging, the n_0 outlier scores from each detector should be standardized to zero mean and unit variance. In other words, we use the Z-scores. This standardization is necessary because subsamples of different sizes will create outlier scores of different raw values for unnormalized k-nearest neighbor algorithms. We refer to this approach as *Variable Subsampling (VS)*. It is noteworthy that the subsampling approach always selects between 50 and 1000 data points irrespective of base data size. For data sets with less than 1000 points, the maximum raw size would be equal to the size of the data set. For data sets with less than 50 points, subsampling is not recommended.

We now analyze the effect of such an approach on parameter choice, by using the k-nearest neighbor algorithm as an example. The merit of this approach is that

it effectively samples for different values of model parameters. For example, varying the subsample size at fixed k effectively varies the *percentile value of k* in the
subsample. In general, holding data size-sensitive parameters fixed, while varying
subsample size, has an automatic effect of parameter space exploration. If we view
each component detector *after* selecting the subsample size, then it has a bias, which
is component dependent. However, if we view the randomized process of selecting
the subsample size as a part of the component detector, then every component has
the same bias, and the variability in the aforementioned component-dependent bias
now becomes a part of this detector variance. One can reduce this variance with
ensembling, with the additional advantage that the underlying component detectors
of variable subsampling tend to be far less correlated with one another as compared
to fixed subsampling. As a result, one can now aim for better accuracy improvements
in the ensemble. Therefore, this approach provides variance reduction not only over
different choices of the training data, but also over different randomized choices of
k (in an implicit way). In other words, the approach becomes insensitive to specific
parameterizations. Although, we have focussed on the parametrization of distance-
based detectors here, it is conceivable and likely that such an approach is also likely
to make ensembles created with other types of base detectors robust to both parameter and data-size-sensitive design choices. This makes the *VS* approach more general
and desirable than simply varying the value of k across detectors; it is independent
of the nature of the parameters/design choices in the base detector and it *concur-
rently* achieves other forms of variance reduction in an implicit way. For example,
the variable subsampling approach would also be helpful for a parameter-free detector in which the effect of data size is highly unpredictable. For data size-sensitive
parameters, it is advisable to select them while keeping in mind that subsample sizes
vary between 50 and 1000 points. Knowledge of subsample sizes eases the parameter selection process to some extent. For example, for distance-based detectors,
we recommend that a value of $k = 5$ will result in a percentile value of k varying
between 0.5 and 10% of data size, which seems reasonable.

It is noteworthy that variable subsampling works with raw subsample sizes
between 50 and 1000, irrespective of base data size. By fixing the subsample size in
a constant range, it would seem at first sight that the approach cannot take advantage
of the larger base data sizes. This is, however, not the case; larger data sets would
result is less overlap across different subsamples, and therefore less correlation across
detectors. This would lead to better variance reduction. The idea is to leverage the
larger base data size for better de-correlation across detectors rather than build more
robust base detectors with larger subsamples; the former is a more efficient form of
variance reduction. After all, the number of points required to accurately model a
distribution depends on the absolute subsample size, rather than on the size of the
original data set obtained by the data collector. Even if we work under the implicit
assumption that a data collector would collect more data for a more complex data
distribution, it is unlikely that the required number of data points to accurately model
the distribution varies linearly with the collected data size. If desired, one can use
other heuristics to increase the robustness of base detector with increasing data size,

such as selecting f from $(\min\{1, \frac{50}{n_0}\}, \min\{1, \sqrt{\frac{1000}{n_0}}\})$. The maximum subsampling rate should always reduce with base data size, to increase the de-correlation benefits rather than using it only to improve the base detector.

Computational Complexity of VS

By focusing on an *absolute* size of the subsample, rather than a subsampling *rate*, we have ensured that each detector requires time *linear* in the base data size, rather than quadratic. This is because points in the full data set need to be scored against a subsample of *constant* size. *Therefore, the relative speed-up increases with increasing data size.* In Fig. 3.13, we have *analytically* shown the number of operations of a quadratic base detector, and two variations of the subsampling approach with 100 trials. One is based on a constant maximum subsample size of 1000, and the other is based on a maximum subsample size of $\sqrt{1000 n_0}$. We assume that the base detector requires $O(n_0^2)$ operations and a 100-trial subsampling approach requires $100 \times \frac{n_{max}+50}{2} \times n_0$, where n_{max} is maximum subsample size in a particular type of variable subsampling. For any data set with more than 50000 points, variable subsampling with constant subsample size has a clear advantage over a single application of the base detector, and it would be 20 times faster for a million point data set, although the figure only shows results up to 200,000 points. If one were to extend the X-axis to beyond 5 million points, even the approach using a maximum subsample size of $\sqrt{1000 n_0}$ would overtake the base detector. For larger data sizes, most of the base data points might not even be included within one of the 100 subsamples; nevertheless, the accuracy could be superior to that of a model on the (full) base data because increasing data size on a single detector is an inefficient way of reducing variance as compared to variable subsampling. The only way of consistently doing better with less data is to use a better designed technique rather than using an identical method on less data.

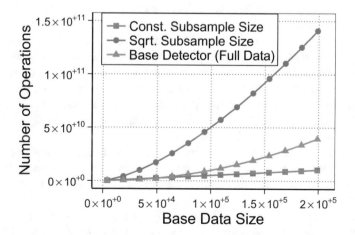

Fig. 3.13 The number of operations required by a quadratic base detector over base data sets of varying size

The Special Case of Raw Distance-Based Detectors

Since distance-based detectors are used often with subsampling, it is worthwhile to examine the properties of this special class of detectors in the context of subsampling methods. Even though we advocate samples of size between 50 and 1000 points for variable subsampling, it is possible that even smaller samples can be used for very simple detectors that are less prone to overfitting. In fact, if a detector is very stable, it is particularly important to use smaller subsample sizes to induce variability. An example is the use of raw nearest neighbor detectors (like the k-nearest neighbor method). Since the value of k for a k-nearest neighbor detector is proportional to the subsample size, and a value of $k = 5$ is advocated for subsamples of size in the range [50, 1000], it stands to reason that one can use subsamples with size in the range [10, 200] while using only $k = 1$. One advantage of this approach is that it makes the individual detectors more efficient and diverse without significantly affecting the bias characteristics. Note that using $k = 1$ with a subsample of size 200 has roughly similar bias characteristics to using $k = 5$ with a subsample of size 1000. However, the former is a more unstable detector with greater diversity across subsamples, because smaller subsamples would tend to have less overlap and correlations with one another when the base data set is small. De-correlated and diverse detectors provide better ensemble-centric improvements (see differences between *ENSEMBLE-F* and *ENSEMBLE-I* in Fig. 2.6b, d). For example, if we have a small base data set of size only 50 points, then variable subsampling with $k = 5$ and samples in the range [50, min{50, 1000}] will result in perfectly correlated base detectors (and therefore no ensemble-centric improvements). On the other hand, using $k = 1$ and samples in the range [10, min{50, 200}] can produce diverse ensemble components. Therefore, the ensemble performance might be even better in such cases by using very small subsamples at $k = 1$. Although the use of $k = 1$ has also been studied in [66], the work mainly emphasizes its efficiency/memory advantage in enabling the use of smaller samples and the anomaly contamination effects of smaller samples (although such effects are largely irrelevant at proportionally chosen k). However, it does not mention that the main (and predictable) accuracy advantage of using $k = 1$ is the *reduction of correlations* among base detectors, which is especially helpful when the original training data is small. These observations also apply to other forms of subsampling such as the *geometric subsampling* method discussed later in this chapter (see Sect. 3.5.1). Raw distance-based detectors are special because of their simplicity and resistance to overfitting; for more complex detectors like the kernel Mahalanobis method (see Chap. 6), we caution against the use of samples that are too small. The key is to understand that the simpler the detector is, the more sense it makes to use smaller samples for more efficient variance reduction. Simple algorithms like k-NN reach the limits of their (excellent) performance on only a small amount of data with typical distributions but incur the risk of poor performance on complex distributions.

A more complex detector can have significant bias deterioration if the sample sizes are too small, and therefore such a strategy is fraught with risk. Clearly, the expected size of the sample (and corresponding model complexity) required to detect outliers from a data set depends on the complexity of the base distribution as well as the complexity of the base method. As shown in Chap. 6, simple detectors work well on many real data sets and therefore small sample sizes are sufficient for *such data sets*. This does not, however, mean that we can make any theoretical assertion based on this experimental observation. In a nutshell, simple data sets require simple detectors with a small amount of data, but it is impossible to know the nature of a data set in unsupervised problems.

An interesting theoretical analysis can also be constructed for the precise effect of using Monte-Carlo sampling with 1-nearest neighbor detectors. As shown in [14, 60, 63], a subsampled 1-nearest neighbor classifier is also a weighted nearest neighbor method on the full data set. This is achieved by using the probability of a point occurring as the 1-nearest neighbor in a subsample as its weight. A similar result can be extended to (raw) distance-based outlier detectors. For simplicity in notation, consider a setting where the test point is not included in the training data of size n. If we subsample with $k = 1$ and fixed subsampling of p points out of n points, then we can show that the unsupervised outlier score $O(\overline{X})$ of a point is equal (in expectation) to the sum of the following weighted distances where D_i is the distance of the ith distant point from the target point in the full data set, and w_i is the weight of this point:

$$E[O(\overline{X})] = \sum_{i=1}^{n} w_i D_i \qquad (3.11)$$

The weight w_i is defined as follows:

$$w_i(\overline{X}) = \begin{cases} \frac{\binom{n-i}{p-1}}{\binom{n}{p}} & \text{if } n - i \geq p - 1 \text{ [Choosing } (p-1) \text{ points from } (n-i) \text{ most distant]} \\ 0 & \text{if } n - i < p - 1 \text{ [Cannot choose } (p-1) \text{ from } (n-i) < p - 1] \end{cases} \qquad (3.12)$$

One can also derive the weights for variable subsampling by averaging $w_i(\overline{X})$ over all possible values of p used in the process. These results imply that one can perform subsampling with 1-nearest neighbor detectors in a deterministic way without actually performing the Monte Carlo procedure. One can also view $w_i(\overline{X})$ as a learned similarity $S(\overline{X}, i$ th distant point). We can therefore write the prediction of subsampled 1-NN as follows in terms of the rank-wise similarity $S(\overline{X}, \overline{Y})$ of target point $\overline{X}$ to training instances:

$$E[O(\overline{X})] = \sum_{\overline{Y} \neq \overline{X}} \underbrace{S(\overline{X}, \overline{Y})}_{\text{Relative Similarity}} \cdot \underbrace{distance(\overline{X}, \overline{Y})}_{\text{Absolute Distance}} \qquad (3.13)$$

Note that the relative similarities sum to 1 for fixed $\overline{X}$ and varying $\overline{Y}$, and depend only on the rankwise distance of $\overline{Y}$ from $\overline{X}$ in exponentially decaying fashion. In other words, subsampling multiplies (rankwise and exponentially decaying) *relative similarities* with *absolute distances* to create an outlier score! A similar observation is true of bagging.

In the classification domain, the theoretical error of a 1-nearest neighbor classifier can be theoretically bounded by twice the Bayes optimal error[16] rate on an infinite data set, and subsampling is simply a way of trying to heuristically achieve a performance close to this rate. However, similar results cannot be shown for nearest neighbor outlier detectors because we are not using the labels of the nearest neighbors, and we are instead using the raw distances as a heuristic for the outlier score. The nearest neighbor of an outlier might easily be another outlier in the subsample. This is particularly common because outliers tend to occur in small clusters in real settings. However, by varying the subsamping rate, one is trying to heuristically achieve a setting where this does not occur in at least some of the base components.

3.4.4.3 Variable Subsampling with Rotated Bagging (VR)

It is possible to combine the base detectors in variable subsampling and rotated bagging to create an even more diverse base detector. This will help in variance reduction. Furthermore, because of the reduction in terms of *both* points and dimensions, significant computational savings are achieved. The combined base detector is created is as follows:

1. Project the data into a random $2 + \lceil \sqrt{d}/2 \rceil$-dimensional space using the rotation method of the previous section.
2. Select a variable size subsample using the approach described in Sect. 3.4.4.2.
3. Score each point using the reduced data set.

The scores of these individual detectors can then be combined into the final ensemble score. It is important to use Z-score normalization of the scores from the base detectors before combination. We refer to this approach as variable subsampling with rotated bagging (*VR*).

This approach also has some clear computational benefits. Rotated bagging already has computational benefits because one is using only $\sqrt{d}$ dimensions. With increasing dimensionality the benefit increases. When combined with variable subsampling, the benefits can be very significant. For example, for a data set containing ten million points and 100 dimensions (i.e., a billion entries), each ensemble component would use a data matrix of size at most 1000×7 (i.e., less than ten-thousand entries). In space-constrained settings, this can make a difference in terms of being able to use the approach at all. For 100 trials, the ensemble (containing quadratic base detectors) would be hundreds of times faster than a single application of the base method on the full data.

---

[16]The Bayes optimal error rate is the smallest possible error that is theoretically achievable by a classifier on a particular data distribution. In other words, the Bayes error rate is the irreducible error caused by the vagaries of the underlying data distribution.

3.4.4.4 Bagging and Bootstrapping (BAG)

In the previous section, we discussed the effect of subsampling on the bias performance. In the case of subsampling, we select only a sample of the data *without replacement*. The subsampling method is a variation on bagging, and the latter was the first data-centric variance reduction technique proposed in [16]. This book provides the first detailed study of this well-known method in the context of unsupervised outlier detection.

In bagging, a *bootstrapped* sample of the data is drawn, in which points from the original data are selected with replacement. Typically, the size of the sample drawn is exactly the same as the size of the original data. The scores of a data point from different ensemble components are then averaged to provide the final result. Since the overlaps among the different training data sets is much larger in such an implementation of bagging than in the case of subsampling, it leads to greater correlation among the base detectors. This correlation hinders variance reduction, and it renders a larger fraction of the data-centric variance irreducible. Furthermore, there are still bias-centric degradations due to the fact that there are repeated points in the data set, and at least some of the original points are lost. When bootstrapping, the probability that any given point in the data set is included is given by $1 - (1 - 1/n)^n \approx 1 - 1/e$. Therefore, a fraction of the points are lost, which could lead to some degradation. The degradation due to loss of points is typically smaller than in the case of subsampling; however, the presence of repeated points in the data set is typically not reflective of the original distribution. The duplicates can be viewed as random weights on the points; clearly, this adds noise to the data set. Depending on the algorithm, this could sometimes lead to significant bias-centric degradation effects if one is not careful about properly handling such points.

One such example of an algorithm is LOF, which could sometimes exhibit significant degradation. LOF sometimes sets the scores of some points in the neighborhood (see Fig. 3.14) of[17] repeated (duplicate) points to be ∞. This is a weakness in algorithm design, especially since many of these ∞ predictions tend to lie in truly dense regions with lots of repeated points. In some unusual cases, this can cause LOF to have worse-than-random bias (in *expectation*), even when its ROC curves show high values of the AUC over individual detectors. This occurs when different points obtain ∞ scores in different ensemble components. It is only upon averaging the scores, that one finds the ensemble to be worse than its base detectors. In other words, the AUCs of individual base detectors do not reflect the full impact of the ∞ scores, whereas the AUC of the averaged score reflects the *expected* bias of the detector more closely. This situation can also occur in feature bagging, because dropping dimensions can lead to repeated instances in the data set in cases where each attribute value is drawn from a small cohort of possibilities. These bias degradation effects can sometimes

---

[17]The LOF paper does suggest the use of k-distinct-distances as a *possibility* to fix this problem. The implementation from the LMU group that proposed LOF [74] also allows ∞ scores. However, this issue only presents an extreme case of a pervasive problem with LOF when k data points are close together by chance at small values of k.

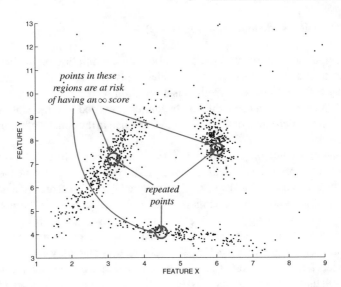

Fig. 3.14 LOF can report very large or ∞ scores (false positives) at small k in very dense regions

be significant; they provide examples of settings in which these heuristic variance reduction techniques simply do not work very well. An example of the poor performance of feature bagging on the Lymphography data set is illustrated in Fig. 3.23b in the experimental section (Sect. 3.7).

In the case of bagging, it is usually possible to compensate for repeated points by excluding its repeated instances during the computation of its neighborhood for all neighborhood-based detectors. This is particularly easy to achieve in the average k-nearest neighbor detector by matching the instance identifier of a test instance with those of the bagged instances in the training data. In the case of LOF, this type of exclusion needs to be performed during the computation of the average distance to its k-nearest neighbors in the process of *reachability distance computation*. Furthermore, the harmonic averaging of reachability distances during the computation of the outlier score also needs to exclude repeated instances of the test point. The reader who is unfamiliar with LOF is referred to Sect. 6.2.5 of Chap. 6 for the definitions of reachability distances and harmonic averaging. It is noteworthy that exclusion of repeated points of a particular test instance is relatively easy with neighborhood methods, but is often not very easy with methods like one-class SVMs that build the entire model up front. This is because such models cannot adjust the outlier detector for specific test instances.

It is also possible to use samples of variable size in bagging, just as we do in the case of subsampling. We propose the *variable bagging (VB)* approach, which is the exact analog of the *variable subsampling (VS)* approach. Like VS, the VB approach always imposes bounds between 50 and 1000 points during the sampling process, although the minimum and maximum number of points are also constrained[18] by the size of the data set.

We present the results of using bagging on the Lymphography, Glass, and Satimage-2 data sets in Figs. 3.15 and 3.16. These data sets are described in detail in Sect. 3.7.1. The box plot AUC performances for the executions of the base detectors at different re-sample rates are shown. Each box plot is defined over 100 different executions of the base detector created by re-sampled bags. Furthermore, the averaged ensemble performance is shown with the use of a triangle marker. In all these experiments (as well as some additional experiments presented in Sect. 3.7), we excluded the repetitions of the point being scored within the training data in order to compute the scores. The effect of bagging at different rates of sampling is shown in Figs. 3.15 and 3.16 for the Lymphography, Glass, and Satimage-2 data sets. The results of bagging are often comparable or better than those of the equivalent sub-sampling results discussed in Sect. 3.7. These results show that that the best quality results are not necessarily obtained by using a bag size equal to the full data set. This is because the use of a bag size equal to the full data set results in too much overlap in the data instances sampled in different ensemble components. As a result, there will be too much correlation between the outlier score vectors from different base detectors, which will reduce the advantages obtained from bagging. These results strongly suggest that one should always use bagging with smaller re-sample sizes; even in classification, it is often recommended to use smaller re-sample sizes for optimal performance [44]. Smaller sample sizes also provide the benefit of better computational complexity. These results are similar to those obtained for subsampling in Sect. 3.7. In a sense, bagging and subsampling are not very different from a conceptual perspective. The results in Sect. 3.7 also show the results for the conventional implementation of bagging with re-sample size equal to the full data set (which are the same as the results in Figs. 3.15 and 3.16 at a re-sample size of 1.0).

Furthermore, the results of variable bagging are shown in Figs. 3.15 and 3.16, which are annotated by VB. As in variable subsampling, the use of variable bagging has the advantage that it makes the ensemble more resistant to the vagaries of parameter choice. It is evident from Figs. 3.15 and 3.16 that there is significant variation in performance between the different re-sample rates over different detectors/data sets, but the variable bagging approach performed robustly in a consistent way.

In practice, it is possible to use relatively small bag sizes with a 1-nearest neighbor detector. If a 1-nearest neighbor detector is to be used, then the variable bagging approach should use re-sample sizes between 10 and 200 points (rather than 50 and 1000 points). Such an approach further reduces the overlap between different base components. As in the case of subsampling, we can show that the Monte Carlo process of bagging with a 1-nearest neighbor detector is equivalent to that of using a weighted distance-based detector on the full data set. In particular, if we perform

---

[18]This constraint is essential for subsampling but not quite as essential for bagging. Even for a data set with 1 point, one can create a data set between 50 and 1000 points by re-sampling it. However, oversampling a data set does not provide significant advantages of diversity, and therefore we maintained exactly the same approach as used in subsampling by constraining the maximum size of the bag to the original data set size.

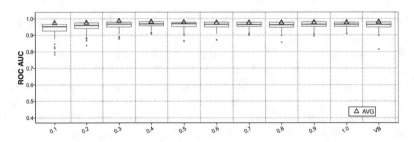

(a) Lymphography, Average k-NN ($k = 5$)

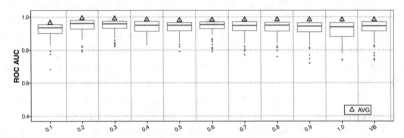

(b) Lymphography, LOF ($k = 5$)

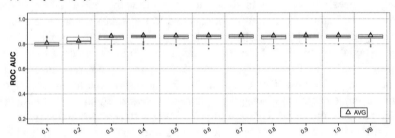

(c) Glass, Average k-NN ($k = 5$)

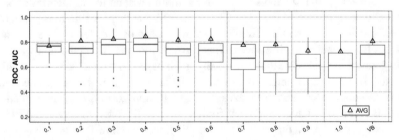

(d) Glass, LOF ($k = 5$)

Fig. 3.15 Performance of bagging at different sampling rates together with variable bagging (VB)– *Lymphography* and *Glass*

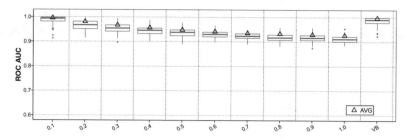

(a) Satimage-2, Average k-NN ($k = 5$)

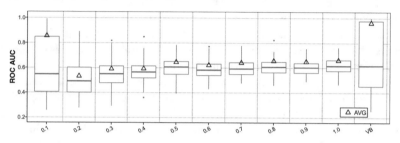

(b) Satimage-2, LOF ($k = 5$)

Fig. 3.16 Performance of bagging at different sampling rates together with variable bagging (VB) –*Satimage-2*

bagging with a 1-nearest neighbor detector with bootstrapped sample of p points out of n training points (and a test point not included in training data), then we can show that the unsupervised outlier score S of a point is equal (in expectation) to the sum of the following weighted distances where D_i is the weight of the ith distant point from the target point in the full data set, and w_i is the weight of this point:

$$E[S] = \sum_{i=1}^{n} w_i D_i \tag{3.14}$$

The weight w_i is defined as follows:

$$w_i = P[\text{Not sampling nearest } (i - 1) \text{ and selecting } i\text{th}] \tag{3.15}$$

$$= P[\text{Not sampling nearest } (i - 1)] - P[\text{Not sampling nearest } i] \tag{3.16}$$

$$= \left(1 - \frac{[i - 1]}{n}\right)^p - \left(1 - \frac{i}{n}\right)^p \tag{3.17}$$

For target points included in training data, the relationship is almost the same for large n but notationally messier. In the case where $p = n$, the (relative) value of w_i over different data points can be shown to be approximately proportional to e^{-i}, where e is the base of the natural logarithm. In other words, bagging with 1-nearest neighbor detectors can be performed in a deterministic way without using a Monte Carlo procedure.

3.4.5 Wagging (WAG)

Wagging is a method that has been used earlier for variance reduction in classification [12]. In bagging, the duplicates in the data set can be viewed as a kind of implicit weight that adds diversity. Furthermore a fraction $1/e$ of the points are dropped. In wagging, all points are retained, but the weights are chosen explicitly from a particular distribution. The scores of a data point from the different ensemble components can then be combined with averaging in order to reduce the variance. In the original version of wagging for classification [12], it was suggested to use a Gaussian distribution with zero mean and standard deviation σ. The classification algorithm is applied to a weighted version of the data. In this book, we will examine the use of wagging in the context of outlier ensembles for the first time. However, in the case of outlier ensembles algorithms, we found the use of a uniform distribution in $[0, 1]$ to be more effective, although the results in the two cases are not very different.

Note that this approach does require some effort in terms of developing weighted versions of outlier detection algorithms. Furthermore, the effectiveness of this approach is highly dependent on the type of base algorithm used. For the case of many algorithms like LOF and average k-nearest neighbor approach, this is not a very difficult task. For example, we can still use the same parameter k to define the two algorithms, but the following changes are made:

1. In the case of the average k-NN algorithm, the average distances are now computed in a weighted way over the k-nearest neighbors. Therefore, the modifications in this case are not very difficult. For the particular case of an exact k-nearest neighbor detector, no advantage is obtained form wagging because the results are identical to those obtained using the full data. This is an example of the fact that the effect of wagging is heavily dependent on the specific base detector and corresponding weighted variation.

2. Note that LOF uses average reachability distances in a locality. The averaging process to compute the reachability distance within a locality is done in a weighted way. Furthermore, the final computation of LOF divides the reachability distance of a point by the harmonically averaged reachability distance in its locality. This harmonic averaging is also done using the same set of weights. For example, if $dist_1 \ldots dist_k$ be the averaged reachability distances in a locality, and $w_1 \ldots w_k$ be the *relative* weights (scaled to sum to 1 so that $\sum_{i=1}^{k} w_i = 1$), then the weighted harmonic mean is given by $1/(\sum_{i=1}^{k}[w_i/dist_i])$.

There are other ways of modifying these algorithms to include weights, although we have suggested the simplest options available. In general, wagging might sometimes require some skill in changing the base detector appropriately.

The incorporation of diversity by addition of noise is a commonly used approach in classification [45]. One nice characteristic of wagging is that it makes the bias degradation in variance reduction algorithms very *explicit*. This is particularly evident when the Gaussian distribution is used with a variance parameter. By increasing the parameter σ of the Gaussian distribution, one typically increases bias but improves diversity. Therefore, there is typically an optimal value of σ at which the performance is optimized. This observation is not very different from the effect of the subsampling parameter f (see Fig. 3.4) in subagging [20]. In the case of subagging, the bias degradation is because of the information loss associated with subsampling, and this is reflected by the first term of Eq. 3.8. In fact, *in virtually every variance reduction algorithm, there is some source of bias loss, when attempting a simulation of data-centric variance reduction with a finite data set.* Very often, this bias loss of many variance reduction algorithm is so subtle (and implicit) that it is ignored by researchers and practitioners; this gives the incorrect impression that such methods would improve the accuracy in every situation.

3.4.6 Data-Centric and Model-Centric Perturbation

Wagging can be viewed as a *weight-centric* data perturbation technique in which the individual data points are multiplied with weights. It is possible to design numerous other types of data perturbation techniques, such as adding noise to the data, or by adding artificial data [45]. For example, the work in [45] discusses a setting in which the points are generated from a base distribution, whose parameters are estimated from the training data. The generated data sets are used to create the models for the base detectors. This can be viewed a a data-centric perturbation technique, which is designed to induce diversity.

It is also possible to perturb the *models* in order to add diversity. For example, instead of determining the average k-NN distance in an outlier detector, one might determine the $\lceil \alpha \cdot k \rceil$ closest neighbors, where $\alpha > 1$. Subsequently, k nearest neighbors are sampled from these $\lceil \alpha \cdot k \rceil$-nearest neighbors. It is not very difficult to see that this approach (very roughly) simulates the process of subagging by choosing the subagging fraction to be $1/\alpha$. However, the correspondence is not exact because one is not fixing the selected fraction of $1/\alpha$ points up front. Nevertheless, the overall effect of variance reduction is very similar. In general, one can understand this approach both from a data-centric and model-centric bias-variance trade-off.

3.4.7 Parameter-Centric Ensembles

Any particular algorithm has numerous choices in terms of the design of the model and the choice of parameters. For example, the k-nearest neighbor algorithm typically uses the parameter k to decide on the model design. By using different values of k

and averaging the results, one can often obtain more robust results. In other words, the uncertainty associated with parameter choice can be reduced with the use of this type of approach. Variations of these types of ensemble methods were discussed in some of the earliest approaches like LOF [17] and LOCI [54]. In fact, some classes of outlier detectors like clustering and histograms are so sensitive to the choice of parameters that it makes sense to use them only in the ensemble-centric setting.

If the number of possible values of the parameters is small, then one can run over all choices of the parameters and average the scores. On the other hand, if the parameter space is large, then one can sample combinations of parameters from a range, and average the outlier scores of a point obtained from the different randomized runs. This type of situation is common in settings in which the algorithm has multiple parameters, and therefore the grid of parameter combinations is too large. In such cases, one simply samples the grid points for the parameter settings of the base detectors. The outlier scores of the different base detectors are then averaged to yield the final result.

Parameter-centric ensembles are particularly helpful when an algorithm is particularly sensitive to a particular choice of parameters. Specific examples of such parameters could include the following:

1. In a k-nearest neighbor algorithm, it is possible to vary the choice of the parameter k.
2. In a centroid-based algorithm, one inputs a parameter k corresponding to the number of clusters. The distance to the nearest centroid provides the outlier score. In this context, the work in [29] is notable because it uses multiple mixture model clusterings in which the number of mixture components is varied over different components. The log-likelihood fits of the points are averaged over the different ensemble components to create the outlier score.
3. In a one-class SVM or kernel logistic regression method, the kernel and regularization parameters can be used to create the ensemble.
4. In histogram-based methods, the data space is divided into a number of buckets, and the number of points in each bucket is used to create the outlier score for all points in the bucket. The width of the histogram buckets, or the number of histogram buckets can be used to create the ensemble.

Since most outlier detection algorithms have parameters associated with them, this approach can make the ensemble more robust to parameter choices. In fact, in the case of unsupervised methods ensembling over "reasonable" ranges of the parameters is often the only realistic approach available, because ground truth is not available for parameter tuning.

3.4.8 Explicit Randomization of Base Models

One can also achieve variance reduction with the use of explicit randomization of base models or with the use of base models that are inherently randomized. In fact, when the base method is an iterative approach with an random initialization point, the final outlier scores will depend on the initialization point.

An example of this setting is the use of the k-means clustering algorithm in order to score outliers. The outlier score of each data point is equal to its distance to the closest cluster centroid. In some settings, the negative logarithm of the number of points in the closest cluster is also used as a component of the outlier score. The scores of such an algorithm may vary significantly from one run to the next because the cluster centroids often depend on the initialization point. Furthermore, the number of points in each cluster may also vary significantly from one run to the next. This is particularly true if the number of clusters is large. This is because clustering-based outlier detection methods naturally have a high variance of prediction, which contributes to the error. In other words, this type of variability is an indicator of a suboptimal detector in which the variance component has not been properly removed. Ensemble methods provide an avenue to remove this type of variability. The scores of a data point from different randomized runs of an algorithm are averaged in order to yield the final result. In general, one creates two n-dimensional vectors of scores, one of which is based on the distance criterion and the other is based on the log-cardinality criterion. Each vector is standardized to zero mean and unit variance, and then the scores in each of the two vectors are averaged across different ensemble components to create two vectors of scores. Then, the average of these two scores is used as the final result.

Randomized clustering ensembles have also been used for outlier detection in graph streams [2]. The basic idea is to create multiple sets of communities from a graph by using the connected components in random subsets of edges. The probability of an edge occurring with its end points in various communities is used to to provide a probabilistic score of its likelihood. The median score across different executions can be used as its outlier score.

The randomization of the base detector may be used in conjunction with various models. For example, while using a k-nearest neighbor detector, one might choose to use an approximate k-nearest neighbor method with Locality Sensitive Hashing [25]. Even though each detector is poorer in terms of quality, the overall ensemble result can be better than a technique that uses the exact k-nearest neighbor method. An LSH method for approximate nearest neighbor outlier detection is discussed in [69]. Therefore, the overall approach may be summarized with the use of the following two steps:

1. Create a suitable randomized variant of the base method. The randomized variant may sometimes be less effective than the base method on a stand-alone basis. Often the randomization is achieved by using an approximate but randomized version of a step that is executed in the base algorithm in an optimal way.
2. Average the normalized outlier scores from multiple runs of the base method.

This approach is often combined with a parametric ensemble method. For example, one can use multiple runs of a k-means algorithm or mixture modeling algorithm with different numbers of clusters. In fact, one can view a random choice of parameters as one way of randomizing the base detector. The scores from the different runs may be averaged. An example of such an approach is provided in [29] in which multiple runs of a mixture modeling algorithm are used with varying numbers of mixture components. The mixture modeling algorithm is itself randomized in terms of the initialization point used for the method.

Another idea for improving the base performance of outlier detection algorithms is the use of autoencoder ensembles [23]. Autoencoders are neural networks that can be used for performing nonlinear dimensionality reduction. The number of input units is exactly equal to the number of output units (with a one-to-one correspondence), and the goal of the neural network is for each output unit to mimic its corresponding input. The outputs of the units in any of the middle layers provide a reduced representation of the data. The aggregate (squared) residual error of the approach provides an outlier score for a single component, and the median score across all components provides the final outlier score. Randomization is achieved in the neural network by sparsifying the connections between computation units. In other words, the connections between units in the middle layers are randomly dropped in each ensemble component. As a result, the reduced representation in each component is quite different, and the median result is much more robust.

3.5 Some New Techniques for Variance Reduction

In the following, we will introduce some new techniques for variance reduction that have not been discussed elsewhere. One of them is an extension of variable subsampling, and the other can be considered a soft generalization of feature bagging. These methods have not been discussed elsewhere, and we will also show experimental results illustrating their effectiveness.

3.5.1 Geometric Subsampling (GS)

The variable subsampling has greater diversity than fixed rate subsampling because of its ability to adjust to varying data-centric bias of different data distributions, with respect to a particular *relative* value of k. However, selecting the number of subsamples points *uniformly* within a particular range $[n_1, n_2]$ is not necessarily the best way of achieving diversity. For example, consider the case where $n_1 = 50$ and $n_2 = 1000$, which is the most common setting in these scenarios. In such a case, the *percentile* value of k corresponding to using a subsample of 50 points is 10 times that obtained by using a subsample of 500 points. On the other hand, the percentile value of k corresponding to the use of a subsample of size 500 points is only twice that obtained by using a subsample of size 5000 points. However, more than half the samples are drawn from the range [500, 1000] even though the diversity in terms of the percentile value of k is much lower. In general, for any given value of $\beta < 1$ and number of points n, we would like the fraction of subsamples with raw size selected from the range $[n\beta, n]$ to depend only on β rather than on $n(1 - \beta)$. This is achieved with the use of geometric subsampling, which uses some of the properties of a memory-less exponential distribution. The basic idea in geometric subsampling is as follows:

1. Select g uniformly at random between $\log_2\left(\min\{1, \frac{50}{n_0}\}\right)$ and $\log_2\left(\min\{1, \frac{1000}{n_0}\}\right)$, where n_0 is the number of points in the original data set $\mathcal{D}$.
2. Set $f = 2^g$.
3. Select $f \cdot n_0$ randomly sampled points from the original data $\mathcal{D}$, and apply the base outlier detector on this sample to create an outlier detection model. Score each point in $\mathcal{D}$ using this model.

As in the case of variable subsampling, the scores of different detectors are averaged in order to determine the overall score. It can be shown that the value of $f \cdot n_0$ is drawn from a partial segment of an exponential distribution between $\min\{n_0, 50\}$ and $\min\{n_0, 1000\}$ points. For example, when all subsamples are chosen between 50 and 1000 points, the relative frequency of the subsamples of various sizes is shown in Fig. 3.17. It is immediately evident that smaller subsample sizes are favored, which reduces the overlap between the subsamples of larger sizes. Furthermore, the true diversity because of varying value of k also increases with this approach. As we will see later in the experimental section of this chapter, there is greater variation in performance between different base detectors with geometric subsampling. Correspondingly, the ensemble performance of the approach is also superior.

Note that the sampling fraction is chosen after first transforming the fraction into the logarithmic space, and then exponentiating after selection. It is easy to see that the fraction of trials in which the selected sampling fraction lies in the range $[f_1, f_2]$ is no longer dependent on $f_2 - f_1$, but on $\log(f_2) - \log(f_1) = \log(f_2/f_1)$. In other words, we obtain a roughly similar number of expected samples containing [50, 100] points, [100, 200] points, [200, 400] points and so on. This property is also evident from the histogram illustrated in Fig. 3.17. This approach tends to make the individual

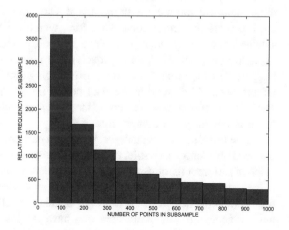

Fig. 3.17 Relative frequency of subsamples of various sizes between 50 and 1000 points in geometric subsampling. A simulation is used to generate this plot. The simulation uses 10000 ensemble components, and reports the number of ensemble components of various subsample sizes on the Y-axis

detectors more diverse, and it therefore helps in better variance reduction. In this case, the average size of the samples is generally smaller than the vanilla version of variable subsampling. Aside from the aforementioned diversity advantages, the smaller size is also beneficial for computational complexity.

3.5.1.1   Geometric Subsampling with Rotated Bagging (GR)

Just as variable subsampling can be combined with rotated bagging, it is also possible to combine geometric subsampling with rotated bagging. The resulting method is referred to as *geometric subsampling with rotated bagging (GR)*. The steps for this method are also analogous to the previous case:

1. Project the data into a random $2 + \lceil \sqrt{d}/2 \rceil$-dimensional space using the rotation method of the previous section.
2. Select a geometric size subsample using the approach described in Sect. 3.5.1.
3. Score each point using the reduced data set.

The scores of these individual detectors can then be combined into the final ensemble score. It is important to use Z-score normalization of the scores from the base detectors before combination. We refer to this approach as geometric subsampling with rotated bagging (*GR*). The GR approach provides one of the most compact representations, and therefore its efficiency advantages are undeniable.

3.5.2 Randomized Feature Weighting (RFW)

The randomized feature weighting method can be viewed as a soft version of feature bagging. Therefore, it shares the same relationship with bagging, as wagging shares with subsampling. In feature bagging, a subset of the dimension are selected in a hard way. In randomized feature weighting, no dimension is dropped. Rather, dimensions are weighted with the use of a specific distribution. These weights are used to scale the dimensions. Therefore, weighting a dimension less will lead to smaller relative importance of the dimension. However, none of the dimensions are explicitly dropped. Such an approach often provides better diversity than feature bagging, in which a large number of overlapping dimensions are used by the various feature bags. After scoring the data points (in multiple ways) with the weighted features in different base detectors, the scores of each data point are averaged over the different ensemble components.

It is noteworthy that feature weighting is a particularly problematic issue in unsupervised problems like outlier detection. In supervised problems, the relative importance of different features can be easily learned by using the ground-truth available in the training data. This is not possible in unsupervised problems like outlier detection. Although one solution is to simply standardize all dimensions to zero mean and unit variance, different dimensions may have varying level of importance for outlier detection. Furthermore, the relative importance of different dimensions may vary for different points. This suggests an inherent representational limitation in selecting a particular set of weights for the different dimensions. This representational limitation can be reduced by applying randomized feature weighting methods. By averaging the scores output by differently weighted detectors, one effectively optimizes the local weighting for each point based on the argument provided in Fig. 3.6.

The overall approach of randomized feature weighting (RFW) is as follows:

1. Scale each dimension to zero mean and unit variance.
2. For each dimension i, select a scaling weight w_i drawn from the Pareto-probability distribution. The density function for the Pareto distribution was defined as follows:

$$f_X(x) = \begin{cases} \frac{\alpha}{x^{\alpha+1}} & \text{if } x \geq 1 \\ 0 & \text{otherwise} \end{cases} \tag{3.18}$$

   The value of α in each ensemble component was chosen uniformly at random from $[1, 2]$.
3. Multiply the values in the ith dimension with w_i.
4. Apply the base-detector to the scaled data set.

The scores from the different detectors are then averaged in order to provide the final ensemble score. It is also possible to use other types of combination functions on the scores output by the various detectors. It is noteworthy that feature bagging can be viewed as a variant of randomized feature weighting, in which all weights are binary, and are chosen from $\{0, 1\}$ in a particular way.

3.6 Forcing Stability by Reducing Impact of Abnormal Detector Executions

So far, we have discussed only the averaging scheme, because it was the prototypical scheme proposed in Brieman's original work [16]. However, there are numerous other central estimators of a given set of points. The mean is one of a large set of estimators, such as the median or the trimmed mean. The main advantage of the mean is that it is an *unbiased* central estimator of any probability distribution; other than symmetric distributions, the median always has some bias. For highly asymmetric distributions, the bias can actually be quite significant. On the other hand, the median is known to be a far more stable estimator; this is especially the case in settings in which the underlying probability distribution has a thicker tail than the normal distribution. In the following, we will explore whether there is any advantage of using this (more stable) central estimator. After all, one of the goals of ensemble analysis is to improve accuracy by creating more stable solutions from the combination. It is also noteworthy that the use of the median instead of the mean in bagging is also referred to as *bragging*, which is short for "robust bagging" in

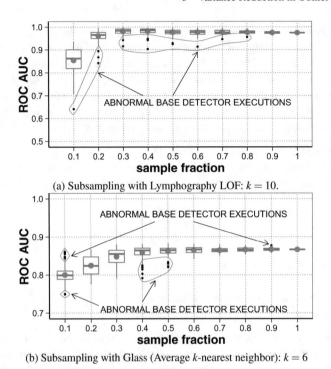

(a) Subsampling with Lymphography LOF: $k = 10$.

(b) Subsampling with Glass (Average k-nearest neighbor): $k = 6$

Fig. 3.18 Most of the abnormal performances are below the box-plot. This is typical in such settings, especially when the underlying data sets are small

the classification domain. Therefore, it is natural to test this approach for the outlier detection problem.

The median not only has lower variance than the mean, but it will also have a different value in *expectation*. In order to understand this point, we replicate the curves in Figs. 3.9b and 3.10d in Fig. 3.18a, b. The box-plots show the AUC performance at different subsampling rates. It is noteworthy that low AUCs correspond to poor performance. Note that outliers in the box-plot (marked in Fig. 3.18) typically have much lower AUC than the rest of the executions. Clearly, the effect of such bad base detectors could not possibly be very helpful for the ensemble. The main issue is that it is hard to precisely identify these component detectors because the ground-truth is not available in unsupervised problems like outlier detection. The main goal of using the median is to reduce the impact of abnormal base detector executions and provide more stable results.

Therefore, we attempted[19] two different methods to remove such base detectors:

---

[19] As we will see later, these attempts to create more stable combination methods were largely unsuccessful because the results did not seem to show a significant improvement over the mean and in fact worsened in many cases. Nevertheless, we include these experiments, because there are some useful lessons one can learn from them. Furthermore, the differences were small enough that we do not consider these results to be definitive in terms of relative performance.

1. *Median*: For each data point, we compute the median of the underlying scores over all components.
2. *Thresholded Trimming*: The median can be viewed as a special case of the trimmed mean, where 50% of the data at both ends of the distribution is trimmed, to yield a single point. One can, in principle, use a much lower trimming parameter such as 1% to reduce the impact of the outliers. In this chapter, we choose to use *thresholded* trimming, in which a *percentage* is not used. Rather, the detectors are scored on the basis of their distance to the ensemble scores; the detectors with abnormally large absolute distance are trimmed. Statistical significance tests are used to determine when a detector is abnormal. Thus, for skewed distributions, the trimming might occur on only one side of the distribution.

The description for the thresholded trimming needs some further explanation. Assume that the total number of detectors is m. The thresholded trimming is computed using the following sequence of steps:

1. Standardize the scores from each detector to zero mean and unit standard deviation. Let the standardized score of the ith point for the jth detector be $O(i, j)$.
2. Compute the average score $a_i = \sum_{j=1}^{m} O(i, j)/m$ of the ith point over all ensemble components.
3. Compute the aggregate detector deviation $\Delta_j = \sum_{i=1}^{n} |O(i, j) - a_i|$ of the jth detector from the mean score for each data point and sum up the deviation over all points.
4. Standardize $\Delta_1 \ldots \Delta_m$ to zero mean and unit standard deviation.
5. Exclude any detector j for which $\Delta_j > 1$. Compute the adjusted average a_i' of the scores of each point over the remaining detectors after this exclusion (trimming) has been performed. Therefore, this trimming approach tends to exclude very unusual detector performance, which are considered suspicious in terms of quality.

It is noteworthy that same set of base detectors is trimmed across *all points*, rather than trimming different detectors for different points; the latter would be similar to the median and therefore it is more interesting to test the former. We refer to this approach as AVG-T, which refers to the fact that it is an average of the detectors, after trimming the abnormal detectors. Here, we are using a conservative threshold of only one standard deviation to magnify the trimming effect, because increasing the threshold too much tends to make the results more similar. However, the basic message from the results is not too different even after increasing the threshold. Another notable variant of this trimming approach is MAX-T, which is similar to AVG-T. The trimming is performed in exactly the same way. However, in AVG-T, we compute the average of the scores over the trimmed set of detectors. On the other hand, we compute the maximum of the scores over the trimmed set of detectors in the case of MAX-T. The MAX-T approach is not a variance-reduction method,

and it can be considered a variant of the maximization scheme, after removing the
abnormal detectors.

3.6.1 Performance Analysis of Trimmed Combination Methods

We evaluated the performance of several combination variants on twelve different
data sets. These data sets are described in detail in Sect. 3.7. We used 100 trials
of the geometric subsampling method[20] over these data sets, and tested the performance of various combination methods. The trimmed average and trimmed maximum are denoted by AVG-T and MAX-T, respectively. The results for the average
k-nearest neighbor method and LOF method are illustrated in Figs. 3.19 and 3.20,
respectively. In each case, we used $k = 5$. In general, we found that these stable
combination methods did not work very well. For example, the median combination
method often showed the worst performance, and trimmed averaging did not typically outperform simple averaging. This was, in part, because of the loss in diversity
associated with trimming. However, the trimming often had a beneficial effect for
the maximization scheme. This is because the maximization scheme often selected
results from the most abnormal base detectors, which could sometimes be poorly
performing. Nevertheless, even for the maximization scheme, the improvement from
trimming was not guaranteed.

The poor results of the median were particularly notable. Although one would
expect the stable combination methods to provide better combination performance
for variance reduction, our experience was exactly the opposite. Furthermore, the

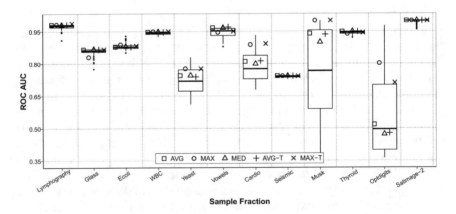

Fig. 3.19 Performance of more stable combination variants (Average k-nearest neighbor at $k = 5$
with geometric subsampling for twelve data sets)

---

[20]We used geometric subsampling because it was one of the best performing variance reduction
methods. However, the basic trends were quite similar over other types of subsampling.

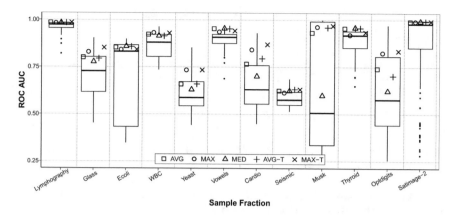

Fig. 3.20 Performance of more stable combination variants (LOF at $k = 5$ with geometric sub-sampling rates for twelve data sets)

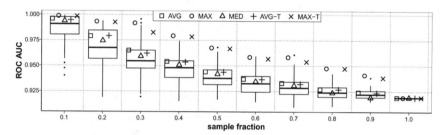

Fig. 3.21 Example of the detrimental effect of trimming (Average k-nearest neighbor at $k = 5$ with varying subsampling rates for the Satimage-2 data set)

trimmed averaging combination provided inconsistent results, and it was difficult to see any advantage on the average. Only in the cases of the trimmed maximum, trimming improved performance (over the maximization combination), although the results were still quite inconsistent. In order to investigate the precise effect of trimming in detail, we selected a particularly pathological case of the Satimage-2 data set and used fixed subsampling in combination with trimming. This data set is described in detail in Sect. 3.7. We used fixed subsampling with varying subsampling rates for both the average k-NN and the LOF algorithms. The corresponding box plots and ensemble combination methods are illustrated in Figs. 3.21 and 3.22, respectively. It is evident that trimming almost always worsens the performance. Furthermore, the median performs particularly poorly in this case. In fact, the median performs worse than the other model combination methods in virtually every case.

In order to understand this phenomenon, we examined the AUCs of the trimmed detectors. Statistics of the AUC-based performance of the trimmed detectors and retained detectors are presented in Table 3.1 for the LOF results of Fig. 3.22. In the table, the AUCs of the retained detectors are illustrated, together with the minimum, median, and maximum of the trimmed detectors. We found that the medians

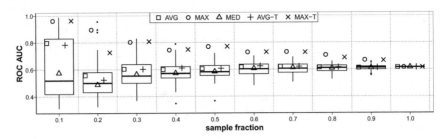

Fig. 3.22 Example of the detrimental effect of trimming (LOF at $k = 5$ with varying subsampling rates for the Satimage-2 data set)

Table 3.1 Performance of trimmed and retained detectors (out of a total of 100 detectors) in terms of AUCs. These results correspond to the LOF run of Fig. 3.22

Sampling Fraction	Number Trimmed	Median AUC (Retained)	Minimum AUC (Trimmed)	Maximum AUC (Trimmed)	Median AUC (Trimmed)
0.1	17	0.511364418	0.375426319	0.988289121	0.527618608
0.2	17	0.492974947	0.341790099	0.956331148	0.518039325
0.3	12	0.560425533	0.469784162	0.73210442	0.542471595
0.4	19	0.58188524	0.347979714	0.636026557	0.559180976
0.5	14	0.584486156	0.504774284	0.684683467	0.574743471
0.6	15	0.609616878	0.504142791	0.628863902	0.569233264
0.7	16	0.608385835	0.536673285	0.683223907	0.593157515
0.8	18	0.611058009	0.527245118	0.661180622	0.611553129
0.9	15	0.613676125	0.564183777	0.628502698	0.604822936

of the trimmed detectors were different from those of the retained detectors to only a minor degree. In some cases, the trimmed detectors had better median AUCs than the retained detectors. In all cases, at least a few highly performing detectors were trimmed as well. This is simple example of how the unsupervised nature of the outlier detection problem makes it difficult to generalize any type of heuristic bias reduction tricks to arbitrary data sets. Furthermore, even in data sets where the trimmed detectors had significantly poorer AUCs, the ensemble method was sometimes unable to gain any advantage because of loss in diversity. On the other hand, the maximization ensemble was more frequently (albeit unreliably) take advantage of trimming, because it is not quite as dependent on diversity. More details on the maximization combination function (together with a justification) are provided in Chap. 5.

Although the results with the median trimmed combination methods gave us unexpected results (to those we originally expected), we have included them to show just how challenging it is to generalize some of these methods to a broader variety of data sets. Certainly, the additional complexity involved in trimming is not justified by its inconsistent performance. It is also noteworthy that these results are specific to the use of subsampling as an approach for ensemble analysis. It is conceivable that the median or the trimmed mean might be useful in settings where other base detectors are used. After all, the median is used quite successfully in the supervised domain in many variance-reduction settings. One issue that it is specific to the outlier detection problem is that extreme scores are often more informative than in the case of classification. Furthermore, one measures error in terms of AUCs rather than MSEs, this sometimes leads to different results than classification (see Sect. 3.3.3). In many cases, the median is unable to benefit from large outlier scores for outlier points, when most ensemble components treat them like false negatives. This might, at least to some extent, explain the differential performance of the median in the two problem settings. We would also like to point out that some of our recent experimental results [23] on using ensembles of autoencoders that the median *can* do better than the mean in some settings. Furthermore, the median has been used successfully in the case of graph data [2]. Therefore, we believe that the effectiveness of the median or the mean will depend on the specific choice of the base detector that used and the specific method used for injecting randomness.

3.6.2 Discussion of Commonly Used Combination Methods

The two most commonly used combination functions are the averaging [40] and the maximization [10, 40] combination functions:

1. *Averaging*: The average of the scores $s_1(i) \ldots s_m(i)$ is reported as the final score of the ith data point. This combination method has already been discussed in detail in this chapter. The averaging function was first proposed in the context of outlier detection by [40], although it had been used earlier for classification ensembles in the context of variance reduction [15].
2. *Maximum*: The maximum of $s_1(i) \ldots s_m(i)$ is reported as the outlier score. A ranking-based equivalent of the maximization function was proposed in [40], and a thresholding-based version of the maximization function for high-dimensional outlier detection was proposed in [10]. For detectors like isolation forests, in which lower scores are indicative of a greater degree of outlierness, the scores are multiplied with -1 before applying the maximization combination function.

Which of these methods of model combination is better? It might seem at first sight that the maximum function overestimates the absolute scores and also picks out the larger errors. On the other hand, the work in [40] shows some comparative experimental results between the averaging function and a rank-based variant of the maximization function (referred to as *breadth-first* combination in [40]). The results are data-dependent and do not seem to show clear superiority of one method over the other.

First, it is impossible to overestimate all the outlier scores, because these are *relative* quantities. In fact, as discussed in Chap. 2, outlier scores need to be converted to a normalized scale before quantifying it bias and variance. When outlier scores are viewed from a relative point of view, it is impossible for all scores to the overestimated at the same time. A subset of overestimated scores always needs to be counterbalanced by another subset of underestimated scores. As discussed in [6], the effect of maximization is often to reduce bias. This argument will also be discussed in detail in Sect. 5.5 of Chap. 5. However, the main problem with maximization is that it can sometimes increase *variance*, because it does pick out the larger errors. This is especially the case when the underlying data sets or subsamples are small. It turns out that one can gain some of the bias advantages of the maximization scheme by combining it variance reduction methods. In the following, we discuss two such variance reduction methods, which are first discussed in [6]. Both these schemes normalize the outlier scores to Z-values before applying the combination:

1. *AOM Method*: For m ensemble components, we divide the components into approximately m/q buckets of q components each. First, a maximization is used over each of the buckets of q components, and then the scores are averaged over the m/q buckets. Note that one does not need to assign equal resources to maximization and averaging; in fact, the value of q should be selected to be less than m/q. For our implementations, we used 100 trials, with $q = 5$. We refer to this method as *AOM*, which stands for *Average of Maximum*.

2. *Thresh Method*: A method suggested in [3], for combining the scores of multiple detectors, is to use an absolute threshold t on the (standardized) outlier score, and then adding the (thresholded and standardized) outlier scores for these components. The threshold is chosen in a mild way, such as a value of $t = 0$ on the standardized score. Note that values less than 0 almost always correspond to strong inliers. The overall effect of this approach is to reward points for showing up as outliers in a given component, but not to penalize them too much for showing up as strong inliers. For our implementations, we always used a threshold value of $t = 0$ on the Z-score. An important point is that such an approach can sometimes lead to tied scores among the *lowest ranked* (i.e., least outlier-like) points having a score of exactly $m * t$. Such ties are broken among the lowest ranked points by using their average standardized score across the m ensemble components. As a practical matter, one can add a small amount $\varepsilon * avg_i$ proportional to the average standardized score avg_i of such points, to achieve the desired tie-breaking. This approach is referred to [6] as *Thresh*.

The *AOM* combination scheme is particularly useful when the maximum number of trials is not a concern from the computationally efficiency perspective. For example, with averaging, we found that it was often hard to do much better by significantly increasing the number of trials beyond a certain point. However, to saturate the benefits of combining maximization and averaging (e.g., *AOM*) one would need a larger number of trials. Nevertheless, it has been shown in [6] that even with the same number of trials, schemes such as *AOM* perform quite well. With faster base detectors, one can run a far larger number of trials to gain the maximum accuracy improvements from *both* bias and variance reduction; indeed, many of the ensemble methods proposed in this paper also provide the dual benefit of greater speed. The

Thresh method can be viewed as a faster way of combining bias and variance reduction, when computational efficiency is important. Other ideas for combining bias and variance reduction include the use of *Maximum-of-Average (MOA)*. For detectors like isolation forests in which lower scores are indicative of a greater degree of outlierness, the scores are always multiplied with -1 before applying any of these maximization-based combination functions.

3.7   Performance Analysis of Methods

In the following, we provide an experimental analysis of the different variance reduction methods. This will provide an understanding of the effectiveness of various schemes. These experimental results provide a comprehensive overview of the relative effectiveness of the different variance reduction methods. We used distance-based detectors as the base detectors in most cases, because of their natural simplicity and high quality performance. As shown in Chap. 6, these simple detectors are very competitive to the best detectors available in the literature. We also present some results for isolation forests in order to show the effect of subsampling on other types of detectors.

3.7.1   Data Set Descriptions

In the following, we describe some data sets for outlier detection that are used throughout this book. Many of these data sets have also been used in [6]. We used twelve data sets from the UCI Machine learning repository.[21] In some cases, further preprocessing was required. In cases where one of the classes was already rare, it was labeled as the outlier class. In cases where a data set contained relatively balanced classes, downsampling was necessary to create an outlier class. In some cases, multiple large classes were combined to create inliers and multiple minority classes were combined to create outliers. In the following, we provide a brief description of the data preparation process.

The Glass data set contained attributes regarding several glass types. Here, points of class 6 were marked as outliers, while all other points were inliers. For the Lymphography data set classes 1 and 4 were outliers while the other classes were inliers. The Ecoli data set contained 8 classes, among which classes 1–5 were included as inliers, whereas classes 6, 7, and 8 were included as outliers. The Wisconsin-Breast Cancer (Diagnostics) data set (WBC) contained *malignant* and *benign* classes, and we started with a processed version[22] of the data set. We further downsampled the *malignant* class to 21 outliers, while points in the *benign* class were considered

---

[21] http://archive.ics.uci.edu/ml/datasets.html.

[22] http://www.ipd.kit.edu/~muellere/HiCS/.

Table 3.2 Summary of the data sets

Data Set	Points	Attributes	Percentage outliers (%)
Glass	214	9	4.2
Lymphography	148	18	4.1
Ecoli	336	7	2.7
WBC	378	30	5.6
Yeast	1364	8	4.8
Vowels	1456	12	3.4
Thyroid	3772	6	2.5
Satimage-2	5803	36	1.2
Cardio	1831	21	9.6
Seismic	2584	11	6.6
Optdigits	5216	64	2.9
Musk	3062	166	3.2

inliers. The Yeast data set contained 10 classes. Classes 1, 6, 7, and 8 were included as inliers, since these classes have the most instances in the data set. From the remaining classes, we sampled 65 points and included them as outliers. In the Japanese Vowels (Vowels) data set, we treat each *frame* in the training data as an individual data point, whereas the UCI repository treats a block of frames (utterance) as an individual point. In this case, class (speaker) 1 was down-sampled to 50 outliers. The inliers contained classes 6, 7 and 8. Other classes were discarded. The ANN-Thyroid data set is the same as that in [38]. The "seismic bumps" data set (Seismic) contained two classes, which were labeled as *hazardous* and *non-hazardous* respectively. The *hazardous* class was selected as the outlier class, whereas the *non-hazardous* class corresponds to the inliers. In the Statlog (Landsat Satellite) data set, the training and test data were combined. Class 2 was down-sampled to 71 outliers, while all the other classes were combined to form an inlier class. Our modified data set is referred to as Satimage-2. The Cardiotocography (Cardio) data set contained measurements taken from foetal heart rate signals. The classes in the data set were *normal*, *suspect*, and *pathologic*. The *normal* class formed the inliers, while the *pathologic* (outlier) class was down-sampled to 176 points. The *suspect* class was discarded. In Optdigits, instances of digits 1–9 where inliers and instances of digit 0 were down-sampled to 150 outliers. The Musk data set contained several musk and non-musk classes. We combined non-musk classes j146, j147, and 252 to form the inliers, while the musk classes 213 and 211 were added as outliers without down-sampling. Other classes were discarded. Refer to Table 3.2 for details of data sets.

3.7.2 Comparison of Variance Reduction Methods

In this section, we will compare several variance-reduction methods on the basis of the ROC AUC. The specific methods that are compared are the following: (i) Fixed subsampling at several subsampling rates, (ii) Variable Subsampling (VS) (iii) Geometric Subsampling (GS) (iv) Bagging (BAG) (v) Wagging (WAG) (vi) Feature bagging (FB), (vii) Randomized Feature Weighting (RFW) (viii) Variable Subsampling with Rotated Bagging (VR), (ix) Geometric Subsampling with Rotated Bagging (GR) (x) Isolation Forests with 256 samples (IF-256). In all cases, 100 trials of the base detector were used. It is noteworthy that even though we used 100 trials for all methods, some methods like GS, VR, GR, and IF-256 are more efficient and it is easy to use a larger number of trials for better variance reduction. Nevertheless, 100 trials is usually sufficient to saturate most of the methods. For bagging, we used bootstrapped samples whose size is equal to the original data as is the traditional use of bootstrapping. It is noteworthy that this is not an optimal setting from a bias-centric point of view because the sizes of the data sets vary. Clearly, a value of $k = 5$ cannot be optimal for all cases. Furthermore, bootstrapping the entire data set leads to inefficient variance reduction because of overlaps between different bootstrapped samples. We would like to point out that there are many ways of improving the performance of bagging such as using smaller sample sizes or even varying the sample size like variable subsampling. Furthermore, for raw distance-based detectors, we can use even smaller subsample sizes at $k = 1$, although LOF requires larger values of k. Therefore, a fixed value of $k = 5$ was used in all settings.

In all cases, we implemented the combination methods corresponding to averaging (AVG), maximization (MAX), average-of-max (AOM), and thresholding (THRESH). For the base detectors, we used either the LOF method or the average k-nearest neighbor method, in both of which we set $k = 5$ in all the experiments. It is fair to say that a value of $k = 5$ induces different types of bias, when subsampling at different rates or when bagging with the full data set. However, each figure also included isolation forests, for which the implementation is independent of these base detectors. In the specific case of isolation forests, one problem is that lower scores are indicative of a greater degree of outlierness. Therefore, the use of a maximization function would have exactly the opposite semantic interpretation to what one might expect. Therefore, we multiplied the scores of the isolation forest with -1 before applying the maximization function. As a result, the use of the maximization function on the sign-flipped scores would have the same semantic interpretation as in the case of the other detectors.

We performed extensive experimental tests on a number of real data sets, which are listed in Table 3.2. The performed experiments were very extensive, and covered the various techniques discussed in this chapter. The experimental results on all the data sets are shown in Figs. 3.23, 3.24, 3.25, 3.26, 3.27, and 3.28. The main observations are as follows:

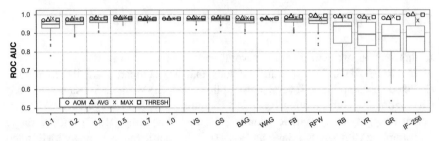

(a) Lymphography, Average k-NN ($k = 5$)

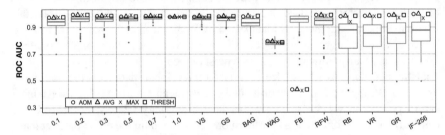

(b) Lymphography, LOF ($k = 5$)

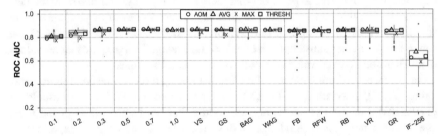

(c) Glass, Average k-NN ($k = 5$)

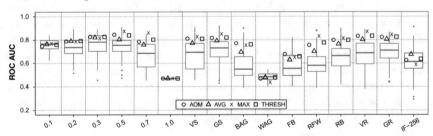

(d) Glass, LOF ($k = 5$)

Fig. 3.23 Performance of different variance-reduction methods

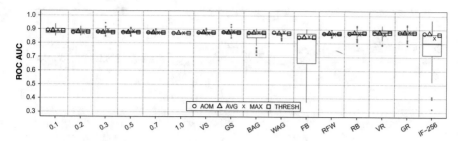

(a) Ecoli, Average k-NN ($k = 5$)

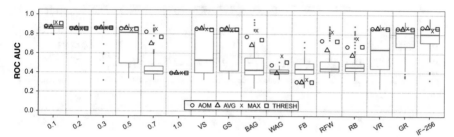

(b) Ecoli, LOF ($k = 5$)

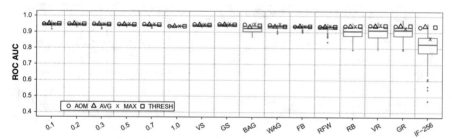

(c) Wisconsin Breast Cancer: WBC, Average k-NN ($k = 5$)

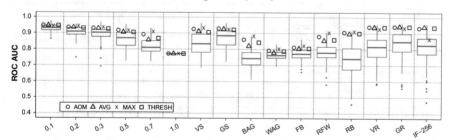

(d) Wisconsin Breast Cancer: WBC, LOF ($k = 5$)

Fig. 3.24 Performance of different variance-reduction methods

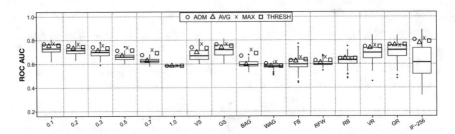

(c) Yeast, Average k-NN ($k = 5$)

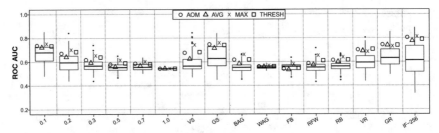

(d) Yeast, LOF ($k = 5$)

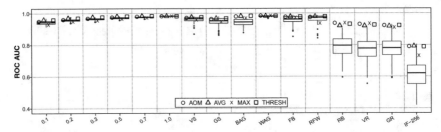

(c) Vowels, Average k-NN ($k = 5$)

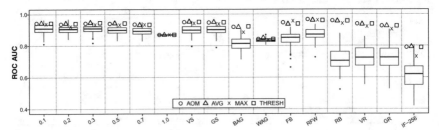

(d) Vowels, LOF ($k = 5$)

Fig. 3.25 Performance of different variance-reduction methods

1. Different fixed subsampling rates are different effects on the *base detectors*. This is because when the value of k is fixed at 5, the size of the base data regulates the *relative* value of k used in the different base detectors. Different data sets work more effectively at different relative values of k. However, lower fixed subsampling rates lead to better *incremental* improvements in performance. This is because the base detectors tend to be more independent at lower subsampling rates. Nevertheless, the performance of the base detector, which was unpredictable, always had an impact on the overall performance. In general, simpler detectors should always be used at lower subsampling rates.

2. The variable subsampling scheme was able to take away some of the unpredictability associated with sample size because it varied the subsampling rate. Therefore, it created an ensemble performance out of more diverse detectors. This was generally helpful to the overall approach because it results in a greater amount of variance that can be reduced. For example, if the anomalies occur in small clusters, these clusters would interfere with the performance of a nearest neighbor detector. However, varying the subsampling rate would ensure that some of the base components would not contain these interfering points.

3. The geometric subsampling approach performed better than variable subsampling. The reasoning for the effectiveness of geometric subsampling is discussed earlier in this chapter. In fact, along with isolation forests, the geometric subsampling schemes was one of the best performing methods. However, some of the effectiveness may also be data set-specific, since the geometric subsampling used different average data set sizes than variable subsampling. This particular effect depends on the trend of AUC with respect to the value of k. However, irrespective of the trend of AUC versus k, we did not find any data set, where geometric subsampling performed significantly worse than variable subsampling. This is most likely the case because geometric subsampling also has diversity advantages in terms of the varying data size effects.

4. The wagging technique (WAG) leads to some improvements in various data sets. However, the improvements were not always significant in every case. This is because this scheme has a high level of correlation between the base detectors. A larger amount of correlation among base detectors hinders variance reduction.

5. In the case of bagging, the proper choice of implementation is crucial in order to obtain high-quality results. Although the results in this section are presented with bag sizes equal to the full data set in order to be consistent with traditional definitions of bagging, such traditional definitions do not achieve the full advantages of bagging. This phenomenon is because of the large overlaps between the data instances of different ensemble components at larger bag sizes, which increases correlation among different components. The results in Figs. 3.15 and 3.16 show that resampling with smaller bag sizes leads to better results. This is particularly evident in the case of the Satimage-2 data set in Fig. 3.16, in which the performance of bagging is significantly better than that of subsampling (cf. Fig. 3.26c, d) at smaller resample sizes (e.g., 10% re-sampling). In all three cases of Figs. 3.15 and 3.16, we observed slight improvements of bagging over subsampling (at comparable resample sizes) over a range of data sets. These improve-

ments of bagging over subsampling might possibly be a result of the fact that bagging promotes greater diversity by allowing repetitions in sampled instances (and therefore fewer overlaps in the samples drawn by different ensemble components). In all cases, the broader trends of bagging and subsampling were similar when the re-sampling rates were fixed to the same values. This is because these two approaches are tightly related to one another, and they should be considered members of the same family.

The results in Figs. 3.15 and 3.16 also show that variable bagging (VB) methods (i.e., variable resample sizes) provide robust results that are comparable to variable subsampling, and they also blunt the effect of specific parameter choice. Although this book does not present detailed results on bagging, we found several data sets in which bagging with smaller sample sizes (or variable bagging) outperformed their subsampling counterparts *as long as one is careful in handling repeated points appropriately*. Refer to Sect. 3.4.4.4 for a discussion on the handling of repeated points with the average k-nearest neighbor and LOF detectors. The special handling of repeated points is the only potential shortcoming of bagging with respect to subsampling, because the specific way of handling repeated points depends on the choice of the base detector. It is generally easier to remove the effects of repeated points when using neighborhood-based methods as compared to other outlier detectors. In this sense, outlier detection is slightly different from classification because outlier detectors tend to more sensitive to the presence of repeated points.

6. The randomized feature weighting (RFW) scheme performs very impressively compared to feature bagging. This is because of the greater diversity among the base detectors when using soft weighting. In the case of feature bagging, the discreteness of the feature selection often results in repetition of similar or even identical models across different ensemble components. This tends to reduce the diversity, which impacts accuracy in a negative way. The randomized feature weighting scheme has the advantage that it uses soft weights on dimensions, which leads to a larger number of possibilities (and therefore greater diversity) for the base components.

7. Rotated bagging usually performed better than feature bagging. This is primarily because rotated bagging provides better diversity benefits than feature bagging although there is generally greater bias deterioration of the individual components. Nevertheless, the diversity benefits trump the bias deterioration. However, rotated bagging generally did not perform as well as subsampling. Rotated bagging can also be combined with subsampling in order to create extremely efficient detectors. In particular, the geometric subsampling with rotated bagging (GR) scheme often provided results that were competitive with the best detectors. This is the main advantage of rotated bagging. For example, for a data set containing 400 dimensions, rotated bagging created a representation with only 12 dimensions. This leads to much more efficient distance computations. When combined with subsampling, one could often represent a very large data set in a tiny amount of space without significant loss in accuracy. This is a significant advantage in big-data settings. For example, when one uses variable subsampling for a data

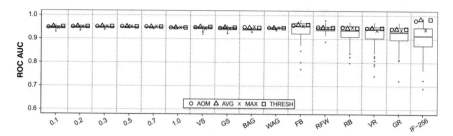

(a) Thyroid, Average k-NN ($k = 5$)

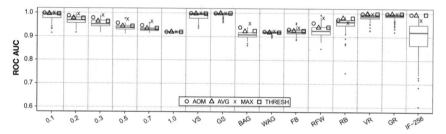

(b) Thyroid, LOF ($k = 5$)

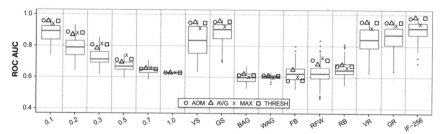

(c) Satimage-2, Average k-NN ($k = 5$)

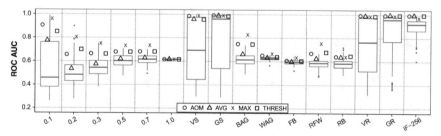

(d) Satimage-2, LOF ($k = 5$)

Fig. 3.26 Performance of different variance-reduction methods

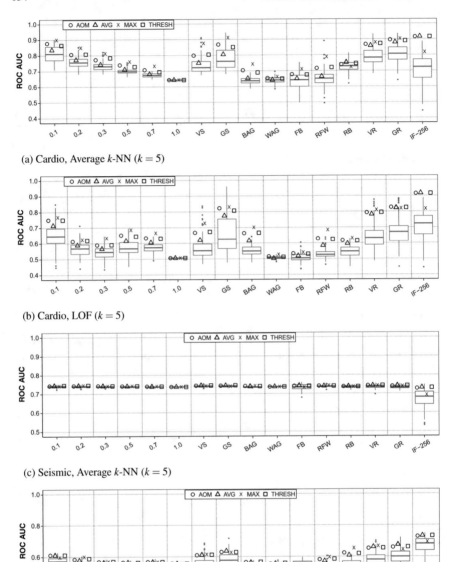

(a) Cardio, Average k-NN ($k = 5$)

(b) Cardio, LOF ($k = 5$)

(c) Seismic, Average k-NN ($k = 5$)

(d) Seismic, LOF ($k = 5$)

Fig. 3.27 Performance of different variance-reduction methods

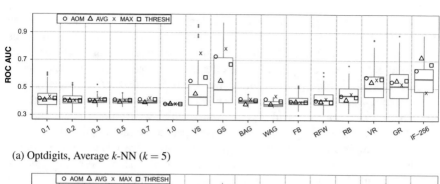

(a) Optdigits, Average k-NN ($k = 5$)

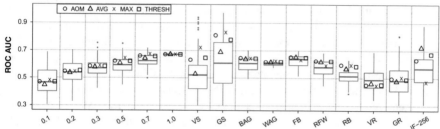

(b) Optdigits, LOF ($k = 5$)

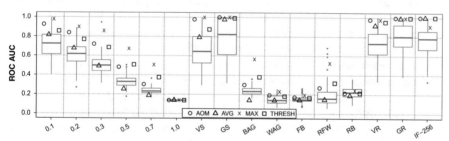

(c) Musk, Average k-NN ($k = 5$)

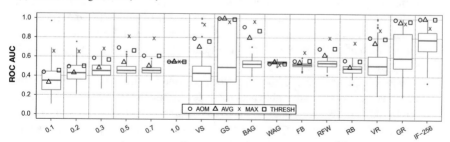

(d) Musk, LOF ($k = 5$)

Fig. 3.28 Performance of different variance-reduction methods

set containing 10^8 points and 400 dimensions, the size of the original data would be of the order of several hundred Gigabytes, but the transformed data would be significantly less than a Megabyte. Clearly, this is very useful from a practical point of view especially since these efficiency and space improvements can be achieved while *improving* accuracy. We also believe that rotated bagging is an effective scheme for other types of base detectors such as density-based methods.

8. The isolation forests provided good results, which were comparable to those of geometric subsampling. For some data sets, geometric subsampling (or geometric subsampling with rotated bagging) was more effective, whereas for others, the isolation forest scheme was more effective. In general, since these two detectors were themselves quite different, it is possible to combine them to gain even better advantages. There is, however, a caveat in the performance of isolation forests, since it tends to favor extreme values. These issues are discussed in Sects. 6.7.5 and 6.7.5.1 (cf. p. 265) of Chap. 6. However, as discussed in Chap. 6, the isolation forest can be a useful component of a broader combination of detectors.

9. The averaging function was robust, in that it always provides consistent improvements with a wide variety of detectors and data sets. However, for distance-based detectors, we found that the maximization function also provided some advantages because of its bias-centric improvements. The maximization function performed particularly poorly with isolation forests; indeed, the authors of the original isolation forest paper did not intend to use such a combination function. Part of the reason for this phenomenon is that the maximization function, which is applied to the negative of the scores in the case of isolation forests, often loses granularity in representation. Most of the scores are (negative) integers, which, when converted to absolute values, are less than 10. This results in a loss of granularity of the scoring mechanism, which is not very desirable. However, even in these cases, the use of the THRESH and AOM functions is able to do reasonably well. Other than in the case of isolation forests, the THRESH and AOM combination methods turn out to be the most effective choices. Another difference of the isolation forest framework from other methods is that each individual detector is extremely weak, as a result of which the maximization function becomes more prone to the increased variance of the result. As we will learn in Chap. 5, the maximization combination function is not very desirable for high-variance detectors.

10. The average k-nearest neighbor detector performed better than LOF both on the base detector and the ensemble performance. Although the LOF provided better ensemble improvements than the average k-nearest neighbor detector because of its ensemble performance, its final performance was not superior to the average k-nearest neighbor detector. This point is discussed in detail in [6]. Furthermore, in some data sets like Lymphography (Fig. 3.23b), the LOF method performed poorly with methods like feature bagging because of the presence of repeated points in the data. In fact, in this particular data set, many points received ∞ scores in the ensemble combination even though the base components generally performed performed well with LOF. The reason for this specific behavior of LOF is explained in Fig. 3.14. This is an interesting example of a setting in which

the averaging worsens performance at least from the perspective of the ROC AUC. It is noteworthy that the averaging combination is intended to optimize MSE rather than the ROC AUC. A detailed explanation of this phenomenon is also provided in Sect. 3.3.3. Indeed, there are many box-plots where the ensemble AUC is lower than the base performance with the averaging function.

In summary, the best performance among various schemes were provided by sub-sampling and bagging methods, with the variable and geometric variants providing good results. However, for many data sets, the feature-wise ensembles were also particularly useful. One caveat is that feature-wise sampling methods do not work quite as well with distance-based detectors as they do with some histogram-like methods. Although we have not presented detailed results on feature-wise sampling methods with histograms, some encouraging results have been presented in [61]. The geometric subsampling method (GR) with rotated bagging was particularly notable for its efficiency, especially if a distance-based method is to be used as the base detector. The GR scheme was also extremely space-efficient because it would compress extremely large data sets in very small space, while retaining a high level of accuracy. Such an approach can be very useful in the big-data and streaming setting.

3.8 Conclusions

In this chapter, we studied the use of variance-reduction methods for outlier detection. Variance-reduction methods are used commonly in classification. The application to outlier detection is fairly straightforward because of the direct applicability of the bias-variance trade-off to the outlier detection problem. However, there are sometime challenges because the unavailability of labels may sometimes hinder the implementation of the base detectors in an optimized way. For example, subsampling methods often show uncertain performance of the base detector with reducing data size. These problems do not arise in classification because of the ability to reduce the uncertainty with cross-validation (in combination with the ground-truth).

These issues related to the unavailability of ground truth are where outlier ensembles are truly different from classification ensembles. Some methods such as variable and geometric subsampling are specifically designed in the context of such unsupervised problems. This chapter also studies a vast array of existing methods (adapted from classification) and new methods for the first time in the outlier detection setting, together with experiments. Our experimental results show that methods like variable subsampling outperform fixed subsampling, whereas rotated bagging techniques outperform feature bagging. More detailed experimental results with different types of base detectors are presented in Chap. 6.

New combination methods such as the use of the median and thresholded trimming are also studied in this chapter. Although these combination methods, such as the median, can often provide superior results in the classification setting, we show that this is not necessarily true in the outlier detection setting. However, other combination functions such as *AOM* and *Thresh* performed very robustly because of their ability to combine bias and variance reduction.

Exercises

1. The variable subsampling box-plots in the chapter show that one obtains a much larger improvement with LOF as compared to the average k-nearest neighbor detector. Explain the possible reasons for this phenomenon.
2. Explain the intuitive similarity between the isolation forest and density-based detectors.
3. Show how both random forests and isolation forests can be used to compute similarities between pairs of points. What is the difference in these computed similarities? How does this result relate an isolation forest to distance-based detectors?
4. Implement an expectation-maximization clustering algorithm in which the log-likelihood fit of a point is reported as the outlier score. Implement an ensemble variant in which the scores over multiple instantiations of the algorithms with different numbers of mixture components are averaged.

References

1. C. C. Aggarwal. Outlier Analysis, Second Edition, *Springer*, 2017.
2. C. C. Aggarwal and P. S. Yu. Outlier Detection in Graph Streams, *ICDE Conference*, 2011.
3. C. C. Aggarwal. Outlier Ensembles: Position Paper, *ACM SIGKDD Explorations*, 14(2), pp. 49–58, December, 2012.
4. C. C. Aggarwal, C. Procopiuc, J. Wolf, P. Yu, and J. Park. Fast Algorithms for Projected Clustering. *ACM SIGMOD Conference*, 1999.
5. C. C. Aggarwal and P. S. Yu. Finding Generalized Projected Clusters in High Dimensional Spaces, *ACM SIGMOD Conference*, 2000.
6. C. C. Aggarwal and S. Sathe. Theoretical Foundations and Algorithms for Outlier Ensembles, *ACM SIGKDD Explorations*, 17(1), June 2015.
7. C. C. Aggarwal. Recommender Systems: The Textbook, *Springer*, 2016. [Chapter 6 on Ensemble-Based Systems]
8. C. C. Aggarwal. Data Mining: The Textbook, *Springer*, 2015.
9. C. C. Aggarwal and C. K. Reddy. Data Clustering: Algorithms and Applications, *CRC Press*, 2013.
10. C. C. Aggarwal and P. S. Yu. Outlier Detection in High Dimensional Data, *ACM SIGMOD Conference*, 2001.
11. F. Angiulli, C. Pizzuti. Fast outlier detection in high dimensional spaces, *PKDD Conference*, 2002.
12. E. Bauer and R. Kohavi. An Empirical Comparison of Voting Classification Algorithms: Bagging, Boosting, and Variants, *Machine Learning*, 36(1), pp. 1–38, 1998.
13. S. Bay. Nearest Neighbor Classification from Multiple Feature Subsets. *Intelligent Data Analysis*, 2(3), pp. 191–209, 1999.
14. G. Biau, F. Cerou, and A. Guyader. On the Rate of Convergence of the Bagged Nearest Neighbor Estimate. *Journal of Machine Learning Research*, 11, pp. 687–712, 2010.
15. L. Brieman. Random Forests. *Journal Machine Learning archive*, 45(1), pp. 5–32, 2001.
16. L. Brieman. Bagging Predictors. *Machine Learning*, 24(2), pp. 123–140, 1996.

17. M. Breunig, H.-P. Kriegel, R. Ng, and J. Sander. LOF: Identifying Density-based Local Outliers, *ACM SIGMOD Conference*, 2000.
18. G. Brown, J. Wyatt, R. Harris, and X. Yao. Diversity creation methods: a survey and categorisation. *Information Fusion*, 6:5(20), 2005.
19. R. Bryll, R. Gutierrez-Osuna, and F. Quek. Attribute Bagging: Improving Accuracy of Classifier Ensembles by using Random Feature Subsets. *Pattern Recognition*, 36(6), pp. 1291–1302, 2003.
20. P. Buhlmann. Bagging, Subagging and Bragging for Improving some Prediction Algorithms, *Recent advances and trends in nonparametric statistics*, Elsevier, 2003.
21. P. Buhlmann, B. Yu. Analyzing Bagging. *Annals of Statistics*, pp. 927–961, 2002.
22. A. Buja and W. Stuetzle. Observations on Bagging. *Statistica Sinica*, 16(2), 323, 2006.
23. J. Chen, S. Sathe, C. Aggarwal, and D. Turaga. Outlier Detection with Autoencoder Ensembles. *SIAM Conference on Data Mining*, 2017.
24. A. Criminisi, J. Shotton, and E. Konukoglu. Decision Forests for Classification, Regression, Density Estimation, Manifold Learning and Semi-Supervised Learning. *Microsoft Research Cambridge, Tech. Rep. MSRTR-2011-114*, 5(6), 12, 2011.
25. M. Datar, N. Immorlica, P. Indyk, V. Mirrokni. Locality-sensitive hashing scheme based on p-stable distributions. *ACM Annual Symposium on Computational Geometry*, pp. 253–262, 2004.
26. M. Denil, D. Matheson, and N. De Freitas. Narrowing the Gap: Random Forests In Theory and in Practice. *ICML Conference*, pp. 665–673, 2014.
27. C. Desir, S. Bernard, C. Petitjean, and L. Heutte. One Class Random Forests. *Pattern Recognition*, 46(12), pp. 3490–3506, 2013.
28. T. Dietterich. Ensemble Methods in Machine Learning, *First International Workshop on Multiple Classifier Systems*, 2000.
29. A. Emmott, S. Das, T. Dietterich, A. Fern, and W. Wong. Systematic Construction of Anomaly Detection Benchmarks from Real Data. arXiv:1503.01158, 2015. https://arxiv.org/abs/1503.01158
30. M. Fernandez-Delgado, E. Cernadas, S. Barro, and D. Amorim. Do we Need Hundreds of Classifiers to Solve Real World Classification Problems?. *The Journal of Machine Learning Research*, 15(1), pp. 3133–3181, 2014.
31. J. Friedman, and P. Hall. On bagging and nonlinear estimation. *Journal of statistical planning and inference*, 137(3), pp. 669–683, 2007.
32. P. Geurts. Variance Reduction Techniques, Chapter 4 of unpublished *PhD Thesis* entitled "Contributions to decision tree induction: bias/variance tradeoff and time series classification." University of Liege, Belgium, 2002. http://www.montefiore.ulg.ac.be/services/stochastic/pubs/2002/Geu02/
33. M. Grill and T. Pevny. Learning Combination of Anomaly Detectors for Security Domain. *Computer Networks*, 2016.
34. S. Guha, N. Mishra, G. Roy, and O. Schrijver. Robust Random Cut Forest Based Anomaly Detection On Streams. *ICML Conference*, pp. 2712–2721, 2016.
35. Z. He, S. Deng and X. Xu. A Unified Subspace Outlier Ensemble Framework for Outlier Detection, *Advances in Web Age Information Management*, 2005.
36. T. K. Ho. Random decision forests. *Third International Conference on Document Analysis and Recognition*, 1995. Extended version appears as "The random subspace method for constructing decision forests" in *IEEE Transactions on Pattern Analysis and Machine Intelligence*, 20(8), pp. 832–844, 1998.
37. T. K. Ho. Nearest Neighbors in Random Subspaces. *Lecture Notes in Computer Science*, Vol. 1451, pp. 640–648, *Proceedings of the Joint IAPR Workshops SSPR'98 and SPR'98*, 1998. http://link.springer.com/chapter/10.1007/BFb0033288
38. F. Keller, E. Muller, K. Bohm. HiCS: High-Contrast Subspaces for Density-based Outlier Ranking, *IEEE ICDE Conference*, 2012.
39. M. Kopp, T. Pevny, and M. Holena. Interpreting and Clustering Outliers with Sapling Random Forests. *Information Technologies Applications and Theory Workshops, Posters, and Tutorials (ITAT)*, 2014.

40. A. Lazarevic, and V. Kumar. Feature Bagging for Outlier Detection, *ACM KDD Conference*, 2005.

41. F. T. Liu, K. M. Ting, and Z.-H. Zhou. Isolation Forest. *ICDM Conference*, 2008. Extended version appears as "Isolation-based Anomaly Detection," *ACM Transactions on Knowledge Discovery from Data (TKDD)*, 6(1), 3, 2012.

42. F. T. Liu, K. N. Ting, and Z.-H. Zhou. On Detecting Clustered Anomalies using SCiForest. *Machine Learning and Knowledge Discovery in Databases*, pp. 274–290, Springer, 2010.

43. C. Manning, P. Raghavan, and H. Schutze. Introduction to Information Retrieval, *Cambridge University Press*, 2008. [Also see Exercises 14.16 and 14.17]

44. G. Martinez-Munoz and A. Suarez. Out-of-bag estimation of the optimal sample size in bagging. *Pattern Recognition*, 43, pp. 143–152, 2010.

45. P. Melville, R. Mooney. Creating Diversity in Ensembles Using Artificial Data. *Information Fusion*, 6(1), 2005.

46. B. Micenkova, B. McWilliams, and I. Assent. Learning Outlier Ensembles: The Best of Both Worlds Supervised and Unsupervised. *ACM SIGKDD Workshop on Outlier Detection and Description, ODD*, 2014.

47. B. Micenkova, B. McWilliams, and I. Assent. Learning Representations for Outlier Detection on a Budget. arXiv preprint arXiv:1507.08104, 2014.

48. F. Moosmann, B. Triggs, and F. Jurie. Fast Discriminative Visual Codebooks using Randomized Clustering Forests. *Neural Information Processing Systems*, pp. 985–992, 2006.

49. R. Motwani and P. Raghavan. Randomized Algorithms. *Chapman and Hall/CRC*, 2012.

50. E. Muller, M. Schiffer, and T. Seidl. Statistical Selection of Relevant Subspace Projections for Outlier Ranking. *ICDE Conference*, pp, 434–445, 2011.

51. E. Muller, I. Assent, P. Iglesias, Y. Mulle, and K. Bohm. Outlier Ranking via Subspace Analysis in Multiple Views of the Data, *ICDM Conference*, 2012.

52. H. Nguyen, H. Ang, and V. Gopalakrishnan. Mining Ensembles of Heterogeneous Detectors on Random Subspaces, *DASFAA*, 2010.

53. H. Nguyen, E. Muller, J. Vreeken, F. Keller, and K. Bohm. CMI: An Information-Theoretic Contrast Measure for Enhancing Subspace Cluster and Outlier Detection. *SIAM International Conference on Data Mining (SDM)*, pp. 198–206, 2013.

54. S. Papadimitriou, H. Kitagawa, P. Gibbons, and C. Faloutsos, LOCI: Fast outlier detection using the local correlation integral, *ICDE Conference*, 2003.

55. T. Pevny. Loda: Lightweight On-line Detector of Anomalies. *Machine Learning*, 102(2), pp. 275–304, 2016.

56. J. Pickands. Statistical inference using extreme order statistics. *The Annals of Statistics*, 3(1), pp. 119–131, 1975.

57. J. Pickands. Multivariate extreme value distributions. *Proceedings of the 43rd Session International Statistical Institute*, 2, pp. 859–878, 1981.

58. D. Rocke and D. Woodruff. Identification of Outliers in Multivariate Data. *Journal of the American Statistical Association* 91, 435, pp. 1047–1061, 1996.

59. L. Rokach. Pattern classification using ensemble methods, *World Scientific Publishing Company*, 2010.

60. R. Samworth. Optimal Weighted Nearest Neighbour Classifiers. *The Annals of Statistics*, 40(5), pp. 2733–2763, 2012.

61. S. Sathe and C. Aggarwal. Subspace Outlier Detection in Linear Time with Randomized Hashing. *ICDM Conference*, 2016.

62. G. Seni and J. Elder. Ensemble Methods in Data Mining: Improving Accuracy through Combining Predictions, Synthesis Lectures in Data Mining and Knowledge Discovery, *Morgan and Claypool*, 2010.

63. B. M. Steele. Exact Bootstrap k-Nearest Neighbor Learners. *Machine Learning*, 74(3), pp. 235-255, 2009.

64. M. Sugiyama and K. Borgwardt. Rapid distance-based outlier detection via sampling. *Advances in Neural Information Processing Systems*, pp. 467–475, 2013.

65. S. C. Tan, K. M. Ting, and T. F. Liu. Fast Anomaly Detection for Streaming Data. *IJCAI Conference*, 2011.
66. K. M. Ting, T. Washio, J. Wells, and S. Arya. Defying the gravity of learning curve: a characteristic of nearest neighbour anomaly detectors. *Machine learning Journal*, Auguest 2016.
67. K. M. Ting, G. T. Zhou, F. T. Liu, and S. C. Tan. Mass Estimation and its Applications. *ACM KDD Conference*, pp. 989–998, 2010.
68. K. M. Ting, Y. Zhu, M. Carman, and Y. Zhu. Overcoming Key Weaknesses of Distance-Based Neighbourhood Methods using a Data Dependent Dissimilarity Measure. *ACM KDD Conference*, 2016.
69. Y. Wang, S. Parthasarathy, and S. Tatikonda. Locality sensitive outlier detection: a ranking driven approach. *ICDE Conference*, pp. 410–421, 2011.
70. D. Wolpert and W. Macready. No free lunch theorems for optimization. *IEEE Transactions on Evolutionary Computation*, 1(1), pp. 67–72, 1997.
71. K. Wu, K. Zhang, W. Fan, A. Edwards, and P. Yu. RS-Forest: A Rapid Density Estimator for Streaming Anomaly Detection. *IEEE ICDM Conference*, pp. 600–609, 2014.
72. Z.-H. Zhou. Ensemble Methods: Foundations and Algorithms. *Chapman and Hall/CRC Press*, 2012.
73. A. Zimek, M. Gaudet, R. Campello, J. Sander. Subsampling for efficient and effective unsupervised outlier detection ensembles, *KDD Conference*, 2013.
74. http://elki.dbs.ifi.lmu.de/

Chapter 4
Bias Reduction in Outlier Ensembles: The Guessing Game

Informed decision-making comes from a long tradition of guessing and then blaming others for inadequate results.

Scott Adams

4.1 Introduction

Bias reduction is a difficult problem in unsupervised problem like outlier detection. The main reason is that bias-reduction algorithms often require a quantification of error in intermediate steps of the algorithm. An example of such a bias reduction algorithm from classification is referred to as "boosting". In boosting, the outputs of highly biased detectors are used to learn portions of the decision space in which the bias performance affects the algorithm in a negative way. Such regions of the data are increased in weight by increasing the weight of incorrectly classified instances in the training data. Note that the identification of incorrectly classified instances requires the availability of ground truth. Unfortunately, such an approach is not possible in unsupervised problems like outlier detection because of the unavailability of ground truth for computing accuracy. The inability to easily adapt a large class of bias reduction methods in classification to the field of outlier detection distinguishes the two fields in a very significant way.

In general, the availability of ground-truth seems to be a pre-requisite in being able to implement bias-reduction methods with *certainty*. In order to understand this point, we repeat the theoretical equation defining the bias-variance trade-off in outlier detection from Chap. 2:

$$E[MSE] = \frac{1}{n} \sum_{i=1}^{n} \{f(\overline{X_i}) - E[g(\overline{X_i}, \mathscr{D})]\}^2 + \frac{1}{n} \sum_{i=1}^{n} E[\{E[g(\overline{X_i}, \mathscr{D})] - g(\overline{X_i}, \mathscr{D})\}^2]$$

(4.1)

© Springer International Publishing AG 2017
C.C. Aggarwal and S. Sathe, *Outlier Ensembles*,
DOI 10.1007/978-3-319-54765-7_4

Here $\overline{X_1} \ldots \overline{X_n}$ correspond to the test points whose outlier scores are computed and $\mathscr{D}$ is the training data. Furthermore, $f(\overline{X_i})$ denotes the "oracle" function generating the unknown ground-truth, and the $g(\overline{X_i}, \mathscr{D})$ denotes the prediction of the detector at hand. An important point here is that the bias term $\frac{1}{n} \sum_{i=1}^{n} \{f(\overline{X_i}) - E[g(\overline{X_i}, \mathscr{D})]\}^2$ cannot be meaningfully estimated without access to the ground-truth $f(\overline{X_i})$. In the case of classification, since examples of the oracle function are available in the form of the dependent variable, one can approximately estimate the bias in some restricted settings. For example, in boosting, one typically uses low-variance base-detectors, and therefore the error term is approximated as the bias. This basic principle forms the raison d'etre of the success of boosting methods; we will discuss this point in detail later. This approach is difficult to replicate in outlier detection because of unavailability of ground truth.

Nevertheless, in spite of these challenges, one can still perform heuristic forms of bias reduction in unsupervised settings. The key idea in unsupervised settings is that the output of outlier detectors provide a kind of "weak" ground truth, which can be used in a limited way to define the steps required for bias improvement. Of course, this weak ground truth could, very easily, be wrong; in this sense, bias-reduction methods are always a guessing game in unsupervised problems like outlier detection. Because of this fact, these heuristic improvements do not always provide better results, although they are useful in many settings.

In this chapter, we will study several methods for bias reduction in outlier ensemble algorithms. Some of these methods proceed by integrating ensemble analysis with some form of pruning or weighting in order to improve the expected performance of the algorithm. In addition, certain combination functions are particularly effective in this context. We will also examine the use of outlier ensembles for bias reduction in the supervised setting. This technique reduces bias by feature engineering with unsupervised outlier detection algorithms. The use of supervision in various ways is a more reliable method for bias reduction. Although this book is primarily focused on unsupervised methods, this chapter will also investigate a number of ways in which mild forms of supervision can be used for bias reduction in outlier detection.

This chapter is organized as follows. In the next section, we will discuss the broad contours of the methods used for bias reduction in classification and their potential applicability to outlier detection. Methods for training data pruning are discussed in Sect. 4.3. Methods for model pruning are discussed in Sect. 4.4. Model weighting can be considered a soft version of model pruning in which high-quality models are given greater importance. The use of bias reduction in model weighting is discussed in Sect. 4.4.3. Most of the existing methods for model pruning can be extended relatively easily to model weighting. Unsupervised feature engineering methods for supervised outlier detection are discussed in Sect. 4.5. Bias reduction with the use of human supervision is discussed in Sect. 4.6. The conclusions are discussed in Sect. 4.7.

4.2 Bias Reduction in Classification and Outlier Detection

Although it is much harder to reduce bias in a controlled way in outlier detection, it is useful to examine some of the common methods for bias reduction in classification. This will also provide an understanding of how such methods can be leveraged in outlier detection. There are several common types of methods used in classification for bias reduction:

1. *Example re-weighting to correct model bias*: In this case, the basic idea is to use a low-variance model in which some of the examples are misclassified (due to the dominant bias component of the model). The weights of such examples are increased in future iterations to perform a bias correction of the model towards classifying such examples correctly. However, other examples which were classified correctly earlier might now be classified incorrectly. A linear combination of the various models is used to create the final ensemble. An example of a classification ensemble approach, which uses this principle, is *boosting* [15, 16, 21].

2. *Example pruning to remove noise*: In this case, examples are pruned or removed because they correspond to noise in the underlying data. The typical approach in classification is to identify mislabeled training data by using a consensus maximization approach [9]. Although this approach is not formally recognized as an ensemble method, it is indeed an ensemble technique in every sense of the word. A soft version of this method would simply weight the noisy examples less, although there are relatively few methods of this nature in the classification literature. Note that this approach can be viewed as the opposite of boosting in that it tends to *reduce* the weight of incorrectly classified training examples. The choice of the base method is crucial in deciding which approach works well. Approaches like boosting work well when the underlying model has low variance, whereas methods like example pruning work best with high-variance models that overfit the training data, and have extremely low bias. In such cases, mislabeled examples (included in the training data) often cannot be classified correctly even after allowing for some overfitting. Using the wrong base detector in either case can lead to disastrous results. Furthermore, the type of data set also has an effect on which approach works well. Boosting generally does not work very well for data sets with a lot of noise because the models tend to overfit the noisy examples and one tends to increase the weight of the bad (noisy) examples in later iterations.

3. *Model pruning to reduce bias*: Different models have different levels of bias on the data. By eliminating the models with very high bias, it is often possible to improve the bias performance of the ensemble. This basic principle is referred to [29, 43] as *"many could be better than all"* in the context of constructing ensembles of neural networks. Recently, the approach has also been used in the context of outlier detection. A very extreme case of this approach is referred to as the "bucket-of-models" technique [3] in which a single model is selected from the data with the greatest accuracy.

4. *Weighted model combination*: A soft version of model pruning is to weight the combination of models in order to down-weight models with poor bias

characteristics [29]. A variation of this approach, which uses Bayesian probabilities for weighting, is also referred to as Bayesian model averaging [12, 19]. In
classification, there are many models that use heuristic combinations of weights
in order to improve the classifier performance [34, 35, 42].

In the following, we will discuss these different methods in the context of classification, and the various ways in which they can be extended to outlier detection.

4.2.1 Boosting

Boosting [15, 16] is a method that uses re-weighting of the instances in order to
reduce the bias of a model. Minor variations of the approach can be used for either
classification or regression modeling. The key in boosting is to use a base model
that has high bias and low variance. For example, in the case of classification, one
would typically use a linear support vector machine (SVM) but never a kernel SVM.
Similarly, one might use a shallow decision tree (e.g., decision stump), but not a
deep decision tree. The goal is to ensure that the errors are caused by bias rather than
variance, when an example is inaccurately predicted.

The approach works iteratively by sequentially modifying the weights of the
examples for training. In the first iteration, the base model is trained. The training
examples that are misclassified (or inaccurately predicted in regression modeling)
are identified. The weights of examples that are inaccurately predicted are increased.
When the target variable is numeric, the increase in the weight of the example depends
on prediction accuracy. The basic assumption here is that the errors are caused by
the bias of the model, rather than the prediction variance or noise in the training data;
this also explains why such models always use low-variance methods. Therefore, the
weights of such examples need to be increased to ensure that the trained model in the
next iteration has lower bias on incorrectly predicted regions of the decision space.
This process is continually repeated, and the process is repeated for a minimum of
T iterations, or if the error rate on the training data drops to 0. The final ensemble
learner is a weighted combination of the base models, where the weight is decreasing
function of the error rate of prediction. By combining models with different bias
characteristics in different regions of the space, one is able to construct a decision
boundary, which is very different from that of the base learner. For example, it is
possible to construct a non-linear decision boundary in the boosted ensemble, while
using a linear SVM as the base learner. Boosting always uses low-variance models to
ensure that inaccuracy is primarily caused by the bias-centric effects of the detector.
This ensures that the increased weight of incorrectly classified training examples
does not lead to overfitting or the emphasis of noisy examples. In cases in which
these conditions are not satisfied, boosting can perform rather poorly because of
the overfitting and noise effects in the data [18]. Boosting methods have also been
used [11, 21] in the context of rare-class learning, which is the supervised analog of
outlier detection.

There are two major problems with using boosting for outlier detection:

1. Without the availability of ground-truth, it is often difficult to determine the error of the outlier score. Although it is possible, in principle, to use a committee of detectors as a robust approximation, the results can be uncertain. This issue is further exacerbated by a factor, which is discussed below.
2. Outlier detection models can be viewed as one-class models of normal points, even though the training data is contaminated with outlier points in the unsupervised setting. If the weights of any data points are increased, they will be automatically assumed to be normal points even if outlier points were misclassified as normal points in the previous iteration. This is different from the supervised setting, where labels are available, and the weights of points in either class can be increased. Given the greater uncertainty in knowing whether or not a point is an outlier point, such an approach can be counter-productive.

These challenges are natural consequences of the fact that boosting relies heavily on *reliable* bias quantification. Furthermore, boosting does not work very well when there is any type of uncertainty about the ground-truth or the source of the prediction error [16] (e.g., bias or variance). An unsupervised setting with missing labels can be viewed as the ultimate form of uncertainty in providing little guidance not only about the source of the error, but also the value of the error. As a result of these issues, it is often hard to generalize boosting to outlier detection in a straightforward way. Even though some methods for boosting have been proposed for 1-class SVMs [30], they rely on heuristic assumptions about the quality of separation between accepted and rejected points. Such assumptions may not be true for specific data sets, and they make the overall performance of the approach uncertain. Furthermore, 1-class SVMs are themselves known to make some assumptions, such as treating the origin as a prior, which makes the use of such approaches controversial in general [4, 10]. Experiments on text and other types of data [14, 26] show that one-class SVMs are notoriously sensitive to the specific representation used and often provide poor performance. In general, it makes little sense to use high-variance methods (like kernel methods) in techniques like boosting.

4.2.2 Training Data Pruning

The use of training data pruning is often leveraged to improve the performance of classifiers [9]. Interestingly, this approach is motivated by an earlier method for removing outliers from the data for regression analysis [38]. In this chapter, we further extend this approach towards formally designing an approach that removes outliers. The work in [9] designs methods to remove mislabeled data. There are many algorithms that are used in these settings:

1. *Single algorithm filters*: A decision-tree based approach was proposed in [20]. This approach uses the pruned leaf nodes of a decision tree. For each (pruned)

leaf node for which the training examples do not belong to the same class, those examples which belong to the minority class are pruned.

2. *Multi-algorithm sequential filters*: In this case, the idea is that one algorithm A serves as a good filter for the output of another algorithm B. Therefore, the training examples that are misclassified by algorithm A are removed. The pruned training data set is used for another algorithm B. For example, an approach in [39] uses a k-NN algorithm to filter the data for a 1-nearest neighbor algorithm.

3. *Ensemble filters*: In this case, an example is pruned if more than a certain percentage of classifiers predict it incorrectly.

Note that all these methods require knowledge of the ground-truth in order to implement them effectively. Nevertheless, some of the ideas underlying these methods can be generalized to outlier detection. The various ways in which these ideas can be generalized are as follows:

1. An outlier detector scores the instances by building a model of the normal data. Therefore, by pruning points with high outlier scores, a more robust model can be created. One can design either a single- or multi-algorithm filter to implement this approach.

2. Instead of using a single- or multi-algorithm filter, an ensemble filter can also be used to remove the instances with high scores, so that outlier points are removed from the model of normal data. In general, ensemble filters are more robust than single or multiple algorithm filters.

By filtering the outlier points, the expected scores of the outlier and non-outlier points are both reduced. As a result, the bias is reduced.

In the classification setting, the labels on the training examples are imperfect, and therefore the approach is viewed as a noise reduction method caused by such a mislabeling. Although this approach can be viewed as a noise reduction method in the classification setting, it can be viewed as a bias-reduction method in the unsupervised setting, since it is assumed that the unobserved outlier scores are ideal. Therefore, the error in the expected outlier scores can only be attributed to bias rather than any mislabeling. Methods for pruning the training data are discussed in Sect. 4.3.

4.2.3 Model Pruning

A complementary approach to training data pruning is that of model pruning. Just as it is desirable to prune bad training examples that hurt the performance, it is also desirable to prune bad models that hurt performance. Within the classification domain, this approach is also referred [29, 43] to as *"many-can-be-better-than-all"*. The basic idea is as follows. One can compute the expected cross-validation error using each of the models. Models with a very high level of error can be pruned because they are likely to have poor bias characteristics. However, many other methods are used in classification for pruning, which incorporate some forms of diversity as secondary goals. Many key pruning methods are classification are discussed in [29, 42].

In the context of outlier detection, the evaluation of the quality of a model is more challenging because of the fact that ground truth is not available. Nevertheless the output of an ensemble learner can sometimes be viewed as a low-bias model, especially when the individual detectors in the ensemble are diverse and have biases in different directions for a given test point. In such cases, the ensemble output can be viewed as a "weak" ground-truth, which can be used in a conservative way for model pruning. This basic idea was first proposed in [31]. It is important to be conservative with model pruning in such settings, because one can easily lose useful information by pruning too aggressively. Methods for model pruning in outlier detection are discussed in Sect. 4.4. Some forms of these models have already been studied as "less-is-more" models for outlier detection [31].

4.2.4 Model Weighting

Model weighting can be viewed as a less aggressive form of model pruning. Less aggressive forms of model pruning can be helpful in settings where there is a greater among of uncertainty. In unsupervised problems, there is always a greater level of uncertainty in the quality of a particular model because of the lack of ground truth. Common forms of model weighting in classification are as follows:

1. Test examples in which one is more certain of the prediction are weighted more heavily.
2. Models that provide low cross-validated error on the training data are weighted more heavily. The main difference from the previous case is that ground-truth is required for computing the error. This makes the implementation of such models more challenging in unsupervised settings like outlier detection.

It is noteworthy that all these forms of the model combination are performed at the final step. These basic ideas can be applied in outlier detection as follows:

1. Models whose outputs are more consistent with other models are weighted more heavily.
2. Outlier scores often show some heuristic characteristics, which tends to make specific combination functions more effective in identifying outliers. For example, the maximization combination function for outlier detection often reduces bias. However, the bias reduction is often at the expense of greater variance [5].

The model weighting techniques for bias reduction will be discussed under the general banner of model combination methods. These methods are discussed in detail in Sect. 4.4.3.

4.2.5 Differences Between Classification and Outlier Detection

At this point, we make a number of general observations about the differences between classification and outlier detection, which is a common theme among all the classes of methods discussed so far. In classification, the ground truth is usually available, and it is used to improve the bias characteristics of the underlying detector. In particular, detectors with high levels of error are also assumed to have high bias for stable detectors and less noisy data sets. Therefore, the computation of the error of the detector on a particular data point is almost always important for estimating the bias.

This is not the case in outlier detection, where such a ground-truth is not available. Therefore, one often uses the output of outlier detectors as a substitute for the ground-truth. As a result, there is an inherent circularity in the approach; the output of the ensemble is used to construct a simulated form of the ground truth, and then this simulated form of the ground-truth is used to improve the ensemble. The improvement of the ensemble may be achieved by modifying either the training data or the choice of detectors in the combination. This inherent circularity in the approach is illustrated in Fig. 4.1. In many cases, this type of circularity naturally leads to an iterative approach in which one uses the output of the algorithm as a kind of *artificial* ground-truth to refine the algorithm for future iterations. However, it is important to use the simulated forms of ground truth in a conservative way to prevent misleading outputs at intermediate stages of the approach from overwhelming the final output. As we will see later in this chapter, this type of broader approach is used in several bias reduction methods in the literature [31].

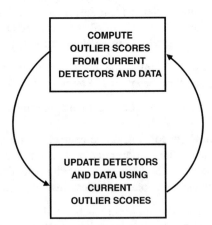

Fig. 4.1 The iterative process of bias reduction used by many outlier ensemble methods

4.3 Training Data Pruning

The notion of training data pruning was proposed as an ensemble method in [1, 5]. However, the discussions in [1, 5] are relatively limited, and they do not provide details of the various ways in which training data may be pruned. The main challenge in pruning data is that ground-truth is not available, and therefore one must be careful about being too aggressive while pruning outliers. There are several variations of this approach, depending on whether deterministic pruning is used, or whether biased sampling is used to emphasize certain types of outliers.

4.3.1 Deterministic Pruning

The simplest form of this approach is to remove the outliers using a deterministic algorithm. The points are then scored again using the pruned data. Therefore, this approach may be described as follows:

1. Use outlier detection algorithm $\mathscr{A}$ to score each point in $\mathscr{D}$.
2. Identify a set S from $\mathscr{D}$ which are scored as outliers using a conservative (high) confidence threshold. For example, one might select S as a set of points whose Z-values (of outlier scores) are greater than 3.
3. Score each point in $\mathscr{D}$ again with algorithm $\mathscr{A}$ by using the set $\mathscr{D} - S$ as the training data.
4. Report updated outlier scores of each point in $\mathscr{D}$.

Note that this is a single algorithm filter. The basic idea here is that by removing the outlier points, one is able to create a better model of the normal points, and therefore reduce the bias in outlier scores. Such techniques have been used in the past for iterative removal of outliers in two passes by refining the model of normal data [7]. Some variations of this approach have also been used in methods such as robust *PCA* [41], although it is formally not considered an ensemble method. Several variations of this basic approach are possible:

- It is important that the first phase of the approach does not make mistakes. A heterogeneous combination of base detectors can be used for both the first phase and the second phase to reduce errors.
- One can construct the initial model with one algorithm $\mathscr{A}$, but perform the final scoring with another algorithm $\mathscr{B}$. Therefore, the two-phase approach uses two different models in the two phases.
- Instead of using a two-phase approach, one might use an iterative technique to score the detectors in which the outliers are iteratively removed from the data in order to create successively refined models.

The iterative technique requires some further explanation. In the iterative technique, we do not remove the outliers in one shot. Rather, the steps of removal are repeated again and again, until convergence is achieved. The basic goal here is to incrementally refine the model so that the outliers removed in the current iteration are more accurately defined than those removed in the previous iteration. This is primarily because the model of normal data often improves from iteration to iteration as more outliers are removed. Therefore, the incremental version of the approach may be described as follows:

1. Use outlier detection algorithm $\mathscr{A}$ to score each point in $\mathscr{D}$.
2. Identify a set S from $\mathscr{D}$ which are scored as outliers using a conservative (high) confidence threshold. For example, one might select S as a set of points whose Z-values (of outlier scores) are greater than 3.
3. Score each point in $\mathscr{D}$ again with algorithm $\mathscr{A}$ by using the set $\mathscr{D} - S$ as the training data.
4. **Convergence check**: If S has changed significantly since last iteration, then goto step 2.
5. Report current outlier scores of each point in $\mathscr{D}$, which were scored in the last iteration before convergence.

The main advantage of the iterative technique is that the model becomes successively more refined in later iterations. Such an approach is likely to be especially effective when the base detector is reliable. Otherwise, it is possible for the approach to be misled by errors made in earlier iterations. However, using multiple phases instead of two phases has the advantage that the outlier removal process is gentler. As a result, it becomes less likely to make mistakes in earlier iteration. This, in turn, also results in fewer mistakes in later iterations.

4.3.2   Fixed Bias Sampling

One problem with most bias reduction methods is that they are often heuristic and are not guaranteed to improve the bias characteristics. On the other hand, variance-reduction methods almost always provide some improvements. It is possible to combine the outlier removal approach in the previous section with variance reduction methods to further improve accuracy. The basic idea is to use the outlier scores to bias the sampling process so that data points are *weighted* rather than *removed*. The scores are used to compute the probability that a data point is an outlier. The cumulative normal distribution is used to convert the Z-value into a probability that a data point is an outlier.

Consider a data set $\mathscr{D}$ containing n data points. Let $s(i)$ be the outlier score of the ith data point. The first step is to compute the mean μ and standard deviation σ of $s(i)$. The scores are then converted to the Z-values $z(1) \ldots z(n)$ as follows:

$$\mu = \frac{\sum_{i=1}^{n} s(i)}{n}$$

$$\sigma = \sqrt{\frac{\sum_{i=1}^{n} (s(i) - \mu)^2}{n - 1}}$$

$$z(i) = \frac{s(i) - \mu}{\sigma} \quad \forall i \in \{1 \ldots n\}$$

The cumulative normal distribution is applied to $z(i)$ to determine the fraction β_i of the standard normal distribution that is larger than z_i. Note that z_i can be either negative or positive. For negative values of z_i, the value of β_i is greater than 0.5. Subsequently, a similar approach to subsampling is used, except that the points are sampled in a biased way from the base data. The probability of sampling point i is proportional to β_i. Therefore, the approach starts with one full application of the base detector to compute the Z-scores, which are converted to $\beta_1 \ldots \beta_n$ with the help of the cumulative normal distribution. Subsequently, these learned values of $\beta_1 \ldots \beta_n$ are used to bias the sampling as follows:

1. Sample a fraction f of the data set $\mathscr{D}$, where the probability of selecting the ith point is proportional to β_i.
2. Score each point using an outlier detector on the subsampled data.

Note that the fraction f is a parameter to the approach, as in subsampling. This base detector is repeatedly applied, and the scores are converted to Z-values. The Z-values of the scores are then averaged over the various biased samples. Therefore, the first phase of the approach is used only to learn the sampling biases, and the subsequent biased ensembles are generated with these learned probability values.

Note that each base detector in the biased sampling method can be implemented only after a first phase of scoring in order to compute $\beta_1 \ldots \beta_n$. One can use a simple application of the base detector to compute $\beta_1 \ldots \beta_n$ (as discussed in Sect. 4.3.1). In other words, we apply the base detector once to compute the outlier scores, and then convert them into Z-values. These Z-values are converted into the probabilities $\beta_1 \ldots \beta_n$ by applying the cumulative normal distribution to them (as discussed in the previous section). A natural question arises as to how one might perform the sampling of fraction f of the points with bias values of $\beta_1 \ldots \beta_n$ for the various points in $\mathscr{D}$. Assuming that the values $\beta_1 \ldots \beta_n$ are provided, this is achieved using the following approach:

1. Define $\gamma_i = \frac{\sum_{j=1}^{i} \beta_j}{\sum_{j=1}^{n} \beta_j}$ for each $i \in \{1 \ldots n\}$ and define $V = \{\}$.
2. Sample r uniformly at random from $(0, 1)$.
3. Determine the largest value of i such that $r < \gamma_i$
4. If the ith point of $\mathscr{D}$ has not yet been added to V, then add the point to V.
5. If V contains $f \cdot n$ points then terminate; else go to step 2.

The main advantage of the sampling approach is that it is able to combine bias reduction with variance reduction. By using sampling, and then averaging the scores, it is possible to reduce the randomness in the final results.

4.3.3 Variable Bias Sampling

One of the disadvantages of fixed bias sampling is that the base detectors become less
diverse. This is because data points with small values of β_i have low probability of
being selected because they are deemed outliers. As a result, the bias characteristics
might improve but the selection of similar subsets of points will limit the variance
reduction advantages. Furthermore, in unsupervised problems, it is hard to fully
control the bias characteristics in any particular setting. In such cases, the ensemble
can get hit be the double whammy of poor bias characteristics and low diversity;
such a trap can become the graveyard of an ensemble method.

A natural solution to address these challenges is to increase the level of diversity
of various samples. The idea is to include a portion of the points that are subsampled
completely at random, and another portion that are subsampled in a biased way. The
proportion of each type of sampling is allowed to vary with the ensemble component.
Such an approach creates additional diversity. Therefore, each base detector of this
approach may be described as follows:

1. **Initialization**: Compute the base detector once on the original data to score the
   points. Convert the outlier scores into Z-scores, and apply the cumulative normal
   distribution on Z-scores to compute outlier probabilities $\beta_1 \ldots \beta_n$.
2. **Iterative sampling step**: Select α uniformly at random from $(0, 1)$.
3. Determine an (unbiased) subsample V_1 of size $\alpha \cdot f \cdot n$ from the original data
   set $\mathscr{D}$.
4. Sample a fraction $(1 - \alpha) \cdot f$ of the data set $\mathscr{D}$, where the probability of selecting
   the ith point is proportional to β_i. Denote this set of points by V_2.
5. Apply the base detector on the subsample of size $f \cdot n$ to score each point. Convert
   to Z-scores.
6. Compute the average Z-scores over all iterations so far. Re-compute $\beta_1 \ldots \beta_n$ by
   applying cumulative normal distribution on averaged Z-score.
7. If more iterations are required, then go to step 2 (iterative sampling step).

At the end of the process, the averaged Z-score is reported. Another difference from
the approach discussed in the previous section is that the values of $\beta_1 \ldots \beta_n$ are
computed iteratively as new outlier scores are computed. Therefore, the estimates
of the bias also changes with time, and further add to the diversity of the various
detectors.

An implementation of this basic idea, referred to as *Filtered Variable Probability
Sampling (FVPS)*, is proposed in [33]. This approach uses variable subsampling in
which the size of the subsample is varied in the same way as discussed in [5]. The
additional step of explicitly filtering the top outliers included in the approach. This
approach uses the following steps:

1. Filter the top outliers found in the previous execution of the base detector. The
   base detector is computed using the biased subsample of the previous iteration.
2. Sample between 50 and 1000 points from the remaining (filtered) data (with the
   data size imposing natural limits on subsample size). The points are sampled

proportionally to their probability of being normal in the previous iteration. Any of a number of probabilistic modeling techniques such as those in [17] can be applied on a point to determine its probability of being normal.
3. Build a base detector on the filtered data.

At the end of the process, the scores from the different detectors are averaged to yield the final result. Another independent work (published at almost the same time) that performs bias reduction with the use of biased sampling is discussed in [37].

4.4 Model Pruning

In model pruning, the basic idea is that ensemble components, which have poor bias characteristics, often have a detrimental effect on the overall result quality. Therefore, it is crucial to remove the poorly behaving components from the ensemble. The basic idea is that ensemble components that vary significantly from the majority behavior are often a result of poor performance of the base detection. Therefore, they should be removed from consideration.

There have been a variety of other methods that have been used in the literature for selective ensemble combination some of which explicitly reduce bias whereas others implicitly reduce bias. An important such technique is the method referred to as *SELECT* [31], which is designed to remove the poorly behaving model components from the ensemble. It is been shown in [32], how the *SELECT* method is a form of bias reduction. Although the *SELECT* algorithm is proposed in a temporal setting, it is possible to envisage scenarios in which it is used in a non-temporal setting.

Before discussing *SELECT* in detail, we first discuss a primitive version of this scheme.

1. Normalize the scores from each detector. One may use any normalization method, although the approach in [32] uses the technique in [17]. Let the normalized score of the ith point for the jth detector be $O(i, j)$.
2. Compute the average score $a_i = \sum_{j=1}^{m} O(i, j)/m$ of the ith point over all ensemble components.
3. Remove any detector whose vectors of scores deviates significantly from the averaged vector of scores.
4. Report the consensus score of the remaining detectors as the final score.

Note that the final two steps of selection and consensus can be executed in a variety of different ways. The particular choices used by the *SELECT* approach are as follows.

- For selection, it uses two different strategies referred to as *vertical selection* and *horizontal selection*, respectively. Furthermore, the selection process does not remove the poorly performing base detectors in one shot. Rather, the pseudo-ground truth of all detectors is used only for the initial ranking of various detectors. Subsequently, the detectors are added iteratively to an initially empty set $\mathcal{L}$, and the ground-truth is correspondingly updated. In each iteration, the detector which is best correlated to the current ensemble score of $\mathscr{L}$ is added to the ensemble $\mathscr{L}$. We will discuss these methods later in this chapter.

- The scores are then combined with the use of a consensus method. Both rank-wise averaging and score-wise averaging methods are used. In the case of score-wise averaging, a mixture modeling approach is used in order to normalize the scores before averaging them.

In the following, we provide an overview of various selection and score combination strategies. Furthermore, we present a simplified version of the basic idea in order to abstract out the key ideas from the low-level details. The broader approach can, of course, be implemented in a variety of different ways.

In vertical forms of model selection, the idea is to select the detectors based on their correlations with the pseudo-ground truth. The first step is to create a pseudo-ground truth by combining the scores of *all* the detectors. The precise method for model combination depends on the domain at hand, although virtually any of the score combination methods discussed in Chaps. 1 and 5 can be used. Let this pseudo-ground truth be denoted by G. For the purpose of this discussion, we assume that averaging may be used. Furthermore, since the detectors may have outputs on different scales (if different algorithms are used), all scores need to be normalized. Virtually any method such as the Z-value may be used, although other methods are discussed in Chap. 1.

We initialize the list $\mathscr{L}$ of selected detectors to be the empty set. Subsequently, all detectors are sorted in order of their correlation with the pseudo-ground truth G. The first step is to add the detector with the highest correlation to the pseudo-ground truth as the first element of the list $\mathscr{L}$. Subsequently, the following greedy approach is iteratively used:

1. Compute the ensemble prediction $\hat{P}(\mathscr{L})$ of $\mathscr{L}$ based on all detectors in $\mathscr{L}$. For example, an average of the normalized scores of each point over various detectors may be used to compute the predicted score of each point.
2. Sort all detectors not in $\mathscr{L}$ based on the correlations of their outputs to $\hat{P}(\mathscr{L})$. The Pearson correlation coefficient is used in [31].
3. If $\hat{P}(\mathscr{L} \cup D)$ is better correlated to the pseudo-ground truth G than $\hat{P}(\mathscr{L})$, then add the top correlated detector D to $\mathscr{L}$. Otherwise, terminate the addition process and report $\mathscr{L}$.

At termination, the value $\hat{P}(\mathscr{L})$ is used for prediction. It is noteworthy that this approach tends to select more correlated detectors, which works *against* variance reduction. On the other hand, the removal of poorly performing base detectors can improve the bias characteristics of the approach.

The vertical selection method focuses on *all* the points when computing correlations. The horizontal selection method focuses only on the anomalous points while computing the relationships between the various detectors. Therefore, in this case, the binary labeling of points into anomalies is used rather than the scores. In general, any statistical thresholding on the scores can yield binary labels. However, the work in [31] uses the mixture-modeling approach proposed in [17] in order to convert the score list from every detector into a binary label. For each outlier point, its ranks are computed across the different detectors. Detectors in which many (pseudo) ground-truth outlier points are ranked very highly are selected. The work in [31] uses a method based on order-statistics to provide a crisp criterion. The basic idea in horizontal selection is that the top-ranked points are more important than the entire list because the anomalies are selected only from the top-ranked points.

For score combination, a variety of score-wise and rank-wise aggregation methods are used. Note that these combination methods are useful not just for the final step of consensus construction, but also within the intermediate steps of creating ensemble predictions. For rank-wise aggregation, a variety of robust rank aggregation methods can be used [13, 23, 24]. For score-wise methods, the main point to keep in mind is to always normalize the scores, so that the heterogeneous scores from diverse detectors can be meaningfully combined. The simplest approach would be to use Z-values, although the work in [31] suggests using other (more complex) methods, such as the score combination methods discussed in [17].

It is noteworthy that such bias reduction methods are essentially a "guessing game" in outlier ensemble analysis. This is because the pseudo ground-truth used by these methods is constructed by using the same algorithms, which are then scored for selection. Clearly, if only a small fraction of the algorithms provide accurate results, it is often possible for the pseudo-ground truth to poorly reflect the outlier scores. In such cases, the selection process can actually harm the ensemble because the (incorrect) ground-truth was used in the selection process. For example, if the very first iteration picks the wrong detector (because the initial pseudo ground-truth is poor), then subsequent additions to this singleton set $\mathscr{L}$ might be increasingly misled by the first mistake. The implicit assumption here is that the majority of methods provide reasonable quality results; therefore, the pseudo ground-truth is useful for the selection process.

Another point to be kept in mind is the choice of correlated detectors in [31]. Although choosing correlated detectors can be helpful in reducing bias, it does have the drawback of not being able to reduce variance. This approach will work best when most of the detectors are of a high quality, and a few detectors behave particularly poorly. This is because this approach depends on the use of the pseudo-ground truth in a crucial way. This type of ground truth will be robust mostly in settings where the vast majority of the detectors are of high quality. On the other hand, if the lower quality is a result of high variance, then choosing correlated detectors might not be helpful. This is, of course, not a specific weakness of the method in [31]. In general, bias reduction methods rely on assumptions about "typical" behavior of detectors; in many cases, such assumptions might be warranted, whereas in others they might not be warranted. It is always helpful to have some understanding of the behavior of outlier detectors on a specific data domain, before choosing to use a particular type of bias-reduction method.

4.4.1   Implicit Model Pruning in Subspace Outlier Detection

An implicit level of model pruning is also performed in the context of subspace outlier detection methods [6]. The original feature bagging method is purely a (model-
centric) variance-reduction method [25]. In this case, the subspaces are selected
randomly from the data. However, several later methods such as HiCS [22] and OUT-
RES [28], suggest that it made sense to bias the subspace sampling process towards
projections that were more likely to contain outliers. For example, the HiCS method
executes a statistical test to estimate the non-uniformity of a subspace. Nonuniform
subspaces are those in which the density differs significantly from the expected density on the basis of attribute-wise independence. It is assumed that such an approach
biases the selection towards subspaces that are more likely to be informative.

Such methods implicitly incorporate bias reduction in a heuristic way through the
selection process. At the same time, they also reduce the variance because they average the scores of points obtained from reasonably diverse subspaces. One can view
these methods as subspace versions of the *"many-could-be-better-than-all"* principle [43], which is known to reduce bias. However, because outlier detection is an
unsupervised problems the corresponding model selection is done in more heuristic
way in the context of outlier detection. Unfortunately, such heuristics are often computationally expensive, and they do not always work in a particular problem setting.
Similarly, many methods [6] that implicitly use the maximization combination for
subspace outlier detection can also be viewed as heuristic bias reduction methods.
For example, the approach in [6] uses only those views of the data discovered by
the genetic algorithm, which are locally sparse beyond a particular threshold. This
can be viewed as a form of subspace pruning. This issue is explained in detail in [4]
and also in Sect. 5.5 of Chap. 5. In that chapter, it is described how the maximization
combination function provides a heuristic combination that can sometimes reduce
bias, albeit at the occasional expense of increased variance.

4.4.2   Revisiting Pruning by Trimming

Another special case of computing the deviation is the methodology of the thresholded trimming (cf. Sect. 3.6 of Chap. 3), which incorporates some of these aspects
of bias reduction. In this case, the final step of model pruning is executed as follows:

1. Compute the aggregate detector deviation $\Delta_j = \sum_{i=1}^{n} |O(i, j) - a_i|$ from the
   mean score.
2. Standardize $\Delta_1 \ldots \Delta_m$ to zero mean and unit variance.
3. Exclude any detector j for which $\Delta_j > 3$. Compute the adjusted average a_i' of
   the scores of each point over the remaining detectors.

This scheme can be viewed as a very simple way of performing bias reduction by
removing the ensemble components that deviate significantly from the normal behavior. Even in methods like subsampling, such variations from the normal behavior are

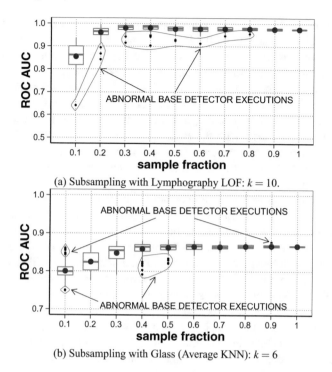

(a) Subsampling with Lymphography LOF: $k = 10$.

(b) Subsampling with Glass (Average KNN): $k = 6$

Fig. 4.2 Most of the abnormal performances are below the box-plot. This is typical in such settings, especially when the underlying data sets are small. This is the same as Fig. 3.18 of the previous chapter

often present. For example, we have replicated Fig. 3.18 from the previous chapter in Fig. 4.2. In this case, the ensemble components are constructed using subsamples from the original data. The area-under-curve (AUC) performance of the receiver operating characteristics (ROC) (with respect to the known ground-truth) is shown as a box-plot. Therefore, even though the ensemble components are probabilistically identical, there are a few ensemble components that deviate significantly from the model of normal behavior. Furthermore, most of the deviations typically lie at the lower end of the box-plot rather than at the upper end. This is common in such setting, although it is not guaranteed. Therefore, from a *heuristic point of view*, it is often desirable to remove the poorly performing detectors. Unfortunately, since the ground truth is not available in real settings, it is not possible to know which ensemble components perform well and which ones perform poorly. However, it is possible to find the detectors, which differ significantly from the average performance by using purely the scores. Unfortunately, it is often possible to lose highly performing detectors along with poorly performing ones when the scores are used instead of the ground-truth. This is, of course, a natural risk in all bias-reduction methods. Indeed, as shown in the previous chapter, this particular method does not work very well when applied to a set of detectors derived from using the same algorithm on subsamples of the data. We believe that these poor results may be a symptom of the reduction in diversity caused by the trimming approach. This is a challenge associated with many bias reduction methods in which heuristic improvements in bias are often accompanied with loss of diversity or increased variance.

The trimming method is related to the *SELECT* scheme. However, the difference is that the *SELECT* scheme uses the pseudo ground-truth to identify the first detector in the ensemble list. Subsequently, new detectors are *added* to the list based on their correlation *similarity* with the ensemble average of current list. In trimming, one works backwards and *removes* detectors from the global list based on their *dissimilarity* with the current list. Furthermore, the trimming is done in one shot rather than in iterative fashion.

Although the trimming scheme does not seem to work very well (as compared to the *SELECT* results reported in [31]), it is fair to say that our tests in the previous chapter used a very different setting than *SELECT* and it also used different types of data sets. While *SELECT* used heterogeneous base detectors, our tests in the previous chapter derived the base detectors using subsampling with a single algorithm. Furthermore, the *SELECT* scheme is designed for time-series data, whereas our trimming tests in the previous chapter were based on multidimensional data. The algorithm in the two cases is also different in terms of the specific details. It is possible that the differences in performance may be attributed to the difference in setting or to the difference in algorithm, although we did not test all the variations in a detailed way. It does need to be kept in mind that model selection leads to a loss of diversity, which has a detrimental effect on ensemble performance. We leave further tests on trimming and model selection to future work on bias reduction.

4.4.3   Model Weighting

In weighted model averaging, the basic idea is that the different models are weighted in a differential way in order to provide more importance to the accurate models. This approach can be considered a soft version of model pruning. Although such methods have not been discussed extensively in the literature, it is relatively easy to convert model pruning methods to model weighting methods. For example, instead of pruning detectors based on their correlation to the pseudo-ground truth, one can weight detectors based on their correlation with the pseudo-ground truth. Detectors with higher levels of correlations with the ground truth are given larger weights, whereas detectors with smaller correlations are given lower weights. Furthermore, the weighting may even be chosen to be a heuristic function of these correlations. Although such methods have not been tested extensively in the literature, the prior experience with model pruning suggests that the use of model weighting may be fruitful in many settings. Nevertheless, an increased weight of such detectors is achieved at the expense of diversity; reduction in diversity is generally not beneficial for outlier detection. Therefore, the overall effectiveness of such a scheme will depend on how well the model weighting process emphasizes the accurate detectors.

A particularly interesting idea in this direction is the *relevance weighted ensemble* in the temporal setting [36]. The basic idea here is that temporal data streams vary in terms of their patterns. For example, the patterns during the morning might not be the same as the patterns during the evening. Therefore, the model of normal data might also change with time. In the relevance-weighted ensemble, the various models are weighted according to their relevance to the current time. The relevance weight is decided based on the similarity in the modeling patterns in the various time-periods.

4.5 Supervised Bias Reduction with Unsupervised Feature Engineering

The majority of this book is devoted to the problem of unsupervised outlier ensembles. This section is a notable exception because unsupervised outlier ensembles are used as a route for feature engineering in rare class detection problems [27].

Rare class detection is the supervised avatar of the outlier detection problem in which information is provided about the class labels (outlier or non-outlier) of data instances. When labels are available, the accuracy of learning algorithms almost always improves. Therefore, supervised methods are always viewed as a valid substitute to unsupervised methods when labels are available. Therefore, at first sight, it would seem that unsupervised methods become useless when labels are available for rare class detection.

However, the answer is not quite as simple, because one can still use representation learning methods with unsupervised outlier detection problems in order to engineer the features into a representation that is more friendly to the learning of rare classes. Representation learning methods [8] are often performed with supervised and unsupervised learning techniques. However, when the amount of training data is small, it often makes sense to use unsupervised methods. In the rare class setting, the amount of training data belonging to the rare class is typically small. Therefore, it makes sense to use unsupervised feature engineering methods.

What type of unsupervised methods make the most sense in the rare-class setting? In this context, the scores of outlier detection algorithms are unsupervised methods that detect "typical" anomalies in real-world settings. Very often, the use of a classifier on the original representation may have model-centric bias that can be reduced with the use of an engineered feature representation. This is the *representational bias* discussed in Chap. 3. In order to understand this point, consider a rare class learning setting in which the pareto-extremes of the data represent outliers. This situation is actually quite common in such settings because anomaly detection and extreme value analysis are intimately related. For example, it might be possible that most points at a large distance from the data mean might be outliers. If one makes the mistake of using a linear support vector machine for this problem, it will almost always result in huge model bias because the decision boundary of this setting is certainly not linear. However, if one used a simple outlier detector such as the Euclidean or Mahalanobis distance from the centroid of the data as one of the engineered features, the data can become (roughly) linearly separable on this feature alone. Therefore, the use of this new feature representation greatly reduces the bias of the classifier.

In general, the scores of outlier detection algorithms have been constructed over the years by researchers and practitioners by testing them over various rare class problems. The bench-marking data sets and evaluation measures of unsupervised outlier detection and rare class detection are identical. Therefore, it is reasonable to believe that the outlier scores encapsulate a (problem) domain-specific understanding of the rare class detection problem. This is *precisely* the kind of features that work well in feature engineering settings.

The work in [27] extracts the outlier scores from different outlier detection algorithms. In addition, different parameter settings of the same algorithm and the outlier scores from different feature bags can be used. This will typically result in a high-dimensional representation of highly correlated features. Many of these features may also be relevant. Therefore, it is crucial to use regularization methods in order to reduce overfitting. In particular, one can use L_1-regularized logistic regression in order to learn the model relating the engineered features to the class label. The use of L_1-regularization also has the implicit effect of feature selection because the coefficients of many of the features are automatically set to 0.

It is also possible to interpret this method from the point of view of outlier ensembles rather than feature engineering. In unsupervised outlier detection, one only uses either a single unsupervised algorithm or a simple average of the scores of these algorithms as the final result because of the inability to perform model selection. However, when labels are available, model selection becomes more possible. Therefore, one can also interpret this approach as an outlier ensemble approach in which a supervised methodology is used for model combination and selection. In such a case, the approach also reduces bias from the point of view of the unsupervised ensemble because of the ability to perform supervised model selection on the ensemble of unsupervised outlier scores. This type of feature engineering is also used by generating each feature in a supervised way. For example, the idea of *stacking* [40] generates each feature with the execution of a classifier on an instance. However, in the method discussed in this section, the features are generated with the use of unsupervised methods.

4.6 Bias Reduction by Human Intervention

Outlier detection is inherently an unsupervised problem in which bias reduction is generally difficult to perform in a controlled way. Human intervention is a natural way to incorporate bias in the process, and one can also view it as a mild form of supervision. Such an approach is the most reliable way of reducing bias, because one is effectively using domain or ground-truth knowledge, albeit in a mild way. There are several ways in which bias can be reduced with human intervention.

1. *Human intervention for selecting relevant ensemble components*: In this case, the results returned by different ensemble components are visually examined by the analyst. A variety of visualization tools, such as scatterplots (or domain knowledge), can be used to identify cases in which the outlier detection algorithm returns high-quality results. In most cases, the user might examine only the top-k outliers returned by each algorithm in order to create a measure of accuracy. The value of k can be a small number such as 20. The poorly performing algorithms can then be removed from the mix of ensemble components. Such an approach will often reduce bias.

2. *Human intervention for selecting model combination methods*: As discussed in Chaps. 1, 3, and 5, the scores of outlier detection algorithms can be combined in various ways such as the averaging and the maximum. Furthermore, it is evident from the experimental results in Chap. 3 that there are large differences in the performance between the various techniques for model combination in different data sets. For example, in one data set, the averaging combination might work well, whereas in another data set, the maximization combination might work well. In such cases, it makes sense to use the same approach of examining the top-k outliers returned by each model combination method on a particular data set. The method that provides the best accuracy on a particular data set is then used. It is also possible to combine this approach with the methodology discussed above for selecting the ensemble components. These methods can be viewed as variants of model-selection methods that use intervention.

3. *Human intervention for converting unsupervised outlier detection to supervised methods*: In many cases, human intervention can be paired with ensemble methods in order to label data points. This is closely related to the problem of *active learning* [2]. The basic idea is to use an ensemble of methods and identify the top-k outliers returned by each of these methods. One can also use the majority vote from an ensemble of different outlier detection methods in order to identify the anomalies in a more robust way. These data points are then visually examined by the analyst and labeled as outliers and non-outliers. In addition, a small random sample of the data is labeled. Once this initial labeling has been done, an active learning approach is used to iteratively label more and more points. Subsequently, supervised classification methods are used on the data in order to identify anomalous data points.

The active learning approach has significant potential, although it is important to use multiple outlier detection algorithms in the first phase in order to identify different types of outliers. In general, combining supervised and unsupervised methods is often valuable in improving the effectiveness of various outlier detection methods.

4.7   Conclusions

Bias reduction is a challenging problem in outlier ensemble analysis because the ground truth is not available. The unavailability of ground truth leads to numerous challenges in the analytical process. Therefore, most bias reduction methods in outlier ensemble analysis are highly heuristic in nature. The idea behind many of these methods is to use an earlier phase of the data analysis to make guesses on the model of the normal data. These guesses are then used to build a more robust model, which is leveraged for outlier detection. A more robust model is usually constructing by either pruning noisy data, or by pruning poorly behaved ensemble components. A soft version of pruning is weighting. Most of the weighting-based methods are closely related to the pruning-based methods. The main danger in bias reduction models is that the heuristic methods often do not work very well for all data sets. As a result, the final results may sometimes be unexpected. Supervised feature engineering methods can also be used for bias reduction in the rare class setting. Furthermore, mild forms of human supervision may also be helpful in reducing bias in a controlled way.

Exercises

1. Suppose you had an oracle, which could tell you the ROC AUC of any particular outlier detection algorithm and you are allowed only 10 queries to this oracle. Show how you can combine this oracle with a subsampling method to reduce bias. [Hint: The answer to this question is not unique.]
2. Implement the biased subsampling method discussed in this chapter.

References

1. C. C. Aggarwal. Outlier Ensembles: Position Paper, *ACM SIGKDD Explorations*, 14(2), pp. 49–58, December, 2012.
2. C. C. Aggarwal. Active Learning: A Survey. *Data Classification: Algorithms and Applications*, CRC Press, 2014.
3. C. C. Aggarwal Data Mining: The Textbook, *Springer*, 2015.
4. C. C. Aggarwal. Outlier Analysis, Second Edition, *Springer*, 2017.
5. C. C. Aggarwal and S. Sathe. Theoretical Foundations and Algorithms for Outlier Ensembles, *ACM SIGKDD Explorations*, 17(1), June 2015.
6. C. C. Aggarwal and P. S. Yu. Outlier Detection in High Dimensional Data, *ACM SIGMOD Conference*, 2001.
7. D. Barbara, Y. Li, J. Couto, J.-L. Lin, and S. Jajodia. Bootstrapping a Data Mining Intrusion Detection System. *Symposium on Applied Computing*, 2003.
8. Y. Bengio, A. Courville, and P. Vincent. Representation learning: A Review and New Perspectives. *IEEE Transactions on Pattern Analysis and Machine Intelligence*, 35(8), pp. 1798–1828, 2013.
9. C. Brodley and M. Friedl. Identifying Mislabeled Training Data. *Journal of Artificial Intelligence Research*, pp. 131–167, 1999.

10. C. Campbell, and K. P. Bennett. A Linear-Programming Approach to Novel Class Detection. *Advances in Neural Information Processing Systems*, 2000.

11. N. Chawla, A. Lazarevic, L. Hall, and K. Bowyer. SMOTEBoost: Improving prediction of the minority class in boosting, *PKDD*, pp. 107–119, 2003.

12. P. Domingos. Bayesian Averaging of Classifiers and the Overfitting Problem. *ICML Conference*, 2000.

13. C. Dwork, R. Kumar, M. Naor, and D. Sivakumar. Rank aggregation methods for the Web. *WWW Conference*, 2001.

14. A. Emmott, S. Das, T. Dietterich, A. Fern, and W. Wong. Systematic Construction of Anomaly Detection Benchmarks from Real Data. arXiv:1503.01158, 2015. https://arxiv.org/abs/1503. 01158

15. Y. Freund and R. Schapire. A Decision-theoretic Generalization of Online Learning and Application to Boosting, *Computational Learning Theory*, 1995.

16. Y. Freund and R. Schapire. Experiments with a New Boosting Algorithm. *ICML Conference*, pp. 148–156, 1996.

17. J. Gao, P.-N. Tan. Converting output scores from outlier detection algorithms into probability estimates. *ICDM Conference*, 2006.

18. https://www.cs.cmu.edu/afs/cs/project/jair/pub/volume11/opitz99a-html/node14.html

19. J. Hoeting, D. Madigan, A. Raftery, and C. Volinsky. Bayesian Model Averaging: A Tutorial. *Statistical Science*, 14(4), pp. 382–401, 1999.

20. G. John. Robust Decision Trees: Removing Outliers from Data. *KDD Conference*, pp. 174–179, 1995.

21. M. Joshi, V. Kumar, and R. Agarwal. Evaluating Boosting Algorithms to Classify Rare Classes: Comparison and Improvements. *ICDM Conference*, pp. 257–264, 2001.

22. F. Keller, E. Muller, K. Bohm. HiCS: High-Contrast Subspaces for Density-based Outlier Ranking, *IEEE ICDE Conference*, 2012.

23. J. Kemeny. Mathematics without numbers. *Daedalus*, pp. 577591, 1959.

24. R. Kolde, S. Laur, P. Adler, and J. Vilo. Robust rank aggregation for gene list integration and meta-analysis. *Bioinformatics*, 28(4), pp. 573–580, 2012.

25. A. Lazarevic, and V. Kumar. Feature Bagging for Outlier Detection, *ACM KDD Conference*, 2005.

26. L. M. Manevitz and M. Yousef. One-class SVMs for Document Classification. *Journal of Machine Learning Research*, 2: pp, 139–154, 2001.

27. B. Micenkova, B. McWiliams, and I. Assent. Learning Outlier Ensembles: The Best of Both Worlds – Supervised and Unsupervised. *Outlier Detection and Description Workshop*, 2014. Extended version: http://arxiv.org/pdf/1507.08104v1.pdf

28. E. Muller, M. Schiffer, and T. Seidl. Statistical Selection of Relevant Subspace Projections for Outlier Ranking. *ICDE Conference*, pp, 434–445, 2011.

29. M. Perrone and L. Cooper. When Networks Disagree: Ensemble Method for Neural networks. *Artifical Neural Networks for Speech and Vision*, Chapman and Hall, pp. 126–142, 1993.

30. G. Ratsch, S. Mika, B. Scholkopf, K. Muller. Constructing boosting algorithms from SVMs: an application to one-class classification. *IEEE Transactions on Pattern Analysis and Machine Intelligence*, 24(9), pp. 1184–1199, 2002.

31. S. Rayana, L. Akoglu. Less is More: Building Selective Anomaly Ensembles with Application to Event Detection in Temporal Graphs. *SDM Conference*, 2015.

32. S. Rayana, L. Akoglu. Less is More: Building Selective Anomaly Ensembles. *ACM Transactions on Knowledge Discovery and Data Mining*, 10(4), 42, 2016.

33. S. Rayana, W. Zhong, and L. Akoglu. Sequential Ensemble Learning for Outlier Detection: A Bias-Variance Perspective. *IEEE ICDM Conference*, 2016.

34. L. Rokach. Pattern classification using ensemble methods, *World Scientific Publishing Company*, 2010.

35. G. Seni and J. Elder. Ensemble Methods in Data Mining: Improving Accuracy through Combining Predictions, Synthesis Lectures in Data Mining and Knowledge Discovery, *Morgan and Claypool*, 2010.

36. M. Salehi, C. Leckie, M. Moshtaghi, and T. Vaithianathan. A Relevance Weighted Ensemble Model for Anomaly Detection in Switching Data Streams. *Advances in Knowledge Discovery and Data Mining*, pp. 461–473, 2014.

37. M. Salehi, X. Zhang, J. Bezdek, and C. Leckie. Smart Sampling: A Novel Unsupervised Boosting Approach for Outlier Detection. *Australasian Joint Conference on Artificial Intelligence*, Springer, pp. 469–481, 2016. http://rd.springer.com/book/10.1007/978-3-319-50127-7

38. S. Weisberg. Applied Linear Regression. *John Wiley and Sons*, 1985.

39. D. Wilson. Asymptotic Properties of Nearest-Neighbor Rules using Edited Data. *Man and Cybernetics*, 2, pp. 408–421, 1972.

40. D. Wolpert. Stacked Generalization, *Neural Networks*, 5(2), pp. 241–259, 1992.

41. H. Xu, C. Caramanis, and S. Sanghavi. Robust PCA via Outlier Pursuit. *Advances in Neural Information Processing Systems*, pp. 2496–2504, 2010.

42. Z.-H. Zhou. Ensemble Methods: Foundations and Algorithms. *Chapman and Hall/CRC Press*, 2012.

43. Z.-H. Zhou, J. Wu, and W. Tang. Ensembling Neural Networks: Many could be Better than All. *Artificial Intelligence*, 137(1), pp. 239–263, 2002.

Chapter 5
Model Combination Methods for Outlier Ensembles

Only government can take perfectly good paper, cover it with
perfectly good ink and make the combination worthless.

Milton Friedman

5.1 Introduction

An important part of the process of creating outlier ensembles is to combine the outputs of different detectors. The precise method for model combination has a significant impact on the effectiveness of a particular outlier detection method because of the varying theoretical effects of different combination methods. For example, the impact of the scheme of averaging is quite different from that of maximization in terms of the bias and variance of the result. Therefore, the choice of model combination has a crucial effect on the results of the ensemble.

It is noteworthy that it is possible for different combination methods to work well different evaluation criteria. For example, most of the outlier analysis evaluations use the Receiver Operating Characteristic (ROC) curve [3] with respect to the ground truth. When using this type of evaluation, the only relevant part of the output is the ranks. As a result combination functions that work with the ranks are sometimes successful with some base detectors. In general, there are three types of outputs that can be used for combining different ensemble analysis methods:

1. *Score-wise combination*: In this case, the raw scores are used as the outputs of various detectors. Subsequently, the raw scores are normalized, and then they are combined.
2. *Rank-wise combination*: In this case, the raw scores are converted into ranks and then combined. Note that the process of transforming scores into ranks loses a significant amount of information. After all, ranks do not retain the same level of information about the degree of outlierness of a data point. For example, the set of scores $\{1, 2, 3, 4, 5\}$ would be considered identical to $\{0.1, 0.15, 0.2, 0.25, 10\}$,

© Springer International Publishing AG 2017

C.C. Aggarwal and S. Sathe, *Outlier Ensembles*,

DOI 10.1007/978-3-319-54765-7_5

even though this pair of scores is very different in terms of the degree of outlierness. For example, the point having a score of 10 is quite likely to be an outlier. This does not seem to be case for the scores in the first case, in which none of the points seems to be a clear outlier. In this case, converting scores to ranks clearly seems to lose a lot of information. Therefore, one would expect that rank-wise combination methods should be relatively rough in terms of their accuracy. However, this is not always the case, and the results often depend on the data set at hand.

3. *Top-heavy combination methods*: In this case, the data points, which appear at the top of the ranked list, are given greater importance in the combination process. The basic idea here is that there is no difference between two sets of scores in which an outlier is ranked in the middle of the list, and one in which an outlier is ranked at the bottom of the list. On the other hand, there is a lot of difference between two detectors in which an outlier is at the top of the list, or in the middle of the list. The area under the receiver operating characteristics curve is often not able to distinguish between these two types of outliers. Therefore, one must use detector outputs in which scoring at the top is weighted more heavily. A specific example of a top-heavy approach is to use the binary output of the outlier detection algorithm after thresholding. Then, one can vote on the outputs of the different detectors to yield the final result. Alternatively, all ranks below a certain threshold can be weighted at the same value.

It is noteworthy that score-wise or rank-wise combination methods are often quite similar. For example, the averaging or the maximization combination schemes work in a very similar way on the score-wise and the rank-wise methods. It is noteworthy that some of the combination methods, such as averaging [8, 19] and maximization [5, 8] are quite old and they date back to the earliest outlier detection algorithms. Some of these methods were proposed even before the outlier ensemble problem had been properly formalized. A historical discussion of some of these combination schemes may be found in [1, 17].

Furthermore, the nature of the combination process often depends on the goals of the underlying ensemble. For example, a technique that emphasizes variance reduction is very different from one that emphasizes bias reduction. In general, the goals of various combination methods may be classified into one of the following groups:

1. *Variance reduction*: Given that outlier analysis is an unsupervised problem, the most common method for improving accuracy is the methodology of variance reduction. Common combination methods that reduce variance include the use of the averaging or the median. As shown in the previous chapter, the averaging combination function seems to be more effective than the median combination function.

2. *Bias reduction*: In bias reduction methods, the idea is to use *heuristic* methods to improve the effectiveness of various outlier detection schemes. For example, the use of the maximization scheme [4] often provides high-quality results in many settings because of heuristic bias reduction effects (of the *relative* scores).

Note that the heuristic approach for bias reduction might not always work. There-fore, there is always an uncertainty in using schemes, although the potential gains could be significant in some of these cases.

3. *Simultaneous bias and variance reduction*: In this case, the combination method is able reduce both bias and variance. For example, the use of the trimmed mean, discussed in Chap. 3, has the effect of reducing both the bias and the vari-ance. However, as shown in that chapter, such heuristic methods are not always successful.

Any of the aforementioned methods of bias reduction or variance reduction can be used in combination with various types of score outputs such as the raw scores, the ranks, or top-heavy outputs. For example, one can use the variance reduction of averaging with either the raw scores, or with the ranks. Therefore, the two ways of classifying score combination methods are mutually orthogonal. The orthogonality of these two methods of classifying combination methods is illustrated in Fig. 5.1. Most of these combination methods have already been introduced in Chaps. 1, 3, and 4.

The combination methods for score-wise outputs and rank-wise outputs are sim-ilar. For example, averaging can be used either with score-wise methods or with rank-wise methods. The combination methods for top-heavy outputs are often some-what different from the score-wise and rank-wise methods. This is because both the score-wise and rank-wise methods essentially deal with sorted lists (but with

	SCORE-WISE COMBINATION	RANK-WISE COMBINATION	TOP-HEAVY COMBINATION
BIAS REDUCTION	**MAX (SCORES)**	**BEST (RANKS)**	———
VARIANCE REDUCTION	**MEAN (SCORES)**	**MEAN (RANKS)**	**MEAN (VOTES)**
BOTH	**AOM: AVERAGE OF MAXIMUM (SCORES)**	**AOM: AVERAGE OF BEST (RANKS)**	**THRESHOLDED MEAN (RANKS OR SCORES)**

Fig. 5.1 Orthogonality of different ways of viewing score combination methods

different values attached to the sorted lists). The top-heavy methods often treat the top candidates differently than the other items in the lists.

In some cases, a small amount of supervision may be available to improve the effectiveness of model combination methods. In cases where the amount of training data is small, the supervision may not be sufficient to use fully supervised rare-class detectors. However, it might still be sufficient to combine the results of different outlier detection algorithms. Such mildly supervised methods will also be discussed in this chapter.

This chapter is organized as follows. In the next section, we will discuss the various evaluation measures for outlier detection. The issue of score normalization will be discussed in Sect. 5.3. Variance reduction methods for model combination are discussed in Sect. 5.4. Bias reduction methods for score combination are discussed in Sect. 5.5. Methods for combining bias and variance reduction are discussed in Sect. 5.6. Supervised methods for model combination are discussed in Sect. 5.7. The conclusions are discussed in Sect. 5.8.

5.2   Impact of Outlier Evaluation Measures

The effectiveness of a particular ensemble method depends on how it is measured. This is an important point because one can often get a different idea of the effectiveness of various outlier analysis methods, depending on which method is used to evaluate it. Most of the outlier evaluation methods use either ranking-based measures across all the ranks, or they use top-heavy measures on the top-ranked points. Often different methods might be more effective, depending on which measure is used. In both cases, we assume that the ground-truth $\mathcal{G}$ is the set of points that are labeled as true outliers. Furthermore, the set of points in the entire data set is denoted by $\mathcal{D}$.

In the following, we provide a brief overview of the common outlier evaluation measures used. Then, we discuss how these evaluation measures impact the different ensemble algorithms. Interestingly, the top-heavy measures are simpler, and the ranking measures are often derived from the top-heavy measures. Therefore, we will discuss the top-heavy measures before discussing the ranking measures.

Top-Heavy Measures

Top-heavy measures often differentially focus on the data points that are ranked at the top of the list, and how they relate to the ground truth. Most outlier detection algorithms output an outlier score. A threshold is applied to this score to convert it into binary labels. While ranking-based measures evaluate the quality of the ranks on the scores with respect the ground-truth, the top-heavy measures evaluate the quality of the output *after* thresholding. For example, for any outlier detection algorithm in which higher values indicate a greater degree of outlierness, one can use a threshold t on the outlier scores, and declare all points with score at or above t as the outliers. This set is denoted by $\mathcal{S}(t)$. If one used the *rank* of the data point as the score, then the threshold can be interpreted as the *number* of outliers that are reported. In the case of ranking, lower values indicate a greater degree of outlierness, because the most outlier point has a rank of 1. Therefore, the threshold t is defined as an upper bound on the score (rank) instead of a lower bound on the score, in which points with rank *at or below* a particular threshold t are reported. In general, the threshold t can be used as a lower bound or an upper bound on the scores, depending on whether or not higher scores indicate a greater degree of outlierness.

The effect of using a particular threshold is quantified in terms of a trade-off between the *precision* and the *recall*. The precision $P(t)$ at a given value of the threshold t is defined as follows:

$$P(t) = \frac{|\mathscr{S}(t) \cap \mathscr{G}|}{|\mathscr{S}(t)|} \tag{5.1}$$

Note that the threshold t can be chosen either on the basis of the raw scores, or on the basis of the ranks. When a specific threshold rank m is chosen, the value of $P(t)$ is often denoted as $P_{@m}$. A second related measure is recall. This measure computes the fraction of ground-truth positives, which are captured at threshold t. In other words, we have the following:

$$R(t) = \frac{|\mathscr{S}(t) \cap \mathscr{G}|}{|\mathscr{G}|} \tag{5.2}$$

When the threshold is chosen on the basis of ranks, and a threshold of m is chosen, the corresponding measure is denoted as $R_{@m}$. Note that the precision and recall are defined completely on the basis of the "top" points defined by the threshold t. The specific behavior of the outliers in the lower ranked points is not relevant. It is often desirable to consolidate the precision and recall into a single measure. A common approach is to use the F_1-measure, which is the harmonic mean between the precision and the recall:

$$F_1(t) = \frac{2P(t) \cdot R(t)}{P(t) + R(t)} \tag{5.3}$$

Note that the F_1-measure also depends on the use of a specific value of the threshold t, and therefore it evaluates a specific point in the precision-recall trade-off.

Ranking-Based Measures

The top-heavy measures use a specific threshold on the scores (or ranks) to provide an evaluation of the quality of the underlying outliers. In ranking-based measures, the entire range of values of the threshold t can be used to plot the precision against the recall. This results in a precision-recall curve.

A more common approach is to use the Receiver Operating Characteristic (ROC) curve. In the receiver operating characteristics curve, we plot the *true-positive rate* against the *false-positive rate*. The true-positive rate $TPR(t)$ is defined in an exactly identical way to the recall at a given threshold t:

$$TPR(t) = Recall(t) = \frac{|\mathscr{S}(t) \cap \mathscr{G}|}{|\mathscr{G}|} \tag{5.4}$$

A closely related notion is that of the false-positive rate $FPR(t)$. The false-positive rate can be viewed as a kind of "bad" recall, where it computes the fraction of ground-truth negatives incorrectly reported by the algorithm at a given threshold t.

$$FPR(t) = BadRecall(t) = \frac{|\mathscr{S}(t) - \mathscr{G}|}{|\mathscr{D} - \mathscr{G}|} \tag{5.5}$$

A nice characteristic of the true-positive rate and false-positive rate is that both of them monotonically increase with increasingly relaxed values of t (i.e., more reported outliers). Therefore, unlike the precision-recall curve, the ROC is monotonic, and it provides an intuitive idea of the performance of the approach. An example of an ROC curve on a 1-NN algorithm on a synthetic data set containing normally distributed data with 2000 points and 3% outliers is illustrated in Fig. 5.2. Note that the false-positive rate is on the X-axis, whereas the true-positive rate is on the Y-axis. The ROC curve also provides a crisp quantification of the quality of the outlier detection algorithm by computing the area under the ROC curve (AUC). The trapezoidal rule can be used to further refine the area, in which the staircase-like ROC curve is approximated with a more convex piecewise linear approximation. A perfectly random algorithm would have performance exemplified by the dashed line in Fig. 5.2. The AUC of such an algorithm would be close to 0.5. As shown in Fig. 5.2, algorithms which perform better than random would have exhibit a *lift* in the ROC above this random performance. For example, the area under the ROC curve for Fig. 5.2 is 0.899. Note that the ROC curve depends only on the ranks of the scores, and the absolute values of the scores are irrelevant. *An intuitive interpretation of the area under the ROC curve is that it is equal to the probability that a randomly chosen outlier and a randomly chosen inlier are inverted in the ranking being evaluated.* This tends to make the AUC intuitively similar to the Kendall rank correlation [18], although the latter computes this value over all pairs of points (i.e., not just outlier–inlier pairs), and maps to a value in $[-1, 1]$ rather than a value in $[0, 1]$.

Fig. 5.2 ROC curve on synthetic data generated by a 1-NN algorithm on normally distributed data with 3% outliers. The points furthest from the mean of the normal distribution are labeled as outliers in the ground truth

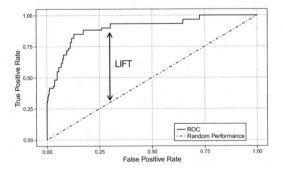

The main problem with such evaluations is that they assign equal importance to all parts of the ROC curve (i.e., top-rated outliers versus bottom-rated outliers). The area under the ROC curve can be viewed as an average performance over all values of the threshold t. In real settings, the performance at restrictive values of the threshold t (with fewer reported outliers) is more important than the performance at relaxed values of t at which many points are reported as outliers. For example, if we choose a value of t at which two-thirds of the data points are chosen as outliers, it provides a very poor idea compared to one in which only 5% of the data points are reported as outliers. There are several ways in which this can be fixed, such as the *trimmed* AUC or the weighted AUC. The trimmed AUC computes the area under the *portion of the* ROC curve only at values of t, at which $FPR(t)$ is less than a given threshold (say 5%). The weighted AUC computes the area under the AUC curve, but it weights each point on the AUC curve by the inverse of the corresponding rank. Other common measures that can be adapted from information retrieval include the normalized discounted cumulative gain (NDCG), in which the utility of a particular candidate list is measured as a weighted score. The weights of the points are defined by their position on the ranked list. Such measures are commonly used in the field of recommender systems [2]. Although we will not investigate many of these top-heavy measures in detail, they are important to keep in mind, because the effectiveness of different ensemble methods often depends on the methodology used for evaluation.

5.3   Score Normalization Issues

Different outlier detection algorithms may often report outputs on different scales. For example, a k-NN algorithm reports the raw distances, whereas the LOF algorithm reports normalized scores, in which a value of 1 indicates break-even behavior. Therefore, before combining the scores of both algorithms, one must normalize them. Otherwise, one of the two algorithms might dominate in the combination score. A second issue is that in some algorithms, lower scores are better, whereas in other cases, higher scores are better. Therefore, it is important to convert minimization scores to maximization ones and vice versa. Several methods have been proposed in the literature for score normalization. A particularly seminal one [16] converts scores into probabilities, so that the results from all the different methods have the same intuitive interpretation. The basic idea behind the method proposed in [16] is to model the outlier scores in the form of a mixture distribution of two components, where one of the components is a normal component and the other is an outlier component. This approach assigns a probability for each point to belong to one of the two components, thereby converting the score into a probability. Specific assumptions are used to model the two components of the mixture distribution, wherein the non-outlier component is assumed to be exponentially distributed, whereas the outlier component is assumed to be distributed according to the Gaussian distribution. In other words, the algorithm uses the following steps:

1. Model the scores from the outlier component to belong to a Gaussian distribution with mean μ and standard deviation σ, and the scores from the normal component to belong to an exponential distribution with parameter λ. In addition, the prior probability of a data point to be an outlier is assumed to be α. The value of α can be viewed analogously to the fraction of points that are expected to be outliers.
2. The values of μ, σ, λ, and α are learned with the use of the EM-algorithm. As shown in [16], this can be achieved with the use of a simple set of update equations.
3. The probability that a data point is an outlier is simply its (posterior) probability that it belongs to the outlier component in the mixture model.

While these choices seem to be reasonable, it is important to point out that the specific choice of the mixture distribution can be sensitive to the data set. Therefore, these assumptions can introduce some bias in the probabilities that have been obtained using this methodology. For example, if the normal component happens to fit the Gaussian distribution better than the exponential distribution for a particular algorithm, it is possible for the outlier scores to be inverted. The main point here is that the work in [16] makes an assertion about the *typical* behavior of outlier scores in real applications, and it therefore makes such an assertion.

A second issue is that the use of probabilities as the outputs, albeit useful from an intuitive point of view, can lead to loss of discrimination among the outlier points. For example, two points which have probabilities of belonging to the outlier component of 0.4 and 0.5, respectively, are not very different from one another. On the other hand, two points that have outlier probabilities of 0.9 and 0.99 are much more different from one another. This can sometimes lead to numerical instability. These situations should be addressed with the use of a damping function. The typical damping function is the logarithm. The use of the logarithms on probability outputs can also be theoretically justified because log-likelihoods are inherently additive like score combination functions. Therefore, it makes sense to damp the scores of the base detector *before* applying the combination function. Although converting scores to probabilities has clear intuitive advantages, it does not always help the ensemble method to use such representations.

It turns out that using simple methods such as the Z-scores can be quite effective in many settings. The idea behind the computation of the Z-score is as follows. Let $s(1) \ldots s(n)$ be the outlier scores of the n data points. The first step is to compute the mean μ and standard deviation σ of these scores. The mean μ is computed as follows:

$$\mu = \frac{\sum_{i=1}^{n} s(i)}{n} \tag{5.6}$$

The standard deviation σ of the n scores is computed as follows:

$$\sigma = \sqrt{\frac{\sum_{i=1}^{n} (s(i) - \mu)^2}{n - 1}} \tag{5.7}$$

Then, the Z-value of the score of the ith data point is defined as follows:

$$z(i) = \frac{s(i) - \mu}{\sigma} \tag{5.8}$$

In the case, where smaller scores indicate greater outlierness, the negative of the Z-value is used. Therefore, the approach always yields scores in which a larger value of the score indicates a greater degree of outlierness. Another simple approach that is sometimes used is to normalize all scores to lie in the range (0, 1) with straightforward scaling. These simple methods can often do reasonably well from a heuristic point of view.

5.4   Model Combination for Variance Reduction

Certain types of combination methods are well suited to variance reduction. The most well-known combination method that reduces variance is the averaging function. A detailed discussion of the effects of averaging on variance reduction is provided in Chap. 3. Some of the common model combination methods for variance reduction are as follows:

1. *Mean of scores*: In this case, the mean is computed over the different scores of a single data point over the various ensemble components, and reported as the combination score. In most cases, normalization is required, when the detectors report outputs from different types of base detectors. Therefore, the scores from each detector are often normalized to zero mean and unit variance before computing the mean.
   Averaging is among the oldest of all schemes and has a rich history of use both in classification and outlier detection. Virtually all the variance-reduction methods in classification use some form of averaging [9–14]. Furthermore, the approach was even used for parameter optimization in some of the older outlier detection algorithms like LOF [8] and LOCI [21].

2. *Median of scores*: A somewhat more stable central representative of the scores is the median, which has been used in the context of outlier detection in graphs [6]. The main advantage of the median is that it is not significantly affected by a few unusual deviations. This makes it a more stable representative. Therefore, for each data point, the median score over the various ensemble components is reported. On the other hand, the disadvantage of using the median is that some of the underlying diversity is lost. In some cases, the few unusual deviations are actually quite informative, and their effects are especially noticed in measures like the AUC (as opposed to the MSE). The varying performance behavior between AUC and MSE is discussed in Sect. 3.3.3 of Chap. 3. We have presented some experiments in Chap. 3 with the use of the median instead of the mean. These results seem to suggest that the loss of diversity has a greater impact than the stability advantages gained from using the median. As a result, the median does

not seem to perform as well as the mean. Nevertheless, we view these results as preliminary because they are presented only over a small number of data sets and detectors. Some of our recent results [15] have also shown that the median can perform quite well in some settings.

3. *Mean of ranks*: In this case, the scores of each detector are ranked, and each point is assigned a rank for each detector. Therefore, each point will have as many ranks as the number of detectors. Then, the average rank of each data point is computed over various ensemble components. This average rank is then reported.

   The use of ranks provides stability because unusual deviations in the scores are ignored. On the other hand, these unusual deviations might sometimes be reflective of the true degree of outlierness of the point. In such cases, valuable information is lost. Nevertheless, averaging with a rank-based output can often provide good quality AUCs with many detectors, because AUCs are measured with respect to the ranks. Furthermore, the use of ranks is better able to handle the instability of detectors such as LOF. This does not, however, mean that the use of ranks will provide universally good scores with all types of detectors and metrics [4]. It is important to keep in mind that the use of ranks often loses a lot of information from the underlying data set.

4. *Median of rank*: In this case, the scores of each detector are ranked, and each point is assigned a rank for each detector. Therefore, each point will have as many ranks as the number of detectors. Then, the median rank of each data point is computed over various ensemble components, and reported as the score for the corresponding data point. However, since ranks are already stable, the use of the median rank is often not very different from the type of output one would obtain with the mean. Therefore, when using ranks, the difference between the median and mean is rather limited.

In general, rank-based combination methods often show very good performance in detectors with unusually high levels of errors for specific points. Furthermore, when the accuracy is measured with rank-centric methods, such combination methods tend to do rather well.

5.5   Model Combination for Bias Reduction

As discussed in the previous chapter, bias reduction is hard to achieve in a controlled way in unsupervised settings like outlier detection. Nevertheless, some methods such as the maximization combination function are able to achieve a limited degree of bias reduction. In the maximization combination function, the scores $s_1(i) \ldots s_m(i)$ of the ith point over the m detectors are standardized to zero mean and unit standard deviation. Then, the maximum value of the score over the various detectors is reported.

It is claimed in [24] that the maximization function overestimates the underlying outlier scores, and it should therefore be avoided. However, outlier scores are *relative*, and it is theoretically impossible to overestimate all scores. If some scores are over-estimated, then others must be underestimated. In fact, outlier scores must always be interpreted after normalizing them appropriately (e.g., standardization). Note that the theoretical results on bias and variance in Chap. 2 are based on standardization of the scores. Once, the scores have been standardized, the issue of consistent overesti-mation does not arise. While there clearly seem to be some stability issues associated with the use of the maximization function, the specific argument provided in [24] seems to be incorrect. In particular, the work provides an argument on the basis of an example that compares the scores on two different data sets. However, outlier scores are relative only within a single data set, and it is impossible to compare the scores across two data sets, unless these scores are normalized in the same way.

The main problematic issue with the maximization score is one of *stability*. The notion of "stability" directly translates to the theoretical impact on the variance. It is possible for the maximization combination function to increase the variance of the underlying scores. At the same time, there are often heuristic bias reduc-tion effects, which we will explain using an argument discussed below. These two effects on bias and variance work against one another. Therefore, the behavior of a pure maximization combination can sometimes be unpredictable. Fortunately, it is possible to reduce the detrimental effects on variance by combining with other variance-reduction methods. Such techniques will be discussed in the next section.

Next, we explain the bias reduction effects of the maximization combination. In many "difficult" data sets, the outliers may be well hidden, as a result of which many ensemble components may give them inlier-like scores. In such cases, the scores of outlier points are often *relatively* underestimated in most ensemble components as compared to inlier data points. In order to explain this point, let us consider the feature bagging approach of [19], in which the outliers are hidden in small subsets of dimensions. In such cases, depending on the nature of the underlying data set, a large majority of subspace samples may not contain many of the relevant dimensions. Therefore, most of the subspace samples will provide significant underestimates of the outlier scores for the (small number of) true outlier points and mild overestimates of the outlier scores for the (many) normal points. This is a problem of *bias*, which is caused by the well hidden nature of outliers. We argue that such kinds of bias are inherent[1] to the problem of outlier detection. The scores of outlier points are often far more *brittle* to small algorithm modifications, as compared to the scores of inlier points. Using a maximization ensemble is simply a way of trying to identify components in which the outlier-like behavior is best magnified. Of course, it is fully understood that any bias-reduction method in an unsupervised problem like outlier detection is inherently heuristic, and it might not work for a specific data set. For example, if a training data set (or subsample) is very small, then the maximization function will not work very well because of its propensity of pick out the high variance in the scores.

---

[1]The original LOF paper recognized the problem of dilution from irrelevant ensemble components and therefore suggested the use of the maximization function.

Clearly, there are trade-offs between the use of the maximization and averaging function and it is difficult to declare one of them as a clear winner. This point also seems to be underscored by the experimental results presented in [19], where the relative behavior of the two methods (i.e., averaging versus maximum rank) depends on the specific data set. In this paper, we will provide experimental results which show further insights.

5.5.1   A Simple Example

In order to illustrate this point, we will provide a simple example of a toy data set $\mathcal{T}$ and ensemble scheme, where outliers are well hidden in the data set. Consider the case, where a data set has exactly n data points and d dimensions. For the purpose of discussion, we will assume that the value of d is very large (e.g., a few hundred thousand). Assumes that the data set contains a single outlier. For the $(n - 1)$ normal data points, the data is uniformly distributed in $[-1, 1]$. The distribution for the outlier point is slightly different in that a randomly chosen dimension has a different distribution. On exactly $(d - 1)$ dimensions, the outlier point is again uniformly distributed in $[-1, 1]$. On the remaining (randomly chosen) dimension, the value of the corresponding attribute is in the range $[2, 3]$.

Note that the single outlier can be trivially discovered by many simple heuristics, although many off-the-shelf distance-based algorithms might not do very well because of the averaging effects of the irrelevant dimensions. In practice, an outlier detection algorithm is not optimized to any particular data set, and one often uses detectors which are not optimized to the data set at hand.

For example, consider the case where the base detector is an extreme value analysis method [22] in which the distance from the data mean is reported as the outlier score. Note that the data distribution of $\mathcal{T}$ is such that the mean of the data can be approximated to be the origin in this case. The ensemble method is assumed to be a variant of the feature bagging scheme [19], in which each dimension in the data is selected exactly once and the detector is applied on this 1-dimensional data set. The process is repeated for each of the d dimensions, and the final score can be reported using either the averaging or the maximum function over these d different scores. Therefore, our simple ensemble-based approach has d components. We will derive the probability that the score for an outlier point is greater than that for an inlier point under both the averaging and maximization schemes. In other words, we would like to compute the probability of a rank inversion in the two cases.

The averaging function will yield a combination score for the inlier points, which has a expected value of 0.5 because each score is randomly distributed in $(0, 1)$. The variance of the score is $1/(12 \cdot d)$ over the different ensemble components. On the other hand, by using the same argument, the outlier point will have an expected score of $[0.5(d - 1) + 2.5]/d = 0.5 + 2/d$, because the irrelevant dimensions contribute $0.5(d - 1)/d$ to the expected value, and the single relevant dimension contributes $2.5/d$ to the expected score. The variance of the score is $1/(12d)$. Therefore, the difference M between the two scores will be a random variable with an expected mean of $\mu = 2/d$ and a variance of $\sigma^2 = 1/(6d)$. Furthermore, this random variable M will be normally distributed when d becomes large. Note that an inversion between the outlier and a randomly selected inlier occurs when M is negative. Let $Z \sim \mathcal{N}(0, 1)$ be a random variable drawn from the standard normal distribution with 0 mean and unit variance. Therefore, we have:

$$P(\text{Inversion}) = P(M < 0) \tag{5.9}$$

$$= P(Z < (0 - \mu)/\sigma) = P(Z < -2\sqrt{6/d}) \tag{5.10}$$

Note that the expression $2\sqrt{6/d}$ tends to zero with increasing dimensionality, and the resulting probability evaluates to almost 0.5. This means that with increasing dimensionality, an inlier is almost equally likely to have a larger outlier score than a truly outlier point. In other words, the averaging approach increasingly provides performance that is similar to a random outlier score for each point. This is because the data point becomes increasingly hidden by the irrelevant dimensions, and the averaging function continues to dilute the outlier score with increasing dimensionality.

Nevertheless, the maximization function always discovers the correct *relative* score of the outlier point with respect to the inlier points because it always reports a value in the range [2, 3], which is greater than the outlier score of the other data points. In other words, the maximization ensemble properly corrects for the natural bias of outlier detection algorithms, in which the scores of well-hidden outliers are often more unstable than inliers. In the easy cases, where most outliers are "obvious" and can be discovered by the majority of the ensemble components, the averaging approach will almost always do better by reducing variance effects. However, if it can be argued that the discovery of "obvious" outliers is not quite as interesting from an analytical perspective, the maximization function will have a clear advantage.

It is not guaranteed that the maximization function will always improve the ensemble accuracy. This is primarily because the maximization function increases variance. Why does maximization increase variance? The primary reason is that the maximum of many random variables can often have a variance, which is much larger than any of the individual variables. However, as we will see in the next section, this increase in variance can often be partially or fully ameliorated by using some combination tricks.

5.5.2 Sequential Combination Methods

All the methods discussed so far discuss the combination of scores from the outputs of independent detectors. However, in data classification, bias reduction methods often use outlier detectors that are not independent from one another. Such types of detectors are referred to as *sequential model combination methods* [1]. An example of sequential model combination method in classification is boosting, in which the different executions of the base detector are not independent of one another. Such types of interdependent detectors also have an impact on the model combination process.

An example of a class of methods in which the model combination depends on the sequential nature of the combination process is that of training data pruning (cf. Sect. 4.3 of Chap. 4). The basic idea behind this class of methods is to remove outliers in successive iterations from the one-class model of normal data, so as to improve the quality of the underlying model. Such an approach was proposed in [7]. In such a case, the final output depends on the *last* execution of the base detector and often does not combine the executions from the previous iterations. The basic idea is that the model is successively refined over many iterations, and therefore the final execution of the base detector provides the best results. However, it is sometimes possible to average the results over the last few iterations in order to increase diversity. This type of approach can sometimes also help in reducing variance, although it is not guaranteed to improve the overall accuracy.

5.6   Combining Bias and Variance Reduction

In this section, we will discuss some combination methods for reducing variance. Some of this discussion has already been provided in Sect. 3.6.2 of Chap. 3. These schemes were first introduced in [4]. For completeness, we replicate some parts of that discussion within this chapter. In particular, all these schemes combine the bias reduction of the maximization scheme with the variance reduction of averaging:

1. *AOM Method*: For m ensemble components, we divide the components into approximately m/q buckets of q components each. First, a maximization is used over each of the buckets of q components, and then the scores are averaged over the m/q buckets. Note that one does not need to assign equal resources to maximization and averaging; in fact, the value of q should be selected to be less than m/q. All implementations in this book used 100 trials, with $q = 5$. We refer to this method as *AOM*, which stands for *Average of Maximum*. The basic idea is that the first phase of maximization reduces the bias, which is subsequently followed by the variance reduction of averaging.

2. *Thresh Method*: A method suggested in [1], for combining the scores of multiple detectors, is to use an absolute threshold t on the (standardized) outlier score, and then adding the (thresholded and standardized) outlier scores for these components. The threshold is chosen in a mild way, such as a value of $t = 0$ on the standardized score. Note that values less than 0 almost always correspond to strong inliers. The overall effect of this approach is to reward points for showing up as outliers in a given component, but not to penalize them too much for showing up as strong inliers. A reasonable choice is to use a threshold value of $t = 0$ on the Z-score. An important point is that such an approach can sometimes lead to tied scores among the *lowest ranked* (i.e., least outlier-like) points having

a score of exactly $m * t$. Such ties are broken among the lowest ranked points by using their average standardized score across the m ensemble components. As a practical matter, one can add a small amount $\epsilon * avg_i$ proportional to the average standardized score avg_i of such points, to achieve the desired tie-breaking. We refer to this approach as *Thresh*.

3. *MOA Method*: Another way of combining bias and variance reduction is the use of the *Maximum of Average (MOA)*. This scheme can be viewed as a complementary version of the AOM scheme. The main difference is that the averaging is done first, which is then followed by the maximization. However, it is generally less beneficial to explore bias reduction as the second step, because the informativeness of the individual detectors has already been blunted by the averaging scheme.

Detailed experimental results illustrating the effectiveness of these methods may be found in [4].

5.6.1 Factorized Consensus

Another approach that uses consensus schemes to de-emphasize the irrelevant detector outputs in an unsupervised way is a low-rank technique based on matrix factorization. The basic assumption here is that detectors that are too different from most of the other detectors might be using an incorrect model, and therefore de-emphasizing them might improve the bias characteristics in addition to the variance.

Consider a setting in which we have m detectors and n data points. The basic idea is assume that the score $s_j(i)$ of the ith point from the jth detector can be expressed as follows:

$$s_j(i) = u_i \cdot v_j + \epsilon_{ij} \tag{5.11}$$

Here, v_j is the adjustment factor for the jth detector, u_i is the true score of data point i, and ϵ_{ij} is the error of detector i on data point j. An additional constraint is that the adjustment factor v_j is non-negative. An additional assumption is that the score outputs of each detector have been standardized to zero mean and unit variance.

The goal of the consensus optimization scheme is to determine the true scores and adjustment factors, so that the sum of the squares of the errors ϵ_{ij} is minimized. Let S be the $n \times m$ matrix of scores for the n points and m detectors. The (i, j)th entry in S contains the score of the jth detector on the ith data point. Let U and V be $n \times 1$ and $m \times 1$ matrices (i.e., column vectors), respectively. Then, Eq. 5.11 can be rewritten in the following rank-1 matrix factorization form:

$$S \approx UV^T \tag{5.12}$$

The goal is to minimize the Frobenius norm $||S - UV^T||^2$ in order to learn the true scores U and adjustment factors in V. This can be achieved by formulating the following optimization problem:

$$\text{Minimize} J = ||S - UV^T||^2$$
$$\text{subject to:} V \geq 0$$

This problem can be solved using gradient descent. We start by initializing U to be the mean score of all the detectors for each point. The matrix V is initialized to set of 1 s. Subsequently, the following $n \times m$ error matrix E is computed:

$$E = S - UV^T \tag{5.13}$$

Subsequently, the gradient descent steps can be performed by using the following matrix-based updates:

$$U \Leftarrow U + \alpha EV$$
$$V \Leftarrow V + \alpha E^T U$$

Here, $\alpha > 0$ is the learning rate. It is important not to select the value of α to be too large to avoid divergence to unbounded values; on the other hand, setting α to be too small will result in very slow convergence. Typically, a few values of α should be tried before selecting its specific value for a particular data set.

After this step of updating U and V, the negative elements in V are set to 0. This is done in order to respect the constraint that V is non-negative. Then, the error matrix is updated according to Eq. 5.13, and the process is repeated to convergence. Interestingly, this entire consensus approach can be shown to be a generalization of the scheme of using the mean as the output of the detector. For example, if this optimization problem is solved while constraining V to only contain values of 1, then the optimal value of the score of each point is equal to the mean score over various detectors.

The overall algorithm for determining the scores nay be written as follows:

1. Standardize the scores output by the various detectors, so that the scores from each detector has zero mean and unit variance. Create an $n \times m$ score matrix S.
2. Initialize U to be an $n \times 1$ matrix (column vector) containing the mean outlier scores of the points. This can be achieved by computing the means of the various rows of S.
3. Initialize V to be an $m \times 1$ matrix containing only 1 s.
4. Compute the error matrix $E = S - UV^T$.
5. Update U and V as follows:

$$U \Leftarrow U + \alpha EV$$
$$V \Leftarrow V + \alpha E^T U$$

Set any negative entries of V to 0.

6. If U and V have not converged, then go to step 4.
7. Report the entries of U as the true outlier scores.

This consensus scheme provides a robust methodology for effectively estimating the scores, as well as the multiplicative factors for various detectors. In a sense, these multiplicative factors regulate the importance of various detectors, and they are learned in a data-driven manner.

5.7 Using Mild Supervision in Model Combination

The reduction of bias during score combination is always somewhat of a challenge. This is because one is always "guessing" when one uses heuristic schemes like maximization or factorized consensus. There are is no certain way in which one can make such schemes provide better results in a fool-proof way, unless some supervision is available. In this section, we study the use of a mild level of supervision in model combination.

In many rare class problems, it is possible for an expert to identify a small number of instances of the rare class and the normal class. With the use of a very small number of instances, a fully supervised algorithm such as a rare-class detector might not be effective because of overfitting. In such cases, the supervision can be restricted to the model combination part of the algorithm [20]. The basic idea is that most model combination methods use a linear combination of the outlier scores in order to determine the final score:

$$S(i) = \frac{\sum_{j=1}^{m} w_j s_j(i)}{m} \tag{5.14}$$

Here, w_j is the weight of the jth detector that needs to be learned in a data-driven manner. Methods like averaging are special cases of this model in which each w_j is set to 1.

Therefore, one can use a logistic regression or SVM model to learn the precise weights given to the different models. Typically, L_1-regularization may be used to avoid overfitting. When L_1-regularization is used, many of the weights from $w_1 \ldots w_m$ are automatically set to 0. This corresponds to the fact that these detectors are excluded from consideration. Regularization is particularly important when the number of detectors to be combined is large, and it is therefore important to avoid overfitting.

This approach is closely related to a supervised ensemble, referred to as stacking [23]. The main difference is that stacking uses supervised rare-class detectors in the first step, whereas this approach uses unsupervised outlier detectors in the first step. When the amount of training data is small, it makes more sense to use unsupervised methods in the first step. One can also interpret this approach from the point of view of unsupervised feature engineering. Such a point of view has been explained in Sect. 4.5 of Chap. 4. The basic idea here is that the outlier scores of the different detectors can be viewed as new features that are used by a rare-class detection algorithm. The feature-engineering point of view therefore views the problem from a supervised rare-class detection point of view, rather than from the outlier model combination point of view. Readers are referred to [20] for more details on these methods.

5.8   Conclusions and Summary

In this chapter, we study the problem of model combination in outlier ensembles. Model combination includes the process of score normalization so that the different detectors can be combined in a meaningful way. Often different detectors might create scores on different scales, as a result of which it is important to normalize the scores before the combination process. This chapter studies several model combination techniques, such as the use of averaging, maximization, and a combination of the two. It was discussed how these different model-combination methods work in different real-world settings. A factorized consensus approach for model combination was also introduced.

The main problem with many model combination methods is that it is hard to perform bias reduction in a controlled way. For example, even though schemes like maximization can heuristically improve bias in many data sets, this is not guaranteed. In some cases, combining with other variance reduction methods like averaging might be a valid choice. In other cases, a small amount of supervision may be available. When supervision is available, it is helpful in learning the weights of different detectors in a controlled way.

Exercises

1. Discuss how the factorized consensus scheme is a generalization of the averaging scheme for outlier ensembles.
2. Implement an algorithm that takes as input a set of scores from an algorithms and then (i) normalizes them using standardization, (ii) combines them using the averaging and maximization schemes, and (iii) combines them using the AOM and Thresh schemes.

References

1. C. C. Aggarwal. Outlier Ensembles: Position Paper, *ACM SIGKDD Explorations*, 14(2), pp. 49–58, December, 2012.
2. C. C. Aggarwal. Recommender Systems: The Textbook, *Springer*, 2016.
3. C. C. Aggarwal. Outlier Analysis, Second Edition, *Springer*, 2017.

4. C. C. Aggarwal and S. Sathe. Theoretical Foundations and Algorithms for Outlier Ensembles, *ACM SIGKDD Explorations*, 17(1), June 2015.

5. C. C. Aggarwal and P. S. Yu. Outlier Detection in High Dimensional Data, *ACM SIGMOD Conference*, 2001.

6. C. C. Aggarwal and P. S. Yu. Outlier Detection in Graph Streams, *IEEE ICDE Conference*, 2011.

7. D. Barbara, Y. Li, J. Couto, J.-L. Lin, and S. Jajodia. Bootstrapping a Data Mining Intrusion Detection System. *Symposium on Applied Computing*, 2003.

8. M. Breunig, H.-P. Kriegel, R. Ng, and J. Sander. LOF: Identifying Density-based Local Outliers, *ACM SIGMOD Conference*, 2000.

9. L. Brieman. Bagging Predictors. *Machine Learning*, 24(2), pp. 123–140, 1996.

10. L. Brieman. Random Forests. *Journal Machine Learning archive*, 45(1), pp. 5–32, 2001.

11. G. Brown, J. Wyatt, R. Harris, and X. Yao. Diversity creation methods: a survey and categorisation. *Information Fusion*, 6:5(20), 2005.

12. P. Buhlmann. Bagging, subagging and bragging for improving some prediction algorithms, *Recent advances and trends in nonparametric statistics*, Elsevier, 2003.

13. P. Buhlmann, B. Yu. Analyzing bagging. *Annals of Statistics*, pp. 927–961, 2002.

14. A. Buja, W. Stuetzle. Observations on bagging. *Statistica Sinica*, 16(2), 323, 2006.

15. J. Chen, S. Sathe, C. Aggarwal and D. Turaga. Outlier detection with ensembles of autoencoders. *In preparation*, 2017.

16. J. Gao, P.-N. Tan. Converting output scores from outlier detection algorithms into probability estimates. *ICDM Conference*, 2006.

17. Z. He, S. Deng and X. Xu. A Unified Subspace Outlier Ensemble Framework for Outlier Detection, *Advances in Web Age Information Management*, 2005.

18. M. Kendall. A New Measure of Rank Correlation. *Biometrika*, 30(1/2), 81–93, 1938.

19. A. Lazarevic, and V. Kumar. Feature Bagging for Outlier Detection, *ACM KDD Conference*, 2005.

20. B. Micenkova, B. McWiliams, and I. Assent. Learning Outlier Ensembles: The Best of Both Worlds – Supervised and Unsupervised. *Outlier Detection and Description Workshop*, 2014. Extended version: http://arxiv.org/pdf/1507.08104v1.pdf.

21. S. Papadimitriou, H. Kitagawa, P. Gibbons, and C. Faloutsos, LOCI: Fast outlier detection using the local correlation integral, *ICDE Conference*, 2003.

22. M. Shyu, S. Chen, K. Sarinnapakorn, L. Chang. A novel anomaly detection scheme based on principal component classifier. *ICDMW*, 2003.

23. D. Wolpert. Stacked Generalization, *Neural Networks*, 5(2), pp. 241–259, 1992.

24. A. Zimek, R. Campello, J. Sander. Ensembles for unsupervised outlier detection: Challenges and research questions, *SIGKDD Explorations*, 15(1), 2013.

Chapter 6
Which Outlier Detection Algorithm Should I Use?

You can't build a great building on a weak foundation. You must have a solid foundation if you're going to have a strong superstructure.

Gordon B. Hinckley

6.1 Introduction

Ensembles can be used to improve the performance of base detectors in several different ways. The first method is to use a single base detector in conjunction with a method like feature bagging and subsampling. The second method is to combine multiple base detectors in order to induce greater diversity. What is the impact of using generic ensemble methods on various base detectors? What is the impact of combining these ensemble methods into a higher-level combination? This chapter will discuss both these different ways of combining base detectors and also various ways in which one can squeeze the most out of ensemble methods.

An interesting observation from the results presented in this chapter is that even though base detectors may vary significantly from one another, ensemble-centric versions of these detectors become more similar with one another. This is, in part, because many ensemble methods reduce the differences contributed by variance component in the detector performance (which can be very different in the original base detector). From the perspective of ensemble-centric performance, not only does the qualitative performance of the detector matter, but its performance gains over the base detector are important. For example, in variance reduction methods, unstable algorithms are known to achieve greater performance gains than stable algorithms. Another observation is that the ensemble-centric avatars of many algorithms have different relative performance than their base detector counterparts.

Although a wide variety of outlier detectors have been proposed in the literature [2], it has often been observed that simple methods like the average k-nearest neighbor method, the exact k-nearest neighbor method, and the Mahalanobis method [54] tend to perform very well. Some experiments have been

© Springer International Publishing AG 2017
C.C. Aggarwal and S. Sathe, *Outlier Ensembles*,
DOI 10.1007/978-3-319-54765-7_6

presented in recent years to compare various outlier detection algorithms [3, 12, 14, 16, 41]. However, many of these comparisons are focused on base detector performance and do not compare natural ensemble-centric variations of these algorithms. In some cases, ensemble algorithms are compared with base detectors; such a comparison is not fair because the ensemble usually has an inherent advantage. Another important observation is that the ensemble-centric variations of algorithms often tend to provide different relative performance than the base detectors because of the varying levels of variance in the different base algorithms (which are typically removed by the ensembles). This work, therefore, provides a broader view of comparing base algorithms by also examining the effect of using ensembles on different base detectors.

Parameter settings create a significant dilemma even for algorithms in which the parameters have semantically similar interpretations. For example, we have shown the performance of the LOF algorithm and the average k-nearest neighbor algorithm on the Lymphography data set for varying values of the parameter k in Fig. 6.1. It is evident that if k is selected between 30 and 50, then LOF is not matched at *any* value of k by the average k-nearest neighbor method. On the other hand, there are several choices of k at which the LOF method performs *much* worse than the average k-nearest neighbor method. An important observation is that the average k-nearest neighbor algorithm shows stable performance across the range of the values of k. Which algorithm should an analyst use? Here, it is important to note that an analyst in a real-world setting would not even have the benefit of a comparison like Fig. 6.1, which is constructed with the assumption of knowing the ground truth. After all, such ground-truth is not available in the unsupervised setting.

In this case, it is evident that the average k-nearest neighbor detector is more stable than LOF and tends to perform better *if it is evaluated over a range of performance settings*. Note that in unsupervised outlier detection problems, it is important to

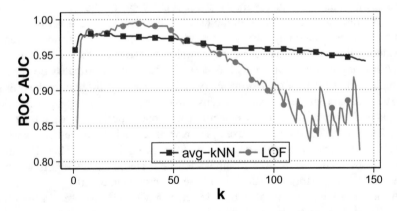

Fig. 6.1 Performance of average k-nearest neighbor and LOF on Lymphography with different values of k. Note that LOF achieves the best performance over all choices of parameters, if the best value of k was selected for each algorithm. However, the performance of LOF is also poorer across the whole range of performance settings

compare the algorithms over a range of "reasonable" parameter values because the best values of the parameters are often not known. Unstable algorithms often have an advantage if the best parameters for each algorithm are used to compare them. This is exactly the opposite of what we want, especially because unstable methods tend to perform poorly over large ranges of values. Excellent performance in a narrow and "hard-to-guess" range is not helpful for an analyst in the unsupervised setting. A second issue is related to the stability of the approach with different choices of *data sets*. The work in [16] suggests that either of LOF or a raw distance-based algorithm could perform better, depending on whether outliers are local or global; however, raw distance-based algorithms are more stable across different types of data sets. This type of trade-off is often observed in many real-world outlier-detection algorithms in which there is wide variation in the relative performances of different algorithms in different data sets, especially when they are used without the variance-reduction tricks of ensemble methods.

Comparing different algorithms is even harder when they use parameters with different semantic interpretations. For example, an average k-nearest neighbor detector uses different parameters than a kernel-based method (like kernel PCA [23]), which is dependent on parameters like the bandwidth of the kernel and the number of dimensions selected. How can one meaningfully compare such methods? Using the best value of the parameters in each case will only favor the most *unstable* algorithm with multiple parameters. For example, a kernel-based algorithm will often win because it is possible to set the kernel parameters and the number of dimensions selected to show excellent results (although this process assumes knowledge of the ground truth). Yet, guessing such parameters (without the benefit of ground truth) turns out to be particularly difficult for unstable algorithms like kernel methods in which incorrect choices can be punished in a severe way. Algorithms with fewer parameters are clearly better in the context of unsupervised problems; yet these algorithms have a consistent disadvantage in bench-marked evaluations because parameters are often (unrealistically) optimized for each baseline algorithm. An algorithm with a large number of parameters can be carefully optimized at the best value to show stellar performance, whereas algorithms with fewer parameters have less scope of optimization. Therefore, even if all algorithms are tuned to the best values of their parameters, it does not provide a fair comparison among them. In the most extreme case of a parameter-free methods (which is highly desirable), only a single performance value will be returned with no scope of optimization. This will typically be outperformed with a highly optimized method. This dilemma has been observed [35] in the context of one-class kernel SVMs [52], where it was found to be notoriously difficult to optimize the parameters. As discussed in [35], this property made the algorithm hard to use in a confident way in the unsupervised setting.

When using ensemble-based methods, another factor to be kept in mind is the particular choice of the algorithm on the ensemble performance. Not all base methods benefit equally from ensemble-based methods. For example, stable methods like the average k-nearest neighbor method would benefit less from a feature bagging or subsampling method, as compared to an unstable method like LOF. Do some algorithms perform poorly on the base detector but very well on the ensemble? The behavior of clustering and histogram-based methods [14, 34, 51] is particularly notable in this respect. Even though the individual base detectors are extremely weak, the ensemble performance of the algorithm often outperforms ensemble-centric variants of other algorithms with much better base performance. Therefore, it often makes sense to use two different ways of comparing outlier detection algorithms:

1. The algorithms are compared using *median base* performance on a set of runs of an ensemble method like variable subsampling. Methods like variable subsampling [3] can often perform implicit parameter space exploration of some detectors by fixing the parameter value to a "rule-of-thumb" value and varying the size of the sampled data set. In the evaluations of this chapter, variable subsampling will play the special role of enabling both diversity and parameter-space exploration.
2. The algorithms are compared using *ensemble* performance in the aforementioned setting. Unstable algorithms are often able to benefit more from the performance jumps achieved in variance reduction. However, in some cases, these performance jumps are not sufficient for the ensemble-centric performance to be different from that of base performance in terms of relative ordering. Furthermore, we will show that ensemble methods like variable subsampling are often able to "close the gap" between the performances of different base detectors and make the different algorithms more similar to one another.

Several aspects of algorithmic choice have little to do with performance. For example, the interpretability of an algorithm [6] is extremely important because the analyst often likes to have an understanding of the causality of the outliers. Some methods like subspace outlier detection provide useful information about relevant features [2, 4]. In fact, as discussed in [2], it makes sense to use such techniques only in conjunction with ensemble-based methods.

We will also explore how to combine different heterogeneous base detectors into an ensemble. Some methods [39, 59] have been proposed in the literature on combining base detectors. However, these methods have explored only a narrow subset of detectors without examining the effect of using a particular base method. In this chapter, we show the effects of using particular types of base detectors, and a principled way to combine detectors of different types. Interestingly, we found that applying generic ensemble methods like variable subsampling on base methods provided large performance jumps, but the additional gain from combining the ensemble-centric versions of different base detector was primarily one of robustness with only slightly improved average performance. This was primarily because different types of algorithms work well on different data sets, and combining the detectors made the ensemble more robust in terms of variability but did not necessarily perform better than the best-performing detector on that data set. Nevertheless, since the best-performing algorithm is unknown to an analyst in the unsupervised setting, it is still advisable to combine these results to make the performance more stable with the choice of data set. In this context, we will examine the behavior of *TRINITY*, which is an ensemble of ensembles; it combines the ensemble-centric variants of three different base algorithms.

This chapter is primarily focused on the setting with multi-dimensional numeric data, because it is the most commonly explored setting in the field of outlier analysis. This chapter will focus on a few distance-based, density-based, soft-PCA and tree-based methods for comparison. These methods are selected for comparison because they often perform competitively in spite of being relatively "older" methods. In particular, we will examine the following classes of methods, which are known to be among the best performing outlier analysis methods in spite of more recent methods being claimed to be superior:

- *Distance-based methods*: These methods use the normalized or unnormalized k-nearest neighbor distance of a data point in order to quantify the outlier score.
- *Linear models*: These methods use principal component analysis (PCA) in order to quantify the outlier score of each data point. Soft versions of PCA, such as the Mahalanobis method, are more appropriate because they properly normalize the different principal component directions and require fewer parameters. We also investigate kernel variations of the Mahalanobis method. These variations are actually more robust versions of 1-class support vector machines and support vector data descriptions because of better normalization of the kernel space and also because of fewer parameters. Furthermore, 1-class SVMs make some assumptions about the origin (in kernel space) being treated as a prior for outliers, which makes the use of such methods controversial [2, 11, 14]. It is noteworthy that even though the Mahalanobis method is well known, we are not aware of any known implementations of the kernel Mahalanobis method. This book therefore provides the first known experimental results on the ensemble-centric variant of the kernel Mahalanobis method.
- *Density-based methods*: Density-based and clustering methods compute the density of specific regions in the data space, but they have very high variability in prediction with the specific parameters used for the implementation. Therefore, these techniques are ideal candidates for ensemble methods. Density-based methods are particularly effective when used in subspaces of the data. An example of such a method is the subspace histogram method referred to as *RS-Hash* [51]. The isolation forest [34] is also a subspace density estimator, although it seems to be quite different at first sight. Many of these methods [17, 51, 56, 62] can also be extended to data streams. In general, histogram and kernel-based density-estimation methods [21, 25, 28, 31] are related to clustering-based ensemble methods.

Therefore, it is a useful exercise to experimentally compare the behavior of these disparate detectors across a wide range of data sets. These results provide significant insights into why selecting particular detectors may be beneficial in various applications.

This book does not explore more complex domains of data such as time-series data, categorical data, or graph data. Nevertheless, some of the general principles of selecting and combining base detectors seem to be invariant across domains. Furthermore, many of the detectors discussed in this chapter, such as distance-based detectors and the kernel Mahalanobis method, can be easily generalized to arbitrary data domains. Therefore, we believe that the general principles discussed in this chapter are also applicable to wider data domains.

This chapter is organized as follows. In the next section, we review some of the classical distance-based detectors that are used for outlier detection. These methods are important; in spite of the numerous advances made in the field of outlier detection over the years, they remain relatively robust over a wide range of data sets. Section 6.3 discusses histogram-based and density-based methods, which are closely related to distance-based methods. Dependency-oriented detectors that leverage inter-attribute correlations are discussed in Sect. 6.4. The issue of choosing evaluation parameters is discussed in Sect. 6.5. Section 6.6 introduces *TRINITY*, which is an ensemble method composed of three different types of base detectors. As we will see, this ensemble method tends to perform better than most of the baseline detectors. Experimental results are presented in Sect. 6.7. The conclusions are presented in Sect. 6.8.

6.2   A Review of Classical Distance-Based Detectors

In the following, we will provide a brief review of classical distance-based detectors. The basic idea in these classical detectors is that outliers are defined as points that are far away from the "crowded regions" based on some commonly used distance measure. While numerous advancements have been made in the outlier analysis domain [2], a group of well-known detectors continue to exhibit a surprisingly high level of robustness under a wide variety of settings. In the following, we review these classical methods, which, in spite of being older methods, have continued to show tremendous robustness with respect to more recent methods. It is likely that the robustness of many of these methods is derived from their simplicity. In unsupervised settings, simpler methods are more easily generalizable across a variety of data sets and data domains than more complex algorithms. Furthermore, even among these detectors, some of them clearly seem to be more dominant than others. One problem with complex detectors is that they tend to have a higher level of variance than simpler detectors, and they can often provide poor results because of overfitting. While it is impossible to test all the complex methods available in the literature, we do investigate the use of some more complex techniques such as kernel methods. An interesting observation from our results is that complexity leads to poorer base detector accuracy, but can often lead to better ensemble-centric *improvements* because of better variance reduction. This fact often leads to all detectors performing more similarly at a performance, which could very well be close to the best achievable performance[1] on a particular data set. We will show several examples of this phenomenon in the experimental section of this chapter.

---

[1]In most learning problems, whether they are supervised or unsupervised, the best achievable performance is unknown. However, if many learning algorithms are used, then the best among them is often close to the best achievable performance. This type of principle has also been used earlier in the context of testing supervised learning algorithms [15].

6.2.1   *Exact k-Nearest Neighbor Detector*

The exact k-NN detector reports the distance of a point to its kth nearest neighbor as the outlier score. Note that the data point is itself excluded while computing the kth nearest neighbor. This is necessary in order to avoid overfitting in the computation. For example, the 1-nearest neighbor distance of a data point is always 0, unless the data point is itself excluded from the computation.

The exact k-nearest neighbor detector was one of the earliest detectors that was developed [29, 30, 47]. The basic version of the detector only outputs an outlier score, which is the distance to the kth nearest neighbor. However, all distance-based methods implement some form of thresholding within the algorithm in order to convert the outlier scores into binary labels. For example, the method in [29] uses an absolute value of the threshold, whereas the method in [47] uses a top-k based thresholding. These different thresholding methods are paired with different data structures in order to make the underlying algorithms more efficient. An important observation is that the exact k-nearest neighbor method requires the computation between all pairs of data points, since the kth nearest neighbor distance needs to be computed for each data point. For a data set containing n points, this process can potentially require $O(n^2)$ time. Therefore, the methods in [29, 47] focus on generating binary scores, in which some clever pruning methods can be incorporated to make the process more efficient. The basic idea in these methods is that one does not need to compute all pairs of distances, if some points can be discarded as non-outliers after computing a subset of their distances. For example, if after computing the distance of point A to the first 100 data points, it is already discovered that its k-nearest neighbor distance is better than the closest outlier found so far, then the point A can be discarded from consideration without computing the distances to all the other data points. Nevertheless, if scores are to be output, then there is no way of avoiding the $O(n^2)$ computation. This is a crucial point because most of the ensemble methods require the computation of the scores from the individual detectors *before* combining them and performing any thresholding. In other words, the computational efficiency advantages proposed in many distance-based detectors [47] cannot be realized in ensemble-centric settings. The computational pruning can be achieved only with voting-based detectors. However, voting-based detectors often lose too much information about the underlying scores to be useful in many settings.

Another key point of variation among distance-based detectors is the specific choice of the distance function that is used. Although we focus on the use of the Euclidean distance (as in traditional settings), significant advantages can sometimes be obtained with the use of data-dependent similarity measures, such as the shared-nearest neighbor distance. Such measures adjust the similarity or distance function to account for the statistical distribution of the data, and achieve similar goals to other locality-sensitive methods like LOF. In fact, some data-dependent measures are more powerful than LOF. A discussion of some data-dependent similarity measures for outlier detection may be found in [63].

6.2.2   Average k-Nearest Neighbor Detector

The average k-nearest neighbor detector [7] is a robust variant of the exact k-nearest neighbor detector. The basic idea in the average k-nearest neighbor detector is to compute the average distance of a data point to its k-nearest neighbors as the outlier score. As in the case of the exact k-nearest neighbor method, the data point is itself excluded while computing the nearest neighbors. The main advantage of the average k-NN detector is that it is more robust to the choice of parameters such as the value of k. This is primarily because the average k-nearest neighbor detector averages the scores of an exact k-nearest neighbor detector over different values of k. If one knew the ideal value of k a priori, it is possible to do better with the exact k-nearest neighbor detector. However, in unsupervised problems like outlier detection, it is impossible to know the "correct" value of any particular parameter such as the value of k. This is where outlier detection problems are different from supervised settings in which one can set the optimal values of the parameters with the use of methods like cross-validation. Therefore, the only way to evaluate such methods is with the use of a range of values over which the evaluation measures are averaged. It is noteworthy that a particular value of k does not mean the same thing for an average k-nearest neighbor detector and an exact k-nearest neighbor detector. For example, if the value of k is 10, then the average k nearest neighbor distance is based on all values of k from 1 to 10, and the *effective* size of the locality is smaller than that of an exact k-nearest neighbor detector. The average k-nearest detector and exact k-nearest detector become the same method at the value of $k = 1$.

6.2.3   An Analysis of Bagged and Subsampled 1-Nearest Neighbor Detectors

As discussed in Chap. 3, the bagged and subsampled 1-nearest neighbor detectors are two detectors that can be implemented without Monte Carlo sampling on the original data set. This is because the expected scores from Monte Carlo sampling can be computed analytically. These expected scores are shown in Eqs. 3.12 and 3.13 of Chap. 3, and we repeat them below. Specifically, if we subsample p out of n points, then the outlier score $E[O(\overline{X})]$ of a point $\overline{X}$, which is not included in the training sample, is expressed in terms of the *relative similarity* of $\overline{Y}$ to $\overline{X}$ with respect to other training data points:

$$E[O(\overline{X})] = \sum_{\overline{Y}:\overline{Y}\neq\overline{X}} \underbrace{S(\overline{X},\overline{Y})}_{\text{Relative Similarity}} \cdot \underbrace{distance(\overline{X},\overline{Y})}_{\text{Absolute Distance}} \qquad (6.1)$$

The relative similarities have the property that they always sum to 1 over a fixed target point $\overline{X}$, and they represent probabilities of each training point $\overline{Y}$ being the nearest neighbor of $\overline{X}$ in the subsample. In other words, we have $\sum_{\overline{Y}:\overline{Y}\neq\overline{X}} S(\overline{X},\overline{Y}) = 1$. It is helpful to think of the relative similarities as relative weights that decay exponentially with increasing distance. The value of $S(\overline{X}, \overline{Y})$ depends on the relative rank $I(\overline{Y}) \in \{1 \ldots n\}$ of the distance of training point $\overline{Y}$ to target point $\overline{X}$ with respect to all the other n training points. To summarize, subsampled 1-nearest neighbor detectors with subsample size of p create a linear, convex combination of all the distances to the remaining points in the set, where the weights of this convex combination are defined as follows (see Eq. 3.12 of Chap. 3):

$$
S(\overline{X}, \overline{Y}) = \begin{cases} \frac{\binom{n-I(\overline{Y})}{p-1}}{\binom{n}{p}} & \text{if } n - I(\overline{Y}) \geq p - 1 \text{ [Choosing } (p-1) \text{ from } (n - I(\overline{Y}))] \\ 0 & \text{if } n - I(\overline{Y}) < p - 1 \text{ [Cannot choose } (p-1) \text{ from } (n - I(\overline{Y}))] \end{cases}
\tag{6.2}
$$

A very similar expression for bagging has also been derived in Eq. 3.17 of Chap. 3, when a bag of p out of n points is used:

$$
S(\overline{X}, \overline{Y}) = \left(1 - \frac{[I(\overline{Y}) - 1]}{n}\right)^p - \left(1 - \frac{I(\overline{Y})}{n}\right)^p
\tag{6.3}
$$

These results show that the scores in subsampling and bagging can be estimated without Monte Carlo sampling. Note that the weights typically decay exponentially with the rank of the distances, although the rate of decay depends on the subsample size p. Choosing small values of p results in slow decay. For example, if we choose $p = 1$, then each $S(\overline{X}, \overline{Y})$ is $1/n$, and the subsampled 1-nearest neighbor detector becomes an average n-nearest neighbor detector. On the other hand, if we choose $p = n$, then $S(\overline{X}, \overline{Y})$ decays so fast that it is only 1 when $\overline{Y}$ is the nearest neighbor of $\overline{X}$ in the whole sample, and 0, otherwise. One can also derive a similar expression for variable subsampling with samples of size between[2] by averaging the value of $S(\overline{X}, \overline{Y})$ over all values of p between n_1 and n_2. As in the case of fixed subsampling, the rate of decay can be shown to be roughly exponential with the ranks of the distances of the training points to the target.

   One observation about the decay of $S(\overline{X}, \overline{Y})$ in the case of the bagged/subsampled 1-nearest neighbor is that it depends only on the rank of the distances to the target. It is also possible to create other exponentially decaying functions for $S(\overline{X}, \overline{Y})$ that depend directly on $||\overline{X} - \overline{Y}||$ although they cannot be directly interpreted as bagged or subsampled 1-nearest neighbors. Nevertheless, the intuition obtained from the bagged/subsampled 1-nearest neighbor detector tells us that such methods are likely

---

[2]If the 1-nearest neighbor detector is used with variable subsampling in the range $[n_1, n_2]$, then the values of n_1 and n_2 are recommended at 10 and 200, respectively. This is because the original variable subsampling method [3] recommends sampling between 50 and 1000 points at $k = 5$. Reducing k proportionately retains the bias characteristics. For smaller data sets, it might make sense to use $k = 1$ simply to reduce the correlations and overlaps between base detectors. This improves the variance reduction.

to be heuristically accurate. The only restriction on selecting $S(\overline{X}, \overline{Y})$ is that it should be normalized to sum to one for fixed target $\overline{X}$ and varying training point $\overline{Y}$.

This goal can be achieved with kernel functions as follows. Let $K(\overline{X}, \overline{Y})$ be any kernel function, such as the Gaussian kernel:

$$K(\overline{X}, \overline{Y}) = e^{-||\overline{X}-\overline{Y}||^2/\sigma^2} \tag{6.4}$$

Then, for target point $\overline{X}$, the value of $S(\overline{X}, \overline{Y})$ can be defined as follows:

$$S(\overline{X}, \overline{Y}) = \frac{K(\overline{X}, \overline{Y})}{\sum_{\overline{Y}:\overline{Y}\neq\overline{X}} K(\overline{X}, \overline{Y})} \tag{6.5}$$

This type of detector has significant potential, although it has not been explored in the literature. Note that if we set $K(\overline{X}, \overline{Y}) = 1/||\overline{X} - \overline{Y}||$, then the approach specializes to the harmonic k-nearest neighbor detector with k set to n. This is because the outlier score is computed as follows:

$$\hat{O}(\overline{X}) = \frac{\sum_{\overline{Y}:\overline{Y}\neq\overline{X}} ||\overline{X} - \overline{Y}|| \frac{1}{||\overline{X}-\overline{Y}||}}{\sum_{\overline{Y}:\overline{Y}\neq\overline{X}} \frac{1}{||\overline{X}-\overline{Y}||}} \tag{6.6}$$

$$= \frac{n}{\sum_{\overline{Y}:\overline{Y}\neq\overline{X}} \frac{1}{||\overline{X}-\overline{Y}||}} \tag{6.7}$$

$$= \text{HARMONIC-MEAN}_{\overline{Y}:\overline{Y}\neq\overline{X}} ||\overline{X} - \overline{Y}|| \tag{6.8}$$

In other words, the harmonic-mean heuristically behaves much like a bagged 1-nearest neighbor detector, except that the decay function is the inverse distance. We discuss this method as a base detector below, along with its connections to density estimation.

6.2.4 Harmonic k-Nearest Neighbor Detector

The harmonic k-nearest neighbor detector is a rarely used method, but it is a technique with several interesting and unusual properties [2]. Like the average k-nearest neighbor detector, the basic idea is to use the mean of all the k distances to the k-nearest neighbors; the main difference is that the *harmonic* mean is used instead of the *arithmetic* mean. Because of the use of the harmonic mean, it is important to remove duplicate points from the data set because the harmonic mean of any set of values including 0 is always 0. When using the harmonic k-nearest neighbor method, it is important to use larger values of k, and one might even use $k = n$ in many data sets with good results. When using $k = n$, the harmonic k-nearest neighbor detector may also be viewed as a density estimator, in which the density-estimation kernel function is the inverse distance of the training point from the target estimation point.

The behavior of a harmonic k-nearest neighbor detector is quite different from that of an average k-nearest neighbor detector when k is set to n. For example, a single outlier at the center of a 2-dimensional ring of points will tend to get an inlier-like score with an average n-nearest neighbor detector. However, a harmonic n-nearest neighbor detector will correctly label it as the strongest outlier, particularly if the value of n is large enough. This is, in part, because the harmonic k-nearest neighbor detector behaves more like a density-based method rather than a distance-based method [2]. Density-based methods become increasingly accurate at large values of n. Interestingly, many density-based methods such as histograms find it difficult to properly score isolated points in central locations (as outliers), particularly when the dimensionality of the data is large. However, kernel-density methods are slightly better than histograms in this respect. It is also possible to combine the harmonic k-nearest neighbor detector with methods like variable subsampling. Because of the density-based interpretation of the harmonic k-nearest neighbor, it makes sense to average the *logarithms* of the outlier scores across different ensemble components (see Sect. 6.3.2).

6.2.5 Local Outlier Factor (LOF)

The *Local Outlier Factor (LOF)* normalizes the k-nearest neighbor distances with distances in its locality. For example, if a locality is expected to contain smaller values of the k-nearest neighbor distances, then the score is adjusted to account for this fact. The basic idea is to adjust the outlier score for the variations in the densities over different data localities.

For a given data point $\overline{X}$, let $D^k(\overline{X})$ be its distance to the k-nearest neighbor of X, and let $L_k(\overline{X})$ be the set of points within the k-nearest neighbor distance of $\overline{X}$. Note that $L_k(\overline{X})$ will typically contain k points, but may sometimes contain more than k points because of ties in the k-nearest neighbor distance. The set $L_k(\overline{X})$ defines the locality over which the distances are averaged to compute the adjustments factor for the outlier score. As we will see later, *harmonic* normalization is used to achieve this goal.

The reachability distance $R_k(\overline{X}, \overline{Y})$ of object $\overline{X}$ with respect to $\overline{Y}$ is defined as the maximum of $dist(\overline{X}, \overline{Y})$ and the k-nearest neighbor distance of $\overline{Y}$.

$$R_k(\overline{X}, \overline{Y}) = \max\{dist(\overline{X}, \overline{Y}), D^k(\overline{Y})\} \tag{6.9}$$

The reachability distance is not symmetric between $\overline{X}$ and $\overline{Y}$. Intuitively, when $\overline{Y}$ is in a dense region and the distance between $\overline{X}$ and $\overline{Y}$ is large, the reachability distance of $\overline{X}$ with respect to it is equal to the true distance $dist(\overline{X}, \overline{Y})$. On the other hand, when the distances between $\overline{X}$ and $\overline{Y}$ are small, then the reachability distance is smoothed out by the k-nearest neighbor distance of $\overline{Y}$. The larger the value of k, the greater the smoothing. Correspondingly, the reachability distances with respect to different points will also become more similar.

Then, the *average reachability distance* $AR_k(\overline{X})$ of data point $\overline{X}$ is defined as the average of its reachability distances to all objects in its neighborhood.

$$AR_k(\overline{X}) = \text{MEAN}_{\overline{Y} \in L_k(\overline{X})} R_k(\overline{X}, \overline{Y}) \tag{6.10}$$

Here, the MEAN function denotes the average of a set of values. The work in [9] also defines the reachability density as the inverse of this value, though this particular presentation omits this step, since the LOF values can be expressed more simply and intuitively in terms of the average reachability distance $AR_k(\overline{X})$. The *Local Outlier Factor* is then simply equal to the mean ratio of $AR_k(\overline{X})$ to the corresponding values of all points in the k-neighborhood of $\overline{X}$.

$$LOF_k(\overline{X}) = \text{MEAN}_{\overline{Y} \in L_k(\overline{X})} \frac{AR_k(\overline{X})}{AR_k(\overline{Y})} \tag{6.11}$$

The use of distance ratios in the definition ensures that the local distance behavior is well accounted for in this definition. A different way of viewing this ratio is as follows:

$$LOF_k(\overline{X}) = \frac{AR_k(\overline{X})}{\text{HARMONIC-MEAN}_{\overline{Y} \in L_k(\overline{X})} AR_k(\overline{Y})} \tag{6.12}$$

The denominator defines the adjustment factor in the normalization process because it is based on the (harmonically) averaged distances in the locality of the data point. As a result, the LOF values for the objects in a cluster are often close to 1, when the data points in the cluster are homogeneously distributed. One can view LOF both as a *relative* distance and as a *relative* density based estimator. Many other local schemes such as LOCI [43] have also been proposed in order to take locality into account during the outlier detection process. Furthermore, many variants of LOF have been proposed in the literature. For example, the LDOF method [67] uses the pairwise distances between data points in $L_k(\overline{X})$ for normalization rather than the harmonically averaged distances. The connectivity-based outlier factor (COF) [57], adjusts the normalization to account for clusters of arbitrary shape in the locality of a data point, whereas the cluster-based local outlier factor (CBLOF) [19] uses the local distances to nearby clusters as well as the sizes of these clusters. These heuristic variants, however, do not always perform better than the original algorithm in spite of their additional complexity. It is also noteworthy that the locality-sensitivity of the LOF can be replicated by using data-dependent similarity measures within exact k-nearest neighbor detectors. For example, one can use the shared-nearest neighbor distance [24] in combination with an exact k-nearest neighbor detector in order to obtain locality-sensitive results.

6.3   A Review of Clustering, Histograms, and Density-Based Methods

Distance-based methods are closely connected to other proximity-based methods such as clustering [42], EM methods (probabilistic clustering) [66], density-based methods [25], and kernel-based methods [21, 31]. In fact, for some distance-based methods like the harmonic k-nearest neighbor detector and LOF, it is sometimes hard to clearly characterize whether these are distance-based methods or density-based methods. All these methods fall in the broader class of proximity-based methods. The main difference between distance-based methods and histogram/kernel-density methods is in the granularity of the analysis. In the latter case, the data space or data points are partitioned into groups and scores are derived from this partitioning.

6.3.1   Histogram and Clustering Methods

These methods partition the data points or data space and score points based on the densities/sizes/distances of the partitions most closely related to them. In practice, these partitioning methods might yield somewhat different anomaly scores from distance-based methods because of their summarization approach to anomaly detection. For example, a summarization technique like clustering has an inherently high variability of the score which makes it an excellent candidate for ensemble-centric implementations. This increased variance is a result of the model-centric uncertainty caused by the specific implementation of the clustering process. In fact, many clustering methods such as k-means and the EM-method are implicitly randomized because of the choice of initialization points. In such cases, it is even more important to use ensemble-centric techniques to reduce the variance of the scores. In fact, the diversity in the summarization process is sometimes more important than the specific quality of the summarization method used within an ensemble-centric implementation. In spite of the poor performance of individual detectors in these settings, the ensemble performance tends to be excellent, when implemented properly.

In histogram methods, the data space is typically partitioned with axis-parallel grid regions. The logarithm of the counts of the points in these grid regions are used to define anomaly scores of the points in these regions. The main problem with histogram methods is that there is a high variability of the scores depending on the sizes of the grid regions used. Furthermore, the approach does not work very well with increasing dimensionality because of the fact that the number of grid regions increases exponentially with data dimensionality. This tends to make it a natural candidate for ensemble methods. In the following, we discuss several implementations of clustering and histograms that address these challenges with use an ensemble-centric implementation.

6.3.1.1 Ensemble-Centric Implementations of Clustering

An effective implementation of an EM-clustering method is reported in [14]. Note that EM-clustering can also be viewed as a parametric density-estimation method. This is not particularly surprising since clustering methods are intimately related to density-based methods. Indeed, there are many methods that have dual or triple interpretations from the algorithmic classes of clustering, histograms, and density-estimation methods because of their close connection. The clustering is implemented with multiple initialization points and choice of parameters (e.g., number of mixture components). The EM algorithm returns fit values as scores in each ensemble component. The logarithms of these scores are then averaged over these different components to yield the final result. Good results have been shown in [14] with this implementation.

Another ensemble-centric implementation of clustering methods is the OutRank method [38]. This approach is focused on high-dimensional data and it therefore focuses on using projected clustering methods as ensemble components. This tends to reveal subspace outliers [4]. A variant, known as *Multiple-Proclus*, uses the PRO-CLUS algorithm [5] within each ensemble component. The data points are scored based on the number of points and the dimensionality of the cluster in which a point occurs. Points that occur in clusters of small size and dimensionality across many ensemble components are deemed as outliers.

6.3.1.2 Subspace Histograms in Linear Time

A subspace-histogram method, referred to as RS-Hash, has been proposed in [51]. In this approach, histograms are built on random subspaces of the data. The dimensionality of the subspace, grid width, and grid placement of grid regions is randomly varied over different ensemble components. Furthermore, the histograms are built on subsamples of size s although all points are scored against these subsamples. A hashing technique is used to efficiently keep track of the counts of the grid regions in each ensemble component, which results in it being called the RS-Hash method. The logarithms of these counts are then averaged over the different ensemble components in order to provide the final result. Lower scores are indicative of a greater degree of outlierness. The varying grid width, grid placement, and dimensionality is helpful in providing high-quality results.

The dimensionality is controlled with a parameter r, the grid size with a parameter f chosen uniformly at random from $(1 - 1/\sqrt{s}, 1/\sqrt{s})$, and random shift parameter α_j associated with dimension j chosen uniformly at random from $(0, f)$. The last parameter controls the grid placement. The value of r is set uniformly at random to an integer between $1 + 0.5 \cdot [\log_{\max\{2, 1/f\}}(s)]$ and $\log_{\max\{2, 1/f\}}(s)$. In each ensemble component, a subset of r dimensions (denoted by V) is sampled up front, and the grid cell for each point is determined. Let min_j and max_j be the minimum and maximum values of dimension j, which are determined from the sample of size s at the time it is selected. The discrete grid cell identifier for any point i and dimension

j, which is included in V, is determined as $\left\lfloor \frac{(x_{ij}+\alpha_j(max_j-min_j))}{f(max_j-min_j)} \right\rfloor$. Thus, each point is represented by r discrete identifiers (representing its grid cell), which can be hashed into the hash table for counting purposes. During the training phase, we scan through the sample, convert them to discrete identifiers and map them into the hash table. During the testing phase, we scan through all n points, convert them using the same approach as the training sample, retrieve their counts, and use the logarithm as the outlier score. An additional value of 1 is added to the retrieved count of points not included in the initial sample S before applying the logarithm function. This is done in order to adjust for overfitting between training and test points. The approach is repeated multiple times over different ensemble components and the average score is returned as the final result. Note that the values of min_j and max_j for conversion are computed only on the training sample, and they are fixed during both training and testing of a single ensemble component.

The subspace histogram requires $O(s)$ time for constructing each histogram in an ensemble component. The value of s is typically a small constant like 1000. Furthermore, since the time for hashing each point is also a small constant, the implementation is extraordinarily fast in practice. The testing time is $O(n)$, since the same process of hashing and retrieving the counts is repeated for each test point. Therefore, the approach requires linear time, and is often extremely fast in practice. The approach has also been extended to data streams, and this variant is referred to as RS-Stream.

6.3.1.3 Isolation Forests

Even though the isolation forest might seem quite different from histograms at first sight, it is a highly randomized histogram and density-estimation method under the covers. Of course, the notion of "density" used here is a slightly different one, but the results tend to be highly correlated with other (subspace) density-based methods. In other words, it would perform well or perform poorly in similar settings and data sets as other (subspace) density-based methods.

The isolation forest[3] is also referred to as *iForest*. An isolation forest is an outlier detection method that shares some intuitive similarities with random forests in the classification domain [10, 22], although the objective of tree construction is quite different. At the same time, isolation forests can also be viewed as a subspace method in which the scoring function quantifies the ease with which a local subspace of low dimensionality can be found to isolate a particular point with a randomized exploration process. In this sense, the isolation forest exhibits intuitive similarities with feature bagging as well.

An isolation forest is constructed using a set of isolation trees. Each isolation tree is constructed like a decision tree in top-down fashion. The algorithm starts with the

---

[3]The description here is almost identical to that provided in Sect. 3.4.3.1 of Chap. 3. The description is repeated in both places for the benefit of readers who have electronic access to only one of the chapters of this book.

entire data set at the root node. An attribute is randomly chosen, and then a binary split is executed at a random point between the minimum and maximum ranges of that attribute. Therefore, the data is split into the two children of that node. This process is recursively repeated until each node contains a single point. This tree will typically not be balanced, because points in dense regions will tend to require a larger number of splits whereas nodes in sparse regions will get isolated earlier on. Therefore, the outlier score of a data point is equal to its depth in the isolation tree. In other words, the number of edges (splits) from the root to the leaf is used as the outlier score. Since an isolation forest is naturally constructed as an ensemble from multiple isolation trees, the scores from the different trees are averaged in order to obtain the final outlier score. In high-dimensional data, the number of splits from the root to the leaf often correlates very well with the dimensionality of the local subspace in which a point is isolated as an outlier. From this point of view, the isolation forest defines outliers as data points that can be isolated easily in lower dimensional subspaces using random splits. Although the original description of isolation forest does not emphasize its connections to subspace outlier detection, this view provides an interesting perspective on the inner workings of the approach.

A single iteration of the recursive splitting process during isolation tree building can be described as follows:

1. Select any node in the (current) isolation tree with more than one point, which has not been split so far.
2. Select any attribute x for splitting.
3. Select a random split point a between the minimum and maximum ranges of that attribute.
4. Create two children of the node based on the random split point and distribute the points to the two children. All points with $x \leq a$ are assigned to one child and all points with $x > a$ are assigned to the other child. Store the split predicate of the form $x \leq a$ or $x > a$ at each of the children. This split predicate can also be used for scoring out-of-sample points that are not included within the training data for *iForest* construction.

The process is repeated until each node in the isolation tree contains exactly one point. For a data set containing n points, this process requires $\theta(n \cdot \log(n))$ time in the average case, although it is possible for it to require $O(n^2)$ time, if the tree is full unbalanced. However, the average case is almost always achieved in practical settings. The approach also requires $O(n)$ space. When the entire data set is used for tree-building (i.e., there are no out-of-sample points), a separate testing phase is not required because the depth of each point can be computed during tree building.

However, to make the approach more efficient, subsampling is used. In some cases, subsampling also improves accuracy because of increased variance-reduction effects, although this improvement is inconsistent. The *iForest* approach samples 256 points from the data set and constructs an isolation tree on this sample. Note that such an approach requires constant time for construction of the isolation tree. When subsampling is used, a separate testing phase is required in order to score the data points. During the training phase, each split point is stored as a split *predicate*.

For example, if the ith attribute is split at value of a, then the two branches of the tree will defined by the condition (or *predicate*) whether $x_i \leq a$ is satisfied. For each test points, we use the split predicates in order to traverse the appropriate path in the isolation tree. The number of edges from the root to the leaf provides the final outlier score. The subsampling approach requires constant space and constant time for training because the tree contains only 256 points. Furthermore, for a tree containing 256 points, the testing time for each point is a small constant, which depends on the depth of the tree. Therefore, the isolation tree requires $O(n)$ time for testing with a small constant factor (for each ensemble component).

From an interpretability point of view, one can view the isolation tree as a randomized test of the ease of being able to isolate a point in a local subspace of low dimensionality. Note that the path length from the root to the leaf node isolates a local subspace, and is roughly[4] indicative of the dimensionality required to isolate the point with randomized partitioning. For example, consider a setting in which we have various physical measurements of an individual, and it is unusual for individuals of height less than 5 ft to have weight greater than 200 pounds. In such a case, a sequence of splits like $Height \leq 5$, $Weight \geq 200$ might quickly isolate a point in a path of length only 2. A closely related subspace interpretation of isolation is with the use of the notion of *mass* [56, 62]. According to this interpretation, minor modifications of isolation forests can also be used to quickly discover subspace regions of low density, although the notion of mass is technically different from density, technically similar quantities are measured in the two cases. Like histogram-based methods, the isolation forest randomly partitions the data *space* (rather than the *points*), and discover sparse regions in the data space to discover outliers. Like histogram-based methods, isolation-based methods tend to be biased against outliers in central regions of the data, and therefore they sometimes miss such points in certain types of data distributions. An example of such a distribution is provided in Sect. 6.7.5. A detailed discussion of the strengths and weaknesses of isolation forests may be found in [8].

Although the original implementation of the *iForest* uses fixed subsampling, it is possible to use variable subsampling to reduce the effect of subsample size on the performance. As shown in [34] with the varying performance on the *Mulcross* data generator [48], the isolation forest's performance can be sensitive to data size. Therefore, by varying the subsample size according to the principles in [3], this effect is diminished.

---

[4]Although the same dimension may be used to split a node along a path of the tree, this becomes increasingly unlikely with increasing dimensionality. Therefore, the outlier score is roughly equal to the dimensionality required to isolate a point with random splits in very high dimensional data. For a subsample of 256 points, roughly 8 dimensions are required to isolate a point, but only 4 or 5 dimensions might be sufficient for an outlier. The key is in the power of the ensemble, because at least some of the components will isolate the point in a local subspace of low dimensionality.

6.3.2   Kernel Density Methods

Kernel-density methods are softer variants of histogram methods. Histogram methods score points depending on their lying within fixed grid regions. A kernel density estimator uses a smooth kernel function to define the "influence" of each data point. For example, consider the case in which we use the Gaussian kernel function with bandwidth σ. In such a case, the density estimation $\hat{f}(\overline{X})$ of the data point $\overline{X}$ is as follows:

$$\hat{f}(\overline{X}) = \frac{1}{n} \sum_{\overline{Y}:\overline{Y}\neq\overline{X}} e^{-||\overline{X}-\overline{Y}||^2/\sigma^2} \tag{6.13}$$

We have omitted some of the constants in the exponent and at the front of the expression for simplicity; however, since outlier scores are relative and σ is an adjustable parameter, this does not affect the overall result. The outlier score of a data point is given by $-\log(\hat{f}(\overline{X}))$ to create a log-likelihood estimate. One can use ensembles with this approach by combining it with subsampling, with feature bagging, or by varying the bandwidth σ. The results of kernel density methods are very similar to histogram methods, and are also closely related to bagged/subsampled 1-nearest neighbors. In fact, as discussed in Sects. 6.2.3 and 6.2.4, the harmonic k-nearest neighbor detector is a heuristic variant of the subsampled 1-nearest neighbor (with an inverse distance kernel function), and it is also a density estimator by using the inverse distance kernel density function. In fact, one can express the density estimator above in terms of Eq. 6.1 by using the kernel function of Eq. 6.4 and setting the distance function $distance(\overline{X}, \overline{Y})$ to the exponentiated Euclidean distance value of $e^{||\overline{X}-\overline{Y}||^2/\sigma^2}$ (which is also the inverse of the kernel function). Note that Eq. 6.1 is a generalized variant of the bagged and subsampled 1-nearest neighbor.

6.3.2.1   Are Specific Ensemble Methods Suitable to Particular Base Detectors?

Different ensemble methods seem to be well suited to particular base detectors. In this context, it is helpful to examine two classes of base detectors corresponding to distance-based methods and density/histogram-based methods. These two classes of base detectors are closely related. Yet, they seem to show completely different performance with respect to point-wise sampling or feature-wise sampling:

1. Distance-based detectors seem to perform well with methods like point-wise subsampling and point-wise bagging. However, when distance-based methods are combined with feature bagging, the performance gains are quite modest. In a few cases, the performance can deteriorate. This is in part because distance-based methods are inherently suited to aggregating the evidence over multiple dimensions, and the bias deterioration from dropping dimensions can sometimes be large. Furthermore, the diversity in the estimation from point-wise sampling is much better than that obtained from feature-wise sampling.

2. Density-based detectors like isolation forests [34] and subspace histograms [51] gain significantly from randomized subspace exploration. However, the effects of point-wise subsampling are often more unpredictable in these cases. This is in part because density-based methods have large bias deterioration with reduction in number of points, and also tend to work particularly poorly in higher dimensionality in terms of estimation accuracy [55]. In fact, density-based methods require an exponentially increasing number of points with increasing dimensionality of the representation. Furthermore, the diversity in estimation from feature-wise sampling seems to be much better than that obtained from point-wise sampling in the case of density-based methods.

These observations suggest that the choice of a base method and its ensemble-centric adaptation are sometimes related in unexpected ways. Blindly applying a particular ensemble method to a base technique can be a recipe for unpredictable results.

6.4   A Review of Dependency-Oriented Detectors

Several detectors use violations in inter-attribute dependencies in order to detect outliers. Some of these techniques use PCA-based methods, whereas others explicitly use learning methods. These models are also referred to as linear models in [2], although the kernel variants of these methods allow for nonlinear distributions.

The basic idea is that the data points are distributed on linear or nonlinear hyperplanes in the underlying data as a result of inter-attribute correlations. Points that violate these inter-attribute correlations should be tagged as outliers. An example of such a point is the point 'A' in Fig. 6.2, in which the data point does not lie on the linear hyperplane on which the remaining data set is distributed. In this sense, principal component analysis [23, 54] is an effective way to discover outliers. For example, the 1-dimensional direction of correlation is shown in Fig. 6.2. The distance of point A to this one-dimensional hyperplane provides the outlier score. Note that if A is projected on this 1-dimensional hyperplane to the new point A', then the distance between A and A' provides the outlier score. One can generalize this idea to discovering the k-dimensional hyperplanes in d-dimensional data. For example, in Fig. 6.2, the 1-dimensional hyperplane with the largest *variance* in 2-dimensional data is discovered and the distance of the data point to this 1-dimensional hyperplane is discovered. In other words, outlier scores are computed along *low* variance directions. This distance can also be viewed as the *reconstruction error* of a dimensionality reduction method. Intuitively, outliers are data points that cannot be reconstructed accurately from a compressed representation (like PCA) because they are not in agreement with the trends in the underlying data. Therefore, the PCA method works as follows:

1. Determine the k orthogonal directions with the largest variance and project the data on this k-dimensional hyperplane. As discussed in the next section, principal

Fig. 6.2 Linear pattern with outliers

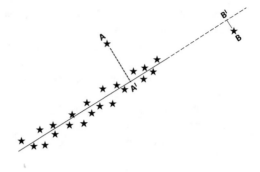

component analysis can be used to discover the k directions with the largest variance.
2. Report the Euclidean distance between each original data point and its projected representation (i.e., reconstruction error) as the outlier score.

An immediate observation is that the value of k is a parameter to the algorithm, which causes some challenges for unsupervised problems. Can we somehow get rid of this parameter? Furthermore, such an approach will miss extreme values along high-variance directions. For example, the outlier B in Fig. 6.2 will be missed. This is because it is an extreme value along the high-variance direction. Such extreme values can exist in real data sets because it is possible for rare instances to also respect the data correlations by simply being extreme values along correlated directions. It turns out that soft versions of PCA use a more gentle approach of *discounting* high-variance directions, but not completely dropping them. Low-variance directions are also treated in a more graceful way by weighing them differentially. Furthermore, such methods preclude the need for specific parameter choices like the value of k because every direction is included in the score, albeit in a discounted way. One such technique is the Mahalanobis method, which is a parameter-free method.

6.4.1   Soft PCA: The Mahalanobis Method

The Mahalanobis method reports the outlier score of a data point as its Mahalanobis distance from the centroid of the data set. The Mahalanobis method has several different interpretations. It can be viewed as a distance-based approach, a probabilistic approach, or as a soft PCA-based approach. While the distance-based interpretation is obvious, the other two interpretations are slightly less obvious. In this discussion, we touch upon the latter two interpretations because they provide a better idea of why this simple approach works so well.

The Mahalanobis method [54] is a multivariate extreme value analysis method, and is often viewed as a relatively rudimentary special case of distance-based methods in which the Mahalanobis distance of a point is computed to the centroid of the data as the outlier score rather than the k-nearest neighbor distance. This simplistic view, however, tends to miss the tremendous amount of knowledge encoded within its use of inter-attribute correlations. The method determines the outliers at the pareto-extremes of the data, and at the same time borrows a number of ideas from principal component analysis. In fact, the Mahalanobis method can also be viewed as a soft version of PCA-based methods. The PCA-based interpretation is more meaningful because the use of inter-attribute correlations tends to have a *more significant* effect on the performance of the technique. This fact is especially important with increasing dimensionality. In the event that locality needs to be incorporated within the technique, one can also use an instance-specific Mahalanobis method [1] by using the locality of the data point rather than all the points. The drawback of doing so is that it can lead to overfitting, and the definition of the locality of a point is itself dependent on the Mahalanobis distance. Therefore, we focus on the global Mahalanobis method in this discussion.

In the probabilistic interpretation, the basic idea is to model the entire data set to be normally distributed about its mean in the form of a multivariate Gaussian distribution. Let $\overline{\mu}$ be the d-dimensional mean vector of a d-dimensional data set, and Σ be its $d \times d$ co-variance matrix. In this case, the (i, j)th entry of the covariance matrix is equal to the covariance between the dimensions i and j. Then, the probability distribution $f(\overline{X})$ for a d-dimensional data point $\overline{X}$ can be defined as follows:

$$f(\overline{X}) = \frac{1}{\sqrt{|\Sigma|} \cdot (2 \cdot \pi)^{(d/2)}} \cdot \exp\left[-\frac{1}{2} \cdot (\overline{X} - \overline{\mu}) \cdot \Sigma^{-1} \cdot (\overline{X} - \overline{\mu})^T\right] \quad (6.14)$$

The value of $|\Sigma|$ denotes the determinant of the covariance matrix. We note that the term in the exponent is (half) the *Mahalanobis distance* between the data point $\overline{X}$ and the mean $\overline{\mu}$ of the data. The computation of the Mahalanobis distance requires the inversion of the covariance matrix Σ. The value in the exponent of the normal distribution above is used as the outlier score. This interpretation is quite powerful, because we can generalize this idea to assume that the data is normally distributed in some transformed kernel space. Such a variation leads to the *kernel* Mahalanobis method, which is discussed in the next section. Although the kernel Mahalanobis method is a natural extension of the Mahalanobis method, we have not seen a detailed experimental analysis of this technique anywhere. This book will provide such an analysis, and also provide an efficient ensemble-centric variant of this technique.

The Mahalanobis distance is similar to the Euclidean distance, except that it normalizes the data on the basis of the inter-attribute correlations. For example, if the axis system of the data were to be rotated to the principal directions (shown in Fig. 6.3), then the data would have no inter-attribute correlations. It is possible to use PCA to determine such directions of correlations in d-dimensional data sets. In order to determine the directions of correlation, the covariance matrix Σ is diagonalized as follows:

$$\Sigma = P\Delta P^T \quad (6.15)$$

Here, Δ is a $d \times d$ diagonal matrix containing non-negative eigenvalues, and P is a $d \times d$ matrix, whose columns contain the d orthonormal eigenvectors. These orthonormal eigenvectors provide the basis system corresponding to the directions

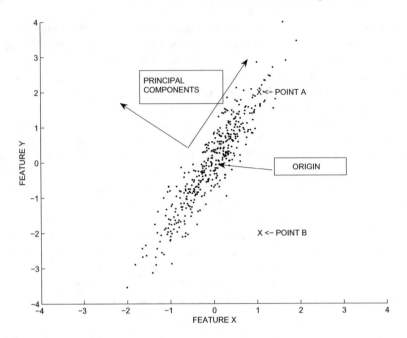

Fig. 6.3 Extreme value analysis in multivariate data with Mahalanobis distance

of de-correlated representation. It is noteworthy that the matrix Δ always contains non-negative elements along the diagonal because of the fact that the covariance matrix is always positive semi-definite.

Since the columns of the matrix P contain the orthonormal basis vectors, one can transform the original $n \times d$ data matrix D by using the matrix product DP.

$$D' = DP \qquad (6.16)$$

The $n \times d$ matrix DP contains the transformed coordinates. The directions corresponding to the orthonormal eigenvectors in P are shown in Fig. 6.3. The Mahalanobis distance is simply equal to the Euclidean distance in such a transformed (axes-rotated) data set *after* dividing each of the transformed coordinate values by the standard-deviation of that direction. Therefore, one simply normalizes the data to unit mean after transforming the data to the coordinate system shown in Fig. 6.3, and then reports the distance from the centroid of the data as the outlier score. Therefore, an alternative method for computing the Mahalanobis distance is as follows:

1. Compute the $d \times d$ covariance matrix Σ of the $n \times d$ data matrix D.
2. Compute the eigenvectors of Σ as follows:

$$\Sigma = P \Delta P^T \qquad (6.17)$$

3. Compute the transformed representation as $D' = DP$.
4. Normalize the data in D', so that each transformed dimension has unit standard deviation.
5. Report the outlier score of each row in D' as its squared Euclidean distance to the mean.

This approach recognizes the fact that the different directions of correlation have different variance, and the data should be treated in a statistically normalized way along these directions. For example, in the case of Fig. 6.3, the data point B can be more reasonably considered an outlier than data point A, on the basis of the natural correlations in the data. On the other hand, the data points A and B are equidistant from the centroid of the data on the basis of the Euclidean distance. The Mahalanobis distance will, however, correctly discover the fact that the data point B is an outlier, as a direct result of the normalization step along the principal components.

We further note that each of the distances along the principal correlation directions can be modeled as a one-dimensional standard normal distribution, which is approximately independent from the other orthogonal directions of correlation. The sum of the squares of d variables drawn independently from a standard normal distributions, will result in a variable drawn from a χ^2 distribution with d degrees of freedom. Therefore, the cumulative probability distribution tables of the χ^2 distribution can be used in order to identify outliers at the appropriate level of significance.

This simple approach is effective for the example of Fig. 6.3, because the entire data set is distributed in one large cluster about the mean. For cases in which the data may have many different clusters with different orientations, such an extreme value approach may not be effective. An example of such a data set is illustrated in Fig. 6.4. In this case, one of the outliers in the interior of the data will be missed by the method. For such cases, one can generalize the probabilistic model of this section (with a single Gaussian) to a mixture model [66] with *multiple* Gaussian components. Unfortunately, this generalization requires the incorporation of an additional parameter in the form of the number of mixture components. This generalization therefore loses one of the important advantages of the Mahalanobis method, which is the fact that it is parameter-free (unlike most other outlier detection methods). Furthermore, if the number of mixture components is overestimated, it is easily possible for a small outlier cluster to overfit one of the mixture components.

Interestingly, in many real data sets, the Mahalanobis method often performs competitively or better than more complex outlier detection algorithms. There are many reasons for this fact. First, the Mahalanobis method is a powerful way of capturing the correlation structure in high-dimensional data without causing excessive overfitting. Second, the Mahalanobis method is also able to detect multivariate extreme values at the pareto-boundaries of the data. Many real applications naturally extract features in which extremes in values correspond to outliers. For example, in a breast-cancer diagnosis application, extremes in clinical measures often correspond to abnormalities, but values in the center of the data are often normal. Therefore, if the analyst has an understanding of the nature of features extracted for a particular data set, it can be used to make a judgement of whether the Mahalanobis method is indeed the best

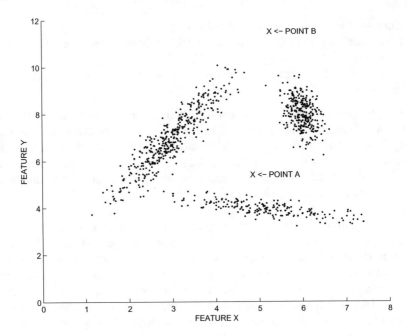

Fig. 6.4 EM-Algorithm can determine clusters with arbitrary correlations

technique to use for a particular data set. Even though the Mahalanobis method may often miss a portion of the outliers, it is beneficial to use it as one of the ensemble components of an outlier detection algorithm.

6.4.1.1 Observations on Parametrization and Computational Complexity

It is noteworthy that there are some significant advantages of the Mahalanobis method over its distance-based counterparts both in terms of parametrization and computational complexity. These advantages are as follows:

1. All the other distance-based methods such as the exact k-nearest neighbor detector, average k-nearest neighbor detector, and the local outlier factor (LOF) require $O(n^2)$ time, because they require the computation of all point-to-point distances. On the other hand, the Mahalanobis method only requires the computation of a covariance matrix, which is linear in the number of points. It does require the computation of a covariance matrix of size $O(d^2)$ and its inversion. However, in most real data sets the dimensionality is much less than the number of points (i.e., $d \ll n$). As a result, it is often computationally much more efficient to apply the Mahalanobis method.

2. All the distance-based methods such as the exact k-nearest neighbor method, average k-nearest neighbor method, and the LOF method require the specification of a parameter k. Unfortunately, the outlier detection approach can often be sensitive to the choice of the parameter k. In unsupervised problems, there is also no way of determining the best value of k beyond selecting the value of k within a range. The Mahalanobis method, however, has the advantage that it is *parameter free*. This makes it extremely robust and stable. On the other hand, one cannot gain too much with the use of variance-reduction methods such as variable subsampling when using stable detectors like the Mahalanobis method. As we will see later, this stability is, nevertheless, very valuable because the Mahalanobis method can perform well both at the base detector level, and at the ensemble level even though it does not gain much from variance-reduction techniques. In cases, where the application of an ensemble is too expensive, the application of even a small number of ensemble components of the Mahalanobis method is usually sufficient.

In later sections, we will explore these different trade-offs between stability and accuracy with the use of experimental analysis.

6.4.2   Kernel Mahalanobis Method

The Kernel Mahalanobis method can be viewed as a soft version of kernel PCA. While hard versions of kernel PCA have been used in the literature for outlier detection [23], they incorporate the additional challenge of having to select a number of dimensions from the data in a hard way. Whenever the number of parameters required to be input to an unsupervised problem increases, it adds an additional layer of uncertainty at execution time because of the difficulty in choosing these parameters in a meaningful way. Furthermore, parameter choice in unsupervised problems often requires some understanding of the physical or semantic interpretation of the underlying data representation, which is notoriously hard for kernel methods. In this book, we discuss the soft version of kernel PCA, which is also referred to as the kernel Mahalanobis method. The approach described here is a natural extension of well-known Mahalanobis method, and we have not seen a detailed analysis of this method anywhere, especially within the ensemble-centric context. However, this discussion does borrow some of the ideas associated with *kernel whitening*, which are discussed in [61]. This approach represents the natural generalization of the Mahalanobis method with a kernel transformation. Although the method in [61] uses the kernel representation in combination with 1-class support vector machines, we present a first ensemble-centric adaptation of the Mahalanobis method in kernel space. The ensemble-centric adaptation of the Mahalanobis method has several advantages over (the more controversial) one-class SVMs, which are sensitive [14, 35] to the choice of kernel and underlying representation. The experimental evaluations in both [14, 35] complain about the difficulty in parameter setting for one-class

SVMs; furthermore, the work in [14] shows that the one-class SVM method frequently provides worse-than-random performance even after good-faith attempts at tuning parameters. Although the work in [35] suggests that the one-class SVM might perform well if the parameters are carefully tuned and the underlying data representation is selected carefully, it is also suggested that the process of doing so is exceedingly difficult without having a deeper semantic understanding of the data. All these issues make the one-class SVM rather hard to use in real settings.

The kernel Mahalanobis method is particularly useful in settings in which the data is distributed along non-linear manifolds of the data. An example of such a data set is illustrated in Fig. 6.5. In this case, the data is arranged along a nonlinear manifold, and the point 'A' is an outlier. In this case, it is evident that the use of PCA will not discover outliers. In such cases, one can use kernel PCA [23] in order to embed the data into a space in which it is linearly correlated. In such a space, the data point 'A' will be exposed as an outlier using PCA. Kernel methods are designed to discover such embeddings. The work in [23] explores the use of hard kernel PCA methods; here we investigate the use of soft kernel PCA methods.

Just as the linear Mahalanobis method models the data in the form of a single Gaussian distribution in *input* feature space, the kernel Mahalanobis method models the data as a single Gaussian distribution in *kernel* feature space. In order to understand the nature of the generalization from the linear Mahalanobis method to the kernel Mahalanobis method, we provide an alternative description of the linear Mahalanobis method, which is implemented using similarity matrices rather than covariance matrices. Let D be an $n \times d$ data matrix which is mean centered. Therefore, the $d \times d$ covariance matrix is defined by $\Sigma = \frac{D^T D}{n} \propto D^T D$. The eigenvectors of this matrix give the principal component directions, and the data is projected on this directions to provide the embedding. However, it is also possible to discover this embedding directly without going through the steps of discovering the principal components by using the $n \times n$ *similarity matrix* $S = DD^T$. Note that the (i, j)th entry in DD^T is the dot product between the ith and jth data points. One can diagonalize the positive semi-definite matrix $S = DD^T$ as follows:

$$S = Q\Lambda^2 Q^T \tag{6.18}$$

Fig. 6.5 Nonlinear pattern with an outlier

When S is set to DD^T, the number of nonzero eigenvectors will be no larger than d. Then, it can be shown that the first d columns of $Q\Lambda$ provide the transformed representation of the data using PCA. This transformed data set is *exactly the same* as the data set $D' = DP$ obtained in Eq. 6.16. Furthermore, we do not need the basis vectors in P to compute the Mahalanobis distance. One can simply standardize each column of D' to zero mean and unit variance, and compute the distance of each data point to the centroid of D' as the Mahalanobis score. Therefore, this alternative approach may be described as follows:

1. Compute the $d \times d$ similarity matrix $S = DD^T$ of the mean-centered $n \times d$ data matrix D.
2. Compute the eigenvectors of S as follows:

$$S = Q\Lambda^2 Q^T \tag{6.19}$$

3. Compute the transformed representation as all the non-zero eigenvector columns of $Q\Lambda$ and define the resulting matrix as D'.
4. Normalize the data in D', so that each transformed dimension has unit standard deviation.
5. Report the outlier score of each row in D' as its squared Euclidean distance to the mean.

However, why would anyone want to use such an approach instead of using the (smaller) covariance matrix? The data set $D' = DP$ can be computed using the eigenvectors of a $d \times d$ covariance matrix, whereas the similarity-based method uses the eigenvectors of an $n \times n$ similarity matrix. Since n is typically much larger than d in real settings, it makes little sense to use such an approach at least for the straightforward case of linear PCA. However, the use of the similarity matrix has the advantage that one can use it to extract nonlinear embeddings like those shown in Fig. 6.5. The key idea is to change the entries in the similarity matrix from the dot product to those obtained by using more carefully chosen kernel functions. Therefore, even though such an approach does not make much sense in the linear setting, it is the only way to implement it in the nonlinear setting.

One can view the use of the dot products in S as a special case of the kernel similarity matrix, in which the (i, j)th entry as the kernel similarity $K(\overline{X}_i, \overline{X}_j) = \overline{X}_i \cdot \overline{X}_j$. This kernel is also referred to as the *linear kernel*. However, this choice of kernel similarity only yields linear PCA. The basic idea in nonlinear PCA is that instead of using the kernel similarity $K(\overline{X}_i, \overline{X}_j) = \overline{X}_i \cdot \overline{X}_j$, we can use[5] functions such as the Gaussian or the polynomial kernel. Some common examples of such kernel functions include the following:

---

[5]Strictly speaking, kernel PCA also requires mean-centering of the similarity matrix. However, this step is not absolutely essential for outlier detection and only adds to the complexity. With certain types of kernels, mean-centering can even be counter-productive for outlier detection. Therefore, it has not been included in our description, and it has also not been used in the experiments.

Function	Form
Gaussian Radial Basis Kernel	$K(\overline{X_i}, \overline{X_j}) = e^{-||\overline{X_i} - \overline{X_j}||^2/\sigma^2}$
Polynomial Kernel	$K(\overline{X_i}, \overline{X_j}) = (\overline{X_i} \cdot \overline{X_j} + c)^h$
Sigmoid Kernel	$K(\overline{X_i}, \overline{X_j}) = \tanh(\kappa \overline{X_i} \cdot \overline{X_j} - \delta)$

The use of such kernel functions is equivalent to using the dot product in some transformed space where nonlinear correlations map to linear correlations. The choice of the kernel function has a critical impact on the type of distribution that the approach can handle. For example, if the small entries of a Gaussian kernel similarity matrix are set to 0, the approach provides an embedding that is similar to that obtained in spectral clustering. Such an embedding will separate out the different clusters well. Furthermore, it is also possible to use a different scoring mechanism [50] once such an embedding has been obtained. The use of the Gaussian kernel[6] is generally recommended [23, 26, 52, 53, 61], although the optimal choice of kernel can be data set-specific. The most commonly used kernel is the Gaussian kernel, which has a parameter corresponding to the *bandwidth* σ. For data sets with less than 1000 points, it is recommended to use between two or three times the median distance between sampled pairs of points as the bandwidth σ.

We cannot easily control the dimensionality of the embedding. When dealing with any kernel function other than the dot product, the dimensionality of the embedding can be as large as the number of data points n because more than d eigenvalues might be nonzero. This type of situation is common with the use of the Gaussian kernel. The embedded representation needs to use all nonzero eigenvalues because outliers are often emphasized along small eigenvalues. There are also some challenges associated with numerical stability; in some cases, zero eigenvalues appear as nonzero eigenvalues as a result of numerical errors made in the computation. Such eigenvalues should not be included in D'. In addition, the errors in smaller eigenvalues are exacerbated to a greater degree in the *relative* sense by numerical errors; this provides an additional reason why they should not be included. Typically using a conservative threshold on the size of the eigenvalue (such as 10^{-8}) is sufficient. One caveat is that the kernel Mahalanobis method sometimes does not work well because of overfitting; for example, one can sometimes obtain poor results when most or all of the eigenvectors are nonzero. In such cases, the best solution is to drop a small number (say about 10) of the *largest* eigenvectors because outliers are emphasized along the smaller eigenvectors. In other cases, dropping large eigenvectors can miss correct outliers, which are emphasized along those directions as extreme values in the original data. These types of quirks are particularly common with the (Gaussian) kernel Mahalanobis method, and they do not occur in the linear kernel setting in which at most $d \ll n$ eigenvectors are nonzero and one can

---

[6]In the table of kernels, we have omitted a constant factor of 2 in the denominator of the exponent of the Gaussian for simplicity. Our discussion throughout this section makes this assumption and it does make a difference while interpreting the selected choice of σ.

use all the nonzero eigenvectors without the risks of overfitting. Nevertheless, the ensemble-centric implementation, which is discussed later, does not have this problem because of its use of *out-of-sample* embeddings. Out-of-sample embeddings are particularly useful in avoiding the pervasive problem of overfitting, and are inherently designed to work in ensemble-centric form.

Note that each of the kernel functions discussed above has a number of parameters associated with it. The choice of the kernel function and its parameters regulates how well the nonlinear shapes in the data can be captured. Herein lies the rub; while kernel functions can be optimized easily using the ground-truth in supervised problems, there is no easy way to do so in unsupervised methods. While some heuristic rules exist for selecting the kernel parameters based on data size, dimensionality, and variance, the results of using these parameters vary significantly over different data sets. For the Gaussian kernel, smaller values of σ can model complex boundaries but will also cause overfitting. Values of σ much larger than the pairwise distances between points will yield results that are similar to the linear Mahalanobis method. A common approach is to use a value of σ somewhere between the median and the maximum pairwise distances between points. When working with larger data sets, one can afford to use smaller values of σ. The optimum value of σ is therefore sensitive to data size, and it is also sensitive to the underlying data distribution.

Although the nonlinear method is *potentially* more powerful, we found that these parameter-setting issues made it exceedingly difficult to use in such a way that we could obtain *consistently* better results than the linear Mahalanobis method when a *single* application of the base component was used. However, the ensemble-centric implementation seems to perform extremely well. This is particularly notable in light of the fact that some kernel methods like one-class SVMs often provide either unpredictable [35] or worse-than-random performance [14]. This is caused in part by the difficulty in tuning the numerous parameters in these methods. In fact, our preference for the kernel Mahalanobis method over many other kernel methods such as hard kernel PCA [23], one-class SVMs [26, 52, 53, 58], one-class kernel Fisher discriminants [23], and support vector data descriptions [58, 60], was motivated by an overwhelming desire to minimize the number of parameters (and underlying uncertainty). The relationship of the kernel Mahalanobis method to these techniques is discussed in Sect. 6.4.2.2. Furthermore, although it was often possible to obtain parameter settings at which some of these methods provide high-quality results, we found it difficult to generalize these settings as robust heuristic rules over various data sets. None of the works in [23, 61] provide clear guidance on how the parameters should be selected. As we will show in Sect. 6.7, it is possible to obtain good results by ensembling over various data sizes, while holding the (data size-sensitive) kernel parameter at a "heuristically" reasonable value; however, there are a few data sets in which the linear method continues to provide better results. The ensemble-centric variation of the nonlinear Mahalanobis method, which is discussed for the first time in this book, is introduced in the next section.

6.4.2.1   An Efficient Ensemble-Centric Implementation

One the challenges with nonlinear kernel methods is its time- and space-complexity. The most important problem is that one needs to construct an $n \times n$ similarity matrix and then diagonalize it, where n is the number of data points. When n of the order of a few hundred thousand points, this can create challenges in terms of both space and computational time. Therefore, to address this problem, we propose to combine the approach with the method of variable subsampling [3]. In essence, the method of Nyström approximation [64] is used for nonlinear dimensionality reduction. This particular method is very convenient because it naturally works with a subsample of rows from the data or kernel matrix to construct the embedding. In each iteration, a value of s is chosen uniformly at random from $(\min\{n, 50\}, \min\{n, 1000\})$. Then, a total of s points are randomly subsampled from the original data matrix. An $s \times s$ similarity matrix S between these sampled points is constructed using the kernel similarity function. This matrix is diagonalized as follows:

$$S = Q \Lambda^2 Q^T \qquad (6.20)$$

All the nonzero eigenvectors of Q are extracted. Let the number of nonzero[7] eigenvectors be k. The corresponding $s \times k$ and $k \times k$ matrices are Q_k and Λ_k, respectively. Then, the extracted embedding of the s points is $Q_k \Lambda_k$. The remaining $(n - s)$ out-of-sample points need to mapped to the same embedding.

Let E_k be the $(n - s) \times k$ matrix representing the out-of-sample embedding. The entries of E_k are determined as follows. First, the $(n - s) \times s$ kernel similarity matrix S_o between the out-of-sample points and in-sample points is constructed. Because of the fact that kernel similarities correspond to dot products in transformed space, we know that the product between the out-of-sample embedding E_k and the transpose of the in-sample embedding matrix $Q_k \Lambda_k$ is given by S_o. This fact can be used to show that the embedding E_k of the out-of-sample points is given by the $(n - s) \times k$ matrix $S_o Q_k \Lambda_k^{-1}$. After the out-of-sample embedding has been determined, it is stacked with the in-sample embedding in order to create[8] a single $n \times k$ embedding.

$$D' = \begin{pmatrix} Q_k \Lambda_k \\ S_o Q_k \Lambda_k^{-1} \end{pmatrix} \qquad (6.21)$$

---

[7]Eigenvalues less than a certain tolerance (e.g., 10^{-8}) are treated as 0 because they could be caused by numerical errors in the eigenvalue computation. Several programming languages like Python provide functions like **numpy.isclose** to discover such "almost zero" entries. Although the small non-zero eigenvectors are important for outlier detection, we do not want them to be nonzero because of numerical errors. Handling numerical errors properly is important in creating a robust implementation of the nonlinear Mahalanobis method because of the importance of small eigenvectors.

[8]An alternative way to create the entire embedding is to compute the $n \times s$ similarity matrix S_a between *all* points and the s in-sample points. Subsequently, D' is given by $S_a Q_k \Lambda_k^{-1}$. In such a case, the in-sample rows of $S_a Q_k \Lambda_k^{-1}$ may not exactly be the same as $Q_k \Sigma_k$ because of minor numerical approximations in the reduction.

Once the embedding D' has been determined, its columns are standardized to zero mean and unit variance. The kernel Mahalanobis score of each point (row) is the squared Euclidean distance to the mean of the rows. This squared Euclidean distance is divided by the number of dimensions in D' (i.e., by k) to ensure that the average score over all points in each ensemble component is 1 unit (because of standardization). This ensures that the scores of a data point from the different components are comparable to one another and no single ensemble component is weighted more than the other.

One drawback is that in-sample scores are often not comparable with out-of-sample scores. Therefore, it is important to repeatedly sample the data set (using variable subsampling) and compute a vector of scores, which is point-specific. Over many samples, a data point receives roughly the same number of in-sample and out-of-sample scores. These scores are averaged to provide the final result. Note that the space-complexity of this approach is of order $O(n \cdot s)$, where the size of s is a constant depending on the chosen subsample size. This is a significant improvement over the $O(n^2)$ complexity of the base scheme without sampling.

Finally, an important issue is the choice of the kernel parameters. This issue will be discussed in Sect. 6.5. Note that this approach can easily be adapted to the linear case simply by using the dot products between pairs of points as the kernel function. In fact, we used almost exactly the same code for both our linear and nonlinear variations. The only difference was in how the kernel similarity matrix was constructed and some specific variations in parameter setting for the nonlinear case. These variations are discussed in Sect. 6.5. As we will see in that section, varying the data size according to variable subsampling actually helps the kernel Mahalanobis method because the parameters are themselves sensitive to the data set size. The feature space normalization in the kernel Mahalanobis description is roughly based on the ideas in [61], although the adaptation to the Mahalanobis method and the ensemble-centric variants are our own. It is noteworthy that these ensemble-centric variants are *essential* to be able to use them in larger data sets; furthermore, they help in avoiding the parameter-centric uncertainty associated with the performance of the nonlinear method. In fact, because of the challenges associated with parameter choice, the nonlinear kernel method is not a practical approach as an *individual base detector* unless it is used in an ensemble-centric setting to reduce uncertainty. Therefore, our results show that ensemble methods can often convert unstable and apparently impractical base detectors to competitive choices when used properly.

6.4.2.2 Relationship of Kernel Mahalanobis Method to One-Class SVMs

Many other kernel methods such as one-class SVMs [52, 53], kernel Fisher discriminants [49], and support vector data descriptions [60] can also be considered variations of the fundamental idea in the kernel Mahalanobis method, although they use many more input parameters and they might seem quite different at first sight. In fact, as we will discuss below, these methods are different only in terms of the relative scaling of the feature space, and the fact that they are focused on finding a hard boundary between outliers and inliers rather than scoring points. Furthermore, the feature scaling assumed by many of these methods is often suboptimal [61] but is unavoidable because they work with the dual SVM formulation without explicitly materializing the transformed data.

The kernel Mahalanobis method models all points to belong to a Gaussian distribution in feature space. In fact, since it scales each direction to unit variance in feature space (i.e., standardizes each column of transformed data matrix D'), all uncorrelated directions of this Gaussian have the same variance. In such a case, it is reasonable to model an outlier score as the distance of a point from the center of the spherical Gaussian. The process of scaling the different directions to unit variance, which is referred to as *kernel whitening* [61], is highly recommended and has clear benefits. A variation of one-class SVMs, known as the support-vector data description (SVDD) [60], also models all inlier points with sphere of radius R (hard boundary) in kernel space. Therefore, it is closely related to the softer approach of the Mahalanobis method that simply reports the distance of the point to the center of the transformed data as the outlier score.

Another key difference between this approach and SVDD [60] is that the latter neglects to scale all directions to unit variance. This is also the case with the original one-class formulations of SVMs [52, 53]. This is primarily because these methods do not explicitly materialize the kernel transformation, but work with well-established practice of using the dual formulation of SVMs. This orthodoxy comes at the price of trying to fit a circular separator in a feature space with directions of widely different variances. As shown in [60], this has the drawback of trying to model a spherical separator for points that really lie within an elliptical shape. Although working with the dual seems to be the common approach to SVMs, one could also use linear SVMs on the representation created in the previous section to obtain better results than the SVDD method; specific examples of this approach are shown in [61] where applying a linear SVM to explicitly transformed and scaled data provides much better results. The sensitivity of one-class SVMs to data representations has also been studied in [35]. The use of the origin as a prior in the one-class SVM also makes the approach sensitive to the choice of the kernel transformation [2, 11, 14]. All these factors tend to make the one-class SVM a rather controversial choice. In fact, the experimental evaluation in [14] shows very poor results for both one-class SVMs and SVDD; furthermore, the evaluation explicitly recommends against using one-class SVMs, which often shows worse-than-random performance.

Another problem with one-class SVMs is that they are focused on finding a hard separator between outliers and inliers, and therefore they require additional parameters regulating the relative proportion of outliers and inliers. This is not optimal for scoring points. Therefore, the kernel Mahalanobis method is the most natural approach for scoring points because the implicit model of the de-correlated transformation of kernel PCA is a Gaussian distribution in kernel space. Therefore, we believe that the kernel Mahalanobis method is an elegant and greatly simplified representative of a very large class of outlier detection methods. Aside from the problems associated with feature scaling in one-class off-the-shelf SVMs [61] explicit transformation becomes extremely efficient in the context of an ensemble-centric implementation (see Sect. 6.4.2.1) because the running time only depends on the square of a small (constant) subsample size. A more detailed discussion of the relationships between these different problems may be found in [2].

6.4.3 Decomposing Unsupervised Learning into Supervised Learning Problems

The PCA method learns the correlations between data points in the aggregate and uses these learned correlations in order to detect violations in dependencies. One can, of course, do this in a more explicit way by using supervised modeling to learn dependencies across attributes. The advantage of this approach is that one can use off-the-shelf classifiers and regression models for outlier detection.

The basic idea of this approach is to decompose an outlier detection problem on d-dimensional data into d supervised problems. These d supervised problems are constructed one by one by selecting each of the d dimensions as the target attribute in turn and using the other $(d - 1)$ attributes to predict it. Since this prediction problem is an off-the-shelf classification/regression modeling problem, one can use any of the hundreds of off-the-shelf classification and regression models such as decision trees, random forests, least-squares regression, and SVMs. The error of the prediction for each point provides an outlier score, although a point receives d different outlier scores, one for each prediction problem. These scores are then combined into a unified outlier score, while giving the more accurate dimensions a greater amount of weight. Cross-validation is used to ensure that each data point receives an out-of-sample score. Therefore, the approach may be summarized as follows:

1. Standardize each dimension in the data set to zero mean and unit variance.
2. Construct d different regression modeling problems by setting each attribute in turn as the target attribute, which is also referred to as the dependent variable. The remaining attributes are predictor attributes or independent variables. Any off-the-shelf regression model can be used for this purpose.
3. For each data point $\overline{X}$, let $\varepsilon_i(\overline{X})$ represent its absolute prediction error, when the ith attribute is set as the target attribute. Cross-validation is used to score each data point, so that all points receive out-of-sample scores. Therefore $\varepsilon_i(\overline{X})$ represents an out-of-sample score.
4. Combine the scores $\varepsilon_1(\overline{X}) \ldots \varepsilon_d(\overline{X})$ into a unified score by weighting the accurately predicted attributes more heavily. In other words, attributes with smaller root-meas-squared-error are weighted more.

It remains to be described how the scores from various base models are combined into a unified score. The weight w_k of the kth attribute is set so that attributes with low predictive power have low weights. Note that the standard deviation of each dimension is 1. Therefore, if an attribute has root-mean squared error (RMSE) greater than 1 on out-of-sample points, it has little predictive power. Therefore, such attributes should be given zero weight.

Let the cross-validated RMSE error on the kth attribute be denoted by $RMSE_k$. Therefore, this error is computed in terms of the errors $\varepsilon_k(\overline{X})$ on individual data points as follows:

$$RMSE_k = \sqrt{\frac{\sum_{i=1}^{n} \varepsilon_k^2(\overline{X_i})}{n}} \qquad (6.22)$$

Therefore, the weight w_k of the kth attribute is set as follows:

$$w_k = 1 - \min\{1, RMSE_k\} \qquad (6.23)$$

Then, one can use the weights on the attributes to compute the final outlier score as follows:

$$Score(\overline{X}) = \sum_{k=1}^{d} w_k \varepsilon_k(\overline{X})^2 \qquad (6.24)$$

Note that the approach is essentially parameter-free, if we consider the fact the parameters of the base learners can be tuned because they are supervised. This approach is referred to as *ALSO* [44], which stands for *attribute-wise learning and scoring outliers*. A similar idea was also proposed in [40], although we follow the approach proposed in [44].

6.4.3.1   An Efficient Ensemble-Centric Variant

An ensemble-centric variant can be constructed using variable subsampling [3]. This variant is being discussed and tested for the first time in this book and has not been presented anywhere else. In each iteration, a value of s is chosen uniformly at random from $(\min\{n, 50\}, \min\{n, 1000\})$. A sample of size s is drawn from the data and a training model is constructed on using an off-the-shelf learner. An attribute is randomly sampled from the data as the target attribute and the remaining attributes are used as the predictors. The RMSE error is computed for this target attribute on the remaining $(n - s)$ out-of-sample points. If the value of $(n - s)$ is less than 10, then all points are used to estimate the RMSE error. This RMSE error is used to compute w_k according to Eq. 6.23. Subsequently, all points are scored using Eq. 6.24 whether they are included in the sample or not. Note that this approach does mix the out-of-sample points with in-sample points during the scoring. However, since the points are repeatedly subsampled and the scores are averaged, each point receives roughly the same number of out-of-sample and in-sample scores. Therefore, the resulting scores are more robust. We refer to this variation as *ALSO-E* to denote the fact that it is an ensemble-centric variant.

6.4.3.2 Relationship to Soft PCA

The *ALSO* approach is closely related to *soft* PCA [54] (i.e., linear Mahalanobis method) in which different uncorrelated directions are inversely weighted by their variance especially when a linear regression model is used as the base learner. Like linear regression, PCA is also an least-squares optimization model; the main difference is that PCA defines the least-squares error with respect to the low-dimensional hyperplane of representation, whereas linear regression defines it with respect to each attribute. Another difference is in the type of weighting function that is used and the specific *representation* of the data that we would like to work with. Imagine a setting in which we transformed the d-dimensional data into d uncorrelated directions using PCA. In such a case, if we tried to apply the technique of the previous section of using supervised learning, it would not make sense to use an off-the-shelf regression model, because we have already taken out almost all the inter-attribute predictive power by de-correlating the dimensions. In such a case, a reasonable approach would be to predict the mean of each dimension as the prediction of each attribute. However, Eq. 6.23 would not work very well because each weight would be set to 0. A less harsh form of the weight-based discounting is required. One such weight w_k is to set it to inverse of the squared RMSE error along each dimension:

$$w_k = \frac{1}{RMSE_k^2} \tag{6.25}$$

This type of discounting does not set the weight of any dimension to be 0. However, this error is simply equal to the variance along the kth attribute. Therefore, by applying Eq. 6.24, one obtains the following:

$$\text{Score}(\overline{X}) = \sum_{k=1}^{d} \frac{\varepsilon_k(\overline{X})^2}{\text{Variance of } k\text{th attribute}} \tag{6.26}$$

It is easy to show that this modified score is *exactly* the same as that obtained using the Mahalanobis method. Note that this form of the weight is useful in finding correlated extreme values in addition to finding dependency-oriented outliers.

The main advantage of the supervised method is that one can use complex base detectors like random forests, which are potentially more powerful than linear regression. Note that linear regression will not work well with decorrelated attributes like those obtained with PCA, especially since the dependent variable was also extracted using the same transformation. However, even in these cases, techniques like random forests can leverage higher-order correlations, whereas PCA only removes second-order correlations. The main advantage of PCA is that by decorrelating the attributes, it consolidates latent concepts in individual dimensions, which allows for a simple scoring mechanism without any explicit learning. The price of this simplicity is that one now loses the ability to use the power of arbitrary supervised learning models which can learn higher-order or nonlinear correlations. The *ALSO* method does not have any parameters beyond those embedded within the specific classification model. However, the parameters of those models can be tuned using cross-validation. Although can achieve similar goalsreplicator neural networks [18, 65], such methods face many challenges because of the increased number of parameters required for learning. Recently, it has been shown [13], how the effectiveness of such replicator neural networks can be improved with the use of outlier ensemble methods.

6.4.4 High-Dimensional Outliers Based on Group-Wise Dependencies

The *ALSO* methodology uses supervision in order to test the violation of dependencies between $(d - 1)$ and a single attribute. However, such an approach works well only work when at least a few attributes can be predicted reliably from other attributes. In some domains such a text, significant dependencies are present across *larger* groups of attributes, but it is often difficult to predict the frequency of a single attribute. For example, it is generally very difficult to predict the frequency of a word based on the frequencies of the other words. On the other hand, since a text collection often contains many *latent concepts*, it is possible to test the presence of these latent concepts based on the words in the document. As we will see, such an approach naturally combines the merits of the PCA-based approach with the supervised decomposition approach in a smooth way. In general, cases in which individual attributes contain very little information in isolation, but there are significant latent correlations *in the aggregate*, are particularly suitable for this approach.

In order to achieve these goals, we propose a *group-wise* supervised learning approach that partitions the d attributes into a set of r target attributes and $(d - r)$ predictor attributes. The approach is inherently designed as an ensemble-centric approach. In each iteration, we randomly sample r target attributes and the remaining $(d - r)$ attributes are treated as predictor attributes. Let the sampled set of r target attributes be denoted by S_r.

To address the issue that the individual attributes are not easily predictable, they are not used in their original form. The r target attributes are then transformed to latent concepts using PCA. Specifically, the eigenvectors of the $r \times r$ covariance matrix are extracted, the data is projected on these eigenvectors to create the new targets. Targets with zero variance are dropped, and the remaining attributes are used as the $r' < r$ targets. Cross-validation is used to determine the error $\varepsilon_k^2(\overline{X})$ of the data point $\overline{X}$ along the kth target, where $k \in \{1 \ldots r'\}$. The cross-validated RMSE error along the kth dimension is denoted by $RMSE_k$. Then, the outlier score for a base detector is computed by aggregating the errors over all r' latent components:

$$\text{Score}(\overline{X}, S_r) = \frac{\sum_{k=1}^{r'} \varepsilon_k^2(\overline{X})}{r'} \qquad (6.27)$$

Note the presence of S_r in the argument of the equation to account of the fact that the score is specific to the sampled set S_r. This is because the approach is an ensemble-centric technique, in which each S_r is sampled to define an ensemble component. The scores of each point are then computed over the various samples $S_1 \ldots S_m$ and then averaged to provide the final ensemble score.

To speed up the approach, we used variable subsampling. For each partitioning into r dimensions and $(d - r)$ dimensions, a sample size s is chosen uniformly at random between $\min\{n, 50\}$ and $\min\{n, 1000\}$, and is used as training data for learning. Therefore, each base detector is sampling both the points and the dimensions. The RMSE error is computed using only the out-of-sample points, as long as at least 10 points are out-of-sample. Otherwise, the RMSE error is computed using all points. Then, all scores are scored using Eq. 6.27 whether they are in-sample or out-of-sample. Note that this approach is not as exact as cross-validation but it is much faster, and can be implemented in linear time for large data sets. Subsequently, the scores over the various base detectors are averaged to provide the final result. This approach is referred to as *Group-wise attribute selection and prediction (GASP)*, and it represents a new algorithm that combines the merits of the two related methods of attribute-wise learning and soft PCA (i.e., the Mahalanobis method). The ensemble-centric implementation is referred to as *GASP-E*.

It is noteworthy that if we set $r = 1$, the approach is similar to the *ALSO* scheme (with some scoring modifications). Furthermore, if we set $r = d$, the approach specializes to the Mahalanobis method because there are no predictor variables and the best any learning algorithm can do in such a setting with no predictor variables is to predict the mean of the targets, each of which is derived using PCA. It is not difficult to see that using the mean of each eigenvector as the prediction would result in the Mahalanobis score. In our implementations of this chapter, we set $r = d/2$ as the compromise scheme, although the value of r should really depend on the dimensionality of the data. For high-dimensional data sets in which attribute-wise correlation is weak, it makes sense to use larger (raw) values of r. However, the value of r should increase sublinearly with increasing data dimensionality. In such cases, the application of PCA on the r targets results in more meaningful latent targets. Even when attribute-wise correlations are weak, the PCA approach can often find a few latent components along which the data varies significantly. For low-dimensional data sets, it makes sense to use smaller values of r.

6.5   The Hidden Wildcard of Algorithm Parameters

Since we will evaluate some commonly used algorithms over a variety of data sets, an important issue is the choice of parameters to be used by the algorithm. The choice of parameters is often not given sufficient attention, although it is clearly a significant wildcard for algorithmic performance. For example, in a k-nearest neighbor algorithm, how should the value of k be selected while comparing two algorithms? For example, a raw k-nearest neighbor algorithm might do better than LOF for a particular value of k, whereas the relative performance might be different for another value of k. As a result, it becomes difficult to reasonably measure the relative performance of the two methods. One possibility is to use the *best* value of k for each algorithm at which optimum results are obtained. However, such an approach often provides a skewed idea of the relative effectiveness of the two algorithms because of the reasons discussed in this section.

An important issue with unsupervised algorithms is that choosing the best value of the parameter (albeit for each compared algorithm) seeds the various algorithms with knowledge that is not available in real settings. Different algorithms are able to use this additional knowledge more effectively, and it turns out that this differential usage unfairly biases the evaluation in favor of unstable algorithms. An algorithm that generally performs poorly at most values of the parameter k, but does very well at a single well-chosen value of k would be highly favored by the approach of selecting the best value of k. This is exactly the opposite of what we want in the unsupervised setting where the user has little idea of the best choice of k.

In order to best understand the effect of a particular type of evaluation, one must view the performance from the point of view of the end user. In most cases, the end user would select the parameters based on the size of the data set within a specific range. Therefore, one needs to average the performance over a "reasonable" range of different values of the parameters. For example, in k-nearest neighbor (or other distance-based) algorithms, one can use different values of k and then compare the box-plot performance of the two methods.

This issue is best exemplified by recent comparisons between LOF and raw distance-based algorithms [3, 12]. When the LOF algorithm is compared with the average k-nearest neighbor method, the latter performs better *on the average* over a range of reasonable choices of the parameters. On the other hand, LOF algorithm is rather unstable (with respect to k) as compared to the average k-nearest neighbor algorithm, and a specific choice of the parameter k might actually overfit the specific data set at hand. As a result, LOF might frequently perform better than the average k-nearest neighbor algorithm, when the best value of k is selected for each algorithm [12]. Which algorithm should be considered better? It is tempting to suggest that the two algorithms should be considered competitive because their relative performance is metric-dependent. This is, however, not a precise picture because the impact of one of these metrics (performance over a broader range) affects the analyst far more than the other (best performance) in real applications. An important practical issue is that it is not possible for an end-user to know the optimal parameter values in the unsupervised setting, and *providing the optimal parameter value as an input to each algorithm works in an unfair way to the advantage of unstable algorithms.* In other words, such an evaluation is biased in favor of an undesirable qualities such as instability and data-specific overfitting. Although the raw experimental results of [12] support this argument, and the importance of using a range of values has also been mentioned in the paper, a majority of the results in [12] have been presented using the best value of k rather than a range of values. As a result, one tends to obtain a more favorable picture of LOF (compared to raw distance-based methods), even though the experimental results in the same paper show that raw distance-based methods perform much better than LOF on a *broader range of parameter values*. The work in [3] also shows the relative performance between LOF and the average k-nearest neighbor algorithms over a range of different ensemble-centric settings and explicitly points out the drawbacks of LOF.

Another particularly interesting example in this context is illustrated by the kernel Mahalanobis technique. This particular method has several choices corresponding to the choice of kernel and the parameters of the kernel. In supervised settings, these choices are easily made using cross-validation. However, in the unsupervised setting, this is often not possible. In our experiments, we often found that by selecting the kernel and the parameters of the kernel carefully in a data-specific way, we could achieve a performance that was not matched by any other method; this is consistent with the results presented in [23] (although their approach is slightly different). The aforementioned observation is especially true in cases where one application of the base detector is used in each case with *optimized* parameters. However, in practice, we found that it was exceedingly difficult to design a heuristic rule for choosing optimized parameters like the Gaussian kernel bandwidth that matched this performance. For example, in the case of the Gaussian kernel, a common heuristic rule is to use the median distance between pairs of points. However, for smaller data sets this distance turns out to be too small (because of overfitting). If one increases the bandwidth too much, the performance becomes more similar to the linear Mahalanobis method. Furthermore, the instability with parameter choice was accompanied by the annoying fact that bad choices were severely punished in a way that could not be predicted a priori for a specific data set. These dilemmas were quite problematic because they show that the experience of the analyst in the unsupervised setting is often different from what a researcher might obtain in a bench-marking setting in which parameters (of each algorithm) are often tuned after the fact (of knowing the ground-truth). In summary, the performance at the best choice of parameters for each algorithm tells us little about the true usability of the approach. In the next section, we discuss how parameter-sensitive methods like the kernel Mahalanobis method can be made more effective by using data-centric ensembles.

6.5.1 Variable Subsampling and the Tyranny of Parameter Choice

An important aspect of many algorithmic parameters is that they are *data size* sensitive. Although data size is not the only factor that influences the choice of parameters, it plays an important role in many settings. For example, in the kernel Mahalanobis method, the pairwise distances between points regulate the bandwidth σ of the Gaussian kernel, but this parameter continues to be sensitive to data set size in a way that also depends on the specific data distribution and is not easily inferred in a heuristic way. Smaller data sets require larger values of σ to avoid overfitting, which makes the results more similar to linear PCA. This is logical because one cannot hope to do much better than linear PCA for very small data sets. Similarly, in a k-distance based detector, the required value of k increases with data size; however the "correct" value of k (for a fixed data set size) also depends on the specific data distribution at hand and it cannot be inferred a priori in a heuristic way as a function of data size. This argument also applies to data size sensitive *design choices*. For example, the choice between polynomial kernel and Gaussian kernel depends both on the data distribution and the data size, and there is no way of validating which kernel is optimal in unsupervised problems; in fact, different kernels might be optimal for different data sizes depending on the overfitting propensity of the various kernels over a particular data distribution.

Variable subsampling [3] helps in using the available heuristic rules for parameter choices in a more confident way by varying the data size between two constant values (typically 50 and 1000). The choices of the parameters are kept fixed, which affects the *relative* effect of these parameters with respect to data size. For example, in our experiments, we used the following heuristic rules for parameter choice in conjunction with variable subsampling:

1. For the case of distance-based detectors, varying the subsample size between 50 and 1000, while fixing $k = 5$, lead to a varying relative value of k between 0.5% and 10% of the data.
2. For the case of the Gaussian kernel the value of the bandwidth σ was set to thrice the median of the pairwise distances between points. The pairwise distances between points were estimated using sampling. Note that we set this bandwidth to thrice the value of what is typically recommended, because sample sizes between 50 and 1000 are quite small. However, such small sample sizes are essential in the case of the kernel Mahalanobis method in order to ensure space efficiency.
3. For the case of the *GASP* technique, the value of r was set to $d/2$. Another possible rule is to allow r to increase sublinearly with data dimensionality. For example, choosing $r = \sqrt{d}$ can often be sufficient. Nevertheless, we leave this issue as an open aspect for further exploration and used the simplest choice of dividing predictors and targets equally as that the approach was exactly midway between PCA and attribute-wise learning.

The other methods such as the Mahalanobis method, the *ALSO* technique and isolation forests did not have algorithm-specific parameters associated with them other than sample size. In spite of this fact, it has been shown in the journal version of [34] that the base detectors are sensitive to the underlying data size. Unfortunately, this optimal data size is not known in advance. Therefore, even for parameter-free detectors, it might sometimes be helpful to use variable subsampling. For the specific case of isolation forests, the effect of using different types of sampling (e.g., fixed or variable) seemed to be smaller than the other methods. This is in part because a lot of the diversity comes from the way in which the isolation forest is constructed with randomized splits, and the specific effect of sampling seems to be marginal as compared to other ensemble methods.

The supervised learning methods did have parameters associated with the base classifier/regression model used, but these parameters can be optimized with cross-validation. Therefore, the *ALSO* approach is technically parameter-free. However, for greater efficiency, we used the simple choice of random forests with 10 trees and 3 bagged features at each node. Note that the supervised learning method uses learners that are obviously quite weak (for efficiency); we observed that the performance was at least somewhat sensitive to the robustness of the underlying learners. Therefore, the performance shown here for these methods is not optimal. However, using stronger learners caused computational problems in some of the data sets and therefore our results are presented with this specific parameter choice in order to provide the same homogeneous setting across all data sets.

6.6 TRINITY: A Blend of Heterogeneous Base Detectors

An important goal of this chapter is to show practitioners how to combine base methods and ensembles in order to obtain results that are robust and practical. In this chapter, we presented a very small subset of the outlier detection algorithms available in the literature. With the exception of isolation forests and a pair of supervised learning methods, almost all these algorithms are more than a decade old. Yet, many of them often outperform most of the recent algorithms. Furthermore, we intentionally presented algorithms of three different types. We presented classical distance-based methods, dependency-based methods, and the isolation forest, which is a space partitioning method. It does not make much sense to combine algorithms of the same type. The best diversity gains may be achieved by combining algorithms of different types. Furthermore, each base detector can be paired with ensemble techniques like variable subsampling (which explores a broader parameter space) or rotated bagging (which explores different subspaces) or both. For simplicity, we restricted ourselves to the use of variable subsampling, although we envisage a broader use of the many variance reduction techniques discussed in Chap. 3. Many of these techniques have the additional benefit of improving efficiency.

In order to create an ensemble that can be used by practitioners with reasonably robust results across many data sets, we make a specific recommendation to create *TRINITY*, which is a heterogeneous combination of three different base detectors. There three components are as follows:

1. *Distance-based component*: The distance-based component corresponds to one of the *raw* distance-based detectors (i.e., not LOF or its variants). This distance-based component is used at $k = 5$, but is applied in conjunction with variable subsampling in order to enable a broader parameter space exploration. For the purpose of our implementation, we used 100 executions of the exact k-nearest neighbor detector with variable subsamples between 50 and 1000 points. The scores output by the 100 different executions were averaged to create the n-dimensional ensemble score vector $\overline{E_1}$.

2. *Dependency-based component*: It is recommended to use either one of the Maha-lanobis methods or the supervised learning methods. The main disadvantage of the supervised learning method is computational efficiency. Although it can *poten-tially* provide better results than the Mahalanobis method, it is hard to achieve this because of the computational difficulty in optimizing the parameters of supervised learning in each ensemble component. Therefore, we recommend the use of the non-linear Mahalanobis method with variable subsampling. A Gaussian kernel is used and the width σ of the Gaussian kernel is set to thrice the median distance between pairs of points. The specific implementation for out-of-sample scoring is provided in Sect. 6.4.2.1. A total of 100 executions of the base detector were used and scores were averaged. The resulting n-dimensional vector of ensemble scores is denoted by $\overline{E_2}$.

3. *Subspace Density-based Component*: It is worthwhile to use a subspace method to account for irrelevant features in the data. Therefore, one can either use subspace histograms [51] or the isolation forest for the subspace density-based component. We used 100 executions of the base detector with a subsample of size between 50 and 1000. Note that this is a different setting than that shown in Chap. 3 in which a subsample of size 256 was always used. Although the approach is parameter-free, variable subsampling is still helpful in ensembling over the implicit diversity created by subsample size. The extended journal version of the paper [34] provides specific examples (using the *Mulcross* data generator [48]) in which it is shown that the optimal performance of this parameter-free approach depends on the data size. Since this optimal data set size is not known for a given data set, variable subsampling has some benefits even in this case. We refer to this variation of isolation forests as IF-VS (as opposed to IF-256) to denote the fact that it uses variable subsampling. The scores over 100 executions of the isolation tree were averaged in order to create the score vector $\overline{E_3}$.

Each of the score vectors $\overline{E_1}$, $\overline{E_2}$ and $\overline{E_3}$ were normalized to zero mean and unit variance and the score vectors were averaged in order to create the final ensemble score of *TRINITY*.

6.7 Analysis of Performance

In this section, we will provide an experimental comparison of several classical detectors. Although many of these distance-based detectors seem to be quite old and apparently outdated, it turns out that they often outperform the more recent detectors. Furthermore, the relative performances of raw distance-based detectors with respect of normalized detectors like LOF are not always what one would expect. These have also been a finding of the recent results presented in [3, 12]. Another interesting observation was that the relative performance on the base detectors did not match the relative ensemble performance because the variance of unstable detectors could often be reduced to a greater degree. The box-plot performance of the base detectors and the ensemble performance therefore provide two different ways of comparing base detectors [3]. For each base detector, one can choose the ensemble most suited to it and compare the final performance. Since many of the detectors were data-size sensitive in terms of performance, we chose to use variable subsampling as the ensemble method of choice. In some sense, the ensemble performance provides a good idea of the "best" performance truly achievable by the algorithm when one combines the effect of base detector performance and ensemble improvements. This type of best performance is truly achievable in real settings. As we will see in this section, some algorithms performed better with respect to the base detector performance, whereas others performed better with respect to ensemble performance. This is also an important factor to keep in mind while selecting an outlier detection technique. For example, in cases where one cannot use too many ensemble components because of computational constraints, it might make sense to use a technique with better base performance.

One of the challenges in comparing different algorithms is the case in which they have parameters with different interpretations. Some detectors like the linear Mahalanobis method and isolation forests are essentially parameter-free for the base detector (if we view subsample size and the number of components as meta-parameters). However, for two methods like the kernel Mahalanobis method and the kth nearest neighbor detector, how do we compare them especially when some parameters are data-size sensitive? The basic idea is to use variable subsampling, in order to vary the data size over a fixed set of parameters that are heuristically chosen. This type of approach implicitly leads to parameter space exploration over a range of reasonable values. Even in the case of parameter-free methods, variable subsampling helps by reducing the uncertain impact of data-size design choices.

After executing the base detector over various subsamples, one can compare the box-plots of various methods over this range of values as well as the final ensemble performance. By comparing box-plots instead of performances at individual parameter choices, one is explicitly treating parameter choice as a wildcard and comparing the numerous outcomes of this wildcard in an aggregated way. We realize that the approach is not perfect, because there is still some residual sensitivity to the specific parameter setting. Nevertheless, such an approach provides the best possible option for a difficult comparison between algorithms with semantically different parameters. The specific details of parameter setting issues are discussed in Sect. 6.7.2.

6.7.1 Data Set Descriptions

The data set descriptions are identical to those discussed in Chap. 3. However, we have repeated these descriptions here for completeness of this chapter. In the following, we describe some data sets for outlier detection that are used throughout this book. Many of these data sets have also been used in [3]. We used twelve data sets from the UCI

Machine learning repository.[9] In some cases, further preprocessing was required. In cases where one of the classes was already rare, it was labeled as the outlier class. In cases where a data set contained relatively balanced classes, downsampling was necessary to create an outlier class. In some cases, multiple large classes were combined to create inliers and multiple minority classes were combined to create outliers. In the following, we provide a brief description of the data preparation process.

The Glass data set contained attributes regarding several glass types. Here, points of class 6 were marked as outliers, while all other points were inliers. For the Lymphography data set classes 1 and 4 were outliers while the other classes were inliers. The Ecoli data set contained 8 classes, among which classes 1 to 5 were included as inliers, whereas classes 6, 7, and 8 were included as outliers. The Wisconsin-Breast Cancer (Diagnostics) data set (WBC) contained *malignant* and *benign* classes, and we started with a processed version[10] of the data set. We further downsampled the *malignant* class to 21 outliers, while points in the *benign* class were considered inliers. The Yeast data set contained 10 classes. Classes 1, 6, 7, and 8 were included as inliers, since these classes have the most instances in the data set. From the remaining classes, we sampled 65 points and included them as outliers. In the Japanese Vowels (Vowels) data set, we treat each *frame* in the training data as an individual data point, whereas the UCI repository treats a block of frames (utterance) as an individual point. In this case, class (speaker) 1 was down-sampled to 50 outliers. The inliers contained classes 6, 7 and 8. Other classes were discarded. The ANN-Thyroid data set is the same as that in [27]. The "seismic bumps" data set (Seismic) contained two classes, which were labeled as *hazardous* and *non-hazardous* respectively. The *hazardous* class was selected as the outlier class, whereas the *non-hazardous* class corresponds to the inliers. In the Statlog (Landsat Satellite) data set, the training and test data were combined. Class 2 was down-sampled to 71 outliers, while all the other classes were combined to form an inlier class. Our modified data set is referred to as Satimage-2. The Cardiotocography (Cardio) data set contained measurements taken from foetal heart rate signals. The classes in the data set were *normal*, *suspect*, and *pathologic*. The *normal* class formed the inliers, while the *pathologic* (outlier) class was down-sampled to 176 points. The *suspect* class was discarded. In Optdigits, instances of digits 1-9 where inliers and instances of digit 0 were down-sampled to 150 outliers. The Musk data set contained several musk and non-musk classes. We combined non-musk classes j146, j147, and 252 to form the inliers, while the musk classes 213 and 211 were added as outliers without down-sampling. Other classes were discarded. Refer to Table 6.1 for details of data sets.

---

[9]http://archive.ics.uci.edu/ml/datasets.html.

[10]http://www.ipd.kit.edu/muellere/HiCS/.

Table 6.1 Summary of the data sets

Data Set	Points	Attributes	Percentage outliers (%)
Glass	214	9	4.2
Lymphography	148	18	4.1
Ecoli	336	7	2.7
WBC	378	30	5.6
Yeast	1364	8	4.8
Vowels	1456	12	3.4
Thyroid	3772	6	2.5
Satimage-2	5803	36	1.2
Cardio	1831	21	9.6
Seismic	2584	11	6.6
Optdigits	5216	64	2.9
Musk	3062	166	3.2

6.7.2   Specific Details of Setting

We compared eight different outlier detectors of different types. Note that the work in [12] only compares detectors of the same type, whereas we compare detectors of different types. In the following, we will provide specific details of the implementations of various methods. As discussed earlier, the different parameters of different methods is a wildcard from the perspective of algorithmic performance. Although three of the detectors were parameter-free, using data sets of varying sizes is helpful even in those cases because the performance of a detector is often sensitive to data size in an unpredictable way. Furthermore, since we are comparing detectors of different types, the parameters become more of a wildcard in terms of relative comparison. Even for detectors of the same type, a specific value of a parameter (e.g., the value of k for distance-based methods) might mean different things for different detectors. For example, a specific value of k at a particular data size might not mean the same thing for an exact k-nearest neighbor detector, average k-nearest neighbor detector, and for LOF. In this sense, variable subsampling is very useful in implicitly ensembling over different data size-sensitive parameter choices by fixing the parameters a priori. For example, by fixing $k = 5$, and varying[11] the data subsample size between 50 and 1000 points one can explore a *relative* value of k between 0.5% to 10% of the data set for all detectors. By examining both the median and the ensemble performance of the various detectors over this randomized choice, we are largely (but not fully) able to ameliorate the impact of parameter choice, when k is fixed to a value such as 5. From a practical point of view, this approach also gives an idea of the median performance over an implicit range of *relative* parameter choices, and also

---

[11]The variation in data subsample size is also limited by the size of the data set, if it contains less than 1000 points.

the *best* possible performance that one can hope to actually achieve with the use of an ensemble. Similarly, in the case of the nonlinear Mahalanobis method, we used a well-known heuristic rule, while varying data size. In each case, 100 executions of the base detector were used. Therefore, in conjunction with variable subsampling, the following settings of various detectors were tested:

1. *Distance-based detectors*: We tested the exact k-nearest neighbor detector (KNN), average k-nearest neighbor detector (AKNN) and Local Outlier Factor (LOF). In each case, the value of k was set to 5, but the size of the data varied between 50 and 1000 points in order to test the impact of different relative values of k. Note that the median performance provided an idea of how the base detectors performed over various relative parameter choices whereas the ensemble performance provided an idea of the best possible performance achievable in practice.

2. *Dependency-oriented Mahalanobis methods*: The linear Mahalanobis method (MAH-L) was parameter-free and therefore, no selection of parameters was required. In the case of the nonlinear Mahalanobis method (MAH-N), a Gaussian kernel was used. The kernel bandwidth σ is normally set to the median pairwise distance between points. Smaller values of the bandwidth can lead to overfitting. Furthermore, the amount of overfitting depends on data size in a distribution-specific way. Smaller data sets (or subsamples) require a larger bandwidth, although the bandwidth also depends on the data distribution. Therefore, we used variable subsampling based on the implementation described in Sect. 6.4.2.1. The bandwidth was fixed to thrice the median pairwise distance between points as a conservative choice, because some of the subsamples contained only 50 points. Larger bandwidths tend to make the approach closer to the linear method, which is generally more stable. We believe that this setting is reasonable across a broad variety of data sets for data sets of size between 50 and 1000 points.

3. *Dependency-oriented learning methods*: Both the *GASP* method and the *ALSO-E* method were implemented according to the variable subsampling approach described in Sect. 6.4.3.1. Similarly, the *GASP* method was implemented according to the description in Sect. 6.4.4. The variable subsampling implementation was referred to as *GASP-E*. The value of r in *GASP-E* was set to $d/2$. In both cases, random forests were used as the base detector with three bagged features at each node and ten trees in the forest. The use of this modest setting was necessitated by computational considerations, although it is possible in principle to optimize these parameters with grid-search (because the underlying subproblems are supervised). Therefore, the *ALSO-E* method is technically parameter-free, although in practice, some pre-setting of the parameters of the supervised learning method might be necessary.

4. *Subspace-density learning method*: We selected the isolation forest from the class of subspace-density learning methods. The isolation forest has been tested with subsamples of size 256 in Chap. 3. Here, we used a somewhat different setting of using variable subsampling, and obtained slightly improved results. The improvement was usually small as compared to the other methods. In fact, as shown in Chap. 3, the subsampled version of isolation forests does not perform very differ-

ently from the version created on the full data. The underlying base detector is parameter-free and the trees are grown to full height. The resulting ensemble is denoted as IF-VS.

Note that many of these methods are parameter-free, and the effect of parameter choice can be largely blunted with the use of variable subsampling. Furthermore, since parameter-free methods often behave unpredictably with data size (see Sect. 3.4.4.1 of Chap. 3), variable subsampling can be helpful in this case as well. Therefore, we believe that this setting provides a reasonable comparison between various detectors both in terms of their base performance and their ensemble-centric potential. As we will see later, the two are not necessarily the same. The *TRINITY* ensemble was set to the average of the Z-normalized scores of the *final ensemble performance* of three of the detectors above. These detectors were the exact k-nearest neighbor detector (KNN), the nonlinear Mahalanobis method (MAH-N), and the isolation forests (IF-VS).

6.7.3 Summary of Findings

In the following, we present the experimental results on all the tested data sets. The results for the various data sets are illustrated in Figs. 6.6, 6.7, and 6.8, respectively. A number of major trends were observed that were common to many data sets. In the following, we provide a summary of our findings over the various data sets:

1. No single method was dominant over all data sets in terms of the *final ensemble performance*. Although the raw distance-based detectors were reasonable robust, the differences between the various distance-based detectors were greater than those across different methods. This suggests that different models are appropriate for different data sets, although distance-based models often work well in real-world settings.
2. The raw distance-based detectors typically performed significantly more robustly than LOF. Furthermore, the box plots of LOF were extremely thick. This is because the LOF detector is unstable with respect to the parameter k. Therefore, as the data size was varied by variable subsampling, the *relative* value of k varied significantly. This lead to extremely thick box-plots for LOF compared to the raw distance-based detectors. Even though the top-end of the box-plot (best LOF performance) was often excellent, it did not perform quite as well on either the median or the ensemble performance compared to the raw distance-based detectors. This is consistent with the observations in [3] in which raw distance-based detectors are shown to be more robust than LOF.

Another important caveat here is that even though variable subsampling blunted the effect of choosing a particular value of k, this blunting effect was not complete because we still restricted ourselves to a range of *relative* values of k (depending on subsample size varying between 50 and 1000). For example, the effective size

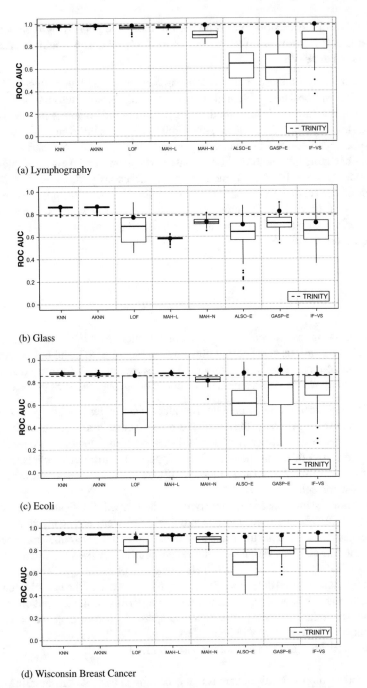

(a) Lymphography

(b) Glass

(c) Ecoli

(d) Wisconsin Breast Cancer

Fig. 6.6 Performance of all detectors on various data sets with variable subsampling. The value of k was set to 5 for distance-based detectors. The Gaussian kernel bandwidth was set to thrice the sampled median distance between points for MAH-N. The random forest detector was used for ALSO-E and GASP-E

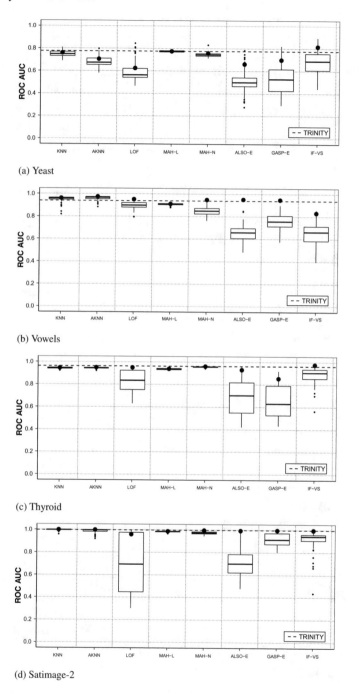

Fig. 6.7 Performance of all detectors on various data sets with variable subsampling. The value of k was set to 5 for distance-based detectors. The Gaussian kernel bandwidth was set to thrice the sampled median distance between points for MAH-N. The random forest detector was used for ALSO-E and GASP-E

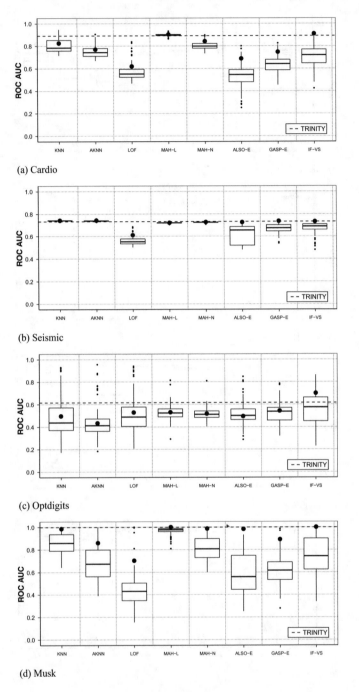

(a) Cardio

(b) Seismic

(c) Optdigits

(d) Musk

Fig. 6.8 Performance of all detectors on various data sets with variable subsampling. The value of k was set to 5 for distance-based detectors. The Gaussian kernel bandwidth was set to thrice the sampled median distance between points for MAH-N. The random forest detector was used for ALSO-E and GASP-E

of the considered locality for an average k-nearest neighbor detector at $k = 5$ is less than the effective locality size for an exact k-nearest neighbor detector at $k = 5$, when the data size is fixed at a particular value. This is because we are averaging over the first five nearest neighbors in the former, whereas we are considering only the fifth nearest neighbor in the latter. By increasing the value of k, it is possible for the relative performance between the average and exact k-nearest neighbor detectors to change even in this parameter-blunted setting. The residual sensitivity to the value of k also affected LOF performance in a negative way to some extent because a value of $k = 5$ might be reasonable for raw distance-based detectors but somewhat small for LOF for data sets varying between 50 and 1000 points; this affects the base performance of LOF more negatively than the raw distance-based detectors. However, while choosing the value of k in the ensemble-centric setting, larger values of k are undesirable because they increase the stability of detectors, and make variance reduction improvements more difficult; therefore, there is a catch-22 in the selection of an appropriate value of k for LOF in the ensemble-centric setting.

Nevertheless, as shown in [3, 12], the LOF method does not perform quite as well as the other distance-based detectors over the entire range of values of k, when looking at the *average* performance over the entire range. Therefore, we believe that the raw distance-based methods might have an advantage in general over the LOF method, even if the LOF performs well at its optimal value of k. Furthermore, since the optimal value of k for LOF seems to vary wildly over different data sets, this stability issue is somewhat of a problem in the unsupervised setting from the perspective of a practitioner without access to the ground truth.

3. There were several cases in which the median base performance was quite different from ensemble performance for various detectors. For example, the median base performance of the linear Mahalanobis method was not matched by any other method for a majority of the data sets, although its ensemble-centric improvements were small. This strongly suggests that methods should be evaluated both on base and ensemble performance while paired with a method like variable subsampling, which largely (but, alas, not completely) blunts the effect of specific parameter choice. As shown in Chap. 3, variable subsampling often reflects the best performance that one can robustly obtain from outlier detectors without worrying (too much) about the effect of parameter choice. The main point is to set the parameters to "reasonable" values while keeping the range of subsample sizes in mind. This is often similar to varying the parameters while keeping the data size fixed. For example, setting $k = 5$ while varying the data set size between 50 and 1000 points seems to be a reasonable choice for a nearest neighbor detector. Similarly, setting the kernel bandwidth to thrice the median distance between points seems to be a reasonable choice for the Gaussian kernel-based detector for these ranges of data sizes. Most of the other methods did not require data-sensitive input parameters, although variable subsampling helps in leveraging the diversity effects of data size even in those cases.

4. A particularly interesting comparison is between the linear and nonlinear Maha-lanobis method. The nonlinear Mahalanobis method occasionally performed poorly on the base performance but performed very well on the ensemble. A spe-cific example of this situation is the *Vowels* data set. The poor base performance is partially attributed to the fact that many points were scored in out-of-sample fashion, and the embedding based on a small subsample did not generalize well to the out-of-sample points. However, since the ensemble performance was based on many different subsamples, the final performance generalized well to the full data and was extremely robust. Furthermore, the performance with the full data set was occasionally very poor, which was not the case with the (more robust) ensemble. This was most likely the result of overfitting and was often caused by the large number of eigenvectors reflecting point-specific adjustments. In this context, it is particularly interesting that the *ensemble-centric* version of the nonlinear Mahalanobis method performed reasonably well (relative to other methods) on all the data sets. These tricky trade-offs and quirks show that the comparison between different outlier detection algorithms is far more subtle than one might imagine, especially if one considers the differences in relative performance between the base and the ensemble-centric setting.

5. The linear Mahalanobis method was very close to the best performer on the *base* performance, but it did not gain much from ensembles. Although the ensem-ble performance was reasonably robust, its performance on *Glass* and *Vowels* was poor. These are typically data sets in which outliers are embedded in the center of complex distributions (e.g., Fig. 6.5). In these data sets, the nonlinear Mahalanobis method performed much better because of its ability to "unfurl" the complex nonlinear patterns in the data. Another interesting observation about the nonlinear Mahalanobis method is that even though it was not the top performer on any data set, its ensemble performance was generally quite robust.

6. The two raw nearest neighbor detectors performed quite robustly although their performance was occasionally poor on a few data sets. Their robust performance suggests that raw distance-based detectors are often under-rated in terms of their robustness. Furthermore, the raw distance-based detectors were stable in their performance with varying subsample size, as shown by the thin box-plots. This is desirable because it shows that the approach is insensitive to different *relative* values of k.

7. The two dependency-oriented detectors *ALSO-E* and *GASP-E* did not win on most of the data sets although they were the winners on the *Ecoli* data set and also performed well on the *Optdigits* data set. It is noteworthy that we used a very weak supervised regressor in these cases (a random forest with only 10 trees, 3 bagged features at each node, and no cross-validated parameter tuning). This was motivated by computational considerations because the technique was rather slow. After all, parameter tuning is one of the privileges of supervised learning methods, which we sacrificed with this approach. We noticed that with sufficient computational resources, these detectors can perform as well as or even better than the other detectors in which the performance gains are already saturated.

8. Although the base performances of *GASP-E* and *ALSO-E* were not very strong, their ensemble performance were robust. One noteworthy fact about these detectors is that the final ensemble did not perform particularly poorly on any of the data sets even when the base performances were poor. The *GASP-E* detector performed better than *ALSO-E* detector in most data sets because of its use of latent correlations. We believe that the main potential of *GASP-E* over *ALSO-E* is in very noisy and high-dimensional domains like text/images in which no single feature has sufficient signal in isolation to be predicted from other features. In such cases, the use of *PCA* on a group of features aggregates the relevant signals from correlated directions. Nevertheless, *ALSO-E* has an advantage over *GASP-E*, in that it is parameter free, whereas *GASP-E* requires an additional parameter r, which is the dimensionality of the predicted latent space. Although we used $r = d/2$ in each case, some additional work is required on the proper heuristics to choose the value of r. Note that we are not counting the parameters of the base (supervised) learning method, because these parameters can be tuned with cross-validation, when sufficient resources are available. However, in our particular case, we used a relatively modest base detector of random forests with three features at each node and 10 trees.

9. Although the isolation forest seemed to be the best performing detector (when averaged over all data sets), its advantage was small compared to the ensemble-centric versions of other detectors. Also, we noticed an extremely high level of correlation between the isolation forest and the linear Mahalanobis method. For example, the only two data sets in which the linear Mahalanobis method performed poorly (i.e., *Glass* and *Vowels*) were also the data sets in which the isolation forest performed poorly. Furthermore, the statistical coefficient of correlation between the (ensemble-centric) AUCs of *IF-VS/MAH-L* was 0.935, which was higher than the correlation of the isolation forest with any other detector (including *TRINITY*). The only other pairs of detectors with higher correlation were the exact-KNN/average-KNN and *GASP-E/ALSO-E*, which were very obviously expected because of methodological similarities. This led us to strongly suspect that the linear Mahalanobis method and the isolation forest (in spite of being seemingly so different) had similar strengths and weaknesses. In particular, when outliers occur in interior regions of the data set, it is a difficult case for both the detectors. It is also noteworthy that the nonlinear Mahalanobis method is quite different from both these detectors in this respect, which is why it was chosen over the linear Mahalanobis method as a component of *TRINITY*. This is an issue that we will examine in greater detail in Sect. 6.7.5.

10. *TRINITY* was almost always among the top-3 performing detectors. This is quite a performance, considering the fact that no single detector was among the top-3 performing detectors. In fact, it was the best performing detector in quite a few cases. Therefore, this detector can form the basis for a robust detector in practical applications in which no ground-truth is available. It is possible to improve the performance of *TRINITY* further by incorporating methods like geometric subsampling discussed in Chap. 3 for the distance-based detector. This is because the ensemble performance of geometric subsampling is superior to that of variable

subsampling, as shown in Chap. 3. However, we only used variable subsampling in *TRINITY* to ensure consistency with the base performance actually shown in the same plots.

6.7.4   The Great Equalizing Power of Ensembles

It is noteworthy that the results presented in the previous section over the twelve different data sets vary significantly in terms of the performance. Therefore, it is natural to ask two questions:

1. Are the difference between the various algorithms statistically significant in terms of either the base performance or the ensemble? In other words, if we used twelve different data sets, would we get different results?
2. Are there any significant differences between the base performance and ensemble performance, while answering the first question?

In order to answer these questions, we first provide a summary table of the performance of different methods over different data sets. The results for the *median base performance* (i.e., median of each box-plot in Figs. 6.6, 6.7 and 6.8) and the *ensemble performance* (from each box plot) are summarized in separate tables. The former is summarized in Table 6.2, whereas the latter is summarized in Table 6.3. In addition,

Table 6.2 Median AUC performance of various detectors over twelve data sets. The median is defined by the horizontal line in the middle of each of the box-plots in Figs. 6.6, 6.7 and 6.8. Summary performance of individual detectors shown in lower four rows

Data	KNN	AKNN	LOF	MAH-L	MAH-N	ALSO-E	GASP-E	IF-VS
WBC	0.948	0.941	0.834	0.929	0.892	0.686	0.788	0.810
CARDIO	0.784	0.743	0.552	0.897	0.798	0.545	0.641	0.720
ECOLI	0.878	0.875	0.530	0.879	0.821	0.607	0.768	0.779
GLASS	0.866	0.864	0.692	0.583	0.726	0.641	0.716	0.649
LYMPHO	0.979	0.983	0.968	0.965	0.897	0.644	0.604	0.849
MUSK	0.859	0.674	0.430	0.976	0.807	0.559	0.616	0.743
OPTDIGITS	0.439	0.413	0.489	0.524	0.511	0.500	0.536	0.574
SATIMAGE	0.998	0.996	0.694	0.986	0.975	0.700	0.914	0.943
SEISMIC	0.742	0.739	0.552	0.721	0.727	0.654	0.676	0.690
THYROID	0.945	0.945	0.835	0.938	0.957	0.703	0.630	0.906
VOWELS	0.959	0.967	0.900	0.911	0.850	0.659	0.758	0.664
YEAST	0.748	0.674	0.565	0.772	0.745	0.500	0.529	0.689
μ_i	0.845	0.818	0.670	0.840	0.809	0.617	0.681	0.751
σ_i	0.155	0.175	0.177	0.156	0.125	0.074	0.112	0.110
$\hat{\sigma}_i$	0.045	0.050	0.051	0.045	0.036	0.021	0.032	0.032
Z_i	2.044	1.270	-1.640	1.916	1.514	-6.466	-2.237	-0.08

Table 6.3 Ensemble AUC performance of various detectors over twelve data sets. This is the same ensemble performance illustrated in Figs. 6.6, 6.7 and 6.8. Summary performance of individual detectors shown in lower four rows

Data	KNN	AKNN	LOF	MAH-L	MAH-N	ALSO-E	GASP-E	IF-VS	TRINITY
WBC	0.949	0.945	0.910	0.931	0.938	0.912	0.924	0.944	0.941
CARDIO	0.825	0.770	0.620	0.902	0.842	0.688	0.747	0.909	0.891
ECOLI	0.881	0.876	0.858	0.879	0.810	0.879	0.902	0.863	0.857
GLASS	0.865	0.868	0.771	0.581	0.729	0.705	0.821	0.719	0.790
LYMPHO	0.980	0.985	0.984	0.977	0.989	0.917	0.913	0.993	0.989
MUSK	0.986	0.860	0.703	1.000	0.987	0.983	0.891	1.000	0.999
OPTDIGITS	0.497	0.434	0.529	0.530	0.517	0.494	0.542	0.699	0.615
SATIMAGE	0.999	0.998	0.959	0.987	0.996	0.993	0.996	0.996	0.998
SEISMIC	0.743	0.744	0.611	0.722	0.728	0.727	0.737	0.733	0.734
THYROID	0.946	0.950	0.950	0.940	0.962	0.932	0.854	0.977	0.963
VOWELS	0.961	0.975	0.952	0.912	0.949	0.952	0.948	0.832	0.939
YEAST	0.759	0.704	0.624	0.775	0.758	0.662	0.699	0.817	0.776
μ_i	0.866	0.842	0.789	0.845	0.850	0.820	0.831	0.873	0.874
σ_i	0.145	0.161	0.166	0.158	0.148	0.159	0.129	0.113	0.122
$\hat{\sigma}_i$	0.042	0.047	0.048	0.046	0.043	0.046	0.037	0.033	0.035
Z_i	0.625	0.057	−1.054	0.110	0.251	−0.422	−0.231	1.032	0.977

the second table also has a column for *TRINITY*. The average performance over each detector is summarized in each of the tables together with the standard deviation over the 12 data sets. Let the mean performance of the ith detector be denoted by μ_i. Note that the standard deviation $\hat{\sigma}_i$ of the average performance over 12 randomly chosen data sets is less than the standard deviation σ_i of the detector over a single randomly chosen data set. Therefore, we convert the detector-specific standard deviation to a *sample-average* standard deviation by dividing σ_i by $\sqrt{12}$.

$$\hat{\sigma}_i = \sigma_i / \sqrt{12} \tag{6.28}$$

The mean performance of all detectors over all data sets is equal to $\mu^{(12)} = 0.754$, when the median performance of the box-plots was used in Table 6.2. When the ensemble performance was considered in Table 6.3, the corresponding mean performance was $\mu^{(12)} = 0.84$. We would like to determine whether the average performance of each detector[12] is greater than these performances by a statistically significant amount. Therefore, we compute the Z-value as follows:

---

[12]This is a simplified and approximate analysis for ease of understanding. Strictly speaking, we should use a paired hypothesis test, although the results are not significantly different by using that approach.

$$Z_i = \frac{\mu_i - \mu^{(12)}}{\hat{\sigma}_i}$$

When the median performance is concerned, we can substitute $\mu^{12} = 0.754$, and when the mean performance is concerned, we can substitute $\mu^{12} = 0.84$. The values of Z_i are illustrated in the last row of each table. Positive values of Z_i indicate detectors that are performing better than average, whereas negative values of Z_i indicate detectors that are performing worse than the average. Absolute values of Z_i, which are less than 1, are too small to be considered statistically significant, whereas values of $Z_i \geq 2$ are quite significant. We make several observations:

1. It is evident from the last row of each of the two tables that the absolute values of Z_i are much greater for the base detector than for the ensemble. This means that there are significant accuracy differences between base detectors, but not as many differences between their ensemble-centric versions. The accuracy performances of the various detectors are also summarized in Fig. 6.9. It is evident that the top five detectors are virtually tied in performance, although there are huge differences in the base versions of these detectors.

   This behavior is because the variable subsampling ensemble can often reduce the variability in performance over different choices of data sizes and parameters. In other words, all detectors become roughly equalized by variable subsampling, because of the reduction of the variance term from each detector. This suggests that different detectors have widely varying levels of variance. Furthermore, even though the performance becomes equalized from the point of view of *median performance over many data sets*, there are still differences on *particular data*

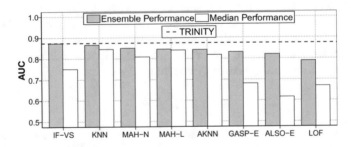

Fig. 6.9 Performance of all detectors in terms of base and ensemble performance. The base performance is evaluated by first computing the median base detector performance (horizontal line in box-plots) over each data set, and then averaging this median over the 12 data sets. The detectors are sorted in order of their ensemble accuracy, which reflects the best performance one can squeeze out of each detector. Note that detectors have very different performances at the base, but equalize with variable subsampling at a high level, which is comparable to *TRINITY*. We believe that *TRINITY* is generally very hard to significantly beat in most settings. However, the almost comparable performances of the individual detector-centric ensembles suggests that variable subsampling can lift most reasonable detectors to their best possible performance which are often comparable. This is in part because of the implicit parameter space exploration (and data-size sensitive robustness) in variable subsampling [3]

sets because of the differences in the bias terms (modeling assumptions) which are more appropriate for different data sets.

We would like to point out that this characteristic is specific to *variable* subsampling because of its implicit exploration of the parameter space [3] and it cannot be achieved by fixed subsampling. This is particularly true for distance-based detectors, which are extremely sensitive to data size, although the nonlinear Mahalanobis and isolation forests are also slightly sensitive. Isolation forests were the least sensitive to whether variable or fixed subsampling was used; this can be observed by comparing our results in this chapter to those in Chap. 3. Fixed subsampling was first introduced by isolation forests, and is reasonably appropriate for that setting; however, as shown in [34] with the *Mulcross* data generator [48], it is possible for even this parameter-free detector to be data size-sensitive. Therefore, we believe that variable subsampling would still have the advantage of being more *robust* even in the setting of isolation forests.

2. The base detector of the linear Mahalanobis method was often the most stable *on a particular data set* (i.e., thin box plots), whereas the nonlinear Mahalanobis was relatively unstable (i.e., thick box plots) and also had poorer (median) performance than the linear method. However, when we view the results for the *ensemble* performance over 12 different data sets in Table 6.3, the value of μ_i was slightly higher (better accuracy) for the nonlinear Mahalanobis method, and the variability $\hat{\sigma}_i$ was also lower (more stable) across different data sets. This shows that the comparison of different methods is far more subtle than one might imagine, especially if we also consider the ensemble-centric setting and the performance variability across different data sets.

3. Although the *TRINITY* detector performed the best, its difference from the ensemble-centric performance of the top five detectors was small. This suggests that the ensemble-centric versions of individual detectors can often saturate the performance gains to the point that there is little additional gains one can make by combining them. This is significant considering the fact that the (nonlinear) Mahalanobis, distance-based detector, and isolation forests seem to be quite different (which is evidenced by the fact that they perform well in different data sets). In other words, the *equalizing power of variable subsampling often brings detectors to near-optimal performance* and squeezes out as much information as possible from the data set. However, there can be some pathological cases where this does not happen.

4. *TRINITY* was only slightly better than the best performing detector (isolation forests) but it was much more robust over different data sets. In particular, *TRINITY* tended to outperform the isolation forest significantly in those data sets in which isolated outliers were present in interior regions of the data. It is also possible for the ensemble-centric versions of individual detectors to outperform *TRINITY* in individual data sets, although not by large amounts (see Figs. 6.6, 6.7 and 6.8).

The use of heterogeneous combinations of base detectors over the best performing detector does not usually improve base performance, but it has the *robustness* advantage shown in Sect. 6.7.5. In this case, isolation forest performs disastrously but *TRINITY* is able to hold up because of greater robustness. Although the situation in Sect. 6.7.5 is a pathological case and does not occur often in real data sets, the isolation forest did degrade in at least a few real data sets like *Glass* and *Vowels*. Therefore, the use of *TRINITY* has the advantage that it provides some protection from the uncertainty inherent in the use of a particular model.

6.7.5 The Argument for a Heterogeneous Combination

The experimental results in the previous sections seem to suggest that isolation forests perform almost as well as *TRINITY* over these data sets. It is, therefore, tempting to suggest that one should simply use the isolation forest in lieu of the combination. However, we have already noticed that there seems to be a strong correlation in performance between a multivariate extreme value analysis method like the (linear) Mahalanobis method and the isolation forest. Therefore, we will investigate this particular aspect as to whether the isolation forest discriminates against interior outliers. It is also possible to misinterpret the statement on the equalizing power of ensembles to suggest that one can use any of the aforementioned detectors (combined with variable subsampling) in lieu of the *TRINITY* method.

A key observation is that every detector has its own weakness in specific types of data sets where it does not work well. Furthermore, the similar performance of the various ensemble methods occurs only in the terms of the median performance over different data sets; there are still performance differences of the detectors on particular data sets. There are many pathological situations in which one or more detectors might perform poorly on a particular data set. From this point of view, a heterogeneous combination of base detectors (like *TRINITY*) provides significant protection. Therefore, it is instructive to examine the pathological cases in which the isolation forest does not perform well. There are two main settings in which the isolation forest performs particularly poorly:

- The isolation forest is essentially a density estimator [62] that uses the path length in an isolation tree as a surrogate for the density. All density-based methods (like histograms and kernel methods) tend to be estimated at higher values at central locations of the data (relative to pareto-extremes), especially when the dimensionality of the data increases and the amount of data is limited. Distance-based methods face less challenges with such outliers, although they are not fully protected with increasing dimensionality. When outliers are placed in sparse, central locations of the data, there is a greater tendency to incorrectly treat them as inliers. An example would be a set of normal points placed on the surface of a sphere and an outlier at the center of the sphere.
- Isolation forests are inherently subspace methods that work well in high-dimensional data when different subspaces of low dimensionality are relevant for the identification of different outliers. However, in cases where all dimensions are relevant, subspace methods can show poor performance with increasing

dimensionality because of the loss of information associated with subspace selection. Therefore, in certain settings, increasing data dimensionality can, in fact, be detrimental for isolation forests.

6.7.5.1   The Ball-and-Speck Data Set

In order to illustrate these effects, we generated a series of synthetic data sets of different dimensionalities. Each data set contained 9999 points on the surface of a unit sphere corresponding to the normal points. In addition, a single point (outlier) was placed at the center of the sphere. In other words, a single *speck* was placed at the center of a *ball* of points, which leads to the "ball-and-speck" name. The points on the sphere were materialized by first generating a uniformly distributed data set in the unit cube and then normalizing each point to unit norm. It is also possible to generalize the ball-and-speck test case to a ball-and-marble test case by using a cluster of outliers at the center rather than a single speck. In the ball-and-speck data set, the rank of the single outlier point can be used to directly derive the AUC of the performance of a detector. An AUC of 1 implies that the outlier is the top-ranked point and an AUC of 0 implies that the outlier is the lowest ranked point. Note that this seems to be a very trivial data set for outlier detection; yet, it turns out to be surprisingly difficult for several off-the-shelf algorithms. For example, such a data set is unsuited to the *linear* Mahalanobis method in virtually any dimensionality; however, the *TRINITY* ensemble uses the *nonlinear* Mahalanobis method, which performs much better in this setting.

We show the performance of the three base components of *TRINITY* with increasing dimensionality in Fig. 6.10. For the base detectors, the ensemble performance with variable subsampling between 50 and 1000 points (and 100 components) is shown. The value of k for the exact k nearest neighbor detector was set at 5, as in all other tests. The settings of the nonlinear Mahalanobis method were the same as all the other tests in this chapter. It is evident from Fig. 6.10 that the isolation forest starts degrading at 3 dimensions and performs worse than random at 4 dimensions. At 7 dimensions, the outlier point is ranked as the strongest inlier, which is the worst possible performance for a detector. The exact k-nearest neighbor detector is more robust than the isolation forest but it too starts degrading between 15 and 20 dimensions. At 20 dimensions, the nearest neighbor detector performs significantly worse than the random detector. Only the nonlinear Mahalanobis method is able to hold on to its good performance up to 20 dimensions. Although we have not shown performance beyond 20 dimensions, the nonlinear Mahalanobis method retains its perfect performance of ranking the sole outlier as the top outlier for dimensionalities up to 100. This is particularly impressive considering the fact that each sample used in the execution of the nonlinear Mahalanobis method contained between 50 and 1000 points. Furthermore, the *TRINITY* detector is also able to achieve the perfect performance in Fig. 6.10 because it uses a robust combination of three different detectors. This perfect performance was retained for dimensionalities up to 90. In general, *TRINITY* may not perform as well as the best detector on any particular data set but

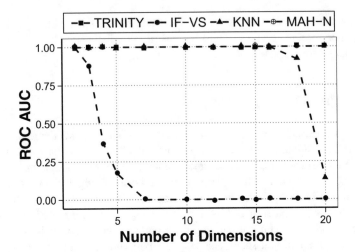

Fig. 6.10 Performance of the base components of *TRINITY* in which a single outlier is placed at the center of a unit sphere with normal points on its surface. Note that the base components of *TRINITY* are themselves ensembles, each of which uses variable subsampling with a particular detector. Therefore, the base performances are also ensemble-centric in nature. Note the poor performance of the isolation forest in comparison with other detectors. Both *TRINITY* and the nonlinear Mahalanobis method retain their effectiveness with increasing dimensionality

it still avoids disastrous performance in most cases. This shows an example of how heterogeneous model combination can often prevent disastrous results in data sets where the use of a particular component is not appropriate. Since the effectiveness of a particular component cannot be known a priori in unsupervised problems, the heterogeneous combination reduces the overall risk of poor results. This suggests that reduction of performance variance (i.e., increased robustness) is a worthy goal in its own right, which can be achieved by methods like *TRINITY*.

Many outlier detection algorithms tend to favor multivariate extreme values (which are not general outliers), and many anomaly detection data sets that were originally designed for bench-marking classification algorithms also tend to place the rare classes far away from the mean of the data. This might not be a problem if this common behavior of rare class data sets does reflect the types of outliers encountered in real settings. However, in practical settings in which rare classes have a chance of being placed near the attribute mean, it becomes more difficult to evaluate the detector quality. In such cases, many algorithms that perform extremely well on these types of benchmarks have hidden weaknesses with interior outliers. Therefore, we believe that outlier detection algorithms should also be tested on difficult synthetic cases like the ball-and-speck test case to evaluate their generality.

6.7.5.2 Subsampling Quirks

This data set is also interesting in another respect– a subsampled ensemble of a k-NN algorithm is always worse than a single execution of the algorithm for fixed k. If the speck is moved to just outside the sphere, then the smallest possible subsample size of k suddenly becomes the best choice for a k-NN algorithm. In general, subsampling with fixed parameters biases distance-based algorithms towards finding multivariate extreme values (see Fig. 3.11 of Chap. 3). For example, a 1-nearest neighbor algorithm on a subsample size of 1 scores data points at their expected average distance to the entire distribution. Such an algorithm can *only* find multivariate extreme values and little else. This behavior is discussed on p. 112 in Sect. 3.4.4.1 of Chap. 3. In general, the preponderance of multivariate extreme values in a data set greatly simplifies outlier detection algorithms, which often occurs in benchmarks related to classification. We discuss this issue below.

6.7.5.3 A Benchmarking Dilemma

Several observations in this book open an important question about the benchmarking dilemmas facing outlier detection algorithms. Many simple algorithms perform exceedingly well on real benchmarks but perform poorly when tested in difficult settings like the ball-and-speck test case. Real benchmarks are often constructed from imbalanced classification data sets in which instances from rare class(es) are designated as outliers and those from the dominant class as the inliers. In most cases, the centroids of the normal and rare classes are likely to be very different, and the centroid of the overall data is likely to be close to that of the normal class. The small size of the rare class (and its different centroid) increases the possibility of its

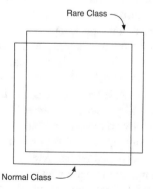

Fig. 6.11 The rare and normal class are distributed in two rectangles that are 90% overlapping. The individual dimensions have relatively weak Fisher scores. However, by increasing the number of dimensions, it is sometimes possible to sharpen separability significantly, so that extreme-value analysis algorithms will work well

separability from the normal class. An important factor is that the features in such data sets are often collected or extracted with the predictive problem in mind. Good features for classification often have high *Fisher's scores* [1], which are indicative of at least partial separability over individual dimensions. This separability is often sharpened by the aggregative effect of multiple dimensions and it is further facilitated by the small size of the rare class. For example, consider a setting in which the rare class occupies a unit square in which each side is 90% overlapping with the unit square of the normal class. In 2-dimensions, this might not look like a very separable situation. This 2-dimensional situation is shown in Fig. 6.11, in which the normal and rare classes do not seem very separable at all, and $0.9 \times 0.9 = 0.81$ of the area of square belonging to the rare class is occupied by the normal class. However, in 10 dimensions, only $(0.9)^{10} \leq 0.35$ of the volume of the rare class is overlapping with the normal class. In 100 dimensions, this fraction reduces to less than 10^{-4}. In many such cases, the anomalous class appears as a separable group from the mean of the normal data, and it becomes increasingly likely for *pareto-extreme* detection algorithms to work really well in detecting outliers in these benchmarks. In fact, even modest separability will often guarantee a very good AUC for pareto-extreme algorithms. Of course, pareto-extreme detectors are generally much simpler than generic outlier detectors, and we really do not need complicated algorithms for outlier analysis in such cases. Note that the linear Mahalanobis method does not gain much from the ensemble, but even its average *base* performance across all data sets was 0.840, which was not much less than the 0.874 average AUC of *TRINITY*. If the rare-class setting is indeed realistic, then it points in the "simpler-is-better" direction for outlier detection algorithms. It is relatively easy to add a bias to any outlier detection algorithm to favor pareto-extremes by using off-the-shelf extreme-value methods [45, 46].

However, many algorithms that perform exceptionally well on real benchmarks fail to pass simple generality tests with interior outliers. For example, the isolation forest performs exceptionally well on the data sets of this chapter (and in other independent evaluations on different data sets [14]), but it cannot even achieve the break-even AUC of 0.5 for a ball-and-speck data set in any dimensionality greater than 3. Placing the speck at an arbitrary position inside the sphere leads to unpredictable and sometimes poor results even in a two-dimensional ring of points, depending on angular placement. Placing the speck outside the sphere leads to a huge jump in performance even when the speck is relatively close to the surface of the sphere. We would like to mention that we have observed these behaviors over many data sets, and the presented results are, by no means, unusual.

This leads to some interesting questions as to whether rare classes represent reasonable benchmarks for unsupervised outlier detection. We do not have a complete answer to this question, although there are some obviously problematic areas with adopting supervised benchmarks in the unsupervised setting. A key issue is that the features in supervised problems are often extracted with particular predictive goals in mind, which might not always be the case in unsupervised settings. This can already change the kind of data sets one might encounter in an unsupervised setting. Another key issue is whether the analyst is looking for outliers associated with a small number or a very large number of abnormal generative mechanisms. Anomalies are more likely to be strongly clustered when the data is collected to model a single rare generating mechanism. For example, in the previous example of the separability of the unit squares, an important assumption was that the normal and rare classes were both coherently clustered in contiguous regions. This may be true in the rare class setting because of the inherent semantic biases in feature extraction, but may not always be true in an unsupervised setting. In some cases, only a small subset of the abnormal instances in the data may be labeled as rare classes, and the extracted features may be discriminative only towards the labeled ones. In such cases, rare-class benchmarks may not be exactly representative of an unsupervised setting. The real problem is that we do not see any viable alternatives to the current benchmarking practices. Supplementing tests on real data with synthetic generality tests might provide a partial answer. A second approach that might help is to create a proper *taxonomy* of the (real) data sets, based on the types of outliers one might find in them. The most fundamental test for the non-triviality of an outlier is an *extreme-value* test. Data sets in which a good fraction of the outliers do not satisfy an extreme-value test [45, 46] should be placed in a different category than the ones in which most outliers are extreme values. The results should be presented separately in the two cases. In any case, it is often difficult to meaningfully compare algorithms with varying levels of extremity bias on a data sets in which most outliers are (trivial) pareto-extreme values. It is important to be aware of where an algorithm is obtaining its performance improvements. On the other hand, if pareto-extremes are indeed ubiquitous for outlier detection, then it is better to recognize it very explicitly and add an extremity-bias to various algorithms as an additional ensemble component.

An important issue in the unsupervised setting is that we have little to tell us whether we have the right predictions or not. A few data sets like *Glass* and *Vowels* were challenging for pareto-extreme detectors like the linear Mahalanobis method, and the performance was poor enough in these cases to be noticeable. This means that the analyst always lives with an inherent uncertainty about her results. This is definitely an argument against algorithms that rely too much on finding pareto-extremes. In such cases, it might make sense to use algorithms or methods that are known to be more general over different data sets, even at the expense of some accuracy. It is possible to design algorithms that ensemble over varying levels of extremity bias. In fact, when variable subsampling is combined with distance-based detectors, this goal is implicitly achieved. In this sense, the field of outlier ensembles provides a partial answer irrespective of the answers to the benchmarking dilemma.

6.7.6 Discussion

Interestingly, in our experiments, we did not find most of the recent algorithms to perform significantly better than raw distance-based detectors, although they did have niche advantages in many settings. However, the *TRINITY* detector generally performed better than the raw distance-based detectors. Therefore, it seems that raw distance-based algorithms should not be underestimated, although a scope for improvement by blending with other algorithms still exists. Furthermore, the robustness of the linear Mahalanobis method was quite notable *in spite of* being parameter free. Another observation is that the use of ensemble methods like *TRINITY* can often avoid disastrous situations like the one discussed in Sect. 6.7.5.

For the two supervised learning methods, their (relatively) poor performance can be attributed to the weak base detectors used for supervised learning. For example, we used a random forest classifier with only 10 trees per component and 3 bagged features per node. Furthermore, we did not use grid search to optimize the parameters of the supervised learning algorithm. The use of weak supervised learning methods was primarily caused by a computational constraint, since we had to run these algorithms multiple times over many data sets. Attempting a (supervised) grid-search of parameters over *each execution of the supervised model* was theoretically possible, but practically unreasonable. On using stronger base learning algorithms, we found that it was possible for the supervised methods to outperform many of the methods on various data sets. Therefore, such methods have significant potential, but they are hampered by computational constraints. Such constraints are, nevertheless, important from a practical point of view.

It needs to be kept in mind that factors other than accuracy play a role in the choice of a particular algorithm. An important factor is that of interpretability [6]. For example, a subspace outlier detection method provides an understanding of the most relevant features that make a data point an outlier. Furthermore, more complex methods often require ensemble methods to improve their performance to a greater degree than simpler techniques such as the average k-nearest neighbor method. This is because complex methods are more prone to model-centric overfitting than simpler methods. For example, it makes sense to use subspace methods [4, 20, 27, 37, 38] with ensemble methods; specific examples are feature bagging or rotated bagging. Furthermore, they are complementary to simpler methods, because they can be used in combination with them. In fact, both feature bagging [32] and rotated bagging [3] are examples of subspace methods, which are used in combination with ensemble techniques. Although we have not shown detailed experimental results on rotated bagging (beyond those in Chap. 3), it is conceivable that rotated bagging may also be useful for various types of base detectors.

When used on a standalone basis as a single base detector, it is preferable to use simpler detectors like the linear Mahalanobis method. More complex methods like the nonlinear Mahalanobis method are reliable only when they are used in an ensemble-centric setting. However, one always incurs a risk in using methods like the linear Mahalanobis method when the data set does not satisfy the strong modeling assumption. This observation further validates the need for model combination methods in outlier detection.

Finally, this book has focused on the multidimensional data type, although many of arguments can also be applied to arbitrary data types, as long as a similarity function between data types can be defined. For example, all the distance-based detectors can be easily generalized to arbitrary data types. The nonlinear Mahalanobis method can also be extended to arbitrary data types with the use of kernel similarity functions. The extension of multidimensional outlier analysis to arbitrary data types would be a worthwhile goal for future research in outlier analysis.

6.8 Conclusions

In this chapter, we presented a comparison of various outlier detection methods in an ensemble-centric settings. The ensemble-centric setting is very useful for comparing outlier detectors with associated parameter choices. This is because some methods like variable subsampling help in ameliorating the effect of specific parameter choice at least to some extent, which makes it easier to compare various base detectors. Furthermore, it is possible to compare both ensemble-centric performance and base performance in these cases.

Our results show that different detectors might be better in terms of base performance and ensemble performance. For example, the linear Mahalanobis method is extremely stable and often does quite well in terms of the base performance. On the other hand, the base detector of isolation forests is extremely weak. However, the ensemble-centric results are quite different because the isolation forests do extremely well in this setting. Furthermore, our results show that distance-based detectors are quite robust; however no detector was able to consistently perform better than all other detectors.

Exercises

1. The shared-nearest neighbor distance is equal to the number of neighbors among the k-nearest neighbors that are shared by two points. Discuss why the shared nearest neighbor distance is locality sensitive, and can be used with the exact k-nearest neighbor detector as an alternative to LOF. What is the disadvantage of this method in terms of the number of parameters and the computational complexity?
2. Use ensembles to design an efficient way to compute the shared-nearest neighbor distance between two points.
3. Discuss how one can use the kernel Mahalanobis method to perform outlier detection in arbitrary data types.
4. Propose an ensemble-centric variant of subsampling for time-series data.

References

1. C. C. Aggarwal. Data Mining: The Textbook, *Springer*, 2015.
2. C. C. Aggarwal. Outlier Analysis, Second Edition, *Springer*, 2017.
3. C. C. Aggarwal and S. Sathe. Theoretical Foundations and Algorithms for Outlier Ensembles, *ACM SIGKDD Explorations*, 17(1), June 2015.
4. C. C. Aggarwal and P. S. Yu. Outlier Detection in High Dimensional Data, *ACM SIGMOD Conference*, 2001.
5. C. C. Aggarwal, C. Procopiuc, J. Wolf, P. Yu, and J.-S. Park. Fast Algorithms for Projected Clustering. *ACM SIGMOD Conference*, 1999.
6. L. Akoglu, E. Muller, and J Vreeken. ACM KDD Workshop on Outlier Detection and Description, 2013. http://www.outlier-analytics.org/odd13kdd/

7. F. Angiulli, C. Pizzuti. Fast outlier detection in high dimensional spaces, *PKDD Conference*, 2002.h

8. T. Bandaragoda. Isolation-Based Anomaly Detection: A Re-examination, *Masters dissertation, Monash University*, 2015. Electronic copy at: http://arrow.monash.edu.au/vital/access/manager/Repository/monash:162299

9. M. Breunig, H.-P. Kriegel, R. Ng, and J. Sander. LOF: Identifying Density-based Local Outliers, *ACM SIGMOD Conference*, 2000.

10. L. Brieman. Random Forests. *Journal Machine Learning archive*, 45(1), pp. 5–32, 2001.

11. C. Campbell, and K. P. Bennett. A Linear-Programming Approach to Novel Class Detection. *Advances in Neural Information Processing Systems*, 2000.

12. G. O. Campos, A. Zimek, J. Sander, R. J. G. B. Campello, B. Micenkova, E. Schubert, I. Assent, and M. E. Houle. On the Evaluation of Unsupervised Outlier Detection: Measures, Datasets, and an Empirical Study. *Data Mining and Knowledge Discovery*, 30(4), pp. 891–927, 2016. http://rd.springer.com/article/10.1007/s10618-015-0444-8

13. J. Chen, S. Sathe, C. Aggarwal, and D. Turaga. Outlier Detection with Autoencoder Ensembles. *SIAM Conference on Data Mining*, 2017.

14. A. Emmott, S. Das, T. Dietteerich, A. Fern, and W. Wong. Systematic Construction of Anomaly Detection Benchmarks from Real Data. *arXiv:1503.01158*, 2015. https://arxiv.org/abs/1503.01158

15. M. Fernandez-Delgado, E. Cernadas, S. Barro, and D. Amorim. Do we Need Hundreds of Classifiers to Solve Real World Classification Problems? *The Journal of Machine Learning Research*, 15(1), pp. 3133–3181, 2014.

16. M. Goldstein and S. Uchida. A Comparative Evaluation of Unsupervised Anomaly Detection Algorithms for Multivariate Data. *PloS One*, 11(4), e0152173, 2016.

17. S. Guha, N. Mishra, G. Roy, and O. Schrijver. Robust Random Cut Forest Based Anomaly Detection On Streams. *ICML Conference*, pp. 2712–2721, 2016.

18. S. Hawkins, H. He, G. Williams, and R. Baxter. Outlier Detection using Replicator Neural Networks. *Proceedings of the International Conference on Data Warehousing and Knowledge Discovery*, pp. 170–180, Springer, 2002.

19. Z. He, X. Xu, and S. Deng. Discovering Cluster-based Local Outliers. *Pattern Recognition Letters*, Vol 24(910), pp. 1641–1650, 2003.

20. Z. He, S. Deng and X. Xu. A Unified Subspace Outlier Ensemble Framework for Outlier Detection, *Advances in Web Age Information Management*, 2005.

21. S. Hido, Y. Tsuboi, H. Kashima, M. Sugiyama, and T. Kanamori. Statistical Outlier Detection using Direct Density Ratio Estimation. *Knowledge and information Systems*, 26(2), pp. 309–336, 2011.

22. T. K. Ho. Random decision forests. *Third International Conference on Document Analysis and Recognition*, 1995. Extended version appears in *IEEE Transactions on Pattern Analysis and Machine Intelligence*, 20(8), pp. 832–844, 1998.

23. H. Hoffmann. Kernel PCA for Novelty Detection, *Pattern Recognition*, 40(3), pp. 863–874, 2007.

24. R. Jarvis and E. Patrick. Clustering Using a Similarity Meausre based on Shared Near Neighbors. *IEEE Transactions on Computers*, 100(11), pp. 1025–1034, 1973.

25. H. Javitz, and A. Valdez. The SRI IDES Statistical Anomaly Detector. *IEEE Symposium on Security and Privacy*, 1991.

26. S. Khan and M. Madden. One-class Classification: Taxonomy of Study and Review of Techniques. *Knowledge Engineering Review*, 29(03), 345–374, 2014.

27. F. Keller, E. Muller, K. Bohm. HiCS: High-Contrast Subspaces for Density-based Outlier Ranking, *IEEE ICDE Conference*, 2012.

28. J. Kim and C. Scott. Robust Kernel Density Estimation. *Journal of Machine Learning Research*, 13, pp. 2529–2565, 2012. http://www.jmlr.org/papers/volume13/kim12b/kim12b.pdf

29. E. Knorr, and R. Ng. Algorithms for Mining Distance-based Outliers in Large Datasets. *VLDB Conference*, 1998.

30. E. Knorr, and R. Ng. Finding Intensional Knowledge of Distance-Based Outliers. *VLDB Conference*, 1999.

31. L. Latecki, A. Lazarevic, and D. Pokrajac. Outlier Detection with Kernel Density Functions. *Machine Learning and Data Mining in Pattern Recognition*, pp. 61–75, 2007.

32. A. Lazarevic, and V. Kumar. Feature Bagging for Outlier Detection, *ACM KDD Conference*, 2005.

33. F. T. Liu, K. M. Ting, and Z. H. Zhou. On Detecting Clustered Anomalies using SCiForest. *Machine Learning and Knowledge Discovery in Databases*, pp. 274–290, 2010.

34. F. T. Liu, K. M. Ting, and Z.-H. Zhou. Isolation Forest. *ICDM Conference*, 2008. Extended version appears in: *ACM Transactions on Knowledge Discovery from Data (TKDD)*, 6(1), 3, 2012.

35. L. M. Manevitz and M. Yousef. One-class SVMs for Document Classification, *Journal of Machine Learning Research*, 2: pp, 139–154, 2001.

36. F. Moosmann, B. Triggs, and F. Jurie. Fast Discriminative Visual Codebooks using Randomized Clustering Forests. *Neural Information Processing Systems*, pp. 985–992, 2006.

37. E. Muller, M. Schiffer, and T. Seidl. Statistical Selection of Relevant Subspace Projections for Outlier Ranking. *ICDE Conference*, pp, 434–445, 2011.

38. E. Muller, I. Assent, P. Iglesias, Y. Mulle, and K. Bohm. Outlier Ranking via Subspace Analysis in Multiple Views of the Data, *ICDM Conference*, 2012.

39. H. Nguyen, H. Ang, and V. Gopalakrishnan. Mining ensembles of heterogeneous detectors on random subspaces, *DASFAA*, 2010.

40. K. Noto, C. Brodley, and D. Slonim. FRaC: A Feature-Modeling Approach for Semi-Supervised and Unsupervised Anomaly Detection. *Data Mining and Knowledge Discovery*, 25(1), pp. 109–133, 2012.

41. G. Orair, C. Teixeira, W. Meira Jr, Y. Wang, and S. Parthasarathy. Distance-Based Outlier Detection: Consolidation and Renewed Bearing. *Proceedings of the VLDB Endowment*, 3(1–2), pp. 1469–1480, 2010.

42. L. Ott, L. Pang, F. Ramos, and S. Chawla. On Integrated Clustering and Outlier Detection. *Advances in Meural Information Processing Systems*, pp. 1359–1367, 2014.

43. S. Papadimitriou, H. Kitagawa, P. Gibbons, and C. Faloutsos, LOCI: Fast Outlier Detection using the Local Correlation Integral, *ICDE Conference*, 2003.

44. H. Paulheim and R. Meusel. A Decomposition of the Outlier Detection Problem into a Set of Supervised Learning Problems. *Machine Learning*, 100(2–3), pp. 509–531, 2015.

45. J. Pickands. Statistical inference using extreme order statistics. *The Annals of Statistics*, 3(1), pp. 119–131, 1975.

46. J. Pickands. Multivariate extreme value distributions. *Proceedings of the 43rd Session International Statistical Institute*, 2, pp. 859–878, 1981.

47. S. Ramaswamy, R. Rastogi, and K. Shim. Efficient Algorithms for Mining Outliers from Large Data Sets. *ACM SIGMOD Conference*, pp. 427–438, 2000.

48. D. Rocke and D. Woodruff. Identification of Outliers in Multivariate Data. *Journal of the American Statistical Association* 91, 435, pp. 1047–1061, 1996.

49. V. Roth. Kernel Fisher Discriminants for Outlier Detection. *Neural Computation*, 18(4), pp. 942–960, 2006.

50. S. Sathe and C. Aggarwal. LODES: Local Density Meets Spectral Outlier Detection, *SIAM Conference on Data Mining*, 2016.

51. S. Sathe and C. Aggarwal. Subspace Outlier Detection in Linear Time with Randomized Hashing. *ICDM Conference*, 2016.

52. B. Scholkopf, R. C. Williamson, A. J. Smola, J. Shawe-Taylor, and J. C. Platt. Support-vector Method for Novelty Detection, *Advances in Neural Information Processing Systems*, 2000.

53. B. Scholkopf, J. C. Platt, J. Shawe-Taylor, A. J. Smola, and R. C. Williamson. Estimating the support of a high-dimensional distribution. *Neural Computation*, 13(7), pp. 1443–1472, 2001.

54. M. Shyu, S. Chen, K. Sarinnapakorn, L. Chang. A novel anomaly detection scheme based on principal component classifier. *ICDMW*, 2003.

55. B. W. Silverman. Density Estimation for Statistics and Data Analysis. *Chapman and Hall*, 1986.
56. S. C. Tan, K. M. Ting, and T. F. Liu. Fast Anomaly Detection for Streaming Data. *IJCAI Conference*, 2011.
57. J. Tang, Z. Chen, A. W.-C. Fu, and D. W. Cheung. Enhancing Effectiveness of Outlier Detections for Low Density Patterns. *PAKDD Conference*, 2002.
58. D. Tax. One Class Classification: Concept-learning in the Absence of Counter-examples, *Doctoral Dissertation, University of Delft*, Netherlands, 2001. http://prlab.tudelft.nl/sites/default/files/thesis.pdf
59. D. Tax and R. Duin. Combining One-Class Classifiers. *Multiple Classifier Systems*, pp. 299–308, 2001.
60. D. Tax and R. Duin. Support Vector Data Description. *Machine learning*, 54(1), 45-66, 2004.
61. D. Tax, and P. Juszczak. Kernel Whitening for One-Class Classification. *Pattern Recognition with Support Vector Machines*, pp. 40–52, 2002.
62. K. M. Ting, G. Zhou, F. Liu, and S. C. Tan. Mass Estimation and its Applications. *ACM KDD Conference*, pp. 989–998, 2010. Extended version of paper appears as "Mass Estimation. *Machine Learning*, 90(1), pp. 127–160, 2013."
63. K. M. Ting, Y. Zhu, M. Carman, and Y. Zhu. Overcoming Key Weaknesses of Distance-Based Neighbourhood Methods using a Data Dependent Dissimilarity Measure. *ACM KDD Conference*, 2016.
64. C. Williams and M. Seeger. Using the Nyström method to speed up kernel machines. *NIPS Conference*, 2000.
65. G. Williams, R. Baxter, H. He, S. Hawkings, and L. Gu. A Comparative Study of RNN for Outlier Detection in Data Mining. *IEEE ICDM Conference*, 2002.
66. K. Yamanishi, J.-I. Takeuchi, G. Williams, and P. Milne. Online Unsupervised Outlier Detection using Finite Mixtures with Discounting Learning Algorithms. *ACM KDD Conference*, pp. 320–324, 2000.
67. K. Zhang, M. Hutter, and H. Jin. A New Local Distance-Based Outlier Detection Approach for Scattered Real-World Data. *Pacific-Asia Conference on Knowledge Discovery and Data Mining*, pp. 813–822, 2009.

Index

© Springer International Publishing AG 2017
C.C. Aggarwal and S. Sathe, *Outlier Ensembles*,
DOI 10.1007/978-3-319-54765-7

Printed in the United States
By Bookmasters